Guns N' Roses FAQ

All That's Left to Know About the Bad Boys of Sunset Strip

Rich Weidman

Backbeat Books

An Imprint of Hal Leonard LLC

Published in 2017 by Backbeat Books
An Imprint of Hal Leonard LLC
7777 West Bluemound Road
Milwaukee, WI 53213

Trade Book Division Editorial Offices
33 Plymouth St., Montclair, NJ 07042

The FAQ series was conceived by Robert Rodriguez and developed with Stuart Shea.

Printed in the United States of America

Book design by Snow Creative

Library of Congress Cataloging-in-Publication Data

Names: Weidman, Rich.
Title: Guns n' Roses FAQ : all that's left to know about the bad boys of Sunset
    Strip / Rich Weidman.
Description: Montclair, NJ : Backbeat Books, 2017. | Includes bibliographical
    references and index.
Identifiers: LCCN 2016046567 | ISBN 9781495025884
Subjects: LCSH: Guns n' Roses (Musical group)—Miscellanea. | Rock
    music—Miscellanea.
Classification: LCC ML421.G86 W43 2017 | DDC 782.42166092/2 [B]—dc23
LC record available at https://lccn.loc.gov/2016046567

www.backbeatbooks.com

To Hailey and Dylan, who have, against all odds, developed
a subtle appreciation for "classic" rock 'n' roll!

Contents

Acknowledgments

F irst and foremost, I would like to thank my wife, Nadine, and kids, Hailey and Dylan, who had to patiently deal with my crazy schedule for the past year as I balanced a full-time job while researching and writing this book at night and on weekends. They also had to endure listening to the entire catalog of Guns N' Roses music on a regular basis (somehow I don't think they will miss "Shackler's Revenge"), as well as some more obscure tracks from groups that influenced GN'R, such as the New York Dolls, the Damned, Rose Tattoo, Hanoi Rocks, and others. I would also like to thank my family—Mom, Dad, Boyd, and Tracy and her family (Cliff, Emma, Jack, and Chris) for all their tremendous support and encouragement.

Thanks to my good friend, Jack Thompson, who has collaborated with me over the years on numerous crazy website projects, including Alternative Reel, which we started way back on July 4, 1999, with a single article on the author Charles Bukowski. For an extremely brief period in 2008–09, I enjoyed what it was like to be a "rock journalist," as we covered a handful of concerts by the likes of Seether, Staind, and Papa Roach at Central Florida venues, such as Hard Rock Live Orlando and House of Blues, as well as the amazing Doors tribute band Peace Frog at the Largo Cultural Center. We also enjoyed watching "Nature Boy" Ric Flair get inducted into the WWE Hall of Fame and hanging out in the press box at WrestleMania 23 at the Citrus Bowl. Great times!

I would like to once again extend my appreciation to my editor at Backbeat Books, Bernadette Malavarca, as well as copy editor Micah White and Robert Rodriguez, Beatles expert and the founder of the FAQ series. Thanks as always to Robert Lecker of the Robert Lecker Agency for everything you do. Special thanks also goes to my supervisors at Westgate Resorts, Robert Jensen and Denise Brookfield, who patiently tolerated my frequent absences from work as I struggled to complete the book.

A special shout-out goes to the folks at Heretodaygonetohell.com for their amazing Guns N' Roses timeline, which serves as a great chronological record of the band's history. Last but not least, I would also like to thank the following individuals for their past and ongoing inspiration: the legendary Tony Fernandez of Peace Frog, Alternative Reel collaborators Bill Chinaski and Jim Foley, Doors expert Jim Cherry, Art "Barfly" Spackle, Bruce "The Mad Hatter" Norris, Jason "DC" Greene, Ben John Smith of HorrorSleazeTrash,

Ben "Scooped" Parker from the *News of Orange* days, JC Pellicciotta for the "Philadelphia Story" and other interesting anecdotes, John Nixdorf for introducing me to his amazing collection of rock and rap cassettes—such as Run-D.M.C.'s "Rock Box"—in the mid-eighties in the Lower A dorm at Stetson University, Dale Nichols of the Flamingo Bar in St. Petersburg, John "Hooch" Lewis for his inspiring Facebook posts, legendary singer-songwriter Michael McCloud of the Schooner Wharf Bar, and, of course, my good old friend, Captain Morgan, who I will be hanging out with very soon at the Golden Lion Café in Flagler Beach.

Introduction

Rock music goes through these surges of really creative, brilliant stuff and then drops into these absolute lows when it almost seems like it's dead . . . We came along at a time when music was at one of those low points. I guess it was almost like a fluke, really, but we seemed to touch a nerve with everybody. —Slash

id you know . . .

- Before he joined Guns N' Roses, Slash actually auditioned for glam rock band Poison in 1984 but lost out to C. C. DeVille?
- Blues legend Etta James recorded a cover of "Welcome to the Jungle" on her final album, *The Dreamer*, in 2011?
- Axl Rose was arrested in 1990 for allegedly hitting his neighbor over the head with "a really good bottle" of Chardonnay, an incident that inspired the song "Right Next Door to Hell," which appeared on the album *Use Your Illusion I*?
- Troubled GN'R drummer Steven Adler was the subject of the song "Wasted Time" by Sebastian Bach that appeared on Skid Row's 1991 album, *Slave to the Grind*?
- Trent Reznor of Nine Inch Nails referred to his band opening for Guns N' Roses during the *Use Your Illusion* Tour in 1991 as "some of the worst performances we ever had in front of the most hostile, moronic audiences I've ever experienced"?

Guns N' Roses FAQ provides a fresh perspective on the legendary rock band that emerged from the West Hollywood club scene in the mid-1980s, skyrocketed to fame with the release of *Appetite for Destruction*, and changed all the rules of rock 'n' roll in the process. In *Guns N' Roses FAQ*, you will learn all about Guns N' Roses' creative influences, recording sessions, song details, most notorious concerts, record-breaking tours, music videos, struggles with drug and alcohol addiction, groupies, feuds, solo efforts, outside projects, "supergroups," and much more. In addition, you will find out about the amazing chain of events that led to Axl Rose, Slash, and Duff McKagan reuniting for the 2016 Not in This Lifetime Tour.

I have been a Guns N' Roses fanatic for nearly thirty years. I bought my first Guns N' Roses cassette, *Appetite for Destruction*, sometime in the fall of 1988. The album had just hit No. 1 on the charts on August 6, 1988, and all you heard on the radio at that time was an endless cycle of "Welcome to the Jungle," "Sweet Child O' Mine," and "Paradise City." I was going for my master's degree in English (Film Studies) at the University of Florida in Gainesville and living in a dingy one-bedroom apartment in the Woods complex, a total dump off Twentieth Avenue that I rented for $245 a month and that overlooked a chain-link fence bordering an endless forest. To top it off, some asshole broke into the place and ripped off all of my meager possessions, including a black-and-white TV, so all I had for entertainment was my cassette player, my *Appetite for Destruction* tape, and a shitload of books. (I was reading my way through Harry Crews novels, such as the appropriately named *All We Need of Hell*, at the time.)

So with nothing but time on my hands, I listened to every track of *Appetite for Destruction* intently and became fascinated with this band, as they depicted all the gritty details of life on the streets of Los Angeles without pulling any punches whatsoever. By the late 1980s, MTV was getting rather bland to say the least—for example, the 1988 Video of the Year was awarded to INXS' "Need You Tonight/Mediate." Guns N' Roses did win "Best New Artist" honors that year, but a glance at their competition for the award gives you a good idea about how lame the music scene was at this time: "Birth, School, Work, Death" by the Godfathers, "Hot, Hot, Hot" by Buster Poindexter, "Breakout" by Swing Out Sister, and "Some Kind of Love" by Jody Watley.

In addition to creating great music, the Guns N' Roses band members seemed to be living the dream—the endless partying, the strippers dancing onstage, and the "not-giving-a-fuck" attitude were all appealing to young college students getting a taste of rebellion by blaring "Welcome to the Jungle" on their boombox while getting totally shitfaced in their dorm rooms. Let's face it, self-destructive behavior hadn't been this cool since the Sex Pistols!

It all started in West Hollywood during the early 1980s as obscure bands—Hollywood Rose, L.A. Guns, Jetboy, Poison, Faster Pussycat, and many others—struggled for prominence as they wandered up and down Sunset Boulevard posting flyers and dreaming about better gigs. Most of these groups had revolving band members, and, through an unlikely set of circumstances, L.A. Guns and Hollywood Rose merged to create Guns N' Roses in the spring of 1985. By the summer of that year, GN'R settled on the "classic" lineup of the band that would create *Appetite for Destruction*: lead singer Axl Rose, lead guitarist Slash, rhythm guitarist Izzy Stradlin, bassist Duff McKagan, and drummer Steven Adler. After embarking on a "Hell Tour" that took them to Seattle, Washington, Guns N' Roses were ready to kick ass and dominate the

West Hollywood club scene at such legendary hotspots as the Troubadour, the Roxy, and Whisky A Go Go, among others.

In the summer of 1987, Guns N' Roses released their debut album, *Appetite for Destruction*, which reached No. 1 on the US charts a year later on the strength of their only No. 1 single, "Sweet Child O' Mine." Today, the album has sold more than 18 million copies in the United States (and 30 million worldwide), making it the best-selling debut album in United States history. The controversial *G N' R Lies* (1988) followed, reaching No. 2 on the US charts and creating much consternation based on the track "One in a Million," which contained blatantly racist and homophobic lyrics. The band soon changed direction with the addition of keyboardist Dizzy Reed and new drummer Matt Sorum (Adler had been fired from the band for severe drug addiction) and the 1991 release of the twin albums *Use Your Illusion I* and *Use Your Illusion II*. Guns N' Roses then embarked on a massive, two-and-a-half-year tour that lasted until 1993, the same year the band released their covers album, *"The Spaghetti Incident?"*

Drug and alcohol addiction (along with the lead singer's ever-increasing megalomania) took its toll on the band, and by 1997 Axl was the only original band member left—Izzy having departed in 1991, Slash in 1996, and Duff in 1997. Over the next eleven years, Axl attempted to replace band members and record the next album, the long-delayed *Chinese Democracy*, which finally appeared in 2008 (fifteen years after GN'R's last release!) at a price tag of $14 million, making it the most expensive rock album in history. In 2012, Guns N' Roses was inducted into the Rock and Roll Hall of Fame (Axl declined to appear or accept the honor).

With Axl and Slash feuding through the media over a span of fifteen years, few people thought that the original band members would ever reunite again (even though Izzy and Duff had sporadically made appearances with the new Guns N' Roses lineup over the years). However, somewhat miraculously (and with a huge financial incentive to boot!), Axl, Slash, and Duff all agreed to reunite in 2016 for amazing shows at the Troubadour, in Las Vegas, and at Coachella, which were followed by the Not in This Lifetime Tour that began in the summer of that year.

Who knows what lies in store for Guns N' Roses in the near future. If their track record tells us anything, it certainly won't be predictable. Whatever happens, it's bound to be innovative, uncompromising, and groundbreaking. There undoubtedly will never be another band even remotely like them. Welcome to the fuckin' jungle, baby!

Free of All the Chains

Key Players in the Guns N' Roses Saga

We were a gang—that's how we thought of ourselves. And we played rock 'n' roll to kick your ass. —Steven Adler

Somehow, amid all of the dozens of faceless bands struggling to make it on the Sunset Strip, Guns N' Roses emerged in the mid-1980s, honed their skills in legendary West Hollywood clubs like the Troubadour and the Roxy, managed to score a contract with Geffen Records, and went on to record *Appetite for Destruction*, which became the best-selling debut album of all time in the United States. Not bad for two small-town "hicks" from Indiana, a punk rocker from Seattle, an ex-BMX racer/skateboarder from England whose first instrument was a one-string flamenco guitar, and a self-taught drummer from Cleveland, Ohio.

Axl Rose, Guns N' Roses Lead Singer/Songwriter (1985–Present)

Love him or loathe him, Axl Rose is simply one of the greatest front men in rock 'n' roll history. The legendary and often notorious Guns N' Roses lead singer was born William Bruce Rose Jr. (he legally changed his name to W. Axl Rose in 1986) on February 6, 1962, in Lafayette, Indiana, to Sharon (Lintner), who was a sixteen-year-old high school student at the time, and William Rose, a local degenerate who soon abandoned the family. (Years later Rose found out that his biological father was murdered in 1984.) Sharon quickly got remarried to a Pentecostal preacher named Rev. L. Stephen Bailey (a.k.a. "Beetle"), and Rose started going by the name William Bruce Bailey. He has two younger siblings: sister Amy and half-brother Stuart. Raised in a strict, oppressive religious household (he later described his stepfather as "a paranoid control freak" who was physically abusive), Rose began singing in the church choir at the age of five and claimed in a 1989 *Rolling Stone* interview that he was "raised on Jimmy Swaggart religious tapes." Rose (who was known as "Bill Bailey" throughout his childhood and adolescence) later remarked to *Rolling Stone* that his upbringing in Lafayette "made me despise people with closed minds. It made me want to break out."

In eighth grade, Rose met Jeffrey Isbell (the future Izzy Stradlin). Around this time, he secretly started listening to rock music, and his early influences included Aerosmith, Nazareth, Queen, Elton John, Led Zeppelin, the Rolling Stones, Electric Light Orchestra, and the Sex Pistols. At the age of seventeen, Rose came across some documents lying around the house and first discovered that Bailey wasn't his biological father. With the knowledge of his true identity, Rose started getting into trouble and was arrested more than twenty times for various misdemeanors ranging from public intoxication and contributing to the delinquency of a minor to criminal trespass/mischief and battery.

Axl and his then girlfriend, Gina Siler, hitchhiked their way to Los Angeles in 1982, eventually hooked up with Stradlin, and performed in a series of pre-Guns N' Roses rock bands, such as AXL, Rapidfire, Hollywood

Guns N' Roses burst onto the Los Angeles rock scene in the mid-1980s with a talented lineup that featured (l–r) lead singer Axl Rose, rhythm guitarist Izzy Stradlin, lead guitarist Slash, drummer Steven Adler, and bassist Duff McKagan.   *Author's collection*

Rose, and L.A. Guns. He also worked a variety of odd jobs, such as night manager at Tower Video on Sunset Boulevard. On June 6, 1985, the "classic" lineup of Guns N' Roses—Axl, Slash, Izzy, Duff McKagan, and Steven Adler—performed live for the first time at the Troubadour in West Hollywood. Axl is the only founding member of Guns N' Roses to take part in the recording of all Guns N' Roses albums, including *Live?!*@ Like a Suicide* (1986), *Appetite for Destruction* (1987), *G N' R Lies* (1988), *Use Your Illusion I* (1991), *Use Your Illusion II* (1991), "*The Spaghetti Incident?*" (1993), and *Chinese Democracy* (2008). Axl was married briefly (1990–91) to Erin Everly, who served as the inspiration for "Sweet Child O' Mine." He then embarked on a relationship with supermodel Stephanie Seymour between 1991 and 1993.

In an August 1989 *Rolling Stone* interview, Axl confessed, "When I was growing up, I was never really popular . . . Now everybody wants to be my friend. I like my privacy, to live alone in my own little world." Indeed, throughout the mid- to late 1990s, Axl became somewhat of a recluse, spending most of his time in his Malibu mansion, and the media even dubbed him the "Howard Hughes of Rock" and "Rock's Greatest Recluse." During this period, Axl worked on a follow-up album, *Chinese Democracy*, and hired a new set of musicians to replace the "classic" Guns N' Roses lineup, who all had left the band: Steven Adler in 1990, Izzy Stradlin in 1991, Slash in 1996, and Duff McKagan in 1997. The rebooted lineup performed at Rock in Rio 3 in 2001 and the 2002 MTV Video Music Awards.

Fifteen years after the release of Guns N' Roses' last album, *Chinese Democracy* finally saw the light of day in 2008. In 2012, Axl was inducted into the Rock and Roll Hall of Fame but did not show up and publicly declined the honor. In 2016, Axl reunited with Slash and Duff for a series of concerts that led to the Not in This Lifetime Tour. He also filled in as lead singer for AC/DC during the spring of 2016 for the remainder of the *Rock or Bust* World Tour after Brian Johnson dropped out due to health issues.

Axl Trivia

Think you know all there is to know about the volatile Guns N' Roses lead singer? Below is a selection of little-known Axl Rose trivia.

- In 1989, Axl appeared on Don Henley's album *The End of the Innocence*, singing background vocals on "I Will Not Go Quietly."

- Axl served as the voice of "Tommy 'Nightmare' Smith," DJ of classic rock station K-DST ("The Dust") in the 2004 video game *Grand Theft Auto: San Andreas.*
- In 2007, Axl made a guest appearance on three tracks that appeared on Sebastian Bach's 2007 solo album, *Angel Down*—"Back in the Saddle" (Aerosmith cover), "(Love Is) a Bitchslap," and "Stuck Inside."
- Axl collects antique crucifixes.
- In 2014, Axl told *SPIN* magazine that his all-time favorite singers are Freddie Mercury, Elvis, Paul McCartney, Dan McCafferty (of Nazareth), Janis Joplin, Michael Jackson, Elton John, Roger Daltrey, Don Henley, Jeff Lynne (of Electric Light Orchestra), Johnny Cash, Frank Sinatra, Jimmy Scott, Etta James, Fiona Apple, Chrissie Hynde, Stevie Wonder, and James Brown.
- One of Axl's favorite books is *James Dean: The Mutant King* (1974) by David Dalton, while Charles Bukowski is one of his favorite authors.
- In 2014, Axl won the Ronnie James Dio Lifetime Achievement Award from *Revolver* magazine.
- Last but not least, "Axl Rose" is an anagram for "Oral Sex."

Slash, Guns N' Roses Lead Guitarist (1985–96, 2016–Present)

Considered one of the greatest guitarists of all time, the laid-back, top-hatted guitar god of Guns N' Roses was born Saul Hudson on July 23, 1965, in London, England, although he was raised in Stoke-on-Trent. Living the complete opposite of Axl Rose's oppressive childhood, Slash grew up in a relaxed, permissive, and artistic household. His mother, Ola, was a costume designer, while his father, Anthony, was a graphic designer who created many album covers, including Joni Mitchell's *Court and Spark* (1973). Ola designed clothes and stage gear for the likes of David Bowie, John Lennon, Linda Ronstadt, and other musicians and celebrities (including the funky outfit Ringo Starr is wearing on the cover of his 1974 album *Goodnight Vienna*). She served as a costume designer for the 1976 cult film *The Man Who Fell to Earth*, which starred Bowie. After his parents divorced, Ola and Slash moved to Los Angeles. (Ola even dated Bowie briefly.) Slash has a younger brother named Albion "Ash" Hudson.

Slash grew up skateboarding and BMX racing. He soon became friends with future GN'R bandmate Steven Adler when they both attended Bancroft Junior High School in Los Angeles. He was given the nickname "Slash" by actor Seymour Cassel (*Rushmore*), the father of his childhood friend Matt, because he was always in a hurry. His early influences included Aerosmith (especially their 1976 album *Rocks*), Led Zeppelin, and Black Sabbath. Slash, who got his first guitar at the age of fifteen (a one-string flamenco guitar gifted to him by his grandmother), started practicing up to twelve hours a day. He later performed with several pre-Guns N' Roses bands during the early 1980s, such as Tidus Sloan, Road Crew (with Steven Adler and Duff McKagan), Klass, and Hollywood Rose (with Axl Rose and Izzy Stradlin). He also auditioned for Poison in 1984 but lost out to C. C. DeVille (not on ability but on "glam" factor).

The youngest member of Guns N' Roses, Slash appears with the band on the following albums: *Live?!*@ Like a Suicide* (1986), *Appetite for Destruction* (1987), *G N' R Lies* (1988), *Use Your Illusion I* (1991), *Use Your Illusion II* (1991), and *"The Spaghetti Incident?"* (1993). In 1995, his side project, Slash's Snakepit, released its debut album, *It's Five O'Clock Somewhere*. Slash's Snakepit also featured Slash's GN'R bandmates Matt Sorum and Gilby Clarke, as well as Mike Inez from Alice in Chains and Eric Dover from Jellyfish. The band's song "Jizz Da Pitt" can be heard in the 1997 Quentin Tarantino film *Jackie Brown*. Slash also formed Slash's Blues Ball, a blues cover band. After leaving Guns N' Roses in 1996, Slash engaged in a feud with Axl that played out in the media over the next two decades.

In 1999, Slash regrouped Slash's Snakepit with an entirely new lineup and released the 2000 album *Ain't Life Grand*. In 2001, at the age of thirty-five, Slash was diagnosed with cardiomyopathy—caused by years of drug and alcohol abuse—and was implanted with a defibrillator after initially being given six days to six weeks to live. In 2003, Slash joined "supergroup" Velvet Revolver, along with former GN'R bandmates Duff McKagan and Matt Sorum, as well as Scott Weiland from Stone Temple Pilots and Dave Kushner from Wasted Youth. The band's first album, *Contraband*, debuted at No. 1 on the US charts and featured the hit single, "Set Me Free."

In 2007, Slash published a self-titled autobiography that reached No. 8 on the *New York Times* Best Seller List. Slash was inducted into the 2012 Rock and Roll Hall of Fame. In 2016, Axl, Slash, and Duff reunited for several GN'R concerts (Troubadour, Las Vegas, and Coachella) before embarking on the heavily publicized Not in This Lifetime Tour. Concerning Axl, Slash remarked in his autobiography, "Axl is a dramatic kind of individual. Everything he says or does has a meaning, a theatrical place in his mind, in a blown-out-of-proportion kind of way."

Slash was married to Renee Suran from 1992 to 1997 and Perla Ferrar from 2001 to 2015. He and Perla have two children: London and Cash. Slash has released three solo albums: *Slash* (2010), which featured an impressive roster of guest musicians, including Ozzy Osbourne, Lemmy of Motörhead, Dave Grohl of Foo Fighters, Chris Cornell of Soundgarden, Iggy Pop, Fergie of the Black Eyed Peas, Adam Levine of Maroon 5, M. Shadows of Avenged Sevenfold, as well as Izzy, Duff, and Steven Adler; and *Apocalyptic Love* (2012) and *World on Fire* (2014), both of which featured Myles Kennedy and the Conspirators.

Slash Trivia

Check out these fascinating tidbits about Guns N' Roses' legendary lead guitarist.

- Slash's least favorite Guns N' Roses song is "Sweet Child O' Mine."
- His signature guitar solo is "The Godfather Theme" ("Speak Softly, Love," originally recorded by Andy Williams).
- He collects vintage Les Paul guitars.
- Slash's favorite live albums are *Live! Bootleg* (Aerosmith, 1978), *Live at Leeds* (the Who, 1970), '*Get Yer Ya-Ya's Out*' (the Rolling Stones, 1970), and *Give the People What They Want* (the Kinks, 1981).
- His favorite West Hollywood hangout is the Rainbow Bar & Grill.
- Slash once owned approximately eighty snakes, as well as a mountain lion cub named Curtis.
- He played guitar on the track "Give In to Me," which appeared on Michael Jackson's 1991 album *Dangerous*. He also collaborated with Lenny Kravitz on "Always on the Run," the lead track from *Mama Said* (1991).
- A gifted artist, Slash designed the famous circular Guns N' Roses logo.
- His favorite book is *Fear and Loathing in Las Vegas* (1971) by Hunter S. Thompson.
- Slash collaborated with the legendary Ray Charles on the song "Baby Let Me Hold Your Hand" for the soundtrack of the 2004 film *Ray*, which starred Jamie Foxx in the title role.
- He has a star on the Hollywood Walk of Fame (located at 6901 Hollywood Boulevard in front of the Hard Rock Café).
- *Time* magazine placed Slash at No. 2, behind Jimi Hendrix, on its list of the "10 Best Electric Guitar Players."
- He collects pinball machines and is an avid horror movie buff.

Izzy Stradlin, Guns N' Roses Rhythm Guitarist (1985–91)

The most mysterious, intensely private Guns N' Roses band member from the "classic" lineup, Izzy Stradlin has been called the "heart and soul" of GN'R. He was born Jeffrey Dean Isbell on April 8, 1962, and grew up in Lafayette, Indiana (also Axl Rose's hometown). Izzy's parents divorced when he was eight years old. He described his childhood as one full of riding bikes, smoking pot, and getting into trouble—"it was pretty *Beavis and Butt-Head* actually." Izzy first met Axl Rose in high school, and the friends started performing covers of their favorite bands in his garage. His earliest influences included the Rolling Stones, New York Dolls, Led Zeppelin, Aerosmith, Pink Floyd, Alice Cooper, and Hanoi Rocks.

After graduating from high school (the only GN'R band member to do so) in 1979, Izzy made his escape from Indiana (which he later described as "a worthless fuckin' place") and headed for Los Angeles. Izzy performed with a slew of pre-Guns N' Roses bands, such as Naughty Women, the Atoms, the Babysitters (where, according to Tracii Guns in a 1999 *SPIN* interview, he "wore a dress, and I think somebody beat his ass"), Shire, Hollywood Rose (with Axl), London, and Stalin. Izzy recorded with Guns N' Roses on the following albums: *Live?!*@ Like a Suicide* (1986), *Appetite for Destruction* (1987), *G N' R Lies* (1988), *Use Your Illusion I* (1991), and *Use Your Illusion II* (1991). Izzy wrote or cowrote many of Guns N' Roses' best-known songs, such as "Sweet Child O' Mine," "Paradise City," "Patience," "Don't Cry," and "You Could Be Mine," among others. He also assumed vocal duties on the likes of "Dust N' Bones," "You Ain't the First, "14 Years," and "Double Talkin' Jive."

After kicking his heroin addiction, Izzy decided to quit Guns N' Roses in the middle of the *Use Your Illusion* Tour. (He was replaced by Gilby Clarke.) He soon started his own band, Izzy Stradlin & the Ju Ju Hounds. In 1992, the band released its self-titled debut album—which *Rolling Stone* called "a ragged, blues-drenched, and thoroughly winning solo debut"—and broke up soon thereafter. Izzy has since released a ton of solo albums, including *117°* (1998), *Ride On* (1999), *River* (2001), *On Down the Road* (2002), *Like a Dog* (2003), *Miami* (2007), *Fire, the Acoustic Album* (2007), *Concrete* (2008), *Smoke* (2009), and *Wave of Heat* (2010). Izzy was inducted into the 2012 Rock and Roll Hall of Fame as a member of Guns N' Roses but declined to attend the ceremony. Although he has performed sporadically with Guns N' Roses since leaving the band in 1991, Izzy is the only member of the classic Guns N' Roses lineup who did not perform at all with GN'R during the 2016 Not in This Lifetime Tour.

Izzy Trivia

Find out more interesting facts about Guns N' Roses' reclusive rhythm guitarist.

*   His guitar hero is Keith Richards of the Rolling Stones.
*   He was the first member of Guns N' Roses to get a tattoo.
*   He was arrested in 1989 for causing a public disturbance (that included urinating in the galley) on a US Airways flight.
*   At the 1989 MTV Video Music Awards, Izzy was sucker punched back-stage by Vince Neil of Mötley Crüe.
*   On his second album, *117°*, which was released in 1998, Izzy covered the Chuck Berry hit "Memphis."
*   Izzy made a guest appearance performing on "Ghost," the first track of Slash's first solo album, *Slash*, in 2010.

Duff McKagan, Guns N' Roses Bassist (1985–97, 2016–Present)

Duff McKagan, who brought a strong punk sensibility to Guns N' Roses (in both his musical style and attitude), was born Michael Andrew McKagan in Seattle, Washington, on February 5, 1964. The youngest of eight children born to Alice and Elmer "Mac" MacKagan, Duff had a near-death experience after a waterskiing accident that was documented in the 1991 book *Closer to the Light: Learning from the Near-Death Experiences of Children*. He discovered punk and glam rock as a teenager and joined his first band, the Fastbacks, as a drummer at the age of sixteen. He dropped out of high school in the tenth grade. His early influences included Prince, the Clash, the Sex Pistols, Johnny Thunders, English post-punk band Magazine, Cameo, Motörhead, Sly and the Family Stone, and Iggy and the Stooges.

In addition to the Fastbacks, Duff performed with the likes of the Vains, the Living, Silly Killers, Cannibal, the Fartz, 10 Minute Warning (which toured the northwestern United States with punk band D.O.A.), and Road Crew (with Slash and Steven Adler), along with a host of other bands. In addition, Duff declined an invitation to join notorious scum-rock band the Mentors. Duff appears on the following Guns N' Roses albums: *Live?!*@ Like a Suicide* (1986), *Appetite for Destruction* (1987), *G N' R Lies* (1988), *Use Your Illusion I* (1991), *Use Your Illusion II* (1991), and *"The Spaghetti Incident?"* (1993). In 1993, Duff released his solo debut album, *Believe in Me*. In 1994, after suffering a life-threatening bout with acute alcohol-induced pancreatitis at

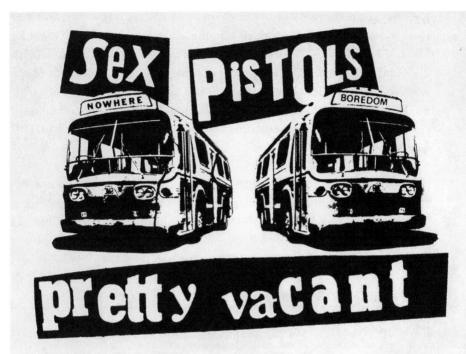

Guns N' Roses infused the blistering hard rock of Aerosmith with a punk sensibility that hearkened back to the onstage anarchy of the Sex Pistols.   *Author's collection*

the age of thirty, Duff sobered up and started a strict workout regimen that involved mountain biking and martial arts/kickboxing.

Duff—along with GN'R bandmate Matt Sorum, ex-Sex Pistol Steve Jones, and John Taylor of Duran Duran—formed the supergroup Neurotic Outsiders the following year. (The band even served a residency at the Viper Room in West Hollywood.) He officially quit Guns N' Roses in 1997 (although the band had been rather inactive for at least three years prior to his decision). In 1999, Duff recorded another solo album, *Beautiful Disease*, but the album was never released due to legal issues involving Geffen Records. That same year, Duff formed the band Loaded with some of his musician friends from Seattle. The band has released one live album, *Episode 1999: Live* (1999), three studio albums—*Dark Days* (2001), *Sick* (2009), and *The Taking* (2011)—as well as the EP *Wasted Heart* (2008).

In 2002, Duff formed another successful supergroup, Velvet Revolver, with Slash, Matt Sorum, Scott Weiland of Stone Temple Pilots, and Dave

Kushner from Wasted Youth. On October 14, 2010, Duff joined Guns N' Roses onstage at the O2 Arena in London and performed "You Could Be Mine," "Nice Boys," "Knockin' on Heaven's Door," and "Patience" with the band. (He joined GN'R again briefly in 2014 for five shows in South America, along with a show at the Joint in Las Vegas that same year.) Duff was inducted into the 2012 Rock and Roll Hall of Fame as a member of Guns N' Roses. He rejoined Guns N' Roses in 2016 for the Not in This Lifetime Tour.

Duff has been married three times: to Mandy Brixx, lead singer of the punk band the Lame Flames (1988–90); to Linda Johnson, a Penthouse Pet (1992–95); and to Susan Holmes, a model (1999–present). Duff and Susan have two daughters. He has published two books: *It's So Easy: and Other Lies* (2011) and *How to Be a Man: (and other illusions)* (2015). The former book was turned into a 2016 documentary of the same name.

Duff Trivia

Below are some interesting facts about the Guns N' Roses bassist.

- In an interview Duff once remarked that his "first musical memory" was hearing "Lovely Rita" by the Beatles when he was around five years old.
- When he first moved to Los Angeles in 1983, Duff worked at the restaurant Black Angus.
- Duff has stated that the fictional "Duff Beer" in *The Simpsons* was named after him but the show's creator, Matt Groening, called the claim "absurd."
- In 1999, Duff appeared in the documentary *Betty Blowtorch and Her Amazing True Life Adventures*, about the all-female hard rock band Betty Blowtorch from Southern California.
- In 2000, Duff enrolled full-time at Seattle University's Albers School of Business and Economics.
- Duff briefly joined Jane's Addiction in 2010. The following year, he founded Meridian Rock, a wealth management firm for musicians.
- Duff served as a columnist for ESPN.com, the *Seattle Weekly*, and Playboy. com.
- Duff occasionally tours with the supergroup Hollywood Vampires, whose members include Alice Cooper, Joe Perry, and Johnny Depp.

Steven Adler, Guns N' Roses Drummer (1985–90)

In a band that exemplified self-destructiveness, Steven Adler was by far the most reckless member of Guns N' Roses and the only one to ever get fired for drug abuse. Adler was born Michael Coletti in Cleveland, Ohio, on January 22, 1965. After Adler's biological father left the family, his mother, Deanna, moved the family to Los Angeles, where she married Melvin Adler and changed her son's name to Steven. Adler has an older brother, Kenny, and younger half-brother, Jamie. Adler first met Slash when both were attending Bancroft Junior High School. His earliest musical influences were KISS, Aerosmith, Queen, Boston, and Mott the Hoople. In 1978, Adler attended his first concert, KISS at Magic Mountain theme park in Valencia, California (which occurred during the filming of the TV movie *Kiss Meets the Phantom of the Park*).

As a teenager, Adler became a fixture of the West Hollywood scene and started hanging out at such legendary hotspots as the Rainbow Bar & Grill, Starwood, Whisky A Go Go, and Barney's Beanery. Adler performed in the pre-Guns N' Roses bands Road Crew (with Slash and Duff) and Hollywood Rose (with Axl, Izzy, and Slash). Adler recorded with Guns N' Roses on the following albums: *Live?!*@ Like a Suicide* (1986), *Appetite for Destruction* (1987), *G N' R Lies* (1988), and *Use Your Illusion II* (1991), on the track "Civil War" only. After getting fired by GN'R in 1990 (his last concert with the band was the Farm Aid IV debacle—see Chapter 14: "Top Ten Most Notorious Guns N' Roses Concerts"), Adler sued the band (and received a $2.5 million settlement and fifteen percent royalties on everything he recorded for the band) and, struggling with severe drug addiction, spent years in and out of rehab facilities. At one point, Adler attempted to reform Road Crew, but the effort was unsuccessful. In 1996, Adler suffered a stroke induced by injecting a "speedball" of cocaine and heroin.

In 2003, Adler formed the band Adler's Appetite (formerly known as Suki Jones), which performed mostly songs from *Appetite for Destruction*. Adler has released three solo albums: *Adler's Appetite* (2005), *Alive* (2012), and *Back from the Dead* (2012). His autobiography, *My Appetite for Destruction: Sex & Drugs & Guns N' Roses*, was published in 2011. Adler was inducted into the 2012 Rock and Roll Hall of Fame as a member of Guns N' Roses. He ended his acceptance speech by quoting from "We Are the Champions" by Queen: "I've taken my bows, my curtain calls, you've brought me fame and fortune and everything that goes with it, and I thank you all." Although Adler was not officially a part of the 2016 Not in This Lifetime Tour, he made a guest appearance and played drums during several songs at two of the shows.

Steven Adler Trivia

Enjoy these little-known facts about Guns N' Roses' original drummer.

- After getting fired from GN'R, Adler was set to join AC/DC, but he claims that an appearance by Axl on the 1990 MTV Video Music Awards where he labeled Adler a drug addict effectively torpedoed the offer.
- Adler was the subject of the song "Wasted Time" by Sebastian Bach that appeared on Skid Row's 1991 album, *Slave to the Grind*.
- In 1998, Adler briefly joined the Los Angeles hard rock band BulletBoys (future Guns N' Roses lead guitarist DJ Ashba was also in the group).
- Adler appeared in seasons two and five of *Celebrity Rehab with Dr. Drew* in 2008 and 2011 respectively, as well as the first season of the show's spin-off, *Sober House* (2009).
- He made a guest appearance on Slash's 2010 self-titled debut solo album, playing drums on the track "Baby Can't Drive."
- Adler once remarked in a 2012 *Rolling Stone* interview that John Mellencamp was "the coolest person I ever met in my whole life."

2

Another Dead-End Street

Pre-Guns N' Roses Bands

Punk pretty much had died and . . . everybody was searching for a thing to do musically.
—Duff McKagan

The road toward the creation of the "classic" Guns N' Roses lineup that recorded *Appetite For Destruction* passed through dozens of bands, most of which are long forgotten today, like the Atoms, Shire, Rapid Fire, Black Sheep, the Babysitters, Vain, and Naughty Women. Dumb luck was also a huge factor. For instance, what would have happened if Duff McKagan had actually entertained the offer from Sickie Wifebeater and El Duce to join scum-rock band the Mentors? If Slash had beat out C. C. DeVille for a spot in Poison? If Izzy Stradlin had decided to hightail it back to Indiana since he had been in Los Angeles for five years without much success and was ready to give up? If L.A. Guns had decided against joining forces with Hollywood Rose to create the early version of Guns N' Roses? Thankfully, everything fell in place for GN'R . . . but the journey was long, arduous, and paved with setbacks and misfortune.

10 Minute Warning

A popular, influential Seattle punk band, 10 Minute Warning was formed by Duff and Paul Solger (both former members of another Seattle band called the Fartz) in 1982. The band also featured Steve Verwolf (vocals) and Greg Gilmore (drums). 10 Minute Warning got their big break when they joined a tour of the northwestern United States with Vancouver punk band D.O.A. (often considered the founders of hardcore punk). Although it was a talented band with much potential, 10 Minute Warning was "decimated" by heroin, according to Duff. In fact, Duff was about the only one in the Seattle music scene *not* doing heroin at the time. According to Duff in *Everybody Loves Our Town: An Oral History of Grunge*, "A friend of mine who was strung out said, 'Man, if you don't get out now, it's going to pass you by. You're the guy, you're our hope.'" Duff made the wise decision to quit the band and decided to head for Los Angeles in 1984. Without any direction whatsoever, 10 Minute Warning broke up soon after. (They had recorded songs for an album that was never released.)

Tidus Sloan

Slash's first true band—Tidus Sloan (no one seems to know what the name meant!), which formed in 1981—consisted of a bunch of his high school friends, including Ron Schneider (guitar), Adam Greenberg (bass), and Louie Metz (drums). The band never found a decent lead singer, so they remained a purely instrumental band. Schneider later became a roadie for Guns N' Roses. One of the band's makeshift flyers read, "Hear the sounds of Rush, Zeppelin, Sabbath, Aerosmith & Hendrix." A typical set included some original material, such as "When the Fire Dies," "Metal on Metal," "What a Change," "Rats Ass Rock N' Roll," "Funky," and "Stormbringer," as well as plenty of covers, including "Heaven and Hell" (Black Sabbath), "What You're Doing" (Rush), "Dazed and Confused" (Led Zeppelin), "Message in a Bottle" (the Police), and "Start Me Up" (the Rolling Stones), among others.

The most memorable Tidus Sloan gig, according to Slash, was a bat mitzvah "in the middle of nowhere." The band arrived the night before and stayed in the guesthouse, where they proceeded to get totally shitfaced and trash the whole place. Someone even barfed in the stew that was simmering overnight in preparation for the celebration. The next morning Slash woke up on the floor "with a raging headache, broken glass stuck to my face, and the odor of warm vomit-infused stew clinging to the air," according to his 2007 autobiography. Tidus Sloan later terrified most of the guests with their heavy metal-inspired set, which consisted mostly of Black Sabbath and Deep Purple covers. According to Greenberg in *Reckless Road*, "We always cranked it up to the limit."

Road Crew

After the breakup of Tidus Sloan, Slash joined forces with his childhood friend, Steven Adler, to form Road Crew (a.k.a. Roadcrew). The name was reportedly derived from the Motörhead song "(We Are) The Road Crew" off of the band's influential 1980 album *Ace of Spades*. According to Adler in his autobiography, the name Road Crew "summed up our warrior attitude about bringing great rock 'n' roll to the masses." Slash, in his autobiography, described the band as "like Metallica . . . but without a singer." Seeking a bass player, they took out an ad in *The Recycler* that read, "Bass player needed for band influenced by Aerosmith, Alice Cooper. Call Slash." It was answered by Duff, who met them at Canter's Deli. They were intrigued by his spiked blonde hair, punk garb, and nonchalant attitude, and joined forces with him on the spot. However, the band was never able to find a decent lead singer and ended up playing just a few gigs.

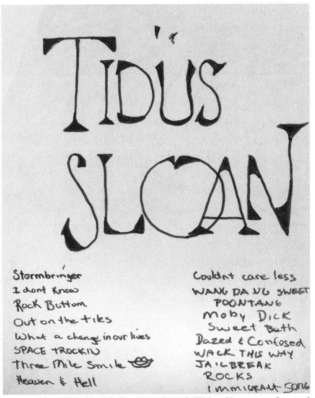

Formed in 1981, Slash's first true band, Tidus Sloan, performed mostly covers of Rush, Black Sabbath, Led Zeppelin, Aerosmith, and Jimi Hendrix.   *Author's collection*

Rapidfire

Axl (still using the name Bill Bailey) was the lead singer for a brief period in this Los Angeles rock band, which also featured guitarist Kevin Lawrence, bassist Mike Hamernik, and drummer Chuck Gordon. Significantly, Rapidfire recorded an EP called *Ready to Rumble* (Axl's first recording) in May 1983, just three days before breaking up. *Ready to Rumble* featured the tracks "All Night Long," "The Prowler," "On the Run," and "Closure." Lawrence finally released the EP in 2014 after struggling with Axl's legal team for several years.

London

At one time or another, London, a revolving-door type of heavy metal outfit that formed in 1978, featured band members that went on to bigger and better things, such as Nikki Sixx (Mötley Crüe), Fred Coury (Cinderella), and briefly, Izzy Stradlin. (In addition, Slash and Steven Adler both tried out for the band before joining Guns N' Roses.) Original band members included Sixx, Lizzie Grey (who cowrote the Mötley Crüe song "Public Enemy #1"), and Dane Rage. Adler and Slash had caught a London show at the Starwood around the time the band first formed and were impressed with Sixx's spiked hair, black leather outfit, and black-and-white striped bass guitar. Adler later claimed, "It was the coolest thing I ever fucking saw."

Izzy was recruited by the second incarnation of London in 1984. At this time, the lineup also featured Grey, Nadir D'Priest, Bobby Marks, and Brian West. During an L.A. Guns gig at the Troubadour on October 5, 1984, Axl started a rant against London, which had performed first, and ripped up one of their posters while remarking, "We'd like to thank them for fuckin' nothing!" He then launched into a cover of Rose Tattoo's "Nice Boys (Don't Play Rock 'n' Roll)." When Slash tried out for London over a four-day period, he couldn't believe how "pompous" the band members, who "behaved like they were larger-than-life," were. London appeared in the heavy metal documentary *The Decline of Western Civilization II: The Metal Years* (1988). In early 2007, Slash was headed to the studio and he spotted one of the guys from London "wearing the same getup, still looking for a gig."

Hollywood Rose

Axl and Izzy formed the band Hollywood Rose in 1983 with guitarist Chris Weber, a Los Angeles native. The band, which initially went by the name

the roots of guns n'roses
feat. axl rose & izzy stradlin

HOLLYWOOD ROSE

In January 1984, Hollywood Rose recorded a five-song demo featuring the tracks "Anything Goes," "Rocker," "Shadow of Your Love," "Killing Time," and "Reckless Life." The demo was released as *The Roots of Guns N' Roses* in 2004.   *Author's collection*

AXL and then simply Rose, later added bassist Rick Mars and drummer Johnny Kreiss. Hollywood Rose's first gig took place on January 3, 1984, at the Orphanage in North Hollywood. Weber soon quit the band and headed to New York City. One early flyer for Hollywood Rose that was designed by Axl and Izzy exclaimed, "There [sic] Living Fast and they'll Die Young! See them now!" Another flyer for Madame Wong's East gig simply announced, "Hell Revisited." In January 1984, the band recorded a five-song demo featuring the tracks "Anything Goes," "Rocker," "Shadow of Your Love," "Killing Time," and "Reckless Life," which was released in 2004 as *The Roots of Guns N' Roses* (generating an unsuccessful cease-and-desist lawsuit from Axl). Guitarist Slash and drummer Steven Adler joined Hollywood Rose briefly as the "new" Hollywood Rose before the band's dissolution. They had previously encountered the band at Gazzarri's, causing Slash to declare Axl "the best singer in Hollywood at the time."

L.A. Guns

Formed in 1983, the group's original lineup featured Axl and Tracii Guns. Just like Hollywood Rose, L.A. Guns was a revolving-door outfit that shared members back and forth with other local bands. After Tracii Guns was later replaced by Slash in Guns N' Roses, he headed back to L.A. Guns, which had continued playing gigs in his absence with Paul Black on vocals. (Black was later replaced by Phil Lewis.) L.A. Guns finally released their debut album in 1988 on Vertigo Records. The band's follow-up album, *Cocked and Loaded* (1989), featured the Top Forty single "The Ballad of Jayne."

Guns N' Roses (Original Lineup)

The original lineup of Guns N' Roses resulted from a merging of the bands L.A. Guns and Hollywood Rose in March 1985. The new band at that time consisted of Axl on vocals, Tracii Guns on lead guitar, Izzy on rhythm guitar, Ole Beich on bass, and Rob Gardner on drums. According to Tracii Guns, the newly formed band desired to evoke "a heavy Aerosmith" sound with "a funky swagger" along with a "punk rock attitude." Proposed band names that were ultimately (and thankfully!) rejected before settling on Guns N' Roses included AIDS and Heads of Amazon. Guns, Beich, and Gardner all left the band shortly before the "Hell Tour" and were hastily replaced by Slash, Duff, and Steven Adler respectively. According to Tracii Guns in a 2010 interview with *The Quietus*, "Axl and I got into an extraordinary fight—and we had never argued ever in the past few years before. [Then] I just kind of went my own way . . . I was probably nineteen then and I thought 'great band, and I love these guys, but they're not worth the headaches.' Even at that age I didn't want to deal with it." Tragically, Beich, who struggled with heroin addiction, drowned in Sankt Jorgens Lake in Copenhagen, Denmark, in 1991.

3

The Price You Pay

"Hell Tour" (Summer 1985)

When we got back from the Hell Tour, from that shared experience, we knew that we had each other's backs. At that point we knew we were a band. We were ready to fuck up L.A.　　　　　　　　　—Duff McKagan

The established lineup of Guns N' Roses that later recorded *Appetite for Destruction* took shape in June 1985 and consisted of lead singer Axl Rose, lead guitarist Slash, rhythm guitarist Izzy Stradlin, bassist Duff McKagan, and drummer Steven Adler. After a couple of days' rehearsals, the band decided to set off on an extremely haphazard "punk tour" along the West Coast with scheduled gigs, arranged by Duff, in Seattle (over one thousand miles away from L.A.), Portland, Eugene, Sacramento, and San Francisco. Former band members Tracii Guns and Rob Gardner had backed out of the epic trip, leaving the door open for Slash and Steven Adler to join the band at the eleventh hour. Plagued with several serious misfortunes from the outset, the misadventure soon became dubbed the "Hell Tour" by band members. However, in hindsight the ill-conceived journey actually turned out to be an incredible bonding experience for Guns N' Roses as the band returned home, prepared to "kick ass," and quickly set their sights on conquering the West Hollywood club scene.

First Gig with the New Lineup at the Troubadour

Before embarking on the notorious "Hell Tour," the new lineup of Guns N' Roses performed for the first time together at the Troubadour in West Hollywood on June 6, 1985. According to Slash in his autobiography, the band had just one rehearsal before the gig, and he claimed, "It really was like a synergy. It was like we'd been playing together for years." The flyer for the show promised "A Rock N Roll Bash Where Everyones [sic] Smashed." During this legendary gig, the band played a standard set of early songs in their repertoire, such as "Reckless Life," "Shadow of Your Love," "Think About You," "Move to the City," "Back Off Bitch," "Anything Goes," and "Don't Cry," along with a smattering of favorite covers that included "Jumpin' Jack Flash (the Rolling Stones), "Nice Boys" (Rose Tattoo), and "Heartbreak Hotel" (Elvis Presley). Three people showed up at the gig.

Stranded Somewhere Outside of Bakersfield

The following day, Guns N' Roses (along with a "roadie" named Joe and another friend Danny Birall, who owned the car and was therefore dubbed

Steven Adler   Izzy Stradlin   Duff "Rose" McKagan   W. Axl Rose   Slash

GUNS N' ROSES

GEFFEN
RECORDS

The Guns N' Roses lineup that would eventually record *Appetite for Destruction* embarked on an incredibly ill-conceived West Coast tour in June 1985 that turned into an amazing bonding experience for the band.   *Author's collection* the "tour manager") headed up Interstate 5 in a beat-up 1977 green Pontiac Catalina and had made it just over 150 miles when the car, which had a U-Haul trailer attached, broke down somewhere between Bakersfield and Fresno, California. According to Duff in *It's So Easy: and Other Lies*, "We were broke, hungry, and sweltering, hunkered down on the side of the highway . . . We had thirty-seven dollars between us." The band was forced to abandon their gear and hitchhike for forty hours to make it the rest of the way to Seattle (getting rides from a trucker who was a total speed freak, an old Mexican farmer and his son, and "two wild hippie chicks").

Playing Gorilla Garden, Seattle

The first and only Guns N' Roses show of "Hell Tour" (the rest of the gigs had been cancelled by the time the band made it to Seattle) took place at the Rock Theater (known locally as Gorilla Garden) in Seattle on June 8, 1985. Duff's former band, the Fastbacks, opened for Guns N' Roses, and just thirteen people showed up. GN'R had to use the Fastbacks' gear for

Duff McKagan was able to book Guns N' Roses at the legendary Gorilla Garden club due to his connections as an ex-member of Seattle punk band 10 Minute Warning.

Author's collection

the show since they were forced to leave theirs behind when the car broke down. One of the flyers for the Gorilla Garden show read, "Guns and Roses Featuring ex-Ten Minute Warning member Duff McKagan with Fastbacks plus 5150, Sat., June 8 Rock Theater 5th & Jackson." To add insult to injury, GN'R received just $50 rather than the $250 they were promised for the gig. Steven Adler later referred to the Gorilla Garden as "a filthy dive bar," while Slash called it "the epitome of a punk-rock shit hole."

Other bands to perform at the legendary Gorilla Garden over the years include the Violent Femmes, Hüsker Dü, and Soundgarden, among many others. After the Gorilla Garden gig, the band caught a ride all the way back to Los Angeles from one of Duff''s friends and made a beeline for Canter's Deli to get some free grub from their old pal, Marc Canter. According to Duff in an October 5, 2011, article for the *Seattle Weekly*, Guns N' Roses arrived back in Los Angeles as "a genuine band—a gang with the shared experience of a road trip gone wrong, an out-of-town gig, and the knowledge that we were all fully committed to Guns N' Roses." Steven Adler concurred, calling the adventure a "ridiculously irrational initiation ceremony, one that no sane person could have tolerated."

Signing with Geffen Records

As their popularity grew based on some amazing live performances at various West Hollywood clubs, Guns N' Roses suddenly found themselves getting pursued by record labels such as Geffen, Warner Bros., Elektra, and Chrysalis. Even after they decided to go with Geffen, GN'R continued to be courted by the other labels so they could continue enjoying the "extravagant liquid lunches," according to Slash. In the VH1 *Behind the Music* special on Guns N' Roses, Geffen's A&R (Artist and Repertoire) representative Tom Zutaut, who had previously signed Mötley Crüe, stated, "I basically went to David Geffen and said, 'I just saw the biggest rock 'n' roll band in the world. They're going to sell more records than maybe Led Zeppelin and the Rolling Stones.'" Zutaut was referring to the band's gig at the Troubadour on February 28, 1986, where "Out Ta Get Me" was performed live for the first time.

Guns N' Roses officially signed with Geffen Records on March 25, 1986, and received a $75,000 advance for a six-record deal. According to Duff, the band members either kept the money in their boots or stashed it under a mattress. Slash later admitted that he spent almost all of his advance on heroin. Each of the band members ran out and got new tattoos (including

Axl, whose new ink read "Victory or Death"). Geffen told the band to lay low and not perform for the next four months, a move that nearly broke up the band, according to Axl, who later remarked during a 2016 Q&A session to promote the Not in This Lifetime Tour, "Everybody got hooked on drugs and stuff [during] whatever the label was doing to figure out who would work with us. Everybody was terrified of us anyway because they thought we were going to die. We were going to leave the label. We wanted to play, we wanted to get out to New York or something. We didn't get signed to sit in an apartment."

New Zealand-born Alan Niven, who had managed Great White, became Guns N' Roses' new manager (providing the band with a steady supply of Jack Daniel's, porno mags, and pizza). Niven replaced Vicky Hamilton, who had gone to bat for the band on many occasions, arranging gigs, initiating contact with record labels like Geffen, and even letting the band crash in her one-bedroom apartment, which they promptly trashed. In 1987, Hamilton sued Guns N' Roses and received an out-of-court settlement of $35,000. Before she was unceremoniously handed her walking papers, Hamilton, who had worked with Mötley Crüe and Poison in their early days, came up with a brief bio of Guns N' Roses that read:

> Wild abandon & streetwise composure are encompassed by the music of the savvy & sexy guns n' roses. Rising from the Hollywood underground, the band has confidence, raw power, and the authenticity of actually surviving the streets . . . Guns n' roses runs on the pure strength of emotion and feeling as can be seen in their highly visual and energetic performances. They aren't afraid to be themselves and refuse to compromise their stance and beliefs for anyone or anything. They've paid their debt to society and are ready to take on the world.

During a March 28, 1986, GN'R gig at the Roxy, Axl dedicated "Mama Kin" to Hamilton, "for putting up with me being a really weird fuck. I am just a pain in the ass."

Release of *Live?!*@ Like a Suicide*

In December 1986, Guns N' Roses released (through Uzi Suicide, actually a subsidiary of Geffen Records) a limited pressing of 10,000 copies of the four-song EP *Live?!*@ Like a Suicide*, which featured two original songs, "Reckless" and "Move to the City," along with two covers that they played the hell out of in early gigs throughout West Hollywood: Aerosmith's "Mama

Kin" and Rose Tattoo's "Nice Boys (Don't Play Rock 'n' Roll)." Izzy, quoted in the Axl Rose biography, considered the EP "an expensive dedication to all the kids who helped us get going when we had no money."

Although billed as a live recording, the four songs on the EP were actually taken from GN'R's demo tapes and overdubbed with crowd noise from the Texxas Jam, a 1970s rock festival, according to Duff. The album cover features the Guns N' Roses logo, along with an image of Duff (who is listed in the credits as Duff "Rose" McKagan) and Axl performing at an early gig. The back cover of the album includes a photo of the entire band straight from one of their early flyers (in this case the July 20, 1985 Troubadour gig), along with the message: "This is dedicated to our friends, for support in the streets as well as the stage." The photo was taken in an alley behind Canter's Deli.

4

In My First Memories

Musical Acts That Influenced Guns N' Roses

We were just following in the footsteps of our heroes growing up and then we just took it one step further.   —Slash

E ach member of Guns N' Roses brought his own set of disparate influences to the band, and somehow it all blended together perfectly. In addition to the influential bands listed below, GN'R idolized both Aerosmith and the Rolling Stones, and they experienced their dream of actually touring in support of both of those legendary bands. (See the chapter "Guns N' Roses as an Opening Act" for more on this.) In a 1986 interview with the *Daily Press*, Axl Rose remarked, "Our favorite music is hard rock—with a blues edge. We used to call ourselves a heavy metal/punk band, [but] I saw a fusion coming together a long time ago . . . The blues edge, the blues riffs, the blues feeling: we're trying to put that back into the music."

T. Rex

Formed in 1967 as Tyrannosaurus Rex, London-based T. Rex was a pioneer in the glitter rock movement and featured the talents of Marc Bolan (Mark Feld), Steve Peregrin Took (Stephen Ross Porter), and Mickey Finn. In the early 1970s, T. Rex achieved several No. 1 singles in the UK, such as "Ride a White Swan," "Bang a Gong (Get It On)," "Jeepster," and "Telegram Sam." The band was also known (just like Guns N' Roses) for their excessive partying, with Bolan once remarking, "I was living in a twilight world of drugs, booze, and kinky sex." Tragedy ensued when Bolan died in a car crash in 1977 and when Took passed away in 1980 after choking on a cocktail cherry while high on morphine. Guns N' Roses' cover of T. Rex's "Buick Makane" appears on *"The Spaghetti Incident?"* (1993). It was actually rhythm guitarist Gilby Clarke who suggested including a T. Rex song on the covers album. According to Clarke in a Songfacts.com interview, "Back then I was wearing a T. Rex T-shirt, like, every single day. Matt [Sorum] used to joke, 'Okay, we got it, we got it. You've worn the shirt every day.' I didn't pick the song that we did. I just suggested doing a T. Rex song. I wanted to do '20th Century Boy' or 'Children of the Revolution' or something."

Led Zeppelin

Ex-Yardbird Jimmy Page initially formed Led Zeppelin (originally named the New Yardbirds) as a way to complete the tour after the band, which featured Eric Clapton and Jeff Beck, broke up. Page then recruited bassist/keyboardist John Paul Jones, singer Robert Plant, and drummer John "Bonzo" Bonham for the endeavor. The band's new name reportedly came from the Who drummer Keith Moon, who declared that the band would go over about as well as a "lead zeppelin." Strongly influenced by American blues music, Led Zeppelin churned out many classics over the years, such as "Stairway to Heaven," "Whole Lotta Love," "Dazed and Confused," "Kashmir," "Black Dog," "Ramble On," "Going to California," and many others. The band was also known for its excessive debauchery on tour. According to Page, "Mild barbarians was how we were once described, and I can't really deny it." Led Zeppelin was inducted into the Rock and Roll Hall of Fame in 1995. As a young teenager, Slash was nabbed for stealing several cassettes, including Led Zeppelin's *Houses of the Holy*, from Tower Records on Sunset Boulevard. Guns N' Roses have covered Led Zeppelin songs such as "Communication Breakdown" and "Rock and Roll" during live performances over the years. Interestingly, *Rolling Stone* described the 2008 GN'R album *Chinese Democracy* as "Led Zeppelin's *Physical Graffiti* remixed by Beck and Trent Reznor."

New York Dolls

With their outrageous, trashed-out, androgynous stage getup (which included plenty of satin, rouge, and high heels) and raunchy, drug-fueled performances, the New York Dolls served as a precursor for the punk rock and glam metal movements. Although certainly not the most talented band (in fact, they bordered on total incompetence at times!), the Dolls strongly influenced the likes of the Sex Pistols, the Damned, KISS, Hanoi Rocks, the Smiths, and Guns N' Roses. The original Dolls lineup—consisting of lead singer David Johansen, guitarists Johnny Thunders (John Anthony Genzale) and Rick Rivets (George Fedorick), bassist Arther "Killer" Kane, and drummer Billy Murcia—performed their first gig rather inauspiciously at a flophouse called the Endicott Hotel in December 1971. The following year, Rivets was replaced by Sylvain Sylvain, and the Dolls got their big break opening for Rod Stewart at Wembley Stadium in London. However, tragedy ensued when Murcia died of a drug overdose after a post-gig bash. He was soon replaced by Jerry Nolan.

The following year saw the release of the Dolls' self-titled debut album, which was produced by Todd Rundgren and peaked at No. 116 on the US charts. It featured such gritty classics as "Personality Crisis," "Trash," and "Jet Boy." Billed as "The Band You Love to Hate," the Dolls captured both "Best New Group of the Year" and "Worst New Group of the Year" honors in *Creem* magazine's annual Readers' Choice Awards. In 1974, the Dolls released *Too Much Too Soon*, which was produced by George "Shadow" Martin and stalled at No. 167 on the US charts. Out of desperation, the Dolls hired Malcolm McLaren as manager, but the self-destructive band started to fall apart in 1975 upon the departure of Thunders and Nolan, both of whom were strung out on heroin. (Kane himself was struggling with severe alcohol addiction at the time.) Thunders went on to create the Heartbreakers with Richard Hell. McLaren got fired from the band, returned to London, and promptly formed the Sex Pistols (and the rest is history).

Johansen later morphed into flamboyant lounge singer "Buster Poindexter" and had a minor hit with "Hot Hot Hot" (which reached No. 45 on the US charts in 1988), while Kane somehow managed to sober up, relocate to Utah, and join the Mormon Church. Thunders died of an apparent drug overdose under mysterious circumstances in Room 37 at the St. Peter House in New Orleans in 1991. In his eulogy for Thunders, Richard Hell remarked, "[The Dolls] mocked the media, threw up on grownups, and kidded with the kids in a language of drugs and sex." Nolan died following a stroke just a few months after Thunders. In 2004, Morrissey organized a reunion of the three surviving band members—Johansen, Sylvain, and Kane—for a performance at the Meltdown Festival in London. Just three weeks after the show, Kane died of leukemia. (His fascinating life story was captured in the 2005 documentary *New York Doll*.)

Guns N' Roses (along with Jetboy) opened for Thunders at Fender's Ballroom in Long Beach, California, on March 21, 1986. According to Duff in *Reckless Road*, "Johnny Thunders was an icon to Izzy and I [sic]. He was the godfather of the type of rock 'n' roll music that we all dug, which was sleazy and in your face." However, frequent sound difficulties and an unruly crowd marred that particular gig. In addition, Axl became enraged when he discovered that Thunders had been hitting on his then girlfriend Erin Everly backstage. The 1993 GN'R album *"The Spaghetti Incident?"* features covers of the New York Dolls' "Human Being" and Johnny Thunders's "You Can't Put Your Arms Around a Memory."

Queen

Expertly fusing glam with hard rock, Queen was formed in London in 1971 and featured the legendary, flamboyant lead singer Freddie Mercury, lead guitarist Brian May, bassist John Deacon, and drummer Roger Taylor. The band's slew of hits over the years include "Bohemian Rhapsody," "Killer Queen," "Somebody to Love," "Crazy Little Thing Called Love," "Don't Stop Me Now," "Another One Bites the Dust," "We are the Champions," and "We Will Rock You." Mercury once exclaimed, "We're the Cecil B. DeMille of rock and roll, always wanting to do things bigger and better." Tragically, Mercury (real name: Farrokh Bulsara) died of complications due to AIDS at the age of forty-five in 1991.

Guns N' Roses performed "Paradise City" and "Knockin' at Heaven's Door" at the Freddie Mercury Tribute Concert for AIDS Awareness at London's Wembley Stadium on April 20, 1992. In addition, one of the highlights of the event was Axl, Elton John, and Queen performing "Bohemian Rhapsody." (Axl and Queen also performed "We Will Rock You.") In 1999, May recorded the lead guitar parts on the Guns N' Roses song "Catcher in the Rye," but his contribution was left on the cutting room floor somewhat controversially when *Chinese Democracy* was finally released in 2008. Queen was inducted into the Rock and Roll Hall of Fame in 2001. During a Q&A session to mark the beginning of the 2016 Not in This Lifetime Tour, Axl remarked, "Queen has always been my favorite band. Freddie is the greatest singer ever is the way I look at it. The other thing about Queen for me is they embraced so many different styles."

AC/DC

Formed in 1973, the hard-rocking band from Sydney, Australia (known for their "no-frills riffing," according to *Rolling Stone*), featured the original

One of Axl Rose's rock heroes, legendary Queen front man Freddie Mercury, composed numerous hits for Queen, such as "Bohemian Rhapsody," "Killer Queen," "We Are the Champions," "Somebody to Love," "Crazy Little Thing Called Love," and others.

Carl Lender/Wikimedia Commons

lineup of brothers Angus and Malcolm Young (lead guitar and rhythm guitar respectively), Bon Scott (vocals), Phillip Rudd (drums), and Mark Evans (bass, replaced by Cliff Williams in 1977). *Highway to Hell* was released in 1979, but tragedy struck the following year when Scott passed away after choking on his own vomit after an all-night drinking binge. Scott was replaced by Brian Johnson, former lead singer of the British band Geordie, and AC/DC's subsequent album, *Back in Black*—which featured such hits as "Back in Black," "You Shook Me All Night Long," "Hell's Bells," and "Rock and Roll Ain't Noise Pollution"—skyrocketed to No. 4 on the US charts. In 2003, AC/DC was inducted into the Rock and Roll Hall of Fame.

According to AC/DC biographer Jesse Fink, Guns N' Roses has "a lot of similar qualities to AC/DC: authenticity, vision, gang mentality, a sound pretty much their own that wasn't going to be fucked with by anyone and an almost feral hostility to the world and outsiders." In fact, in many of their earliest shows, GN'R covered "Whole Lotta Rosie," one of AC/DC's most popular songs from their 1977 album, *Let There Be Rock*. According to legend, the song refers to a one-night stand Bon Scott had with an extremely obese Tasmanian woman weighing over 300 pounds.

In 2016, Axl joined AC/DC's *Rock or Bust* World Tour, filling in for Johnson, who was forced to stop touring due to hearing issues. The move to replace Johnson with Axl drew a mixed reaction from fans and fellow rockers alike, with the Who's Roger Daltrey dismissively remarking to the *London Free Press*, "I mean, go and see karaoke with Axl Rose? Give me a break."

Motörhead

Formed in 1975 in England, Motörhead featured Lemmy Kilmister (bass/vocals), Eddie Clark (guitar), and Phil "Philthy Animal" Taylor (drums). Lemmy once remarked, "Metal is the bastard son of rock and roll. If Eddie Cochran was playing today, he'd probably be in a garage playing with a metal band." In 1980, Motörhead released their seminal album *Ace of Spades*, which featured the highly influential title track. In the March 2005 issue of *Q* magazine, "Ace of Spades" was ranked No. 27 on the magazine's list of the "Top 100 Greatest Guitar Tracks of All Time." According to Duff in a May 5, 2015, *Esquire* interview, all of the "classic" GN'R band members idolized Motörhead: "That's probably our root band . . . I think when *Ace of Spades* first came out, that was a real conjoining of punk, hard rock, rock 'n' roll, and some metal, and it was kind of a touchstone for everyone, especially if you're playing hard rock music." Motörhead actually opened for Guns N'

Roses during several dates on their ill-fated 1992 US tour with Metallica. According to Lemmy in a 1999 *SPIN* interview, "We played with Guns N' Roses at the Rose Bowl . . . and they were already fragmenting. Axl was on his own—it didn't feel like they were thinking as a band anymore."

Sex Pistols

Izzy Stradlin once declared, "Rock 'n' roll in general has just sucked a big fucking dick since the Pistols." Who can argue with Izzy? Equally influential and controversial, the Sex Pistols sparked the punk revolution in the mid-1970s. Formed in 1975 in London, the band's original lineup consisted of Johnny Rotten (vocals), Steve Jones (guitar), Glen Matlock (bass), and Paul Cook (drums). Rotten (real name: John Lydon) had been discovered by the band's manager, Malcolm McLaren, wandering around London wearing a Pink Floyd T-shirt with the words "I HATE" scrawled on it. In 1977, the outrageous Sid Vicious (who was so untalented on bass that his amplifier was kept unplugged during many shows) replaced Matlock, and the Pistols released their highly influential debut album, *Never Mind the Bollocks, Here's the Sex Pistols*, which *Rolling Stone* labeled "the Sermon on the Mount of UK punk." The seminal album featured such punk classics as "Anarchy in the UK," "God Save the Queen," "Pretty Vacant," "Holidays in the Sun," and "Bodies." Although the album reached No. 1 in Britain, it stalled at No. 106 on the US charts.

The Sex Pistols then embarked on a disastrous US tour that started in the South and concluded at the Winterland in San Francisco, where the group broke up. Rotten's last words on stage were, "Ever get the feeling you've been cheated?" A drug-addled Vicious (real name: John Simon Ritchie) remained in New York City (residing in the Chelsea Hotel with girlfriend Nancy Spungen) and released the single "My Way," an amazingly decadent punk remake of the Frank Sinatra classic. (Axl Rose reportedly loved to watch Vicious singing "My Way" over and over again on MTV during the mid-1980s.) On February 2, 1979, Vicious died of a heroin overdose at the age of twenty-one while out on bail for murder charges related to the mysterious stabbing death of Spungen in October of the previous year. The eminently strange relationship between Vicious and Spungen was expertly captured in the remarkable 1986 film *Sid and Nancy*, which starred Gary Oldman and Chloe Webb. Interestingly, Slash served as an extra in the film for a concert scene that was shot at the Starwood in West Hollywood. Other classic Sex Pistols-related films include *The Great Rock* 'n' *Roll Swindle* (1980) and *The Filth and the Fury* (2000). In 1995, Duff and Matt Sorum joined Steve Jones of the Sex Pistols and John Taylor of Duran Duran in the supergroup Neurotic Outsiders. The group, which frequently jammed at the Viper Room in West Hollywood, released a self-titled album in 1996.

Rose Tattoo

Formed in Australia in 1976 and fronted by George Stephen "Angry" Anderson, Rose Tattoo maintained a cult following as an outlaw band that strongly influenced Mötley Crüe and Guns N' Roses, who covered the track "Nice Boys (Don't Play Rock 'n' Roll)" on both *Live ?!*@ Like a Suicide* (1986) and *G N' R Lies* (1988). "Nice Boys" was also a mainstay of the band's early setlist during West Hollywood club gigs. Rose Tattoo's self-titled debut in 1978 featured such classics as "Rock 'n' Roll Outlaw" and "Bad Boy for Love." The band evinced a raw blues rock style led by the bald, five foot two Anderson, who one critic compared to a "sawed-off Sumo wrestler." Axl first encountered Rose Tattoo when the band opened for Aerosmith in 1982. According to former band member Robin Riley in *The Youngs: The Brothers Who Built AC/DC*, "Rose Tattoo has been ignored by the Australian music business, criminally . . . Guns N' Roses coming out and saying we inspired them was a beautiful thing but fucking nothing got done about it." Rose Tattoo even reunited to support Guns N' Roses at Sydney and Melbourne concerts during their 1993 Australian tour.

The Damned

Punk rock band the Damned achieved a number of milestones, including releasing the first punk single ("New Rose") in 1976, appearing on the bill during the first-ever Sex Pistols concert, and being the first British punk band to tour the United States. In addition, most rock critics consider the Damned's 1977 release, *Damned Damned Damned*, as the first punk album. The band's initial lineup consisted of Dave Vanian (vocals), Brian James (guitar), Captain Sensible (bass), and Rat Scabies (drummer). Guns N' Roses paid tribute to the Damned by covering "New Rose" on the 1993 album *"The Spaghetti Incident?"* When asked about the Guns N' Roses cover in a 2015 interview, Captain Sensible responded in a 2015 *NME* article, "The truth is, I haven't heard it, because I don't listen to any music made after 1980."

Guns N' Roses covered "New Rose" by English punk rock band the Damned on their 1993 album, "*The Spaghetti Incident?*" Cofounded by the enigmatic Captain Sensible, the Damned was the first UK punk band to release an album, *Damned Damned Damned*, in 1977.

Johnny Jet/Wikimedia Commons

Hanoi Rocks

A groundbreaking Finnish rock band that formed in 1979, Hanoi Rocks carried the influence of the Rolling Stones, the Stooges, New York Dolls, and Alice Cooper. According to the *Rough Guide to Punk*, Hanoi Rocks was "self-consciously trashy but in a good way." However, the once-promising band collapsed after the tragic death of drummer Nicholas "Razzle" Dingley in a car accident in December 1981 during a beer run with Mötley Crüe's

Hanoi Rocks served as a major influence for Guns N' Roses, who acknowledged their debt to the band by reissuing the Finnish hard rock band's back catalog on their own Uzi Suicide label.
Tuomas Vitikainen/Wikimedia Commons

front man Vince Neil, who was at the wheel. Hanoi Rocks never fully recovered from Razzle's death and disbanded in 1985 (although they reformed in 2002). Guns N' Roses' UZI Suicide label rereleased Hanoi Rocks' albums on CD in the early 1990s. In addition, Hanoi Rocks front man Michael Monroe played the harmonica and saxophone on the GN'R song "Bad Obsession" for the 1991 album *Use Your Illusion I* and sang on the cover version of "Ain't It Fun," which appeared on the 1993 album *"The Spaghetti Incident?"* In addition, Hanoi Rocks bassist Timo Caltia cowrote (with Izzy and Axl) "Right Next Door to Hell," which appeared on *Use Your Illusion I*.

5

Taste the Bright Lights

Earliest Guns N' Roses Venues

GNR was a fucking whack-job gang that was ready to rumble. We would fight tooth and nail to get a gig.　　　　　　　　　—Steven Adler

West Hollywood in the 1980s was flooded with countless up-and-coming bands fighting for prominence among the sea of faceless, booze- and drug-addled denizens wandering aimlessly along the bustling Sunset Strip. In the early years as they struggled to get recognition, Guns N' Roses took the stage at just about every one of the Sunset Strip area clubs, including such legendary venues as the Troubadour, Whisky A Go Go, the Roxy, Gazzarri's, and the Cathouse. The band also performed at several lesser-known venues, like the time they took the stage before an extremely sparse crowd (and earned just $200) at the Reseda Country Club (which served as the disco-era club Hot Traxx in the 1997 film *Boogie Nights*). According to Duff in *Everybody Loves Our Town: An Oral History of Grunge*, "I was living in a cockroach-infested single-room apartment. L.A. at the time was Quiet Riot, Ratt, some really terrible bands. In L.A., Guns N' Roses was considered a punk-rock band. We were huddled in this corner of Hollywood, snapping viciously at any gig we could get."

At this time, bands were forced to spend all of their time plastering flyers everywhere in a desperate attempt to get the word out about their next gig. Meanwhile, some of the most popular clubs placed into effect notorious pay-to-play rules whereby bands themselves were responsible for selling tickets in order to take the stage. Axl described early Guns N' Roses as "a sore thumb on the glam scene" that displayed a "fuck-you attitude." However, according to legendary rock producer Kim Fowley in *Waiting for the Sun*, by the late 1980s everything had gone downhill and the Strip had devolved from "lip-gloss to cock-stink . . . Suddenly a lot of cock-stink bands showed up. . . . By 1988, we had to deal with the clones of Guns and Poison. The tits got bigger, the men got dumber, and the music got uglier." *Reckless Road: Guns N' Roses and the Making of Appetite for Destruction* (2007) by Marc Canter serves as the definitive illustrated guide to the band's Los Angeles club years up to the release of *Appetite for Destruction*.

With a lack of early material, Guns N' Roses filled their setlists with a variety of popular covers, such as "Jumpin' Jack Flash" (the Rolling Stones), "We're an American Band" (Grand Funk Railroad), "Nice Boys" (Rose Tattoo), "Mama Kin" (Aerosmith), "Heartbreak Hotel" (Elvis Prelsey), "Whole Lotta Rosie" (AC/DC), and "Goodnight Tonight (Paul McCartney & Wings). Both "Nice Boys" and "Mama Kin" eventually ended up on the band's second studio album, *G N' R Lies*, in 1988.

In addition to the clubs listed below, Guns N' Roses also took the stage at a UCLA frat party (July 21, 1985), the eighth annual Los Angeles Street Scene Festival (September 28, 1985), Radio City in Anaheim (October 31, 1985), the Central, which later became the Viper Room (May 1, 1986), Bogart's in Long Beach (July 21, 1986), Club Lingerie (July 24, 1986), Scream (August 1, 1986), Stone in San Francisco (August 28, 198), and others.

The Troubadour

Founded as a coffeehouse on La Cienega Boulevard by eccentric visionary Doug Weston in the 1950s, the Troubadour soon moved to 9081 Santa Monica Boulevard and played a pivotal role in the burgeoning 1960s folk music scene and the singer-songwriter movement in the early 1970s. A slew of legendary performers—Bob Dylan, Joni Mitchell, James Taylor, Carly Simon, Neil Young, Carole King, Tim Buckley, Jackson Browne, Gordon Lightfoot, Linda Ronstadt, Kris Kristofferson, Tom Waits, Van Morrison, Tim Hardin, Billy Joel, and many others—took the stage here, as well as prominent comedians, such as Lenny Bruce, Richard Pryor, Steve Martin, Cheech & Chong, and George Carlin. Just a few landmark events that took place at the Troubadour over the years include Lenny Bruce getting arrested for saying "schmuck" onstage in 1962, the Byrds performing "Mr. Tambourine Man" for the first time in 1965, Buffalo Springfield making their live debut in 1966, Elton John performing his first US show in 1970, John Lennon and Harry Nilsson getting kicked out of the club for heckling the Smothers Brothers in 1973, Miles Davis recording *Live at the Troubadour* in 1975, and cult author Charles Bukowski ("The Poet Laureate of Skid Row") meeting his future wife, Linda Lee Beighle, during one of his typically anarchic poetry readings in 1976.

In the late 1970s and early 1980s, the Troubadour hosted a number of up-and-coming punk and metal bands such as Mötley Crüe, Metallica, Poison, Warrant, and W.A.S.P. On March 26, 1985, an early Guns N' Roses lineup featuring Axl, Izzy, Tracii Guns (guitar), Ole Beich (bass), and Rob Gardner (drums) made its debut at the Troubadour. The setlist consisted of early classics such as "Reckless Life," "Shadow of Your Love," "Think About You," "Move to the City," "Don't Cry," "Back Off Bitch," and "Anything Goes," as well as covers of the Rolling Stones' "Jumpin' Jack Flash," Rose Tattoo's "Nice Boys," and Elvis Presley's "Heartbreak Hotel." According to Duff in a 2012 *New York Times* interview, "There were three people there [at the Troubadour], and one of them was our friend, and one was one of our girlfriends, and the other was the girlfriend's friend. But we believed in ourselves from the first chord we played together."

On July 20, 1985, Guns N' Roses returned to the Troubadour and performed "Welcome to the Jungle" live for the first time, followed by a September 20, 1985 performance where they debuted "Rocket Queen." On October 10, 1985, the band gave their first live performance of "Paradise City" at the club. Their first sold-out performance at the Troubadour took place on November 22, 1985. For the band's January 4, 1986, show at the Troubadour, the distributed flyers exclaimed, "Get Yourself Together, Drink Till You Drop, Forget About Tomorrow, Have Another Shot. Happy New Year! From the boys who brought you the most chaotic shows of 1985." During this show, "My Michelle" was performed live for the first time. GN'R performed "Out Ta Get Me" live for the first time at the Troubadour on February 28, 1986. Axl introduced the song with one of his classic rants: "Like every time you turn around, someone is trying to screw you over financially, or the cops are banging on your door and you didn't do anything. It's just being railroaded into something and trying to get out from underneath. You know, parents, teachers, and preachers." Most importantly, Tom Zutaut, A&R representative for Geffen Records, attended the show and then raved about GN'R to his boss David Geffen, who later signed the band.

The *Appetite for Destruction* lineup of Guns N' Roses performed their last show at the Troubadour on July 11, 1986, with an accompanying flyer that promised "brand new songs, cool props . . . girls, and the rest as a tribute to

HOLLYWOOD prior to the production of our debut album on GEFFEN RECORDS!" With so many GN'R milestones taking place at the Troubadour over the years, it certainly was no accident that when the newly reunited GN'R band members (Rose, Slash, and Duff) decided to play an impromptu warm-up show on April 1, 2016, they chose the old, reliable Troub as their venue of choice, and the show featured a flyer claiming, "From the Boys Who Will Bring You the Most Chaotic Tour of 2016."

Stardust Ballroom

In 1975, bandleader Orrin Tucker converted a former roller skating rink at 5612 Sunset Boulevard into the Stardust Ballroom. (The name was derived from a 1974 TV movie, *Queen of the Stardust Ballroom*, which Tucker had appeared in.) For most of the decade, ballroom dancing was the main attraction here, but in the late 1970s a cash-strapped Tucker made the venue available to punk rock and new wave concerts. On June 28, 1985, Guns N' Roses received bottom billing at the Stardust Ballroom below the Elektra Records act the Unforgiven, along with two other bands, the Joneses and London. The show is notable for having GN'R's first live performance of Aerosmith's "Mama Kin." At one point during the show, Slash exclaimed, "Yo, this place has cockroaches going through the PA system." The subject of a record label bidding war, the show's headliner, the Unforgiven, faded into obscurity after their self-titled album bombed. According to a 2009 article by John C. Hughes in *Popdose*, the Unforgiven were "a power-pop/ alterna-country/cowpunk act . . . Dressed up in their best Western gear, the group emerged from the ashes of a more straight-ahead Cali punk act, the Stepmothers. A little U2, a little Alarm, and a lot of look, the Unforgiven signed to Elektra Records."

The Gunners returned to the Stardust on August 30, 1985, to perform a benefit gig for the Muscular Dystrophy Association, along with Poison, Ruby Slipper, the Joneses, and Mary Poppinz. The concert was billed as "A spectacular night of 'Glitter-Glam and Rock' as Hollywood and 'Rock-n-Roll' rally to show there [sic] support with a special Dress to Kill Party." David Lee Roth and Bret Michaels both attended the GN'R performance that night. The setlist featured "Reckless," "Welcome to the Jungle," "Jumpin' Jack Flash," "Think About You," "Move to the City," "Don't Cry," "We're an American Band" (Grand Funk Railroad), "Back Off Bitch," "Anything Goes," and "Heartbreak Hotel."

Madame Wong's East

As improbable as it seems, Madame Wong's East was a Chinatown restaurant with live entertainment owned by Esther Wong (a.k.a. the "Godmother of Punk"), an immigrant from Shanghai. In the late 1970s, Wong started booking punk and new wave bands such as Black Flag, Fear, Fishbone, X, the Alley Cats, the Bangs, Naughty Sweeties, Bad Actor, and Los Illegals. In addition, up-and-coming rock and new wave bands such as the Police, the Motels, the Go-Gos, and Oingo Boingo took the stage here before their careers took off.

The pre-Guns N' Roses band Hollywood Rose took the stage at Madame Wong's East and its sister establishment, Madame Wong's West (which was located in Santa Monica) on several dates in 1984. The collage-style flyer for the June 16, 1984, show announced, "Warning: The Surgeon General Has Determined That Hollywood Rose is Dangerous to Your Health, but Worth the Risk." The gig featured Axl, Slash, Steven Adler, and Steve Darrow (bass) performing in front of a sparse crowd. The setlist included "Reckless Life," "Shadow of Your Love," "Jumpin' Jack Flash," "Think About You," "Move to the City," "Don't Cry," "Nice Boys," "Back Off Bitch," "Mama Kin," "Anything Goes," and "Heartbreak Hotel." In a July 1999 *SPIN* article, "Appetite for Self-Destruction," Bret Michaels recalled attending the Hollywood Rose gig at Madame Wong's East: "There were maybe fifteen people in the club and Axl was playing as if he were in front of a million people."

Madame Wong's East closed its doors for good in the mid-1980s. In a November 23, 1986, article in the *Los Angeles Times*, Wong remarked, "I just think the club scene is burning out. . . . I really miss the days when the Plimsouls and the Motels were here all the time. But those days are gone. . . . The kids that come here now, they drive me crazy. . . . They come here and act like spoiled brats. Some of them plugged up my toilets, and one band set fire to some paper towels and set off our sprinkler system, flooding the whole basement. They write graffiti everywhere."

Bogart's

A popular Long Beach alternative rock club in the 1980s and early 1990s (it closed its doors for good in 1993), Bogart's was located in a nondescript strip mall and featured up-and-coming bands and cutting-edge acts, such as the Jesus Lizard, Weezer, Melvins, Uncle Tupelo, Screaming Trees, Stone Temple Pilots, Tool, Sublime, Goo Goo Dolls, Hawkwind, Sonic Youth,

Nirvana, Faith No More, and Soul Asylum. Guns N' Roses performed here on July 21, 1986, along with a long-forgotten local band called Marshes of Glenny. Axl dedicated "Rocket Queen" to "all the women here who are out to dress to impress."

The Roxy Theatre

Opened in 1973 by Elmer Valentine and Lou Adler at the site of a former strip joint called the Largo, the Roxy Theatre at 9009 West Sunset Boulevard has hosted a multitude of legendary performers over the years, such as Neil Young, Genesis, Prince, Muddy Waters, David Bowie, Duran Duran, Lou Reed, Bruce Springsteen, Van Morrison, Linda Ronstadt, Jimmy Buffett, Patti Smith, Jane's Addiction, and Pearl Jam. Classic live albums recorded at the Roxy include Frank Zappa and the Mothers of Invention's *Roxy & Elsewhere* (1974), Bob Marley and the Wailers' *Live at the Roxy* (recorded in 1976 but not released until 2003), George Benson's *Weekend in L.A.* (1978), and Warren Zevon's *Stand in the Fire* (1980). In addition, the concert scene from the 1979 musical comedy *Rock 'n' Roll High School* ("Where the three R's stood for Rock, Roll, and Rebellion!") featuring the Ramones was shot here. Struggling comedian Paul Reubens introduced his "Pee-wee Herman" character on stage at the Roxy in 1981. Ratt recorded the video for their hit song "Back for More" at the Roxy in 1984. The bar above the Roxy, On the Rox, served as a notorious gathering place for celebrity debauchery. John Lennon reportedly hung out there with Harry Nilsson during his fabled "Lost Weekend" period in the mid-1970s. One of the characters in Bret Easton Ellis' nihilistic 1985 novel *Less Than Zero* hits the Roxy just in time to hear X perform "Sex and Dying in High Society."

The "classic" lineup of Guns N' Roses first performed at the Roxy on August 31, 1985, with a setlist that included "What's That Noise" (Stormtroopers of Death), "Reckless Life," "Shadow of Your Love," "Welcome to the Jungle," "Jumpin' Jack Flash," "Anything Goes," and "Heartbreak Hotel." GN'R again performed at the Roxy on January 18, 1986, with L.A. Guns and Plain Jane. After scoring their record deal with Geffen, GN'R took the stage at the Roxy once again for two shows on March 28, 1986, before an audience of mostly record executives who did not know that the band had already been signed. The show's flyer exclaimed, "Dance Your Ass Off, Drink Your Face Off, Get Your Rocks Off." On March 29, 1987—shortly after recording *Appetite for Destruction*—GN'R played the Roxy for "1 Final Blowout Show," according to the flyer. Before the last song,

"Mama Kin," Duff announced to the audience, "The after-party is free if you show your fucking tits." In 2014, Slash featuring Myles Kennedy and the Conspirators released the album *Live at the Roxy 9.25.14*, which included six Guns N' Roses tracks: "Nightrain," "You Could Be Mine," "You're Crazy," "Rocket Queen," "Sweet Child O' Mine," and "Paradise City."

Arlington Theatre

Built in 1930 on the former site of the Arlington Hotel in Santa Barbara, the historic Arlington Theatre has served as both a movie theater and concert venue over the years. It is also home to the annual Santa Barbara International Film Festival. Guns N' Roses opened for Alice Cooper at the Arlington Theatre in support of his Nightmare Returns Tour. However, Axl arrived late to the gig and wasn't granted access since his name did not appear on the list for some odd reason. Izzy took over vocal duties on the set, except for "It's So Easy," which was handled by Duff. At one point, Duff even asked the audience if anyone knew the lyrics for AC/DC's "Whole Lotta Rosie."

Music Machine

An eclectic venue to say the least, Music Machine at 12220 Pico Boulevard hosted everything from blues and acoustic to punk rock and thrash metal bands during the 1980s. On December 20, 1985, Guns N' Roses performed "Nightrain" live for the first time at Music Machine. Introducing the song, Izzy explained, "It's about that cheap shit that everybody drinks." Cowpunk band Tex & the Horseheads—whose members included Texacala Jones, Smog Vomit, and Rock Vodka—served as the opening act.

Guns N' Roses returned to Music Machine on September 13, 1986, with a show that was marred by technical difficulties and a set that featured "Welcome to the Jungle," "Think About You," "Mr. Brownstone," "Rocket Queen," "Nightrain," "My Michelle," "Sweet Child O' Mine," "Paradise City," "Mama Kin," and "Nice Boys." Axl kicked off the show by announcing, "Ladies and gentlemen, we're Guns N' Roses. This song is 'Welcome to the Fucking Jungle.'" At another point during the show, Axl exclaimed, "In honor of our fuckin' technical difficulties, we're gonna get some of our frustration out of our systems now. I hope you can live with it. This is a song called 'Nice Boys Don't Play Rock 'n' Roll.'" The show's opening acts were the Unforgiven and King Kan Klub.

Whisky A Go Go

Opened in 1964 at 8901 Sunset Boulevard and briefly a hangout for the Hollywood elite such as Cary Grant and Steve McQueen, the world-famous Whisky A Go Go quickly evolved into a hub for psychedelic rock 'n' roll in Los Angeles and possibly the entire West Coast during the mid-1960s. Legendary bands such as the Doors, Love, the Byrds, Frank Zappa and the Mothers of Invention, the Turtles, Buffalo Springfield, and Them (featuring Van Morrison) took the stage here during the 1960s. The Whisky, as it was known, was also one of the centers of the notorious "Sunset Strip Riots" in 1966 (which were documented for posterity in Stephen Stills's stirring anthem "For What It's Worth"). The unfairly neglected Los Angeles band Love immortalized the Whisky in their song "Maybe the People Would Be the Times or Between Clark and Hilldale," which appeared on the band's brilliant 1967 album *Forever Changes*.

Guns N' Roses first took the stage at the Whisky on April 5, 1986. The flyer for the show announced, "When was the last time you saw a real rock 'n' roll band . . . at the Whisky A Go Go?" The event was paired with the "Wettest, Wildest Bikini Shake Off of 1986 with a $50 Cash Prize to the Winner." According to Marc Canter in *Reckless Road*, "This show was prime Guns N' Roses: raunchy, rowdy and raucous." During an August 23, 1986, performance at the Whisky, Guns N' Roses performed "Sweet Child O' Mine," "Mr. Brownstone," and "Ain't Going Down" live for the first time ever. The flyer for the show announced, "The rock 'n' roll event of the year w/an all star jam including the superstars of hollywood's unrivaled growing r&r scene!" Slash reportedly wore his top hat on stage for the first time at this show. After they finished recording *Appetite for Destruction*, GN'R made a triumphant return to the Whisky for "2 Lethal Nights" on March 16 and 29, 1987.

Gazzarri's

Owned and operated by the white-hatted, cigar-chomping Bill Gazzarri, the "Godfather of Rock and Roll," Gazzarri's first opened in 1961 as an Italian restaurant with live entertainment and was originally located at 319 North La Cienega. In the early years, Gazzarri's hosted such musical acts as the Standells, Johnny Rivers (who would become a fixture at Whisky A Go Go), Jackie DeShannon, and the McCoys. In 1967, the Doors played at the grand opening of Gazzarri's new location at 9039 Sunset Boulevard on the Sunset Strip in West Hollywood. Other notable bands that took the stage at Gazzarri's over the years include Buffalo Springfield, Van Halen, Ratt, Cinderella, Quiet Riot, Mötley Crüe, Poison, Warrant, and Guns N' Roses. (Slash first heard Axl onstage performing with Hollywood Rose at Gazzarri's in the early 1980s and, according to his autobiography, proclaimed him to be "the best singer in Los Angeles at the time.")

Slash later admitted in his autobiography that he hated Gazzarri's, where the "really plastic glam metal" bands were staples. On May 31, 1986, GN'R performed at Gazzarri's under the alias "Fargin Bastydges," which was derived from a line that appears in the 1984 Michael Keaton comedy *Johnny Dangerously*. The setlist featured "Out Ta Get Me," "Welcome to the Jungle," "Think About You," "Move to the City," "Rocket Queen," "Nightrain," "My Michelle," "Jumpin' Jack Flash," "Don't Cry," "You're Crazy," "Paradise City," and "Mama Kin." Steven Adler, in his autiobiography, remembered the night as an "epic show" characterized by "extended solos, long jams, and fucking loud."

Los Angeles hard rock band Shark Island served as the house band at Gazzarri's in the mid-1980s. It is alleged that Axl appropriated some of the unique dance moves of Shark Island's lead singer, Richard Black, into his own stage routine. Shark Island released three albums—*S'cool Buss* (1986), *July 14, 1989 Bastille Day – Alive at the Whiskey* (1989), and *Law of the Order* (1989)—before going their separate ways in 1992. (They reunited briefly for one last album, *Gathering of the Faithful*, in 2006.)

Debauchery reigned at Gazzarri's. For example, in his 2014 autobiography, *Sex, Drugs, Ratt & Roll: My Life in Rock*, Stephen Pearcy of Ratt claimed, "I saw so many people fuck on the lawns behind Gazzarri's that I actually got bored of watching and started to throw empty beer cans at them." In the 1988 heavy metal documentary *The Decline of Western Civilization, Part 2: The Metal Years*, Gazzarri himself can be viewed organizing a "sexy rock and roll" dance contest and predicting that the long-forgotten hair metal band Odin was "going to be bigger than David Lee Roth!" In 1991, Gazzarri died, and the club closed in 1993.

Raji's

A total dive located at 6162 Hollywood Boulevard on the site of a former Greek restaurant known as the King's Palace, Raji's hosted an eclectic range of bands (some of which achieved greatness and many of which faded into obscurity), such as Nirvana, Jane's Addiction, Green Day, Redd Kross, Thelonious Monster, Arab and the Suburban Turbans, the Mentors, Pussy

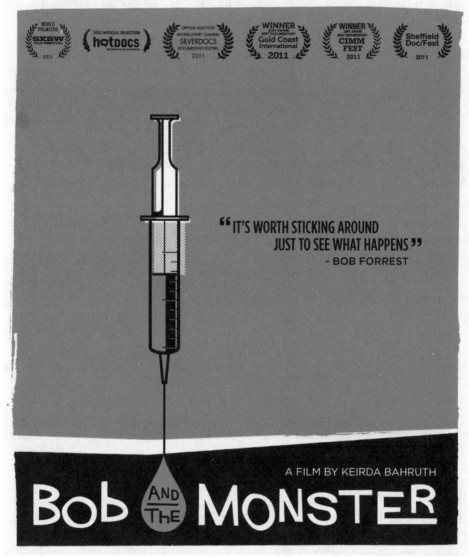

Bob Forrest, lead singer of Thelonious Monster, and Axl Rose clashed during a Guns N' Roses set at Raji's in 1986. Years later, as a drug counselor on *Celebrity Rehab*, Forrest would attempt to assist Steven Adler with his drug addiction.   *Author's collection*

Galore, Tex & the Horseheads, Social Distortion, Mary's Danish, Los Lobos, and even the notorious GG Allin and the Murder Junkies (the subject of a truly disturbing 1993 documentary called *Hated*—watch at your own risk!), among countless other bands. Raji's, which "reeked of beer and piss" according to Slash in his autobiography, was owned by Danny "Dobbs" Wilson, who once remarked in a 1990 *Los Angeles Times* interview, "We're the McDonald's of nightclubs."

On May 13, 1986, Guns N' Roses (under their standard alias "Fargin Bastydges") took the stage at Raji's and performed "You're Crazy" live for the first time. An overzealous female fan in the front row started spraying beer in Axl's face and then threw a bottle at him. Axl reportedly hit her over the head with the mic stand and yelled, "Somebody get this stupid bitch out of here." After the set, Axl got into a fistfight with her boyfriend, who just happened to be Bob Forrest, lead singer of the band Thelonious Monster (and who, many years later, was a drug counselor on *Celebrity Rehab with Dr. Drew* who would attempt to help Steven Adler overcome his addiction). In his 2005 memoir, *Scar Tissue*, Anthony Kiedis of the Red Hot Chili Peppers recalled Forrest during this period as "Lunatic Bob, the then King of Exaggerations, Rumors, and Lies . . . a drunken wreck . . . bitter and angry." Meanwhile, Slash, who according to a 2007 *Seattle Times* article had just done "a big hit of smack," ended up blowing chunks "over the back of [his] amps every five minutes." Paul Stanley of KISS was also in attendance at Raji's that evening and commented in his 2014 autobiography, *Face the Music: A Life Exposed*, "Guns N' Roses were stupendous . . . I immediately realized I was witnessing true greatness." A photo of the infamous gig at Raji's can be viewed on the inside sleeve of the *Appetite for Destruction* album.

Timbers Ballroom

An early version of Guns N' Roses took the stage at Timbers Ballroom in Glendora, a suburb of Los Angeles, on April 27, 1985. The show was notable for being the last known live GN'R performance of Tracii Guns on lead guitar and Rob Gardner on drums. (The two would later back out of the "Hell Tour" less than two months later, leaving the door open for Slash and Steven Adler to join the band.)

On July 31, 1986, Guns N' Roses opened for Lords of the New Church—a post-punk/gothic rock supergroup that featured Stiv Bators of the Dead Boys, Brian James of the Damned, Dave Tregunna of Sham 69, and Nick Turner of the Barracudas—at Timbers Ballroom (the Flamethrowers were third billed). Perhaps setting the tone for later concert debacles, Axl arrived late for the Timbers show, and the band was forced to start without him after they were told that they wouldn't get paid if they didn't take the stage. Rose finally made it to the gig at the end of the song "Anything Goes" and announced to the audience, "I'm sorry about being late. I was told 11 [p.m.] and turn this shit up."

Other bands that performed at Timbers Ballroom over the years include the Dickies, Stryper, Great White, Blitzkrieg, and the Cramps. An influential punk band led by Lux Interior (Erick Lee Purkhiser) and Poison Ivy (Kristy Wallace), the Cramps churned out such memorably outrageous tunes as "Don't Eat Stuff off the Sidewalk," "I Wanna Get in Your Pants," "Let's Get Fucked Up," and "Can Your Pussy Do the Dog?" Interior sang on "I Ain't Nuthin' but a Gorehoud" that "I don't know about art, but I know what I like."

Club Lingerie

Known for its rather eclectic booking policy, Club Lingerie at 6507 Sunset Boulevard hosted the likes of Guns N' Roses, the Red Hot Chili Peppers, Jane's Addiction, Chris Isaak, Butthole Surfers, R.E.M., the Minutemen, Sonic Youth, Fishbone, and Nirvana during the 1980s and early 1990s. Guns N' Roses took the stage at Club Lingerie under their pseudonym "Fargin Bastydges" on July 24, 1986. Slash and Axl had gotten into a fight that afternoon, causing Axl to quit GN'R, but he rejoined the band in time for the set. During the late 1970s, the club was known as the Masque and catered to the burgeoning Los Angeles punk scene by hosting performances by the Germs, Weirdos, Dickies, X, Bags, Black Randy and the Metrosquad, Go-Go's, Zeros, Avengers, Skulls, and others.

Cathouse

Opened in 1986 by Riki Rachtman and Taime Downe (lead singer of sleaze rock band Faster Pussycat) on the site of a rundown disco called Osco's (featured in the 1978 movie *Thank God It's Friday*), the Cathouse catered to the Hollywood underground rock scene. The club was located at 333 North La Cienega (but soon relocated to 836 North Highland Avenue) and was only open on Tuesdays. According to LA.com, the Cathouse "was known for its edgy, underground, dirty rock 'n' roll vibe that was rooted in punk. It reeked of raunch and pure decadence." Fortunately for all involved, the Cathouse obeyed a strict no-cameras-allowed policy. The ever-humble Rachtman even claimed that the Cathouse "did for rock and roll what Studio 54 did for cocaine."

Opened in 1986 on the site of a rundown former disco, the Cathouse evolved into one of West Hollywood's most happening (and decadent) clubs. Guns N' Roses band members hung out at the Cathouse and even shot the controversial music video for "It's So Easy" here.   *Author's collection*

Named after the 1965 Russ Meyer cult classic *Faster, Pussycat! Kill! Kill!*, which starred the incomparable Tura Satana, Faster Pussycat was one of the most popular early bands that took the stage at the Cathouse. Faster Pussycat even wrote a song, "Cathouse," that appeared on their 1987 self-titled debut album and featured the lyrics: "Let's go down 'cross the tracks/ Where a pussy ain't no feline." In addition, Alice Cooper name-dropped the club in the opening line of his 1989 song "Trash"—"It ain't the way you crawl across the Cathouse floor." Guns N' Roses held their raucous "Live Like a

Named after the 1965 cult classic *Faster, Pussycat! Kill! Kill!*, Faster Pussycat emerged out of the West Hollywood scene in the mid-1980s and hung out with Guns N' Roses frequently during the early years.   *Author's collection*

Suicide Release Party" at the Cathouse on December 23, 1986. According to Slash in his autobiography, Guns N' Roses "fuckin' ruled" at the Cathouse, and some of the most embarrassing things he ever did in public took place there, such as passing out "naked in a booth with some chick" and "fuck[ing] so many girls on the floor while people were walking over us." Steven Adler remembered getting drunk and "stair-diving" at the club with Duff and others.

The Cathouse was featured prominently in the 1988 rockumentary *The Decline of Western Civilization II: The Metal Years*. Guns N' Roses (fortunately!) declined the opportunity to appear in the film, and Detroit rock band Seduce was added at the last minute in their place. *Decline* features some classic, thoroughly decadent interviews with the likes of Steven Tyler, Joe Perry, Alice Cooper, Gene Simmons, Paul Stanley, Ozzy Osbourne, Bret Michaels, and Lemmy, who remarks at one point, "If you think you got what it takes, shove it out, run it up the flagpole, and see who salutes you." The outrageous rockumentary also includes footage of a couple of bands that didn't quite reach mainstream success, such as Seduce, Lizzie Borden, London, and Odin, whose lead singer Randy "O" boldly proclaims with delusional glee (from a bubbling hot tub surrounded by several bikini-clad babes), "I want to be as big as Zeppelin or the Beatles . . . go down in history like Jim Morrison or Robert Plant—it's gonna happen." However, by far the most disturbing scene in *Decline* involves a severely inebriated Chris Holmes, lead guitarist of W.A.S.P., babbling incoherently, guzzling vodka, and dumping the rest over his head while floating on a raft in the middle of a pool as his horrified mother looks on in total despair.

The very first live performance at the Cathouse included an acoustic set by Guns N' Roses and performances by Faster Pussycat, L.A. Guns, and Jetboy in 1986. In addition, GN'R played live at the Cathouse the night before opening for the Rolling Stones at the Los Angeles Coliseum in 1989. GN'R's sleazy music video for "It's So Easy" (featuring Axl's future wife, Erin Everly, dressed in bondage gear) was shot during the show. A drunken David Bowie was milling around the club during the concert and reportedly tried to pick up Everly. An enraged Axl punched Bowie and then chased him out of the club and down the street (threatening to kill him the entire time). After Bowie apologized, he invited Axl out for drinks. In addition, Axl can be seen wearing a Cathouse T-shirt in the "Paradise City" music video.

Another Cathouse lowlight involved the "Queen of Heavy Metal" herself, Lita Ford, puking her brains out in the bathroom on opening night. Cathouse cofounder Riki Rachtman (with a major assist from Axl Rose) later became host of MTV's *Headbanger's Ball* from 1990 to 1995 and can be seen in a cameo as a wedding guest in GN'R's "November Rain" music video. The Cathouse closed its doors for good in 1993, but its legacy lives on. A music festival—Cathouse Live—took place at Irvine Meadows Amphitheatre in Southern California on August 15, 2015, and featured live performances by former Gunner Gilby Clarke, L.A. Guns, Faster Pussycat, Saigon Kick, Dokken, Sebastian Bach, and Jetboy, among others.

6

Fun 'n' Games

West Hollywood Landmarks Associated with Guns N' Roses

The survival of early Guns N' Roses [is] pretty much comprised of [a] little hustling here and there, a lot of really nice girls, a couple of odd jobs and a drive to survive. —Slash

In the early to mid-1980s, Guns N' Roses was just one of the dozens of anonymous up-and-coming bands wandering Sunset Boulevard in West Hollywood and attempting to just eke out a living by while desperately struggling to get recognition and gigs. Survival meant scraping together a couple of bucks for biscuits and gravy at Denny's, bumming some chow at Canter's Deli, grabbing a meal at the local homeless mission, crashing the five a.m. all-you-can-eat buffet at a gay club called Rage, sitting down to a cheap breakfast at Hamburger Hamlet, or splitting a cheeseburger five ways at the Sunset Grill. Known for its famous "Flaming Margarita," the dimly lit El Compadre was a cheap Mexican joint, making it a favorite hangout for the members of GN'R during those lean, mean days. Meanwhile, the band rehearsed and crashed in squalor at a series of total shitholes that they dubbed "Sunset & Gardner Hotel & Villa" (a modified storage unit just off Sunset Boulevard) and "Hell House" on North Fuller Avenue.

The Starwood

Although the Starwood in West Hollywood only lasted between 1973 to 1981, the nightclub proved to be a highly influential addition to the Los Angeles music scene, hosting such acts as Van Halen, Mötley Crüe, Black Flag, the Germs, X, Quiet Riot, the Runaways, Judas Priest, Fear, Circle Jerks, the Motels, and Kool & the Gang, among others. Both Slash and Steven Adler frequently snuck into the club as teenagers. According to Adler in his autobiography, the Starwood was "the number one gathering spot for everyone. We goddamn lived there." The Starwood (previously known as P.J.'s, a jazz club) was owned by Eddie Nash, who was known primarily as the alleged mastermind behind the notorious "Wonderland Murders" that took place in Laurel Canyon in 1981. The Red Hot Chili Peppers name-dropped the club—"Got to sneak into the Starwood"—in their song "Deep Kick" off the 1995 album *One Hot Minute.*

Gardner Street

Guns N' Roses gelled as a band in the most unlikeliest of places—a twelve-by-twelve-foot rehearsal space (actually a converted storage unit) on Gardner Street just off of Sunset Boulevard without toilets or showers that was sarcastically dubbed the "Sunset & Gardner Hotel & Villa." The "front door" was a corrugated aluminum roll-up panel and the place was literally crawling with cockroaches. A charcoal hibachi grill was acquired for the rare times that somebody actually made the effort to cook a meal here. Most of the band members had no place to crash so they also built a makeshift loft in the rehearsal space in order to have a spot to take strippers for sex, get drunk, and pass out. Slash compared the "studio" to "an uncomfortable prison cell" although the band had many great early rehearsals there. In addition, some of the most enduring Guns N' Roses songs—such as "Rocket Queen," "My Michelle," and "Nightrain"—were reportedly written at Gardner Street. According to Steven Adler in a 1999 *SPIN* interview, "The rehearsal space we lived in on Sunset and Gardner was disgusting. No toilet, no nothing, but who cared? We didn't have jobs. We lived off girls—off strippers. We were doing what we wanted to do. We had women, and we were playing rock 'n' roll."

The rehearsal space opened onto an alley that was the site of many raucous parties involving other bands, such as Faster Pussycat and Jet Boy, as well as assorted strippers, drug addicts, and wannabes from the Sunset Boulevard scene. Someone could always be counted on to hawk beer out of a trunk for a dollar each. Of course, heroin use was also rampant here. As might be expected, the police were called to the locale on dozens of occasions and became quite familiar with the inhabitants here.

"Hell House"

A total dump at 1139 North Fuller Avenue in West Hollywood dubbed "Hell House" served as a place to crash for the members of Guns N' Roses, along with their assorted friends, such as West Arkeen and Del James. All types of total debauchery involving alcohol, drugs, and strippers took place at the three-bedroom ranch house. Band members survived on cheap wine and handouts. Slash, in his autobiography, referred to Hell House as "a pit that embodied our collective mind at the time," while Steven Adler, in *My Appetite for Destruction*, called it "the band's official headquarters" where Guns N' Roses and their friends "hung out, partied, puked and passed out." According to Adler in his autobiography, the informal jam band Drunk Fux—the "ultimate superband of the eighties"—was formed here and included GN'R band members (excepting Axl), Tommy Lee from Mötley Crüe, Lemmy from Motörhead, and others.

Rainbow Bar & Grill

One of the most legendary hangouts on the Sunset Strip, the Rainbow Bar & Grill at 9015 Sunset Boulevard in West Hollywood was originally opened as the Mermaid Club Café in the 1920s. The Mermaid later morphed into the nautical-themed Villa Nova restaurant (owned by silent film actor-director Allen Dale) in the 1940s and was later owned by film director Vincente Minnelli (husband of Judy Garland and father of Liza). Minnelli had reportedly proposed to Garland at the restaurant in 1945. At that time, the Villa Nova's celebrity clientele included Charlie Chaplin, John Wayne, Bing Crosby, Henry Fonda, Mickey Rooney, Dean Martin, and Don Knotts, among others. The bar upstairs, known as Villa Up, attracted the likes of mobsters Bugsy Siegel and Mickey Cohen. According to legend, Marilyn Monroe first met Joe DiMaggio at the Rainbow in 1953. The couple got married the following year. The Villa Nova relocated to Newport Beach in 1968.

In 1972, music producer Lou Adler and his partners Elmer Valentine and Mario Maglieri (the same masterminds behind Whisky A Go Go) purchased the former Villa Nova space and rechristened it the Rainbow Bar & Grill. The Rainbow quickly evolved into a notorious hangout for rock musicians, including the likes of Elvis Presley, John Lennon, Ringo Starr, Mick Jagger, Keith Moon, Elton John, Alice Cooper, Neil Diamond, Billy Idol, and Lemmy of Motörhead, as well as members of Black Sabbath, Led Zeppelin, Guns N' Roses, Mötley Crüe, and Poison. Musician and actress Cheryl Smith (*Caged Heat*) became known as "Rainbeaux" as a result of her frequenting the Rainbow, and the name of Ritchie Blackmore's rock band Rainbow was reportedly inspired by the establishment. According to legend, actor John Belushi ate his last meal (lentil soup) at table No. 16 at

One of West Hollywood's most legendary hangouts, the Rainbow Bar & Grill on Sunset Boulevard served as a salacious stomping ground for members of Guns N' Roses, along with a host of other rock musicians and celebrities alike.   *Mike Dillon/Wikimedia Commons*

the Rainbow before his fatal overdose at the Chateau Marmont Hotel on March 5, 1982, at the age of 33. In a 1985 profile of the Rainbow for *Hustler* magazine, Lonn Friend wrote, "One patron spoke of getting a blow job on the crowded dance floor upstairs . . . another talked about walking into the bathroom and seeing a girl snorting cocaine off the paper towel dispenser."

In a July 16, 2014, interview with *Los Angeles Magazine*, Maglieri remarked, "Axl Rose was thrown out of here about eleven times. David Lee Roth . . . was tossed out about thirteen times. I think they were trying to break a record. They were literally thrown out, like, 'Get the hell out and don't come back!' They would just get so screwed up and out of control. It was off the hook." Slash could always be found at the Rainbow getting drunk on vodka and cranberry juice. (As an underage teenager, he had actually dressed as a woman to get past the bouncers!) The Rainbow appears as the backdrop in the Guns N' Roses music videos for "November Rain," "Estranged," and "Don't Cry." In addition, the Rainbow has been referenced in several songs, including "Poor Poor Pitiful Me" by Warren Zevon, "Sunset and Babylon" by W.A.S.P., "Vampire" by L.A. Guns, and "Peach Kelli Pop" by Redd Kross. Last but not least, the Cheech & Chong album *Let's Make a New Dope Deal* includes the track "Rainbow Bar & Grill." In 2015, *LA Weekly* named the Rainbow as the "Best Place to Drink with Aging Rock Stars," claiming the establishment "seems to be single-handedly keeping hair metal alive" with a lively bar that boasts crimson booths, which "have seen more T&A than an Alice Cooper concert."

"Riot House" (Continental Hyatt Hotel)

A venerable West Hollywood establishment, the Hyatt first opened in 1958 as the Gene Autry Hotel at 8401 Sunset Boulevard in West Hollywood. In 1966, after being sold and renamed the Continental Hyatt Hotel, it earned an infamous reputation as a favorite anarchic stopover for local and touring rock bands, such as the Doors, Led Zeppelin, the Rolling Stones, the Who, Motörhead, Poison, Guns N' Roses, and others. According to legend, Keith Richards mooned passersby from his Room 1015 balcony, and a booze-addled Jim Morrison dangled from one of the balconies here. In addition, members of Led Zeppelin were notorious for renting up to six floors of the hotel for their entourage, throwing TVs out hotel windows, and even driving Harley-Davidsons through the hotel lobby, into the elevator, and down the corridors. Robert Plant himself allegedly screamed out "I am a Golden God!" from one of the hotel balconies in the mid-1970s (inspiring a similar scene from the 2000 film *Almost Famous*).

In 1986, Axl Rose reportedly set off a smoke detector at Riot House while cooking steaks on a balcony. As fire trucks arrived on the scene, he ended up throwing the steaks to a crowd of gawkers gathered below. Little Richard reportedly lived in Room 319 of the hotel for seventeen years in the 1980s and 1990s. In addition, scenes from both *This is Spinal Tap* (1984) and *Almost Famous* (2000) were filmed at the Riot House. Now known as the Andaz West Hollywood, the hotel pays tribute to its storied rock 'n' roll past at the onsite Riot House Restaurant, and at the front desk a poster featuring a scraggly haired musician reads: "Be kind to this customer. He may just have sold a million records."

Canter's Deli

Believe it or not, Canter's Deli, a Fairfax Avenue institution since 1948 and a longtime favorite among celebrities, played a pivotal role in the early development of Guns N' Roses. It was here that Duff met Slash (who briefly worked at the deli) and Steven Adler for the first time to form the short-lived pre-GN'R band Road Crew. After the infamous "Hell Tour" in June 1985, Guns N' Roses headed straight to Canter's and chowed down for free since they hadn't eaten a real meal the whole time they were away. Rock photographer Jack Lue took the famous picture of the band hanging out in a booth at Canter's that day (which ended up on a flyer for the band's second official gig with the classic lineup, as well as on the cover of Canter's 2007 book, *Reckless Road: Guns N' Roses and the Making of Appetite for Destruction*). Another image from the photo shoot that was taken in an alley behind Canter's ended up on the back cover of the 1986 EP *Live ?!*@ Like a Suicide.*

A childhood friend of Slash and an amateur photographer (the target of his first obsession was Aerosmith), Marc Canter (now the deli's owner) documented the rise of GN'R as they performed early gigs at such venues as Stardust Ballroom, Madame Wong's East, the Troubadour, the Roxy, Music Machine, Fender's Ballroom, Raji's, Gazzarri's, Whisky A Go Go, and others. The liner notes for *Appetite for Destruction* feature the line, "Marc Canter—without you?" In addition, Axl performed "November Rain" on piano during Canter's wedding.

Tower Video

As they fought tooth and nail to get gigs, the members of GN'R each took odd jobs simply for survival. Axl actually worked his way up to night manager at Tower Video at 8844 Sunset Boulevard in 1984. He would allow all the other members of Hollywood Rose to hang out at Tower Video after hours, getting drunk and watching porno movies. Axl often slept under the stairway at Tower Video when he had nowhere else to go. He also managed to get Slash a job here as a counter clerk in 1984. Years later, during the height of his feud with Vince Neil, Axl challenged the Mötley Crüe lead singer to a fight in Tower Video's parking lot. (Unfortunately it never took place.)

During a 2012 appearance on *Jimmy Kimmel Live!*, Axl remarked, "I became manager [at Tower Video] for a very short amount of time . . . I let everybody have beers after work." Kimmel responded, "You know, it's funny, because I think every video store employee thinks they're going to be a rock star one day—you're the one that actually did." Tower Video was the sister store of the legendary Tower Records, which was located just across the street. As a teenager, Slash was banned from the establishment for trying to

As an up-and-coming band trying to survive on the Sunset Strip in West Hollywood, Guns N' Roses' members lived in total squalor, worked odd jobs at places like Tower Video, and bummed meals and alcohol from local strippers who danced at the Seventh Veil.   *Author's collection*

steal some cassettes. The 2015 documentary *All Things Must Pass: The Rise and Fall of Tower Records* highlights the legacy of this fabled Sunset Boulevard institution.

Seventh Veil

When they were totally down and out, the struggling band members of Guns N' Roses owed a debt to the strippers of the Seventh Veil and other West Hollywood-area strip clubs who helped them out in their time of need. According to Slash in a 2007 *Rolling Stone* interview, "Strippers were our main source of income . . . They'd pay for booze, sometimes you could eat, shit like that. Really a great bohemian, gypsy lifestyle . . . I have great memories for those renegade strippers that took their chances with us." At early gigs, some of the strippers actually joined the band onstage and danced to "Rocket Queen." On a typical Seventh Veil night, Slash would drop by the club, collect some tip money from the dancers, head to the liquor store for some Jim Beam, and get a party started for when their shift ended. A Seventh Veil stripper named Adriana Smith, an on-again/off-again girlfriend of Steven Adler, provided the memorable, sexual sound effects (accompanied by Axl Rose) for "Rocket Queen." Other Seventh Veil strippers who hung out with the band included Gabby (nicknamed "GabaGabaHey") and Adriana Barbour, who Steven Adler revealed "could drink any man under the table." Another dancer, Cameron, slept with every band member at one time or another according to Slash. "[She] gave every one of us crabs," he said, which led to her nickname becoming "Craberon." The Seventh Veil itself became infamous when it appeared in Mötley Crüe's decadent music video for the band's 1987 stripper anthem "Girls, Girls, Girls." It's one of those rare music videos where the crude lyrics perfectly complement the sleazy visuals. The strip club was also name-dropped in the song itself ("Raising hell at the 7th Veil") along with the Dollhouse in Fort Lauderdale, Tattletails in Atlanta, Crazy Horse in Paris, and others. The inspiration for this classic music video was rather simple according to Mötley Crüe's Nikki Sixx: "We seemed to be hanging out in strip clubs and drinking a lot, so we thought, hey, what about making a video of one?" Mötley Crüe even released an X-rated version of the music video that can be found on *Mötley Crüe: Greatest Video Hits*.

Comedy metal band Steel Panther also penned a humorous, overly raunchy tribute to the strip club called "Stripper Girl," which features the lyrics: "I met you down at the Seventh Veil/The first night that I got out of jail."

Retail Slut

Founded in 1983 by Helen O'Neill, Retail Slut was located on Melrose Avenue and specialized in "punk, goth, and underground fashions." Many rock stars such as Axl Rose, Cyndi Lauper, and Billy Idol frequented the store. According to Slash in a 2014 *MOJO* interview, he "liberated" his signature top hat from the store "out of desperation." He added, "The top hat appealed to me, and it seemed to make sense to walk out of the store with it. Looking back on it, there were a lot of people working in that store, and I'm not sure how I managed it. But let's just say that a lot of people working in that place were not necessarily shop-keeper types." He also swiped a belt that he wrapped around the hat for better effect. The hat appealed to Slash since he "could see everything but no one could really see me." Discussing the GN'R lead guitarist's unique look, rock biographer Danny Sugerman called Slash "a rock 'n' roll hybrid of the Mad Hatter and Cousin Itt." Retail Slut, which closed its doors for good in 2005, appears in the 2008 underground experimental film *The Lollipop Generation* by Canadian artist G. B. Jones.

Turner's Fine Wine & Spirits

Founded in 1953 by Gil Turner ("Mr. Sunset Strip") at the corner of Sunset Boulevard and Doheny Drive, Turner's Fine Wine & Spirits was a frequent pit stop for Guns N' Roses and other up-and-coming bands, and it remains one of the most well-known liquor stores in Los Angeles. Turner's was conveniently located near the Roxy, Rainbow Bar & Grill, Troubadour, Whisky A Go Go, and Tower Video. According to Slash in a 1987 GN'R press release, "We had no money but we could usually dig up a buck to go down to this liquor store, which happened to sell this great wine called Nighttrain that would fuck you up for a buck. Five dollars and we'd all be gone. We lived off this stuff." In a 2002 *Metal Sludge* interview, Tracii Guns of L.A. Guns stated that the last time he saw Axl Rose was in 1989 at Turner's: "I said 'Rock and Roll' and he said 'Rock and Roll.'"

Sunset Marquis Hotel

Ideally located at 1200 Alta Loma Drive, the hip, boutique-style Sunset Marquis is a true rock 'n' roll hotel that over the years has hosted the likes of James Brown, Elton John, Bruce Springsteen, Ozzy Osbourne, Neil Diamond, Bob Marley and the Wailers, the Clash, Blondie, the Runaways, the Ramones, Metallica, Iron Maiden, KISS, Aerosmith, the Red Hot Chili Peppers, and Guns N' Roses (especially Slash, who has been a fixture at the hotel since the late 1980s). Courtney Love's band Hole recorded the song "Sunset Marquis," which documented her time at the hotel. In a 1978 profile of Springsteen for *Rolling Stone*, Dave Marsh wrote, "If God had invented a hotel for rock bands, it would look like the Sunset Marquis." According to Slash in a 2015 interview with *The Man Guide*, "The Marquis was the stomping grounds for a lot of crazy shit . . . Overindulgent, hedonistic, whatever you want to call it. It still is. From the bar to the bathrooms to the rooms to the pool, it was all going on." In the 1990s, many rockers could be found partying at the hotel's Whiskey Bar (now known as Bar 1200).

Today, the Sunset Marquis's lobby features the Morrison Hotel Gallery, which boasts an incredible collection of rock photography from the likes of Henry Diltz (who took the famous photo of the Doors that appears on the cover of their 1970 album *Morrison Hotel*), Timothy White, and Bob Gruen. The hotel also features its own world-class recording studio called Nightbird.

Barney's Beanery

Guns N' Roses band members could often be found getting drunk at Barney's Beanery, and it is where they posed for the photo that appears on the back cover of *Appetite for Destruction*. A favorite hangout for musicians, authors, screenwriters, and actors, Barney's Beanery was first opened in 1920 by John "Barney" Anthony in Berkeley, California. In 1927, Anthony relocated Barney's Beanery to its present location as a roadhouse diner at 8447 Santa Monica Boulevard. Legendary film stars such as Jean Harlow, Clark Gable, Bette Davis, John Barrymore, Clara Bow, Judy Garland, Bette Davis, Lou Costello, and Errol Flynn frequented the famous landmark during the 1930s and 1940s.

During the late 1950s, Barney's evolved into more of a beatnik hangout and then became a popular hotspot for rock stars during the mid- to late 1960s. According to legend, it was here that Janis Joplin bashed Jim Morrison over the head with a bottle of Southern Comfort. On another occasion, Morrison urinated on the bar and was kicked out. (The bar later commemorated the event with a memorial plaque!) On October 4, 1970, Joplin sat down at her favorite booth (#34) at Barney's and guzzled two screwdrivers before heading down to the Landmark Hotel, where she overdosed on heroin the next morning. Author Charles Bukowski (*Ham on Rye*) used to drink beer at Barney's and write lines of poetry on cocktail napkins, according to legend. A scene from the 1991 Oliver Stone movie *The Doors* was shot here. In addition, director Quention Tarantino reportedly wrote most of the script for *Pulp Fiction* (1994) while sitting at his favorite booth at Barney's.

The Central/The Viper Room

According to the *Los Angeles Times*, the Viper Room at 8852 Sunset Boulevard in West Hollywood is "the most consistently hip club in town." The Viper Room (Tom Waits reportedly suggested the name) opened on August 14, 1993, with Tom Petty and the Heartbreakers taking the stage. Actor Johnny Depp (*Fear and Loathing in Las Vegas*) was part-owner of the club until 2004. During the early morning hours of October 31, 1993, actor River Phoenix (*Stand By Me*) collapsed outside of the Viper Room and died of a drug overdose at the age of twenty-three. In 1994, the supergroup Neurotic Outsiders—which featured a newly sober Duff McKagan, Matt Sorum, John Taylor of Duran Duran, and Steve Jones of the Sex Pistols—got their start at the Viper Room and performed there regularly on Monday nights. Duff's later band, Loaded, also performed at the Viper Room. Other musicians who have performed at the Viper Room over the years include Johnny Cash (who debuted many of the songs that would later appear on his 1994 album, *American Recordings*), Bruce Springsteen, Stone Temple Pilots, Green Day, Counting Crows, Billy Idol, Sheryl Crow, Red Hot Chili Peppers, Run-D.M.C., Iggy Pop, Lenny Kravitz, Oasis, Everclear, Concrete Blonde, the Black Crowes, Pussycat Dolls, Matchbox 20, and the Go-Go's, among many others. Gonzo journalist Hunter S. Thompson took the stage with Depp and John Cusack at the Viper Room in September 1996 for an impromptu discussion, portions of which would end up in the 2003 documentary *Breakfast with Hunter*. The Viper Room also appears in the 2004 documentary *Dig!*, which documents the competitive relationship

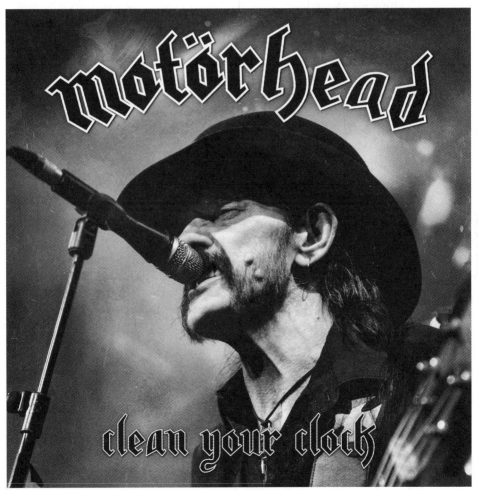

Led by the indefatigable Ian Fraser "Lemmy" Kilmister, the English rock band Motörhead heavily influenced the sound and attitude of early Guns N' Roses. According to Duff McKagan, "Motörhead forged the way as leaders to all of the rest of us."   *Author's collection*

between two bands, the Brian Jonestown Massacre and the Dandy Warhols. In a November 21, 2015, article in the *Telegraph*, musician Bob Forrest of the bands Thelonious Monster and the Bicycle Thief remarked, "When you were in LA, the Viper Room is where you would go. Every night somebody was there—Tom Petty, Tom Waits—everybody just hung out there . . . It was a really special, magical thing. There was a love of music and a love of each other, because we all loved the same things: *Exile on Main St.* and Jack Kerouac and Bob Dylan and Leonard Cohen. It was like finding your people."

The space currently occupied by the Viper Room has a storied history starting in the 1950s with the opening of a jazz club called the Melody Room, which featured acts such as Billy Ward and His Dominoes and was frequented by actors like Cesar "The Joker" Romero and Jackie "Uncle Fester" Coogan, as well as notorious gangsters such as Mickey Cohen. In 1973, the Melody Room morphed into Filthy McNasty's, which counted none other than Tom Waits and Evil Knieval among its regular customers. The outside of Filthy McNasty's was featured on the cover of British glam rock band Sweet's 1974 album, *Desolation Boulevard*. During the 1980s, Filthy McNasty's morphed into the Central, which featured a variety of live musical acts, along with Chuck E. Weiss and the Goddamn Liars every Monday night. The Go-Go's filmed the music video for "Our Lips Are Sealed" at the Central, which was also featured in the 1983 comedy *Valley Girl*, during the scene where the Plimsouls perform "A Million Miles Away." Guns N' Roses performed a rare acoustic set at the Central on May 1, 1986, performing (without Steven Adler) "Move to the City," "Don't Cry," and "Jumpin' Jack Flash." It was the first time the band played "Don't Cry" acoustically in front of a rather unappreciative, chattering crowd. In Oliver Stone's 1991 film *The Doors*, the Central was used to represent the long-defunct London Fog nightclub.

7

Climbin' Through the Wreckage

Appetite for Destruction (1987)

The whole album is about someone we've known and hung out with or something we've done.
                                                                    —Axl Rose

A raw, powerful, and uncompromising chronicle of the struggles Guns N' Roses faced as they tried to survive on the gritty streets of West Hollywood during the early 1980s, *Appetite for Destruction* would eventually become the best-selling debut album in US history (with more than 30 million copies sold worldwide to date). However, with little fanfare, *Appetite for Destruction* made its debut on August 29, 1987, and promptly stalled at No. 182 on the *Billboard* charts. Help came in the form of David Geffen of Geffen Records, who asked for a little favor from MTV, which eventually started placing the music videos of "Welcome to the Jungle" and "Sweet Child O' Mine" into heavy rotation. Before long, the album finally reached No. 1 on the US charts on August 6, 1988, nearly a year after it was first released. Rounding out the top five were *Hysteria* (Def Leppard), *Roll with It* (Steve Winwood), *Tracy Chapman* (Tracy Chapman), and the *Dirty Dancing* soundtrack. Guns N' Roses was on tour opening for Aerosmith at the time. Slash summed it up best in his autobiography when he remarked, "It was the right band at the right time with the right message."

Produced by Mike Clink (who had worked on Survivor's No. 1 hit "Eye of the Tiger" from the 1982 *Rocky III* soundtrack), *Appetite for Destruction* was recorded at Rumbo Studios in Conoga Park, Take One Studios in Burbank, and Can Am Studio in Tarzana, and mixed at Media Sound in New York City. A series of producers were considered before settling on Clink, such as Paul Stanley of KISS, Nikki Sixx of Mötley Crüe, and Manny Charlton of Nazareth, among others. Songs that were considered and inevitably rejected

At one time Manny Charlton of Scottish hard rock band Nazareth was considered as producer of *Appetite for Destruction*. Growing up, Axl Rose was such a big fan of Nazareth that he asked the band to play "Love Hurts" at his wedding to Erin Everly.

Author's collection

for *Appetite for Destruction* include "November Rain," "You Could Be Mine," "Don't Cry," and "Back Off Bitch." In the album's liner notes, Guns N' Roses thank some of their favorite early West Hollywood venues such as the Troubadour, Whisky A Go Go, and the Roxy.

Appetite for Destruction encountered controversy right out of the gates, as its album cover featured the disturbing artwork of Robert Williams depicting a woman apparently being raped by a robot while some kind of large predator looms above, possibly to wreak vengeance. (The album's name came from the painting's title.) Williams, who went on to found *Juxtapoz Art*

& Culture Magazine in 1994, later remarked that since "none of the guys in the band were too articulate," they directed the media to him to "defend the cover." Since Geffen Records believed quite correctly that many retailers would balk at displaying *Appetite for Destruction* on their shelves, the offensive album cover was quickly replaced with tattoo art created by artist Billy White Jr. The new image depicted skulls representing each GN'R band member. (The original cover art was included inside the album's booklet as a compromise.) Believe it or not, Axl Rose originally wanted to use a photo of the 1986 Space Shuttle Challenger explosion on the album cover.

By the way, the album's liner notes are very entertaining as well. They feature thanks to Geffen A&R representative "Tom 'Balls Out' Zutaut," "West (Smith and Wesson GN'R #6) Arkeen," "Richard Caballero (for keeping Axl and Slash out of jail)," manager "Alan Niven (for comin' in and kickin' ass when it was needed!)," "Todd Crew for putting Slash up and taking care of his snakes: Clyde and Cranston (Slash's snakes from hell)," and, saving the best for last, "all those who taught us hard lessons by attempted financial sodomy, the teachers, preachers, cops, and elders who never believed."

Interestingly, *Appetite for Destruction* reached No. 1 just one day before *Straight Outta Compton*, the debut album of gangsta rappers N.W.A., was released. The groundbreaking rap album featured such incendiary tracks as "Fuck tha Police" and "Gangsta Gangsta." In a 2006 *New York* magazine interview, Axl commented, "We thought we were so badass . . . Then N.W.A. came out rapping about this world where you walk out of your house and you get shot. It was clear what stupid little white-boy poseurs we were."

Appetite for Destruction received mostly positive reviews from rock publications such as *Kerrang!*, which enthusiastically exclaimed, "Rock is at last being wrestled from the hands of the bland, the weak, the jaded, the tired, the worn, and being thrust back into the hands of the real raunch rebels." However, some critics weren't so receptive. For example, Dave Ling of *Metal Hammer* dismissed the band as a second-rate rehash of Aerosmith, Hanoi Rocks, and Johnny Thunders, while Robert Christgau of the *Village Voice* gave the album a B minus. Many of Guns N' Roses' peers, however, were impressed by the album's potency. One such peer was Lars Ulrich of Metallica, who remarked in a July 1999 *SPIN* interview, "['It's So Easy'] just blew my fuckin' head off. I had never heard anything with that kind of attitude. It wasn't just what was said—it was the way Axl said it. It was so venomous. It was so fucking real and so fucking angry." *Appetite for Destruction* later placed No. 62 on *Rolling Stone's* list of "The 500 Greatest Albums of All Time."

"Welcome to the Jungle"

"If you got the money honey/We got your disease." The first song cowritten by Axl and Slash, "Welcome to the Jungle" peaked at No. 7 on the US charts and depicts a harrowing journey through the dark side of the American Dream. Allegedly written in just three hours, the song was inspired by Axl's frightening encounter with a homeless man in New York City who shouted, "You know where you are? You're in the jungle, baby. You're gonna die!" *SPIN* magazine stated that Axl sounded like a "West Coast Ratso Rizzo giving a tour of Hollywood." Simply one of the most powerful, hardest-rocking songs

Known as "America's Loudest Lounge Singer," Richard Cheese covered a swinging Vegas-style version of "Welcome to the Jungle" on his 2005 album, *Aperitif for Destruction.*   *Author's collection*

of the 1980s, "Welcome to the Jungle" served as the album's first single (the B-side offered a live cover of AC/DC's "Whole Lotta Rosie" recorded at the Marquee Club in London) and featured an accompanying music video that quickly became one of MTV's most requested videos during the summer of 1988. Often used as an opener at GN'R concerts, "Welcome to the Jungle" begins with the lines: "Do you know where the fuck you are? You're in the jungle, baby! Wake up! Time to die!" The song can still be heard frequently to announce teams at various sporting events throughout the country. *Rolling Stone* ranked "Welcome to the Jungle" No. 467 on its list of the "500 Greatest Songs of All Time."

Believe it or not, "Welcome to the Jungle" also played a pivotal role in the capture of Manuel Noriega in December 1989. With the former military dictator of Panama holed up in the Vatican embassy, the US military installed some powerful stereo speakers around the building and blasted "Welcome to the Jungle," "I Fought the Law" by the Clash, "Too Old to Rock 'n' Roll: Too Young to Die" by Jethro Tull, and other classic rock songs as a form of psychological warfare that actually worked—within a few days Noriega surrendered.

"It's So Easy"

"I drink n' drive everything's in sight." Duff McKagan and West Arkeen initially cowrote "It's So Easy"—a song about groupies that includes some seriously misogynistic lyrics—in an acoustic style. According to Axl, it was Slash's idea to turn it into a rock song, and it became one of Guns N' Roses' live staples, serving as the band's show opener during the *Appetite for Destruction* Tour. It was released as a single with the B-side "Shadow of Your Love." Duff later titled his 2011 autobiography, *It's So Easy: and Other Lies,* after the song. A raunchy "It's So Easy" music video (which was filmed at the Cathouse and featured Axl's then girlfriend and future wife Erin Everly in bondage gear) can only be found on YouTube these days.

A talented musician and songwriter in his own right, West Arkeen was an early friend of Guns N' Roses who cowrote other songs—such as "Yesterdays," "Bad Obsession," and "The Garden"—that ended up on the *Use Your Illusion* albums. Arkeen, who was part of a side project with Duff and Izzy called the Drunk Fux, also played guitar on three songs—"Man in the Meadow," "Swamp Song," and "Fuck You"—that appeared on Duff's 1993 solo debut album *Believe in Me.* In 1995, Arkeen formed his own band, the Outpatience, which released an album called *Anxious Disease* the following year. Axl, Slash, and Duff made guest appearances on the album and Izzy co-wrote one of the songs. Tragically, Arkeen died of an accidental drug overdose in 1997 at the age of thirty-six. In his autobiography, Slash called Arkeen "the only one that always came through when any of us needed anything; for a long time he literally was the only one we could trust."

"Nightrain"

"Said I'm a mean machine/Been drinkin' gasoline." A favorite among skid row bums and struggling musicians, Night Train Express is a fortified wine with 17.5 percent alcohol by volume that featured artwork of a locomotive rumbling through the night on its label. A bottle sold for just $1 plus tax during the early 1980s, making it highly appealing to aspiring rock stars wandering along the Sunset Strip. According to Slash, the song simply came together as band members stumbled their way down the street toward the Troubadour one shitfaced evening yelling "Night Train" as they brazenly chugged from a bottle of the cheap wine.

A straightforward track with lots of energy in the hard-rocking vein of mid-1970s Aerosmith, "Nightrain" perfectly exemplifies the brash, in-your-face, don't-give-a-fuck attitude of the band in the early days as they drunkenly made their way from bar to bar in the early morning hours on the Sunset Strip. "Nightrain" is about "the attitude" and how one feels "invincible" when drinking the cheap wine, according to Slash, who later admitted it was his favorite Guns N' Roses song. "Nightrain" was released as a single, reaching No. 93 on the US charts. *Guitar World* named "Nightrain" No. 8 on its list of the "Top Drinking Songs" (with "Tequila" by the Champs at No. 1).

"Out Ta Get Me"

"Been hidin' out/And layin' low." An Axl-penned tune, "Out Ta Get Me" depicts his deeply instilled paranoia that resulted from his frequent run-ins with authority figures during a very troubled childhood in Lafayette, Indiana. According to Duff, the song was also inspired by an incident where L.A. cops were searching for Axl on a "bogus rape charge" that forced him to go into hiding until the charges were eventually dismissed. The raw immediacy of tracks such as "Out Ta Get Me" resulted in the fact that most songs on the album were first, second, or third takes, according to Steven Adler. "Out Ta Get Me" made its live debut during a Guns N' Roses gig at the Troubadour

on February 28, 1986. While introducing the song, Axl remarked, "I wanna dedicate this to the LAPD and any young girls that like to fuck around." During a performance of "Out Ta Get Me" when GN'R opened for the Rolling Stones at the Los Angeles Coliseum on October 18, 1989, Axl fell off the stage. It was the same night as his notorious "Mr. Brownstone" speech (see below), which admonished his fellow bandmates for their drug use.

"Mr. Brownstone"

"Now I get up around whenever/I used ta get up on time." A mainstay of Guns N' Roses live performances, this powerful song depicts a day in the life of a heroin addict ("Mr. Brownstone" being slang for the drug). At one time or another, just about every GN'R band member (with the exception of Axl) was addicted to heroin. Slash and Izzy reportedly came up with the lyrics, which they scrawled on the back of a paper bag. According to Slash, a friend of his thought the song "was about a building." However, "Mr. Brownstone" became truly infamous when it served as a backdrop for Axl's infamous onstage rant when the band opened for the Rolling Stones at the Los Angeles Coliseum on October 18, 1989: "Unless certain people in this band get their shit together, these will be the last Guns N' Roses shows you'll fucking ever see. Cause I'm tired of too many people in this organization dancing with Mr. Goddamn Brownstone."

In addition, "Mr. Brownstone" was one of three songs (along with "Sweet Child O' Mine" and "Paradise City") performed by Slash, Duff, Gilby Clarke, Matt Sorum, and Myles Kennedy during the 2012 induction of Guns N' Roses into the Rock and Roll Hall of Fame. "Mr. Brownstone" placed No. 7 on Alternative Reel's list of the "Top 10 Heroin-Inspired Songs," behind "Under the Bridge" by the Red Hot Chili Peppers, "Sam Stone" by John Prine, "The Needle and the Damage Done" by Neil Young, "Hurt" by Nine Inch Nails, "Hotel California" by the Eagles, and "Heroin" by the Velvet Underground.

"Paradise City"

"Captain America's been torn apart/Now he's a court jester with a broken heart." As a hit single, "Paradise City" reached No. 5 on the US charts and was often used as a closing song during the *Appetite for Destruction*, *Use Your Illusion*, and *Chinese Democracy* tours. "Paradise City" is also the only track on the album that uses a synthesizer. According to Slash, the band came up with the

popular stadium anthem while riding in a rental van on the way back from an early gig in San Francisco. Slash's preferred lyrics were: "Where the girls are fat and they've got big titties." (The rest of the band thankfully squashed that idea!) VH1 placed "Paradise City" at No. 21 on its list of the "40 Greatest Metal Songs of All Time," and it also ranked No. 453 on *Rolling Stone's* list of the "500 Greatest Songs of All Time." According to *Rolling Stone*, GN'R's performance of "Paradise City" at a 1988 gig at the Ritz in New York City "captured the band at its most primal . . . [The performance] culminated with Axl diving into a sloshing, jostling sea of fans . . . It remains the definitive live version of the decadent anthem."

"My Michelle"

"Drivin' your friends crazy/With your life's insanity." A gritty biographical sketch of the rather chaotic life of one of Axl Rose's former girlfriends, Michelle Young, "My Michelle" opens with the infamous lines: "Your daddy works in porno/Now that mommy's not around." According to Young in a July 1999 *SPIN* interview, "I was driving Axl to a gig and 'Your Song' by Elton John came on the radio. I said that I wished somebody would write a beautiful song about me. But, you know the song. At the time, I didn't care because I was so fucked up, but what it says is all true: My dad does distribute porno films and my mom did die." "My Michelle" was covered by punk rock band AFI for the 2000 compilation album *Punk Goes Metal*.

"Think About You"

"Funny how I never felt so high." Written by Izzy, "Think About You" reportedly concerned one of his former girlfriends (although, according to one theory, it's about heroin, his true love at the time). Izzy assumed rhythm and lead guitar duties on the song, as well as backing vocals. "Think About You" served as a frequent staple of early, pre-*Appetite for Destruction* GN'R gigs (but only appeared sporadically thereafter).

"Sweet Child O' Mine"

"I hate to look into those eyes/And see an ounce of pain." The third single released from *Appetite for Destruction* (after "It's So Easy" and "Welcome to the Jungle"), "Sweet Child O' Mine" skyrocketed up the US charts due to the heavy

rotation of its accompanying music video by MTV, and it became the band's first and only No. 1 single. Slash came up with the iconic opening riff (one of the most famous in rock 'n' roll history), describing it in a *Rolling Stone* interview as "a combination of influences. From Jeff Beck, Cream, and Zeppelin to stuff you'd be surprised at: the solos in Manfred Mann's version of 'Blinded by the Light' and Gerry Rafferty's 'Baker Street.'"

Axl wrote the lyrics about his then girlfriend and future wife Erin Everly, the daughter of Don Everly of the Everly Brothers ("All I Have to Do is Dream") and actress Venetia Stevenson (*Horror Hotel*). According to Axl, "Sweet Child O' Mine" was the "first positive love song" he had ever written, and he turned to an unlikely source for inspiration according to a 2005 *Q* magazine article: "I went out and got some old [Lynyrd] Skynyrd tapes to make sure that we'd got that heartfelt feeling." As for Slash, he felt the song was a "joke" and he was "just fuckin' around" when he came up with the riff. In a 2015 *Guitar World* interview, Slash remarked, "To me it was a nightmare because, for some strange reason, everyone picked up on it and, the next thing you knew, it had turned into a song. I hated it forever!"

At the 1989 MTV Music Video Awards, "Sweet Child O' Mine" won "Best Heavy Metal Video" over "Rag Doll" (Aerosmith), "Pour Some Sugar on Me" (Def Leppard), and "One" (Metallica). The song also beat out both "Never Gonna Give You Up" by Rick Astley and "Roll with It" by Steve Winwood to capture the "Favorite Pop/Rock Single" Award at the 1989 American Music Awards. In addition, "Sweet Child O' Mine" later ranked No. 198 on *Rolling Stone's* "500 Greatest Songs of All Time." Slash's guitar solo ranked No. 37 in *Guitar World's* list of the "100 Greatest Guitar Solos." (Not surprisingly, "Stairway to Heaven" by Led Zeppelin ranked No. 1.)

Sheryl Crow's cover of "Sweet Child O' Mine" for the Adam Sandler comedy *Big Daddy* regularly appears in lists of the "Worst Covers of All Time" (although somehow she received a Grammy Award for her efforts!). "Sweet Child O' Mine" also appeared on the soundtrack of the 2008 film *The Wrestler*, which starred Mickey Rourke. In the movie, Rourke's character, Randy "The Ram" Robinson, exclaims, "Bet your ass, man. Guns N' Roses fuckin' rules!" In the 2008 comedy *Step Brothers*, Derek (Adam Scott)—the obnoxious brother of Brennan (Will Ferrell)—and his family sing a hilariously cheesy version of "Sweet Child O' Mine" in the car. The song has also appeared on the soundtracks of *Bad Dreams* (1988) and *State of Grace* (1990). In 2015, Australian music TV channel MAX published an article on its website noting some striking similarities between "Sweet Child O' Mine" and a 1981 song called "Unpublished Critics" by an Australian band called Australian Crawl.

As far as the relationship between Axl and Erin Everly, it ended disastrously. The couple got married in April 1990, and Axl filed for divorce less than a month later. They reconciled, but the marriage was finally annulled in January 1991. According to Axl, as quoted in a 2015 *Rolling Stone* article, "Erin and I treated each other like shit. Sometimes we treated each other great, because the children in us were best friends. But then there were other times when we just fucked each other's lives completely up." Everly eventually filed a civil lawsuit against Axl that was settled out of court.

"You're Crazy"

"Lookin' for a lover in a world that's much too dark." Originally written as an acoustic song (the way it appears on the 1988 Guns N' Roses release *G N' R Lies*), "You're Crazy" was initially known as "You're Fucking Crazy" during early gigs. *Appetite for Destruction* features a harder-rocking version of the song than originally intended, which ended up being perfect for the album.

"Anything Goes"

"Always hungry for somethin'/That I haven't had yet." One of Guns N' Roses' oldest songs (originally known as "My Way Your Way"), "Anything Goes" is a raunchy little number that dates from the Hollywood Rose days and was written by Izzy and Chris Weber. It includes some of the band's most offensive, misogynistic lyrics, such as "Panties 'round your knees/With your ass in debris." During early club dates at places like the Troubadour, Axl would introduce "Anything Goes" as the band's "theme song."

"Rocket Queen"

"I'm a sexual innuendo/In this burned out paradise." The final track on *Appetite for Destruction*, "Rocket Queen," ends with a bang (no pun intended) due to the inclusion of the notorious sexual "sound effects" featuring Axl and nineteen-year-old Adriana Smith (who happened to be Steven Adler's girlfriend at the time). According to Axl, "I wrote this song for this girl [later identified as Barbi Von Greif] who was gonna have a band and call it Rocket Queen. She kinda kept me alive for a while. The last part of the song is my

message to this person, or anybody else who can get something out of it. It's like there's hope and a friendship note at the end of the song." One of the recording engineers later commented that the studio was "like a Ron Jeremy set." Smith agreed to participate in the recording to help out the band and for a bottle of Jack Daniel's. Today, Smith is reportedly a drug and alcohol counselor.

8

Gone on a Binge

Appetite for Destruction Tour

Guns was a band that might break apart at any second; that was half of the excitement. —Slash

The *Appetite for Destruction* Tour served as the only Guns N' Roses tour in which the "classic" lineup of Axl Rose, Slash, Izzy Stradlin, Duff McKagan, and Steven Adler performed together (excluding the four shows in support of the Rolling Stones at the Los Angeles Coliseum in October 1989). The grueling, sixteen-month-long *Appetite for Destruction* Tour, which comprised 180 shows, featured Guns N' Roses opening for such bands as the Cult (August 14–September 17, 1987), Mötley Crüe (November 3–29, 1987), Alice Cooper (December 3–27, 1987), Iron Maiden (May 13–June 8, 1988), and Aerosmith (July 17–August 17 and August 24–September 15, 1988) with varying degrees of success.

Several bands, many of which have since faded into total obscurity (with a few exceptions), opened for Guns N' Roses during the *Appetite for Destruction* Tour, such as Faster Pussycat, L.A. Guns, the Quireboys, Ezo, Funhouse, Junkyard, Knightshade, T.S.O.L., Zodiac Mindwarp and the Love Reaction, Kings of the Sun, U.D.O., and the Angels. Below are some of the highlights (and various lowlights!) of the legendary *Appetite for Destruction* Tour.

August 1–2, 1987: Two weeks before embarking on the *Appetite for Destruction* Tour, Guns N' Roses film the music video—their first—for "Welcome to the Jungle" in Los Angeles.

August 14, 1987: Guns N' Roses embark on the *Appetite for Destruction* Tour in support of the Cult at the Halifax Metro Centre in Halifax, Nova Scotia. (Ironically, during the band's 2016 Not in This Lifetime Tour, it would be the Cult that would serve as opening act for Guns N' Roses.)

September 2, 1987: While opening for the Cult at the Warfield Theater in San Franciso, Gun N' Roses discover that *Appetite for Destruction* has cracked the Top 100 on the *Billboard* charts.

September 29, 1987: The first Guns N' Roses concert of the European leg of the tour takes place at the Markthalle Hamburg Auditorium in Hamburg, West Germany, with Faster Pussycat as the opening act.

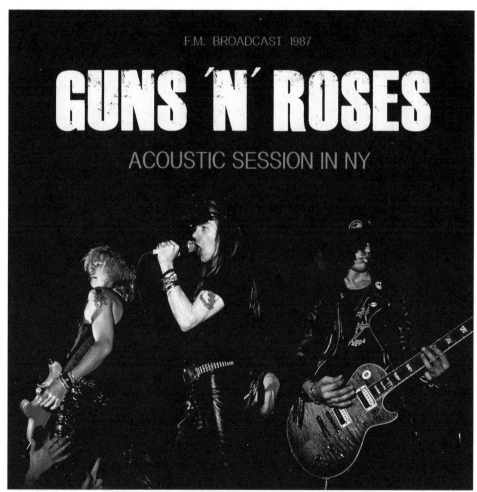

Guns N' Roses played an acoustic set at CBGB's Record Canteen in New York City on October 30, 1987, that featured "One in a Million," one of only two times the band would perform the controversial song live.   *Author's collection*

October 24, 1987: The GN'R members stop by the set of MTV's *Headbangers Ball* and get invited by VJ Adam "Smash" to destroy the set, which they promptly do before making a hasty retreat from the studio.

October 30, 1987: Approximately one hundred fans cram into CBGB's Record Canteen in New York City as Guns N' Roses perform an acoustic set where they debut songs from *G N' R Lies*, including "Patience" and the controversial "One in a Million." Axl tells the crowd that he hasn't slept in two days.

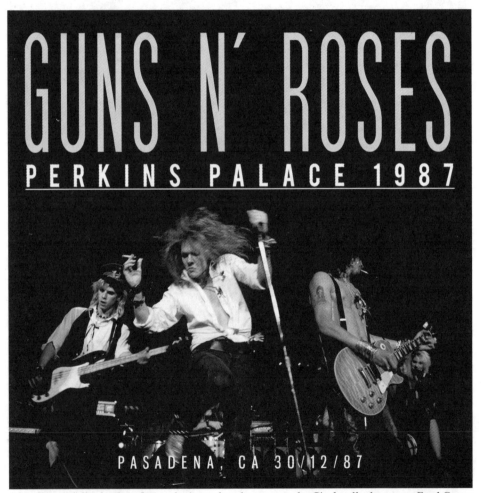

After Steven Adler broke a finger during a drunken escapade, Cinderella drummer Fred Coury filled in for him for a set at Perkins Palace in Pasadena, California, in support of Alice Cooper.

Author's collection

November 3, 1987: The Municipal Auditorium in Mobile, Alabama, serves as Guns N' Roses' first concert in support of Mötley Crüe during their *Girls, Girls, Girls* Tour.

November 20, 1987: Axl gets arrested onstage for assaulting a security guard (who reportedly shoved one of his friends near the stage) at a concert opening for Mötley Crüe at the Omni Coliseum in Atlanta. A roadie named "Big Ron" (Ronnie Schneider) fills in on vocals.

December 3, 1987: Guns N' Roses' first concert in support of Alice Cooper takes place at the La Villa Real Convention Center in McAllen, Texas.

December 18, 1987: Opening for Alice Cooper at the UIC Pavilion in Chicago, Axl tells the audience, "Bon Jovi can suck my dick!" The day before he had been harassed in a hotel lobby by an obnoxious fan who claimed Axl looked just like Jon Bon Jovi.

December 26, 1987: During this Guns N' Roses show in support of Alice Cooper at Perkins Palace in Pasadena, California, drummer Fred Coury of Cinderella fills in for Steven Adler, who had recently broken a finger during a barroom brawl.

January 31, 1988: At the Limelight in New York City, Guns N' Roses perform the raunchy "Cornshucker" for the first (and reportedly only) time with Duff assuming vocal duties.

February 2, 1988: Guns N' Roses perform a legendary set at the Ritz in New York City. MTV films the concert and later broadcasts an edited version of the show titled *Guns N' Roses: Live at the Ritz*. Axl, Slash, and Duff all stage-dive during the intense performance. Footage from the concert later appears in the music video for GN'R's "You Could Be Mine." Slash later admitted in his 2007 memoir that the Ritz appearance "wasn't one of our greatest shows by any means, it was loose and out of tune and punk rock . . . That [MTV] footage is important because it is the essence of the band."

March 31, 1988: Guns N' Roses appear on Fox's *The Late Show* and performs "You're Crazy" and "Used to Love Her."

May 13, 1988: At the Moncton Coliseum in Moncton, New Brunswick, Canada, Guns N' Roses join Iron Maiden's Seventh Tour of a Seventh Tour.

May 27, 1988: British rocker Kid Chaos (a.k.a. Haggis) fills in as bassist for Duff during the Guns N' Roses show at the Saddledome in Calgary. Duff has taken a leave from the band to marry Mandy Brixx of the Lame Flames.

June 8, 1988: Axl loses his voice and Guns N' Roses are forced to cancel their appearance as opening act for Iron Maiden at Irvine Meadows Amphitheatre in Irvine, California. Ironically, L.A. Guns are tapped to fill in for GN'R (and Izzy and Slash join them onstage for the gig).

August 6, 1988: *Appetite for Destruction* reaches No. 1 on the US charts while Guns N' Roses perform in support of Aerosmith's *Permanent Vacation* Tour at the Saratoga Springs Performing Arts Center in Saratoga Springs, New York.

August 11, 1988: Guns N' Roses film the music video for "Sweet Child O' Mine" at Huntington Ballroom in Huntington Beach, California.

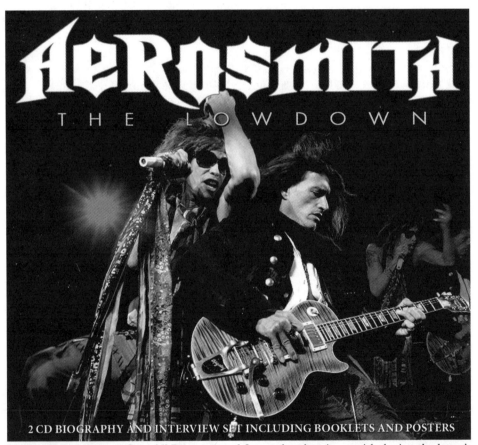

2 CD BIOGRAPHY AND INTERVIEW SET INCLUDING BOOKLETS AND POSTERS

Hard partying upstarts Guns N' Roses opened for newly sober Aerosmith during the latter's *Permanent Vacation* Tour during the summer of 1988. By the end of the tour, the opening act was bigger than the headliner, and Guns N' Roses even supplanted Aerosmith on the cover of *Rolling Stone.*   *Author's collection*

August 16, 1988: Footage for the "Paradise City" music video is shot during a GN'R concert opening for Aerosmith and Deep Purple at Giants Stadium in East Rutherford, New Jersey.

August 20, 1988: Tragedy ensues during Guns N' Roses' performance at the Monsters of Rock Festival at Castle Donington, England, as two fans are trampled to death in the sea of more than 100,000 people surging toward the stage (and ignoring Axl Rose's pleas for the crowd to move back). Footage from this concert was also used in the "Paradise City" music video.

September 7, 1988: Guns N' Roses perform "Welcome to the Jungle" at the 1988 MTV Video Music Awards and win "Best New Artist" for the song, beating out the Godfathers ("Birth, School, Work, Death"), Buster Poindexter ("Hot, Hot, "Hot"), Swing Out Sister ("Breakout"), and Jodi Watley ("Some Kind of Love").

September 10, 1988: "Sweet Child O' Mine" reaches No. 1 on the US charts while Guns N' Roses perform at the Shoreline Amphitheatre in Mountain View, California.

September 17, 1988: The final show of the US leg of the *Appetite for Destruction* Tour takes place at Texas Stadium in Irving, Texas, and also features INXS, Iggy Pop, Ziggy Marley, and the Smithereens. According to Steven Adler in his autobiography, it was "the absolute *worst* show we ever played."

September 24, 1988: *Appetite for Destruction* reaches No. 1 on the US charts.

November 17, 1988: With the tagline "Hard Rock Heroes," Guns N' Roses appear on the cover of *Rolling Stone* for the first time.

November 30, 1988: GNR's second studio album, *G N' R Lies*, is released, featuring the tracks "Reckless Life," "Nice Boys," "Move to the City," "Mama Kin," "Patience," "Used to Love Her," "You're Crazy," and the extremely controversial "One in a Million." The only single released from the album, "Patience," rises to No. 4 on the US charts.

December 10, 1988: Guns N' Roses perform for the first time at the legendary Nippon Budokan in Tokyo, Japan.

December 19, 1988: The *Appetite for Destruction* Tour culminates with a Guns N' Roses show at Mount Smart Stadium in Auckland, New Zealand.

9

When Your Innocence Dies

G N' R Lies (1988)

Basically, it was a live session. I recorded everyone in the same room in a circle and they all played together. And it was pretty magical.
— *G N' R Lies* producer Mike Clink

resh off the overwhelming success of their 1987 debut album, *Appetite for Destruction*, Guns N' Roses released a patchwork follow-up, *G N' R Lies*, in November 1988 and immediately got mired in controversy for the inclusion of the final track, "One in a Million," which contained both racist and homophobic lyrics. The eight-song album featured four recordings from the band's 1986 EP *Live?!*@ Like a Suicide*— "Reckless Life," "Nice Boys" (Rose Tattoo cover), "Move to the City," and "Mama Kin" (Aerosmith cover), along with three new songs—"Patience," "Used to Love Her," and the still-notorious "One in a Million"—as well as an acoustic remake of "You're Crazy." The only single from the album, "Patience," reached No. 4 on the US charts.

Orginally titled *G N' R Lies: The Sex, the Drugs, the Violence, the Shocking Truth*, the album featured a tabloid-style cover (think vintage *Weekly World News*) full of outrageous headlines such as "Elephant Gives Birth to Midget," "Sue's Toes Shot Off by Snatch Gang," "Man Sues Ex-Wife, 'She Took My Sperm Without Permission,'" "Heir to Throne Caught with Trousers Down in Lurid Lust Pit," and "She Broke My Heart . . . So I Ripped Hers Out." The *Live?!*@ Like a Suicide* album cover that features Axl Rose and Duff McKagan appears on the inside jacket of *G N' R Lies*, which also includes a blonde centerfold with the bogus headline "The loveliest girls are always in your GN'R L.P."

"Reckless Life"

The first track on *G N' R Lies* opens with Slash exclaiming, "Hey fuckers! Suck on Guns N' fuckin' Roses!" Originally performed by the pre-Guns N' Roses band Hollywood Rose, "Reckless Life" was written by Axl, Izzy, and Hollywood Rose bandmate Chris Weber. The song also appears in *The Roots of Guns N' Roses*, a compilation album released by Deadline Music in 2004 and produced by Weber. The *Roots* album also contains early versions of "Killing Time," "Anything Goes," "Rocker," and "Shadow of Your Love."

Writers: Axl, Izzy, Slash, Duff, Steven Adler, Chris Weber. **Personnel:** Axl (vocals), Slash (lead guitar), Izzy (rhythm guitar), Duff (bass), Steven Adler (drums).

"Nice Boys"

The Australian rock band Rose Tattoo proved to be a significant influence on Guns N' Roses, and the band acknowledged their debt by recording "Nice Boys" (as well as making the song a standard at most of their early gigs). Formed in Sydney in 1976, Rose Tattoo released its 1978 self-titled debut album, which featured "Nice Boys," as well as other favorites such as "Rock 'n' Roll Outlaw" and "Bad Boy for Love." The band released its second album, *Scarred for Life*, in 1982 and embarked on a US tour in support of Aerosmith and ZZ Top. Rose Tattoo received international attention with the success of their rock anthem "We Can't Be Beaten," off their third album, *Scarred for Life* (1983). The band has opened for Guns N' Roses on several occasions over the years (including on the Australian leg of GN'R's *Use Your Illusion* Tour in 1993).

Angry Anderson has been the lead singer of Rose Tattoo since 1976. (He got his start with hard rock/blues band Buster Brown.) According to Anderson, Australia has produced only three "great hard rock 'n' roll bands" in its history: AC/DC, the Angels, and Rose Tattoo. Australian rock historian Ian McFarlane, quoted in a 2015 interview on Triplem.com, has called Rose Tattoo "one of the most revered bands of all time," claiming, "The Tatts played peerless, street-level heavy blues with the emphasis on slide guitar and strident lyric statements." In 2006, Rose Tattoo was inducted into the Australian Recording Industry Association Hall of Fame. Other bands that have covered Rose Tattoo songs include L.A. Guns,

Atlanta-based sleaze rockers Nashville Pussy, and Los Angeles heavy metal band Keel, among others.

Writers: Angry Anderson, Mick Cocks, Geordie Leach, Dallas "Digger" Royalle, Peter Wells. **Personnel:** Axl (vocals), Slash (lead guitar), Izzy (rhythm guitar), Duff (bass), Steven Adler (drums).

"Move to the City"

One of the earliest Guns N' Roses recordings, "Move to the City" features the novelty of sax accompaniment and was one of the staples of the band's early sets. In its 2016 ranking of all Guns N' Roses songs, *SPIN* magazine placed "Move to the City" at No. 70, stating, "It's slight for early Guns, but it's a better early-band invocation of the Toxic Twins' streetwise strut than their 'Mama Kin' cover." During a Guns N' Roses performance at Madame Wong's East on July 4, 1985, Axl introduced "Move to the City" as "a song dedicated to anybody that got tired of wherever the fuck they were and moved to a big city such as L.A."

Writers: Izzy, Chris Weber. **Personnel:** Axl (vocals); Slash (lead guitar), Izzy (rhythm guitar), Duff (bass), Steven Adler (drums).

"Mama Kin"

An edgy cover of the Aerosmith classic, "Mama Kin" was performed by GN'R at most of their early gigs. Written by lead singer Steven Tyler, "Mama Kin" first appeared on Aerosmith's 1973 self-titled debut album, which also featured such classics as "Dream On," "Make It," "Somebody," "Write Me a Letter," "One Way Street," "Movin' Out," and "Walkin' the Dog." In *Walk This Way: The Autobiography of Aerosmith* (2003), Tyler remarked, "I stole the opening lick [for 'Mama Kin'] from an old Blodwyn Pig song." In addition to being Aerosmith's first-ever single, "Mama Kin" became a signature tune for the legendary band, and it appears on the live albums *Live! Bootleg* (1978), *Classics Live* (1986), and *A Little South of Sanity* (1998).

When Guns N' Roses opened for Aerosmith during the latter's *Permanent Vacation* Tour, Aerosmith brought GN'R onstage during the last show for an amazing performance of "Mama Kin." Guns N' Roses also performed "Mama Kin" with Steven Tyler and Joe Perry during a pay-per-view show on June 6, 1992, in Paris, France (the same concert where Axl launched into a rant against actor Warren Beatty). Interestingly, Buckcherry also covered the song as a bonus track on their 2014 EP *Fuck*. "Mama Kin" is the only song on the album that does not use "fuck" in the title or in the song lyrics. The album includes the tracks "Somebody Fucked with Me," "Say Fuck It," "The Motherfucker," "I Don't Give a Fuck," "It's a Fucking Disaster," and "Fist Fuck."

Writer: Steven Tyler. **Personnel:** Axl (vocals); Slash (lead guitar), Izzy (rhythm guitar), Duff (bass), Steven Adler (drums).

"Patience"

Written by Izzy about a former girlfriend and remembered by many due to Axl's distinctive whistling intro, the acoustic ballad "Patience" was released as the only single from *G N' R Lies* and became one of the band's biggest hits, reaching No. 4 on the US charts. Guns N' Roses biographer Danny Sugerman called the song "an acoustic song Gram Parsons influenced by way of the Stones circa *Beggar's Banquet*." The band made an accompanying music video that was filmed on Valentine's Day 1989 at the Ambassador Hotel in Los Angeles, where Democratic presidential candidate Robert F. Kennedy was assassinated in 1968. Steven Adler, who did not play on the recorded track, can be seen twiddling his thumbs in the music video. (Ironically, it would be the last GN'R music video Adler would ever appear in.)

Guns N' Roses performed "Patience" at the American Music Awards in 1989 with the Eagles' Don Henley filling in on drums for Adler, who was in rehab at the time. When asked about the performance in an interview with *Modern Drummer* magazine, Henley replied, "Fortunately it was a ballad that we played, not a balls-to-the-wall number. I rehearsed with Axl a couple of days, although the whole band never showed up. But it was a piece of cake. There was really nothing to it." In addition, "Patience" was featured in the soundtracks of the Martin Scorsese thriller *Cape Fear* (1991) and the zombie comedy *Warm Bodies* (2013).

During a November 13, 2010 episode of VH1 Classic's *That Metal Show*, Tesla guitarist Frank Hannon claimed that "Patience" was a rip-off of an early Tesla track, "Better Off Without You." According to Hannon, "We were labelmates with Guns N' Roses on Geffen. There's a demo of a song that we wrote called 'Better Off Without You.' It is 'Patience' note for note . . . I don't know if they ripped us off or [then Geffen A&R executive] Tom Zutaut or

Geffen or somebody passed them the tape." Upon hearing the accusation, Slash immediately returned fire on his Facebook page: "I heard that one of the guys from Telsa claimed GN'R stole 'Patience' from them. I'm assuming he's smoking super crack. Or dreaming out loud." Hannon quickly took to Tesla's official forum to "clarify" his remarks: "The song 'Patience' is a great song that they wrote themselves, and it is only the end part that has any similar part to the guitar chords we used."

Writers: Izzy, Axl. **Personnel:** Axl (vocals, whistling), Slash (lead acoustic guitar), Izzy (rhythm acoustic guitar), Duff (bass), Steven Adler (drums).

"Used to Love Her"

Due to its blatant misogyny, "Used to Love Her" would qualify as the most controversial track on just about any other rock album. However, *G N' R Lies* also contains the track "One in a Million," so the controversial lyrics here—"I used to love her/But I had to kill her"—were pretty much dismissed as a lighthearted joke. Guns N' Roses even performed the song on Fox's *The Late Show* in 1988. Izzy reportedly wrote the song on a whim after hearing a breakup song on the radio. However, Slash joked that "Used to Love Her" was actually about Axl's dog. Vancouver garage-punk trio White Lung covered the song during a performance at Sirius XMU in 2016.

Writers: Axl, Izzy, Slash, Duff, Steven Adler. **Personnel:** Axl (vocals), Slash (lead acoustic guitar), Izzy (rhythm acoustic guitar), Duff (bass), Steven Adler (drums).

"You're Crazy"

A version of "You're Crazy" (originally called "You're Fucking Crazy") with electric guitars appeared on *Appetite for Destruction*. However, this mainly acoustic track is how it was originally written just after the band signed with Geffen Records in March 1986. Guns N' Roses performed the slower-paced, bluesy version of "You're Crazy" on Fox's *The Late Show* in 1988.

Writers: Axl, Izzy, Slash, Duff, Steven Adler. **Personnel:** Axl (vocals), Slash (lead acoustic guitar), Izzy (rhythm acoustic guitar), Duff (bass), Steven Adler (drums).

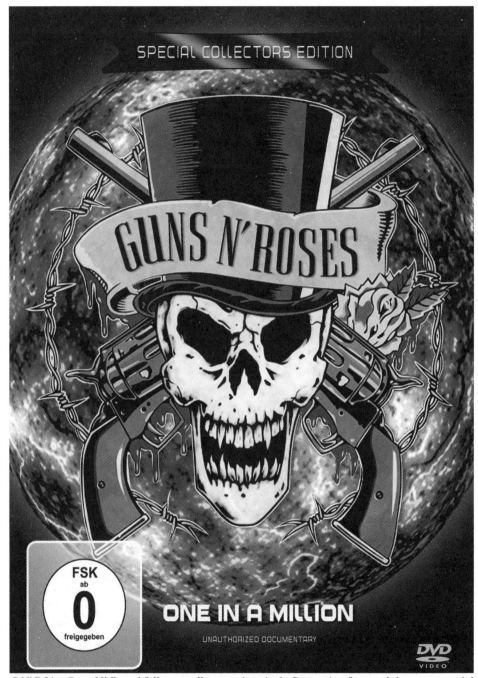

G N' R Lies, Guns N' Roses' follow-up album to *Appetite for Destruction*, featured the controversial song "One in a Million," which was widely condemned for its racist and homophobic lyrics.

Author's collection

Disturbed by the fact that Axl Rose had apologized for "One in a Million," shock rocker Marilyn Manson performed the song during soundchecks on his *Guns, God and Government* Tour in 2000 and 2001.   *Author's collection*

"One in a Million"

Simply one of the most controversial rock songs of all time, "One in a Million" features lyrics to offend just about everyone—including "Police and Niggers, that's right/Get out of my way" and "Immigrants and faggots/ They make no sense to me." One critic went so far as to say it was music for "[former Grand Wizard of the Klu Klux Klan] David Duke's America." Axl defended the song by claiming that he had simply written an honest account of a "small town white boy" finding himself overwhelmed as he tried to adjust to big city life in Los Angeles.

In a 1989 *Rolling Stone* interview, Axl remarked:

> I used words like police and niggers because you're not allowed to use the word nigger. Why can black people go up to each other and say 'nigger,' but when a white guy does it all of a sudden it's a big put-down? I don't like boundaries of any kind. I don't like being told what I can and what I can't say. I used the word nigger because it's a word to describe somebody that is basically a pain in your life, a problem. The word nigger doesn't necessarily mean black. Doesn't John Lennon have a song 'Woman is the Nigger of the World'? There's a rap group, N.W.A., Niggers with Attitude. I mean, they're proud of that word. More power to them.

However, addressing the issue onstage when opening for Guns N' Roses and the Rolling Stones at the L.A. Coliseum in 1989, Vernon Reid of Living Colour stated, "If you don't have a problem with gay people, don't call them faggots. If you don't have a problem with black people, don't call them niggers."

Most of the rest of the band (especially Slash, whose mother was African-American) were reportedly extremely uncomfortable with the idea of including the track on the album—but Axl was insistent. In an interview with the *San Diego Union-Tribune*, Slash remarked, "I was offended. That was a brash, ignorant kind of statement Axl made. I knew where he was coming from, once he explained it, but that didn't validate it to make it worthy of putting on a record. We had issues. But the more issues we had, the more adamant he was about putting the song on there. I was hugely embarrassed that it was on something that my name was on. It was a tough little period." According to Duff in *It's So Easy: and Other Lies*, "When [Axl] showed [the lyrics] to us, I cringed at some of the words—especially *niggers*. It wasn't that I thought Axl held racist views—there was never any question on that front. I realized Axl's lyrics represented a third-person observation about what Reagan-era America had become: a nation of name-callers, a nation of fear.

It was just a word my mouth would not form. Among my earliest memories as a child was my mom pulling me out of kindergarten to march in a peace rally after Martin Luther King was shot and killed." However, Steven Adler, in *My Appetite for Destruction*, defended the inclusion of "One in a Million" on the album, remarking that "it was a great song that needed strong words. It expressed a heavy sentiment that had to be delivered with no punches pulled . . . It simply described the scumbags of the world."

In his 2015 list of "The 10 Worst Guns N' Roses Songs" in the *Houston Press*, Jef Rouner placed "One in a Million" at No. 2, writing: "To this day Axl says he doesn't see what all the fuss is about, but you could play this song at a Tea Party rally and get a standing ovation." Timothy White of *Billboard* summed up how a lot of critics reacted to the song when he wrote, "['One in a Million'] is still a piece of racist, gay-bashing garbage, a brainless screed affronting any humane person who believes in art's mandate to articulate the truth." Interestingly, none other than actor Sean Penn chimed in as a defender of the song in a September 24, 1989, letter to the *New York Times*, stating, "Guns N' Roses' song 'One in a Million' is like a Capa photo of war. It's a no-holds-barred reminder that hatred, fear, and bigotry are as alive today as they were when the American media called this war of domestic unrest a finished cause."

As a side note, shock rocker Marilyn Manson performed "One in a Million" during soundchecks on his *Guns, God and Government* Tour in 2000 and 2001. (He also had plans to record a cover of the song that never materialized.) In a July 6, 2002, interview with *The Heirophant*, Manson explained his reason for performing the song, claiming that he wanted "to do it simply because Axl Rose apologized" and because he didn't "think you should ever make something you will have to say 'sorry' for."

Writers: Axl, Izzy, Slash, Duff, Steven Adler. **Personnel:** Axl (vocals, piano), Slash (lead acoustic guitar), Izzy (rhythm acoustic guitar), Duff (bass), Steven Adler (drums).

10

Always on the Edge

Guns N' Roses as Opening Act

We were the wanton offspring of Aerosmith and the Rolling Stones,
delivering the goods with a hardcore rock attitude. —Steven Adler

G uns N' Roses honed their live performing skills at various West Hollywood clubs while occasionally opening for more established acts, such as Cheap Trick, Red Hot Chili Peppers, Alice Cooper, and Duff's idol Johnny Thunders. They even got the chance to party with Mötley Crüe. However, by the time GN'R joined the *Permanent Vacation* Tour in support of Aerosmith during the summer of 1988, *Appetite for Destruction* was skyrocketing up the charts. Guns N' Roses started getting more attention than the headliners, which culminated in GN'R "stealing" the cover of *Rolling Stone* from their idols.

Johnny Thunders

Both Duff and Izzy were big fans of ex-New York Doll and former Heartbreaker Johnny Thunders (who was born John Anthony Genzale Jr.). In a 2015 *Village Voice* interview, Duff remarked, "When people talk about Guns N' Roses these days, punk rock is a term that's rarely used . . . But in truth, we were those kids who benefited directly from early groundbreaking bands who played CBGB . . . Without the Ramones and Johnny Thunders and CBGB, I would have not had the career that I have." Therefore, Duff was elated when Guns N' Roses got the opportunity to open for Thunders (along with Jetboy) at Fender's Ballroom in Long Beach, California, on March 23, 1986. However, Duff's respect for his hero diminished when Thunders (a "sloppy heroin addict," according to Duff) started hitting on Axl's then girlfriend Erin Everly and when he tried to score dope backstage. Thunders, who struggled with heroin addiction most of his life, died alone in a cheap New Orleans hotel room in 1991 under mysterious circumstances. Guns N'

Roses ended up recording Thunders's "You Can't Put Your Arms Around a Memory" for their 1993 album *"The Spaghetti Incident?"*

Ted Nugent

Years before he became primarily known as a rightwing polemicist and rabid hunting advocate, Ted Nugent was a rock guitar legend known as the "Motor City Madman." Guns N' Roses opened for Nugent at the Santa Monica Civic Center on August 30, 1986. It had a sold-out crowd of approximately 3,000 people and was GN'R's first arena show, and, according to Slash, it was also the first time the band performed "Sweet Child O' Mine" live. However, Slash spent the whole afternoon before the concert desperately trying to score drugs, and he just barely managed to get to the show on time. He later regretted that he didn't even get the chance to meet Nugent.

Red Hot Chili Peppers

Formed in Los Angeles in 1983 and known for their electrifying live concerts, the Red Hot Chili Peppers (RHCP) created a unique sound that blended funk with elements of punk and psychedelic rock. Along the way, the band sold more than 80 million albums worldwide, won six Grammy Awards, and was inducted into the Rock and Roll Hall of Fame in 2012 (the same year as Guns N' Roses). The original RHCP lineup consisted of lead singer Anthony Kiedis, guitarist Hillel Slovak, bassist Flea (a childhood friend of both Slash and Steven Adler), and drummer Jack Irons. Later members included guitarist John Frusciante, guitarist Josh Klinghoffer, and drummer Chad Smith. RHCP scored their first Top 10 hit with the immensely popular "Under the Bridge," which appeared on the band's fifth studio album, *Blood Sugar Sex Magik* (1991). The song captured the "Breakthrough Video" and "Viewers Choice" awards at the 1992 MTV Video Music Awards. However, both bands were relatively unknown outside Los Angeles when Guns N' Roses (along with punk bands the Dickies and Thelonious Monster) opened for RHCP in the Ackerman Hall at UCLA on Halloween, 1986.

Cheap Trick

On December 21, 1986, Guns N' Roses opened for Cheap Trick at Fender's Ballroom (quite a step down from Budokan!) in Long Beach. GN'R's setlist that night included several early compositions intertwined with the usual covers: "Reckless Life," "Mr. Brownstone," "Move to the City," "Welcome to the Jungle," "Don't Cry," "Nice Boys" (Rose Tattoo), "It's So Easy," "Perfect Crime," "Shadow of Your Love" (Hollywood Rose), and "Mama Kin" (Aerosmith). Formed in 1973, Cheap Trick achieved a slew of hits over the years such as "Dream Police," "Surrender," "I Want You to Want Me," "The Flame," and others. One of the bestselling live albums of all time, *Cheap Trick at Budokan*, was released in 1978, reached No. 4 on the US charts, and has sold more than 3 million copies. The "classic" Cheap Trick lineup consisted of lead singer/rhythm guitarist Robin Zander, lead guitarist Rick Nielsen, bassist Tom Petersson, and drummer Bun E. Carlos. Cheap Trick was inducted into the Rock and Roll Hall of Fame in 2016.

As an amusing side note, Nielsen reportedly once invited the GN'R band members over to his house, where he promptly challenged Slash to a tequila-drinking contest. Slash proceeded to drink Nielsen under the table, and the Cheap Trick lead guitarist got so drunkenly belligerent that Izzy kicked him in the balls. Nielsen later admitted to having the band over to his place for drinks (but denied getting kicked in the nuts).

The Cult

Originally known as Southern Death Cult, then Death Cult, and finally simply the Cult, this British rock band formed in 1983 and featured a lineup that included lead singer Ian Astbury, guitarist Billy Duffy, and bassist Jamie Stewart, along with a succession of drummers over the years (including Matt Sorum, who was briefly a member of the Cult before replacing Steven Adler as Guns N' Rose' drummer in 1990). The *Rolling Stone Album Guide* dismissed the Cult as "essentially a heavy-metal band for folks who think they're above such things" with a "sound out of equal parts post-punk guitar aggression and neo-hippie mysticism, a combination that quite naturally results in some of the most pompous and silly music rock has seen since the heyday of the Doors."

Starting in August 1987 and with Guns N' Roses in support, the Cult embarked on a headlining tour through Canada and the West Coast of the United States that featured such lowlights as Astbury frequently trashing the band's equipment in an alcoholic stupor during concerts. According to some reports, Astbury spent more time in Guns N' Roses' dressing room than his own. By all reports, Guns N' Roses upstaged the Cult virtually every night. (It got so bad that the Cult's roadies even tried sabotaging some of

As an up-and-coming band in the pre-*Appetite for Destruction* days, Guns N' Roses got the opportunity to open for such acts as Cheap Trick, Red Hot Chili Peppers, Alice Cooper, Ted Nugent, Johnny Thunders, and others.   *Author's collection*

GN'R's equipment during performances.) Adler, in his autobiography, thought that Astbury "was great," while Duffy "seemed distant, maybe a bit egotistical." While opening for the Cult at Warfield Theater in San Francisco on September 2, 1987, Guns N' Roses discovered that *Appetite for Destruction* had cracked the Top 100 on the *Billboard* charts. According to a 2014 TeamRock.com article, Slash exclaimed, "We've made it!" Axl responded derisively, "Made what? We've done nothing yet!"

Mötley Crüe

Formed in 1981, Mötley Crüe was one of the most respected (and notorious!) bands to come out of Los Angeles in the 1980s. (They had come a long way, their first gig being at a Pasadena deli called Pookie's.) The band's debut album, *Too Fast for Love*, was released in 1981. However, 1983's *Shout at the Devil* served as Mötley Crüe's true breakthrough album, spawning such hits as "Looks That Kill" and "Too Young to Fall in Love."

All of the up-and-coming bands in Los Angeles envied Mötley Crüe's decadent rock 'n' roll lifestyle. The band consisted of lead singer Vince Neil, guitarist Mick Mars (real name Bob Deal), bassist Nikki Sixx (born Frank Ferrano), and drummer Tommy Lee. In his 2005 autobiography *Tommyland*, Lee boasted, "I joined Mötley Crüe and we became one of the baddest-ass rock bands in history . . . We drank oceans of liquor, snorted and shot mountains of drugs, crashed cars, watched people die, and watched one another fight, make up, break up, reunite, and break up again." As Mötley Crüe gained more fame and notoriety, the relationships within the band started to splinter. In his memoir *This Is Gonna Hurt*, Sixx lamented, "I don't really understand how we went from best friends in a garage band to not really knowing one another and living in mansions."

Guns N' Roses enjoyed partying with Mötley Crüe (in a particularly notorious incident, Sixx OD'd one night while hanging out with Slash and Steven Adler), but they didn't think much of their music. For instance, in a 1987 *Sounds* magazine interview, Izzy commented, "Mötley Crüe was more teen metal. We go for a more roots-oriented sound than most other bands around here." For his part, Sixx remarked that "[Slash] is up there with Mick Mars among my favorite guitar players." GN'R toured in support of Mötley Crüe throughout the South starting in November 1987. At a November 20 show at the Omni in Atlanta, Axl was arrested for punching a security guard (see the "Top Ten Notorious Guns N' Roses Concerts" chapter). Slash remembered the stint opening for Mötley Crüe as a "learning experience" and recalled that "at the end of every single night, Tommy was usually so fucked up that he looked like he was on the brink of dying." Interestingly, Slash later stated that he never even saw Mick Mars during the whole tour.

Alice Cooper

Early in the band's career, Guns N' Roses got the opportunity to open for the "Godfather of Shock Rock" himself, Alice Cooper, at the Arlington Theatre in Santa Barbara on October 23, 1986, but they had to perform without Axl, who was refused entry because for some reason he wasn't on the artist list. According to *Reckless Road*, Izzy was forced to make up absurd lyrics during "Nightrain," such as "elephant dick under my arms" instead of "rattlesnake suitcase," while Slash pleaded with the audience for someone who knew GN'R's song lyrics to join them onstage and sing. The band, which made $500 for the gig, ended up totally trashing their dressing room in frustration at the shitty performance. Guns N' Roses (along with Megadeth) also joined the Alice Cooper tour starting in December 1987. (By this time a lot of fans were showing up just for the opening act, so Cooper was forced to perform in front of several half-empty venues.) Guns N' Roses also helped rerecord "Under My Wheels" with Cooper for the soundtrack of the 1988 rockumentary *The Decline of Western Civilization Part II: The Metal Years*.

Born Vincent Damon Furnier, Cooper was the son of a preacher who joined a series of rock bands—such as the Earwigs, the Spiders, and the Nazz—in the 1960s before forming the Alice Cooper Band in 1968. They soon earned a reputation as "the worst band in Los Angeles." At the Toronto Rock 'n' Roll Festival in 1969, someone threw a live chicken onstage during the band's set. Unaware that chickens could not fly, Cooper hurled it off the stage, and the poor bird was torn to pieces by the unruly crowd. Unable to gain any momentum in Los Angeles, the Alice Cooper Band returned to Cooper's hometown of Detroit, Michigan, and befriended other local bands, such as the Stooges and MC5.

In 1971, the band released the album *Love It to Death*, which featured the hit single "Eighteen"—an instant teen anthem that reached No. 21 on the US charts.

By this time, Cooper started indulging in rock theatrics and incorporating elaborate stage props—black makeup, fake blood, guillotines and electric chairs, live boa constrictos, and six-foot-long inflatable phalluses—into live shows. During a concert rehearsal in 1988, Cooper nearly hanged

Guns N' Roses (sans Axl Rose, who arrived late and was denied entrance) opened for "Godfather of Shock Rock" Alice Cooper at the Arlington Theatre in Santa Barbara, California, in 1986. Cooper later shared vocal duties on GN'R's "The Garden," which appeared on *Use Your Illusion I*.
Author's collection

himself when a safety rope broke but was saved by a quick-thinking roadie. Even Johnny Rotten was an Alice Cooper fan: "I've referred to the Sex Pistols as 'musical vaudeville' and 'evil burlesque,' and for me there was definitely Alice Cooper influence there."

No stranger to excess, Cooper and his band boasted of spending $300,000 a year on booze alone. Cooper later remarked, "We were the *National Enquirer* of rock 'n' roll." *Love It to Death* was followed by *Killer* (1971); *School's Out* (1972), which reached No. 2 on the US charts; and *Billion Dollar*

Babies (1973), which reached No. 1. Cooper's first solo effort, *Welcome to My Nightmare* (1975), featured narration by the "Merchant of Menace" himself, Vincent Price, and the controversial ballad "Only Women Bleed." (Guns N' Roses often sampled this song in concert as an intro to "Knockin' on Heaven's Door.") Cooper's 1989 album *Trash* featured the hit single "Poison," which skyrocketed to No. 7 on the US charts. Cooper was inducted into the Rock and Roll Hall of Fame in 2011, a year before Guns N' Roses.

Iron Maiden

Formed in 1975, British heavy metal band Iron Maiden scored a major hit in both the United Kingdom and the United States with their 1982 album *The Number of the Beast,* the first Iron Maiden release to feature Bruce Dickinson on vocals. Hit songs off the album included the title track, as well as "Run to the Hills" and "Hallowed Be Thy Name." Considered one of the most successful heavy metal bands in history (and known for their famous demon/zombie-like mascot, "Eddie"), Iron Maiden has sold more than 90 million albums worldwide. Guns N' Roses was tapped to open for Iron Maiden's North American Tour in the spring of 1988. Things went relatively smoothly, although the bands had little rapport. At a sold-out show at the Felt Forum, Axl showed up late and drunk because, as he later explained to *RIP* magazine, he'd "passed out from drinking Night Train and doing an MTV interview." Duff ditched the tour at one point to marry his girlfriend Mandy Brixx of the punk band Lame Flames (the marriage lasted less than two years), and British rocker Kid Chaos (Haggis), a founding member of hard rock band Zodiac Mindwarp and the Love Reaction, filled in for him on bass. GN'R was forced to pull out of the Iron Maiden tour due to problems with Axl's vocal cords. (Ironically, L.A. Guns was tapped to finish out the tour.)

Aerosmith

"Kick ass and leave a footprint" was Aerosmith's philosophy. It's safe to say that every Guns N' Roses band member grew up idolizing Aerosmith—"The Bad Boys from Boston." GN'R ended up covering their signature song, "Mama Kin," on the 1986 EP *Live?!*@ Like a Suicide* and later released the song on their 1988 album *GN'R Lies.* In a 1987 interview with *Sounds* magazine, Axl remarked, "[I]n my mind, the hardest, ballsiest rock band that ever came out of America was Aerosmith. What I always liked about them was that they weren't the guys you'd want to meet at the end of any alley if you'd had a disagreement." Steven Adler concurred in his 2010 autobiography, *My Appetite for Destruction*: "Aerosmith are my heroes. Period. I respect Steven Tyler more than any other front man in the world. He really was the coolest, greatest, most down-to-earth guy."

Known for their excessive rock 'n' roll lifestyle during the 1970s and their amazing comeback in the 1980s, Aerosmith has over the years continually churned out hit after hit, such as "Dream On," "Walk This Way," "Janie's Got a Gun," "Sweet Emotion," "Livin' on the Edge," "I Don't Want to Miss a Thing," "Cryin'," "Crazy," "Back in the Saddle," "Love in an Elevator," and many more. The band has sold more than 150 million albums, achieved nine No. 1 hits, and won four Grammy Awards and ten MTV Video Music Awards. In fact, Slash revealed in his autobiography that Aerosmith's 1976 album, *Rocks*, changed his life: "*Rocks* is as powerful to me today as it was then: the screaming vocals, dirty guitars, and relentless grooves are bluesy rock and roll as it is meant to be played." The following Aerosmith band members were inducted into the Rock and Roll Hall of Fame in 2001: Steven Tyler, Joe Perry, guitarist Brad Whitford, bassist Tom Hamilton, and drummer Joey Kramer. Quoted on the Rock and Roll Hall of Fame website, Tyler exclaimed, "We weren't too ambitious when we started out. We just wanted to be the biggest thing that ever walked the planet, the greatest rock band that ever was." Perry concurred, "We were America's band . . . We were the garage band that made it really big—the ultimate party band."

In the mid-1980s, Aerosmith enjoyed a resurgence in part due to the 1986 music video for "Walk This Way," which featured Run-D.M.C. and helped take rap music into the mainstream. Before this, Aerosmith was on the verge of fading into obscurity precipitated by years of alcohol and drug abuse. At the 1987 MTV Video Music Awards, "Walk This Way" was nominated for "Best Concept Video" and "Best Overall Performance in a Video" but lost out both times to Peter Gabriel's "Sledgehammer."

Guns N' Roses was absolutely thrilled to get the opportunity to hit the road as the opening act for their heroes during Aerosmith's *Permanent Vacation* Tour in the summer of 1988. According to Aerosmith lead guitarist Joe Perry in his 2014 memoir *Rocks*, "I was blown away by their sound and flattered when they talked about our influence on their music. Slash talked about *Rocks* as the most important album in his development as a guitarist. Axl praised Steven [Tyler] to the sky." Released the year before, Aerosmith's comeback album, *Permanent Vacation*, had yielded several hits, including "Dude (Looks Like a Lady)," "Angel," and "Rag Doll." It was Aerosmith's first tour since both Tyler and Perry had completed drug rehabilitation, and their manager was wary about the former "Toxic Twins" hanging out with the young, heavy-partying upstarts. In fact, Geffen A&R representative Tom Zutaut remembered Aerosmith's manager making a rule that no one in GN'R could be seen with drugs or alcohol in front of Aerosmith or they would be thrown off the tour, "so all the insanity was happening behind closed doors," according to Zutaut in a 1999 *SPIN* interview. As for Aerosmith, they saw in Guns N' Roses their former selves and attempted to serve as mentors to the band. To no avail, the partying raged on with more intensity than ever from their younger counterparts. The "Paradise City" music video features footage from the August 16, 1988, show at Giants Stadium in East Rutherford, New Jersey, at which Guns N' Roses opened for Aerosmith and Deep Purple. (Duff wears an Aerosmith T-shirt in the video.)

An interesting phenomenon took place on the *Permanent Vacation* Tour: As *Appetite for Destruction* skyrocketed up the charts (and "Sweet Child O' Mine" became a No. 1 single), Guns N' Roses started to become more popular than Aerosmith. For example, *Rolling Stone* joined the tour to do a story on Aerosmith, but it was GN'R that ended up on the magazine's cover. According to Slash, by the end of the *Permanent Vacation Tour*, Guns N' Roses was "absolutely fucking huge, generating the kind of excitement that pretty much baffled [him] night after night." Several years later, Tyler and Adler ended up in the same rehab facility together. In his 2011 autobiography, *Does the Noise in My Head Bother You?*, Tyler recounted, "The poor guy. Talk about an appetite for destruction . . . Steven was a total wreck, he was slurring his words so badly, I could barely understand him . . . I was stunned. 'You sound good, man,' I said, 'Nice goin'!' And I walked out. I wanted to throw up."

The Rolling Stones

The opportunity to open for the Rolling Stones at the L.A. Coliseum for four dates in October 1989 should have been the fulfillment of a dream for the members of Guns N' Roses. However, heroin addiction was taking a heavy toll on several band members—primarily Slash, Izzy, and Steven Adler—and the appearance turned out to be disastrous. On just the first night, Axl stopped the show and gave his famous "Mr. Brownstone" speech warning the other band members that if they didn't stop "dancing with Mr. Brownstone" the band would be playing its last concert. (See the "Top Ten Most Notorious Guns N' Roses Concerts" chapter for more on this incident.)

In a 1988 interview with the *Los Angeles Times*, Axl had acknowledged GN'R's debt to the Stones: "We have lots of influences, but the Stones are more definitely a big part of it . . . As a band, we haven't seemed to wear out the Stones yet. We keep learning more and more from them . . . about the fact you are able to do anything you want in your music." Rock journalist Mick Wall (who later gained notoriety for being targeted in GN'R's venomous song "Get in the Ring" off the *Use Your Illusion II* album) once referred to Axl and Slash as "the Jagger and Richards of their generation." A 1988 *Rolling Stone* article compared the two bands and speculated that "if the Gunners go beyond the Stones . . . it's because times are rougher; they are a brutal band for brutal times. Unlike the Stones, they don't keep an ironic distance between themselves and their songs."

A Heaven Above

Use Your Illusion I (1991)

I just want to bury Appetite. I don't want to live my life through that one
album. I have to bury it.   —Axl Rose

For the *Use Your Illusion* albums, Axl had a vision of something much more elaborate, so the rawness and immediacy that made *Appetite for Destruction* so successful would have to be abandoned. In the VH1 *Behind the Music* special on Guns N' Roses, Slash remarked, "We had a horn section and pianos and all this other crap, which we didn't necessarily want as a band but it was something Axl still wanted." GN'R manager Alan Niven considered the *Use Your Illusions* albums as a cross between Led Zeppelin's 1975 *Physical Graffiti* and Pink Floyd's 1979 *The Wall*. From then on, everything would get bigger—production values, massive stadium tours, and the introduction of epic ballads such as "November Rain" (which ran nearly nine minutes long). However, it sometimes seemed like the heart and soul of the band was left behind, somewhere back in the smoky dive clubs in West Hollywood.

With Steven Adler getting fired in 1990, the *Use Your Illusions* albums, which were once again produced by Mike Clink, featured Matt Sorum (formerly of the Cult) on drums (except for Adler on one track, "Civil War"), as well as the addition of Dizzy Reed on keyboards. Slash recalled in his autobiography that recording sessions now seemed to be like "a fuckin' chore." Guns N' Roses actually considered *GN'R Sucks* and *Buy Product* as two potential titles (that were thankfully rejected!). The cover art on both albums featured an interpretation of a detail from Raphael's *School of Athens* by Estonian-American artist Mark Kostabi, who also designed album covers for the Ramones' *¡Adiós Amigos!* (1995) and Seether's *Holding Onto Strings Better Left to Fray* (2011), among others. Both *Use Your Illusion* albums' liner notes contain the message "Fuck You, St. Louis!" in reference to the infamous "Riverport Riot" concert at the Riverport Amphiteatre on July 2, 1991.

Among the most anticipated albums in rock 'n' roll history, *Use Your Illusion I* (which contained sixteen tracks) and *II* (which contained fourteen tracks) were ceremoniously released at midnight on September 17, 1991. Due to the rampant profanity in songs like "Back Off Bitch" and several other tracks, Walmart and K-Mart both refused to stock the albums. Guns N' Roses retaliated by adding their own warning sticker to the albums that read: "This album contains language which some listeners may find objectionable. They can F?!* OFF and buy something from the New Age section."

At the Freddie Mercury Tribute Concert for AIDS Awareness at Wembley Stadium in London in 1992, Axl Rose joined Queen (with Elton John) for "Bohemian Rhapsody" and "We Will Rock You."
Author's collection

None of this mattered—an estimated 500,000 copies of the two albums were sold in just two hours. Buoyed by the single "You Could Be Mine," *Use Your Illusion II* hit No. 1 on the *Billboard* charts, followed closely by *Use Your Illusion I* at No. 2. "November Rain" became the most popular song on either album, reaching No. 3 on the US charts (and became the band's last Top 10 single), while "Don't Cry" peaked at No. 10 on the charts. *Billboard* magazine raved about the *Use Your Illusion* albums, exclaiming, "Guns N' Roses' readily anticipated double-barreled studio opus is remarkable in nearly every way. Astonishingly rich . . . Artistic verdict: A brilliant vindication of America's top hard rock band." *Rolling Stone* also gave the albums a positive review, stating, "Guns N' Roses fire on all comers and take no prisoners. Was *Use Your Illlusion* worth the wait, the traumas, and the onstage tantrums? Yes." Interestingly, the *Use Your Illusion* albums were released exactly a week before Nirvana's *Nevermind* hit the shelves with a lot less fanfare on September 24, 1991. However, with its hit single "Smells Like Teen Spirit," *Nevermind* would go on to supplant Michael Jackson's *Dangerous* at No. 1 on the US charts in January 1992 and would help revolutionize the music industry.

"Right Next Door to Hell"

One of Axl's most bizarre feuds involved his ongoing battle with a neighbor, Gabriella Kantor, at his West Hollywood condo. Things escalated and on October 30, 1990, Kantor claimed that Axl hit her over the head with "a really good bottle" of Chardonnay (along with a piece of chicken) and threw her apartment keys off of his twelfth-story balcony, so she had him promptly arrested. As for Axl, he spent four hours in jail before being released on $5,000 bail, denied the charge, and dismissed her as an "obsessed fan." He later told *People* magazine, "Frankly, if I was going to hit her with a wine bottle, she wouldn't have gotten up."

The case against Axl was ultimately dismissed due to lack of evidence. MTV even held an "Evict Axl" contest to give away Axl's condo with an accompanying commercial featuring Axl himself giving an amusing, impromptu tour of the residence (a must-watch video that can be viewed on YouTube). "Right Next Door to Hell," which deals with Axl's feud with his neighbor, was cowritten by Rose, Izzy, and Timo Caltia, a Finnish guitarist and songwriter who had worked with Hanoi Rocks. At one point in the song, Rose simply exclaims, "Fuck you, bitch!"

Writers: Izzy, Timo Caltia, Axl. **Personnel:** Axl (vocals), Slash (lead and rhythm guitars, 6-string bass), Izzy (rhythm guitar), Duff (bass), Matt Sorum (drums), Slash, Duff, Izzy (background vocals).

"Dust N' Bones"

Izzy provided the lead vocals (with a little help from Axl) on this bluesy rock song that he cowrote with Slash and Duff. "Dust N' Bones" features the classic line, "Time's short, your life's your own, and in the end we're just dust and bones." It's simply one of the most underrated tracks in the Guns N' Roses repertoire. Dust N' Bones, a Guns N' Roses tribute band from the Midwest, took its name from this song.

Writers: Izzy, Duff, Slash. **Personnel:** Izzy (vocals, rhythm guitar), Slash (lead and rhythm guitars, voice box), Duff (bass), Matt Sorum (drums/percussion), Dizzy Reed (piano/organ), Axl, Slash, Duff (background vocals).

"Live and Let Die"

Originally recorded by Paul McCartney and Wings (and written by McCartney and his wife, Linda) for the soundtrack of the 1973 James Bond film of the same name, "Live and Let Die" served as the second single from *Use Your Illusion I.* An accompanying music video featured a collage of live performances intermixed with old photos of GN'R band members (making it the last video that Izzy appeared in before his departure from the band in 1991). Guns N' Roses' version of "Live and Let Die" was nominated for "Best Hard Rock Performance" at the 1993 Grammy Awards but lost out to the Red Hot Chili Peppers' "Give It Away." Other nominees included Alice in Chains ("Dirt"), Faith No More ("Angel Dust"), Nirvana ("Smells Like Teen Spirit"), and Pearl Jam ("Jeremy").

GN'R's cover of "Live and Let Die" also ended up on the soundtrack for the 1997 action comedy *Grosse Pointe Blank,* which starred John Cusack and Minnie Driver. At the June 6, 1992, pay-per-view Paris concert (the same show where he ranted against Warren Beatty), Axl introduced "Live and Let Die" onstage by dedicating the song to "those who try to control and manipulate you . . . the powers that be, the government, your family, your friends, or anything else that chooses to fuck with you. You can even try to talk to some of these people. You can try to be friends. You can try to work it out . . . but if you can't save nobody else, you'll be lucky if you can save your own ass. But we'll dedicate this to these fucking people."

During another extended rant at a Guns N' Roses show at Myriad Arena in Oklahoma City, Oklahoma, on April 6, 1992, Axl introduced "Live and Let Die" by exclaiming:

> I believe that deep inside everybody, there's something inside you that knows what the fuck you're supposed to do with our life. And no matter what anybody tells you, if you keep looking and you keep digging, you're gonna find it . . . you can, when the going gets real rough, you can think of a theme song that somebody else wrote. Namely Mr. Paul McCartney. And when they're trying to keep you down, just hold on and know someday you'll bust out, you'll get onto your own shit and they won't be able to fuckin' keep up with your ass. And you can be thinking Live and Let Die motherfucker!

Writers: Paul and Linda McCartney. **Personnel:** Axl (vocals, keyboard), Slash (lead and rhythm guitars, 6-string bass), Izzy (rhythm guitar), Duff (bass), Matt Sorum (drums), Dizzy Reed (piano), Axl, Shannon Hoon (background vocals), Johann Langlie, Axl (synthesizer programmers), Matthew McKagan, Rachel West, Robert Clark, Jon Trautwein (horns).

"Don't Cry"

The original version of the power ballad "Don't Cry" appeared on *Use Your Illusion I*, while a version with alternate lyrics can be found on *Use Your Illusion II*. The song was written about one of Izzy's former girlfriends, Monique Lewis, who Axl soon fell for. (Her face is tattooed on his right bicep.) "Don't Cry" peaked at No. 10 on the US charts. The elaborate music video for "Don't Cry" served as the first chapter of an unofficial trilogy (inspired by Rose's friend Del James's short story "Without You") that includes "November Rain" and "Estranged." It features a scene where Axl and his then girlfriend, supermodel Stephanie Seymour, fight over a gun, which was allegedly based on a real-life incident between Axl and Erin Everly. Shannon Hoon of Blind Melon assisted Axl with the vocals on "Don't Cry."

Writers: Izzy, Axl. **Personnel:** Axl, Shannn Hoon (vocals), Slash (lead and rhythm guitar), Izzy (rhythm guitar, background vocals), Duff (bass), Matt Sorum (drums).

"Perfect Crime"

An early Guns N' Roses song credited to Izzy, Slash, and Axl, the frantic, insanely confrontational "Perfect Crime" clocks in at just 2:36, making it the shortest track on the album. It features the refrain, "Goddamn it, it's a perfect crime! Motherfucker, it's a perfect crime!" The song was performed live for the first time when Guns N' Roses opened for the Red Hot Chili Peppers on Halloween, 1986, at the Ackerman Ballroom at UCLA.

Writers: Izzy, Slash, Axl. **Personnel:** Axl (vocals, sound effects), Slash (lead and rhythm guitars), Izzy (rhythm guitar), Duff (bass), Matt Sorum (drums).

"You Ain't the First"

A rock ballad written by Izzy that, according to *Ultimate Classic Rock*, is the "least Guns N' Roses-sounding song the band ever produced" and "more like a boozy acoustic blues." It's a simple goodbye song: "I think you've worn out your welcome honey."

Writer: Izzy. **Personnel:** Izzy, Axl, Shannon Hoon (vocals); Izzy (acoustic guitar); Duff (bass/acoustic guitar); Slash (slide dobro); Matt Sorum (drums); Tim Doyle (tambourine).

"Bad Obsession"

A song about the horrors of heroin addiction, "Bad Obsession" was cowritten by Izzy and West Arkeen. The track features a guest appearance by Hanoi Rocks lead singer Michael Monroe on tenor saxophone and harmonica. During a GN'R concert at the Tokyo Dome on February 22, 1992, Axl introduced this song by taking a subtle dig at Izzy, who had recently departed the band: "This is a song that we wrote about one year before 'Mr. Brownstone' with the help of our old friend West Arkeen and some guy that just, I don't know, his name just escapes me."

Writers: Izzy, West Arkeen. **Personnel:** Axl (vocals), Slash (slide lead and rhythm guitars), Izzy (rhythm guitar, percussion, background vocals), Duff (bass), Matt Sorum (drums), Dizzy Reed (drums), Mike Monroe (saxophone, harmonica).

"Back Off Bitch"

Written by Axl and his old friend, Paul Tobias, during the Hollywood Rose days in the early 1980s, this extremely misogynistic tune ("nasty ballbreaker stay out of my bed") was one of the main reasons that Walmart and K-Mart refused to stock the *Use Your Illusion* albums. During a Hollywood Rose show at Madame Wong's West on July 20, 1984, Axl dedicated "Back Off Bitch" to "every guy that's got [sic] some girl who just bugs the fuck out of them." Interestingly, a "safe" single-disc version of *Use Your Illusion* was released in 1998 that omitted "offensive" tracks such as "Back Off Bitch," "Pretty Tied Up," and "Get in the Ring," while preserving twelve songs: "Live and Let Die," "Don't Cry," "You Ain't the First," "November Rain," "The Garden," "Dead Horse," "Civil War," "14 Years," "Yesterdays," "Knockin' on Heaven's Door," "Estranged," and "Don't Cry" (alternative lyrics).

Writers: Paul Tobias, Axl. **Personnel:** Axl (vocals), Slash (lead and rhythm guitars, background vocals), Izzy (rhythm and lead guitars), Duff (bass, background vocals), Matt Sorum (drums).

"Double Talkin' Jive"

Written and sung by Izzy, this dark, disturbing song begins with the morbidly curious line, "Found a head and an arm in da garbage can." It turns out that while Guns N' Roses were recording the album at the Record Plant, the police actually discovered a dismembered arm and head in a dumpster behind the studio. Listen for the classical Spanish flamenco-type guitar solo by Slash at the end of the song. Rock journalist Mick Wall (who was one of the subjects of the venomous GN'R track "Get in the Ring" on *Use Your Illusion II*) remarked that this song "sounds like an old Johnny Rotten lyric sung by Iggy Pop to an ancient T. Rex riff, with guitar solos by Carlos Santana." At an August 3, 1991, Guns N' Roses show at the Great Western Forum in Inglewood, California, Axl dedicated "Double Talkin' Jive" to "some asshole at CBS News who likes to call me a punk."

Writer: Izzy. **Personnel:** Izzy (vocals, lead and rhythm guitars); Slash (classical guitar solo, acoustic rhythm guitar); Duff (bass, acoustic rhythm guitar); Matt Sorum (drums/percussion); Axl (background vocals).

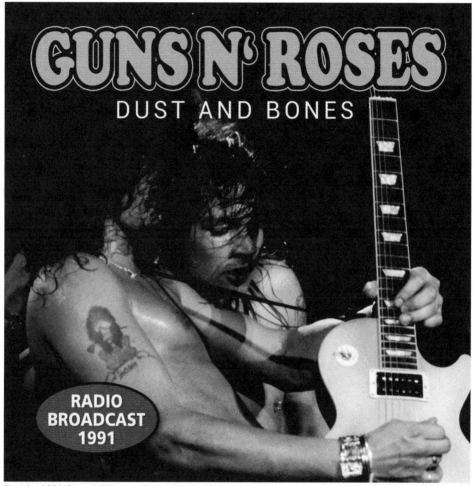

For the 1991 Guns N' Roses album *Use Your Illusion I*, rhythm guitarist Izzy Stradlin assumed vocal duties for "Dust N' Bones," as well as "You Ain't the First" and "Double Talkin' Jive."

Author's collection

"November Rain"

A nearly nine-minute-long power ballad, "November Rain" was actually considered at one point for inclusion on *Appetite for Destruction*, as Axl had started writing the song before the release of that album. Slash revealed in his autobiography that an 18-minute version of the song was recorded before the *Appetite for Destruction* recording sessions even began. At 8:57 long, "November Rain" is the second-longest song on the album (the longest being "Coma," which clocks in at 10:14). "November Rain" reached No. 3 on the US charts (behind Sir Mix-a-Lot's "Baby Got Back" and Boyz II Men's "End of the Road"), making it the longest song ever to reach the Top 10 of the *Billboard* Hot 100. *Guitar World* ranked Slash's guitar solo on the track as No. 6 on its list of "50 Greatest Guitar Solos." GN'R biographer Danny Sugerman referred to "November Rain" as "an epic song along the lines of 'Stairway to Heaven' or 'The End.'"

Guns N' Roses performed "November Rain" with Elton John and full orchestral backing during one of the highlights of the 1992 MTV Video Music Awards. The epic music video for "November Rain" serves as the second chapter in the unofficial trilogy that includes "Don't Cry" and "Estranged." Costing more than $1 million, the video featured an extravagant wedding between Axl and Stephanie Seymour, a rained-out reception followed by a funeral, and, somewhere along the line, Slash playing a guitar solo in front of a tiny church in the desert for no apparent reason. It won an MTV Video Music Award for "Best Cinematography." Slash later admitted in an interview with HuffPost Live that he had no idea what the video was about.

Writer: Axl. **Personnel:** Axl (vocals, piano, keyboard orchestra); Slash (lead and rhythm guitars); Izzy (rhythm guitar); Duff (bass); Matt Sorum (drums); Axl, Johann Langlie (synthesizer programmers); Axl, Matt Sorum, Shannon Hoon, Stuart Bailey, Izzy, Duff, Reba Shaw (background vocals, choir).

"The Garden"

Written by West Arkeen, Del James, and Axl Rose prior to the release of *Appetite for Destruction*, "The Garden" is an eerie little song with surreal lyrics that features guest vocals by "Godfather of Shock Rock" Alice Cooper and Shannon Hoon of Blind Melon. In a 1999 *SPIN* interview, Cooper remembered that he was staying at the Sunset Marquis in Los Angeles when Axl called him to do the vocals on the song, claiming, "When you're in the studio one-on-one with him, he's really amazing—the guy can really sing. I did my bit three times, but Axl was a perfectionist—almost to the point where you want to say, 'At some point, Axl, it's gotta be good enough.'" A rather bleak, mostly black-and-white music video accompanied the song and was filmed in New York City at several locales, such as Times Square and Washington Square Park.

Writers: West Arkeen, Del James, Axl. **Personnel:** Axl, Alice Cooper (vocals), Slash (lead and rhythm guitars, slide guitar, acoustic guitar), Duff (bass), Matt Sorum (drums), West Arkeen (acoustic guitar), Axl, Shannon Hoon (background vocals).

"Garden of Eden"

Written by Slash and Axl, "Garden of Eden" attacks organized religion. In a *RIP* magazine interview, Axl remarked, "I was brainwashed in a Pentecostal church. I'm not against churches or religion, but I do believe, like I said in 'Garden of Eden,' that most organized religions make a mockery of humanity." A bizarre accompanying music video filmed with a fish-eye lens featured an extreme close-up of Axl singing while the band performed and danced wildly in the background.

Writers: Slash, Axl. **Personnel:** Axl (vocals, keyboards, effects), Slash (lead and rhythm guitars), Izzy (rhythm guitar), Duff (bass), Matt Sorum (drums), Axl, Johann Langlie (synthesizer programmers), Dizzy Reed, Duff, Slash (background vocals).

"Don't Damn Me"

Written by Slash, Dave Lank (a longtime friend of the band), and Axl, "Don't Damn Me" is the only song on the album that was never performed live.

Writers: Slash, Dave Lank, Axl. **Personnel:** Axl (vocals), Slash (lead and rhythm guitars), Izzy (rhythm guitar), Duff (bass), Matt Sorum (drums).

"Bad Apples"

One of the sadly overlooked songs on the *Use Your Illusion I* album, the funky "Bad Apples" was credited to Slash, Duff, Izzy, and Axl. It features background vocals by Izzy, Duff, Matt Sorum, and Dizzy Reed. Slash claimed to have worked the song up during the band's "exile" in Chicago.

Writers: Slash, Duff, Izzy, Axl. **Personnel:** Axl (vocals), Slash (lead and rhythm guitars), Izzy (rhythm guitar), Duff (bass), Matt Sorum (drums), Dizzy Reed (piano/clavinet), Izzy, Duff, Matt Sorum, Dizzy Reed (background vocals).

"Dead Horse"

An early Axl song, "Dead Horse" featured an accompanying music video. According to the *Los Angeles Weekly*, "If past lives are a thing, then Axl is the reincarnated Billy the Kid, or Janis Joplin with a penis. Which is utterly useless thinking as it relates to a song that isn't about an actual horse, or an 'old cowboy,' but Axl's frustration with a woman."

Writer: Axl. **Personnel:** Axl (vocals, acoustic guitar); Slash (lead and rhythm guitars); Izzy (rhythm guitar); Duff (bass); Matt Sorum (drums); Mike Clink (nutcracker).

"Coma"

A classic Slash/Axl collaboration that runs 10:14 long, "Coma" is the longest song on either *Use Your Illusion* album (and, in fact, the longest GN'R song to date). It features hospital sound effects and an actual defibrillator. The 1996 book *The Sex Revolts: Gender, Rebellion, and Rock n' Roll* by Simon Reynolds and Joy Press describes "Coma" as "a sort of 'Gimme Shelter' for the MTV blank generation," and claims, "The song sees Axl in several minds about seeking refuge from reality: numb the pain or thrive on its edge?" In a 2011 interview with *Ultimate Classic Rock*, Slash remarked that he wrote "Coma" in a "heroin delirium." According to Slash, "We were just fucking around, but the song is heavy, and Axl's vocals are gorgeous. I mean really amazing." During the 2016 Not in This Lifetime Tour, Guns N' Roses brought "Coma" back into the set list, with Axl commenting during a Q&A session to kick off the tour at the China Exchange in London that he "knew it would make Slash happy."

Writers: Slash, Axl. **Personnel:** Axl (vocals), Slash (lead and rhythm guitars), Izzy (rhythm guitar), Duff (bass), Matt Sorum (drums/percussion), Bruce Foster, Johann Langlie (sound effects), Suzanne Filkins, Patricia Fuenzalida, Rose Mann, Monica Zierhut-Soto, Michelle Loiselle, Diane Mitchell ("bitches" providing background rants during the song).

12

These Dreams Are Swept Aside

Use Your Illusion II (1991)

When our record comes out, I know it's going to be really different—whether it's accepted or not I couldn't give a shit.   —Slash

Bolstered by the strength of its hit single "You Could Be Mine" off the *Terminator 2: Judgment Day* soundtrack, *Use Your Illusion II* debuted at No. 1 on the *Billboard* charts, with its sister album, *Use Your Illusion I*, at No. 2. It is the last Guns N' Roses album to feature both Steven Adler (who played drums on one track, "Civil War") and Izzy Stradlin, who left the band less than two months after the *Use Your Illusion* albums were released on September 17, 1991.

The eclectic list of individuals that Guns N' Roses thank in the album's liner notes includes the likes of "Dick Fuckin' Clark," "Bill Gazzarri—The Godfather R.I.P.," "all at Geffen who've worked their fuckin' asses off," "Sean Penn," "Arnold Schwarzenegger," "Stephanie Seymour," "Lars Ulrich," and "the West Hollywood Sheriff's Dept. for all dat priceless news footage."

"Civil War"

A powerful political anthem written by Axl, Slash, and Duff, "Civil War" was first publicly performed at Farm Aid IV, which also served as Steven Adler's last live appearance with the band before he was fired. In addition, the song appeared on the 1990 charity album *Nobody's Child: Romanian Angel Appeal.* "Civil War" served as the B-side of the single "You Could Be Mine." In a 1993 *Rockline* interview, Duff discussed the origin of the song: "Basically it was a riff that we would do at sound-checks. Axl came up with a couple of lines at the beginning . . . I went in a peace march, when I was a little kid, with my mom. I was like four years old. For Martin Luther King . . . It's just true-life experiences, really."

"Civil War" samples the speech of the "Captain" (Strother Martin) in the critically acclaimed 1967 prison drama *Cool Hand Luke*: "What we've got here is . . . failure to communicate. Some men you just can't reach. So you get what we had here last week, which is the way he wants it . . . well, he gets it. I don't like it any more than you men." In addition, "Civil War" quotes from a guerilla general in the Shining Path (the Peruvian revolutionary organization): "We practice selective annihilation of mayors and government officials, for example, to create a vacuum, then we fill that vacuum. As popular war advances, peace is closer." At the song's beginning and end, Axl whistles "When Johnny Comes Marching Home."

Writers: Slash, Duff, Axl. **Personnel:** Axl (vocals), Slash (lead and rhythm guitars, acoustic guitar), Duff (bass), Steven Adler (drums), Dizzy Reed (piano), Duff, Dizzy Reed (background vocals).

"14 Years"

According to competing theories, the ambiguous, Izzy-penned "14 Years" either describes his turbulent friendship with Axl or a failed relationship/marriage. Take your pick. (I go with the latter.) Either way, GN'R stopped playing the song when Izzy left the band.

Writers: Izzy, Axl. **Personnel:** Izzy (vocals, rhythm guitar), Slash (lead and rhythm guitars), Axl (piano, background vocals), Duff (bass), Matt Sorum (drums), Dizzy Reed (organ).

"Yesterdays"

An exercise in pure nostalgia, this powerful ballad was written by Axl, West Arkeen, Del James, and Billy McCloud. "Yesterdays" appeared on the 1999 live album *Live Era '87–'93* and the 2004 *Greatest Hits* album, which was released by Geffen Records without the approval of any existing or former GN'R band members. The accompanying black-and-white music video for "Yesterdays" was directed by Andy Morahan and featured the band performing in an abandoned warehouse.

Writers: West Arkeen, Del James, Billy McCloud, Axl. **Personnel:** Axl (vocals, piano), Slash (lead and rhythm guitars), Izzy (rhythm guitar), Duff (bass), Matt Sorum (drums), Dizzy Reed (organ).

"Knockin' on Heaven's Door"

Originally written and performed by Bob Dylan for the soundtrack of the 1973 Sam Peckinpah-directed Western *Pat Garrett and Billy the Kid*, "Knockin'

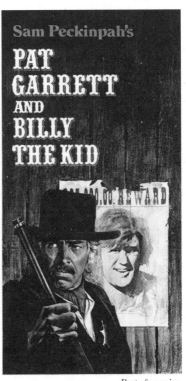

Best of enemies.
Deadliest of friends.

Guns N' Roses covered Bob Dylan's "Knockin' on Heaven's Door" on *Use Your Illusion II*. Dylan's version of the song first appeared on the soundtrack of the 1973 Sam Peckinpah–directed western film *Pat Garrett and Billy the Kid*. *Author's collection* on Heaven's Door" reached No. 12 on the US charts. Dylan appeared in the film in a bit role as "Alias." Before *Use Your Illusion I* was even released, the Guns N' Roses cover of "Knockin' on Heaven's Door" had already appeared on the soundtrack of the stock car racing drama *Days of Thunder* (1990), which starred Tom Cruise and Nicole Kidman. Guns N' Roses also played this song, along with "Paradise City," at the April 20, 1992, Freddie Mercury Tribute Concert for Aids Awareness at London's Wembley Stadium. The version on *Use Your Illusion II* features background vocals by the Waters, a family group out of Los Angeles consisting of Julia, Maxine, Luther, and Oren, who, according to their official bio, "have been heard on more gold and platinum recordings than anyone in the history of the music industry."

In addition, the spoken word section of the song ("You just better start sniffin' your own rank subjugation, Jack . . .") was performed by actor Josh Richman, who also directed the Guns N' Roses music video for "Live and Let Die." Richman may be best remembered for his role as "Tony" in the 1986 film *River's Edge*, which also starred Keanu Reeves, Ione Skye, Crispin Glover, and Dennis Hopper as "Feck," a burned-out Vietnam veteran and drug dealer who takes an inflatable sex doll along for a ride in arguably the funniest beer run in film history. Directed by Tim Hunter, written by Neal Jimenez (*The Waterdance*), and billed as "the most controversial film you will see this year," *River's Edge* is a nihilistic, post-punk view of angst involving teenagers who live out the Sex Pistols' creed—"No future, no future for you."

Writer: Bob Dylan. **Personnel:** Axl (vocals); Slash (lead and rhythm guitars); Izzy (rhythm guitar); Duff (bass); Matt Sorum (drums); Axl, the Waters (background vocals); Josh Richman (spoken word section).

"Get in the Ring"

"And in this corner weighing in at eight hundred fifty pounds, Guns N' Roses." A blistering attack on GN'R's media critics, "Get in the Ring" (original title: "Get in the Ring Motherfucker") began as a simple punk-inspired song by Duff called "Why Do You Look at Me When You Hate Me." Axl went to the trouble of naming specific journalists who he felt had wronged the band, such as Mick Wall of *Kerrang!*, Andy Secher of *Hit Parader*, and especially *SPIN's* Bob Guccione Jr., whose father was the *Penthouse* magazine magnate. Wall later claimed he made Axl's "shit list" by reporting on the ongoing feud between the singer and Vince Neil of Mötley Crüe that originated

at the 1989 MTV Video Music Awards. "Get in the Ring" has never been performed live. (The crowd noises heard in the song were added from a 1991 concert in Saratoga Springs, New York.) Guns N' Roses dedicated the song "to all the Guns N' Fuckin' Roses fans who stuck with us through all the fuckin' shit."

Writers: Slash, Duff, Axl. **Personnel:** Axl (vocals), Slash (lead and rhythm guitars), Izzy (rhythm guitar), Duff (bass, background vocals), Matt Sorum (drums), Dizzy Reed (piano).

"Shotgun Blues"

"An now you're blowin' smoke/I think you're one big joke." Written by Axl, "Shotgun Blues" is said to concern his ongoing feud with Vince Neil of Mötley Crüe. In his list of the "10 Worst Guns N' Roses Songs," Jeff Rouner of the *Houston Press* referred to "Shotgun Blues" as "a really, really pointless song" with "Rose phoning in some very predictable rhymes and a solo that sounds like Slash was inspired by a need to finish recording and get to the bathroom."

Writer: Axl. **Personnel:** Axl (vocals, rhythm guitar); Slash (lead and rhythm guitars); Duff (bass); Matt Sorum (drums); Izzy, Duff (background vocals).

"Breakdown"

The "Breakdown" track uses quotes by blind DJ "Super Soul" (Cleavon Little, best known from *Blazing Saddles*), but recited by Axl, from the 1971 existential road movie *Vanishing Point*, including "There goes the challenger being chased by the blue, blue meanies on wheels." Basically an extended car chase with a nihilistic ending and accompanied by a great soundtrack, *Vanishing Point* starred Barry Newman as the mysterious, pill-popping "Kowalski," who makes a bet that he can drive a 1970 Dodge Challenger from Denver to San Francisco in fifteen hours. Meanwhile, an extremely inept array of law enforcement officers fails miserably in their efforts to arrest him.

Writer: Axl. **Personnel:** Axl (vocals, piano); Slash (lead and rhythm guitars, banjo); Izzy (acoustic guitar); Duff (bass); Matt Sorum (drums).

"Pretty Tied Up"

Subtitled "The Perils of Rock N' Roll Decadence," this Izzy tune delves into the depraved world of bondage and discipline and involves a chick that "lives down on Melrose." Izzy plays rhythm guitar and Coral Sitar on the track. Duff told rock journalist Mick Wall that "Pretty Tied Up" was "actually a factual story about this chick down on Melrose we know, she's like a dominatrix chick, you know? You pay her and you're pretty tied up. It's a great song."

Writer: Izzy. **Personnel:** Axl (vocals); Slash (lead and rhythm guitars); Izzy (rhythm guitar/coral sitar); Duff (bass); Matt Sorum (drums); Dizzy Reed (piano).

"Locomotive"

An exercise in misogyny courtesy of Slash and Axl, "Locomotive" is subtitled "Complicity" and makes reference to "prejudiced illusions." It is easily one of the most underrated songs in the entire Guns N' Roses repertoire with its killer riff perfectly complementing some of Axl's finest lyrics.

Writers: Slash, Axl. **Personnel:** Axl (vocals), Slash (lead and rhythm guitars), Izzy (rhythm guitar), Duff (bass, percussion), Matt Sorum (drums, percussion), Dizzy Reed (piano).

"So Fine"

Duff provides the vocals on "So Fine," his only solo writing credit for Guns N' Roses. "So Fine" was dedicated to one of Duff's early musical idols, Johnny Thunders of New York Dolls and Heartbreakers fame. Guns N' Roses opened for the by-then-smacked-out Thunders—who died of a drug overdose in 1991—at the Fender's Ballroom in 1986. "So Fine" features a guest appearance by artist/session musician/tattooist Howard Teman on piano. He is also credited with percussion work on *G N' R Lies*. Teman started out as a T-shirt designer for acts such as Iron Maiden, Lynyrd Skynyrd, Bon Jovi, and others. He owns the upscale tattoo parlor T-Man Tattoo in Studio City, California.

Writer: Duff. **Personnel:** Duff (vocals, bass); Axl (vocals); Slash (lead and rhythm guitars); Izzy (rhythm guitar); Matt Sorum (drums, percussion, background vocals); Howard Teman (piano).

"Estranged"

Axl wrote this song about lost love (his marriage to Erin Everly had just ended) and Slash provided the "killer guitar melodies." Introducing "Estranged" in concert, Axl would comment, "As the Stones would say, this song's about a girl who's just a memory." Part of an unofficial trilogy that includes "Don't Cry" and "November Rain," the accompanying music video for "Estranged" reportedly cost $4 million to produce. The insanely extravagant video features Axl leaping off an oil tanker and being rescued by dolphins (which definitely has to be seen to be believed). Featured under the album's liner notes is the line, "Slash, thanks for the killer guitar melodies."

Writer: Axl. **Personnel:** Axl (vocals, piano); Slash (lead and rhythm guitars); Izzy (rhythm and lead guitars); Duff (bass); Matt Sorum (drums).

"You Could Be Mine"

Written by Axl and Izzy (and once considered for inclusion in *Appetite for Destruction*), "You Could Be Mine" was featured on the soundtrack of *Terminator 2: Judgment Day*. Because of its association with the hit movie, "You Could Be Mine" served as the first single from either of the *Use Your Illusion* albums. In the accompanying music video, Arnold Schwarzenegger as T-800 stalks the band during a live performance. The end of the first verse of "You Could Be Mine" references the title of the Bernie Taupin/Elton John song "We've Seen That Movie Too" from John's 1973 album, *Goodbye Yellow Brick Road*. (The credits above the lyrics for the song read "Thanks to Bernie Taupin and Elton John.") "You Could Be Mine" appeared on the 2004 *Greatest Hits* album. Interestingly, the lyrics—"With your bitch slap rappin' and your cocaine tongue you get nothin' done"—appear on the inside jacket of *Appetite for Destruction* (1987), although the song does not appear on that album.

Writers: Izzy, Axl. **Personnel:** Axl (vocals), Slash (lead and rhythm guitars), Izzy (rhythm guitar, background vocals), Duff (bass, background vocals), Matt Sorum (drums).

"Don't Cry" (Alternate Lyrics)

A different version of "Don't Cry" appears on each of the *Use Your Illusion* albums. This is the alternate version, which also features guest vocals by Shannon Hoon of Blind Melon.

Writers: Izzy, Axl. **Personnel:** Axl (vocals), Slash (lead and rhythm guitars), Izzy (rhythm guitar, background vocals), Duff (bass), Matt Sorum (drums), Shannon Hoon (vocals).

"My World"

"You ain't been mindfucked yet." A strange rock/rap hybrid, "My World" was written by Axl and performed solely by Axl and electronic musician Johann Langlie, who later worked on the scores of several TV shows and video games. Jef Rouner of the *Houston Press* placed "My World" at the top of his list of "The 10 Worst Guns N' Roses Songs," citing it as "a strange hybrid of industrial and bad rap that had no place on one of the last great rock records."

Writer: Axl. **Personnel:** Axl (vocals); Johann Langlie (keyboards, drums, effects).

13

Such a Lonely Place

Use Your Illusion Tour

A lot of drugs and yes men came in, and that killed the band . . .
But on certain nights, we were the fucking greatest band on the planet.
—Duff McKagan

In 1991, Guns N' Roses embarked on the twenty-eight-month-long *Use Your Illusion* Tour (considered the longest tour in rock 'n' roll history), which featured 194 performances in twenty-seven countries in front of more than seven million fans. The *Use Your Illusion* Tour will be long remembered for its pure excess (even by rock 'n' roll standards!). For instance, GN'R leased a private plane, which turned out to be an actual 727 from MGM Las Vegas. In addition, as bizarre as it sounds, Axl started traveling with his own psychic, Sharon Maynard, who the other band members dubbed "Yoda."

The *Use Your Illusion* Tour was also marred by frustrating delays that in some cases led to riots, including the notorious "Riverport Riot" (a.k.a. "Rocket Queen Riot") at Riverport Amphitheatre near St. Louis, Missouri, on July 2, 1991. Within four months after the Riverport Riot, Izzy Stradlin called it quits and was replaced by Gilby Clarke. According to Geffen A&R representative Tom Zutaut in a July 1999 *SPIN* interview, Guns N' Roses ended up paying hundreds of thousands of dollars in curfew violation fees: "Izzy finally had it and went over to Axl's house and told him that if he insisted on going on late, the late fees should be charged to him. That was it—Izzy was out of the band."

Among the tour's opening acts were Soundgarden (nicknamed "Frowngarden" by GN'R for their somber disposition), Skid Row, Nine Inch Nails (which received a disastrously negative response from GN'R fans), Smashing Pumpkins, Faith No More, Rose Tattoo, Body Count (Ice-T's metal band, which got dropped from the tour in a controversial fashion), Dumpster, the Quireboys, Suicidal Tendencies, and Raging Slab. Below are

ESTÁDIO DO MARACANÃ,
RIO DE JANEIRO - BRASIL

11-20 DE JANEIRO, 1991

PRINCE/ GUNS N' ROSES/
GEORGE MICHAEL/ A-HA/ INXS
RUN DMC/ NEW KIDS ON THE BLOCK/ JUDAS PRIEST/
BILLY IDOL/ FAITH NO MORE/ SANTANA/ JOE COCKER/
MEGADETH/ LISA STANSFIELD/
HAPPY MONDAYS/ QUEENSRYCHE/JIMMY CLIFF/ SEPULTURA/ DEEE LITE/COLIN HAY/ DEBBIE GIBSON/
INFORMATION SOCIETY/ TITÃS/ ROUPA NOVA/ CAPITAL INICIAL/ENGENHEIROS DO HAWAII/ MORAES
MOREIRA E PEPEU GOMES/ ELBA RAMALHO/ LOBÃO/ ALCEU VALENÇA

Before embarking on the *Use Your Illusion* Tour, Guns N' Roses performed at Rock in Rio 2 in January 1991 along with the likes of Judas Priest, Queensryche, and Megadeth.
Author's collection

some of the highlights, along with some of the controversies, riots, rants, and complete insanity, that marked the massive *Use Your Illusion* Tour, the likes of which may never be seen again.

May 24, 1991: Although the *Use Your Illusion* albums had not been released yet, the tour (dubbed the "Get in the Ring, Motherfucker Tour") officially begins at the Alpine Valley Music Theatre in East Troy, Wisconsin.

May 28, 1991: During a "homecoming show" at the Deer Creek Music Center in Noblesville, Indiana, Axl compares young people growing up in Indiana to being "prisoners in Auschwitz."

June 10, 1991: At a performance at Saratoga Performing Arts Center in Saratoga Springs, New York, Axl implores fans to shout "Get in the ring!" over and over again. The chant was recorded and can be heard in the song of the same name (a classic rant against rock journalism) that appears on the Use *Your Illusion II* album.

July 2, 1991: The so-called "Riverport Riot" unfolds at the Riverport Amphitheatre in Maryland Heights, Missouri (just outside St. Louis). After leaping off the stage into the crowd to retrieve a camera from an errant fan, and after blaming the venue's security for not being responsive enough, Axl storms off the stage with the band soon following in his wake. A riot ensues, resulting in sixty injured fans and damages totaling $200,000.

July 11, 1991: Axl, who had recently watched Oliver Stone's newly released film *The Doors*, starts an onstage rant against the media during a concert at McNichols Sports Arena in Denver, exclaiming, "Well, they fucking killed Jim Morrison, didn't they? And now they're trying to kill me!"

August 3, 1991: At the L.A. Forum, Guns N' Roses perform an amazing, three-and-a-half-hour show, the longest concert of the *Use Your Illusion* Tour. The show lasts until 3:30 a.m. and features a total of thirty-one songs. Special guests include Shannon Hoon of Blind Melon on "Don't Cry" and Sebastian Bach of Skid Row on "You're Crazy."

August 13, 1991: The "Get in the Ring, Motherfucker Tour" makes its way to Europe with a first stop at Helsinki Ice Hall in Helsinki, Finland.

August 19, 1991: Someone throws a firecracker onstage during GN'R's concert at Forum Copenhagen, in Copenhagen, Denmark. Axl abruptly stops the show and rants at the crowd—"I didn't come here for anyone in the band to get hurt or for any people in the crowd to get hurt, because somebody wants to be an asshole"—before the whole band retreats backstage for fifteen minutes and returns to resume "Sweet Child O' Mine."

August 24, 1991: Nine Inch Nails open for Guns N' Roses in front of an extremely antagonistic crowd at May Market in Mannheim, Germany. Trent Reznor later calls the crowd one of "the most hostile, moronic audiences I've ever experienced."

August 31, 1991: Izzy performs his last show as a member of Guns N' Roses at Wembley Stadium in London.

September 17, 1991: *Use Your Illusion I* and *Use Your Illusion II* make their debut at No. 2 and No. 1 on the US charts respectively.

November 7, 1991: Izzy Stradlin quits Guns N' Roses in the middle of the *Use Your Illusion* Tour and is replaced by Gilby Clarke.

December 5, 1991: Gilby Clarke makes his debut as GN'R's new rhythm guitarist (replacing the recently departed Izzy) at the Worcester Centrum in Worcester, Massachusetts. The Worcester show serves as the first concert since Guns N' Roses released the *Use Your Illusion* albums.

December 28, 1991: Axl shows up late for a Guns N' Roses concert at the Suncoast Dome in St. Petersburg, Florida, because he allegedly got sidetracked watching *Teenage Mutant Ninja Turtles II: The Secret of the Ooze*.

January 3, 1992: At a Guns N' Roses show at the LSU Assembly Center in Baton Rouge, Louisiana, Axl embarks on a rant about disgraced TV evangelist Jimmy Swaggert: "When I was growing up, I had to listen to his tapes . . . I was so glad when he went down."

February 1, 1992: Guns N' Roses play a prank on opening act Soundgarden during their last show together at Compton Terrace in Phoenix, Arizona, by interrupting their set with several inflatable sex dolls. (Slash takes it one step further by getting completely naked onstage.)

April 20, 1992: Guns N' Roses perform "Paradise City" and "Knockin' at Heaven's Door" at the Freddie Mercury Tribute Concert for AIDS Awareness at Wembley Stadium in London. In addition, Axl and Elton John perform "Bohemian Rhapsody," Axl sings "We Will Rock You" with Queen, and Slash joins Queen for a rendition of "Tie Your Mother Down."

May 20, 1992: Del James announces the Guns N' Roses concert at Strahov Stadium in Prague, Czechoslovakia, with the words, "Okay, you ex-Commie bastards, get ready to rock!"

Rapper Ice T's heavy metal band, Body Count, briefly served as opening act during the Guns N' Roses/Metallica stadium tour in 1992. Body Count's 1991 self-titled debut album contained the extremely controversial song "Cop Killer," which Ice-T later stated is sung "in the first person as a character who is fed up with police brutality."

Victoria Perez/Wikimedia Commons

June 2, 1992: "November Rain" is released as a single and reaches No. 3 on the US charts.

June 6, 1992: During an HBO pay-per-view event in Paris, France, Axl dedicates "Double Talkin' Jive" to Warren Beatty and delivers a blistering rant against the *Bonnie and Clyde* actor, who had briefly dated Axl's then girlfriend Stephanie Seymour before marrying actress Annette Bening (*American Beauty*). Lenny Kravitz joins Guns N' Roses onstage for a performance of "Always on the Run." Steven Tyler and Joe Perry from Aerosmith join GN'R for renditions of "Train Kept A-Rollin'" and "Mama Kin."

June 13, 1992: Queen lead guitarist Brian May joins Guns N' Roses onstage at Wembley Stadium in London for a performance of "Tie Your Mother Down" and "We Will Rock You."

July 12, 1992: As Guns N' Roses return from the latest European leg of the tour, Axl is arrested at the JFK Airport in New York City on charges stemming from the "Riverport Riot" a year earlier. He is eventually given two years' probation and forced to donate $50,000 to charity.

July 29, 1992: Axl gets struck in the nuts with a cigarette lighter while performing "Knockin' on Heaven's Door" during a GN'R concert at Giants Stadium in East Rutherford, New Jersey.

August 8, 1992: Metallica front man James Hetfield suffers second- and third-degree burns during a pyrotechnic mishap at Olympic Stadium in Montreal, Canada. A desperate call goes out to touring partners Guns N' Roses to immediately head from their hotel to the stadium and start their set. Three hours later, Guns N' Roses start their set but after just nine songs Axl storms off the stage (later citing a sore throat along with a monitor malfunction as the reasons for his departure). The ensuing riot results in more than a dozen injuries and damages estimated at more than $300,000.

September 9, 1992: At the 1992 MTV Video Music Awards, Axl gets into a verbal battle backstage with Kurt Cobain of Nirvana and performs a duet of "November Rain" with Elton John. Duff almost gets into a fist-fight with Nirvana bassist Krist Novoselic. Guns N' Roses win "Best Cinematography in a Video" for "November Rain" and also the "Michael Jackson Video Vanguard Award."

September 27, 1992: Body Count (rapper Ice-T's metal band) is replaced as opening act for the Guns N' Roses/Metallica stadium tour at the Los

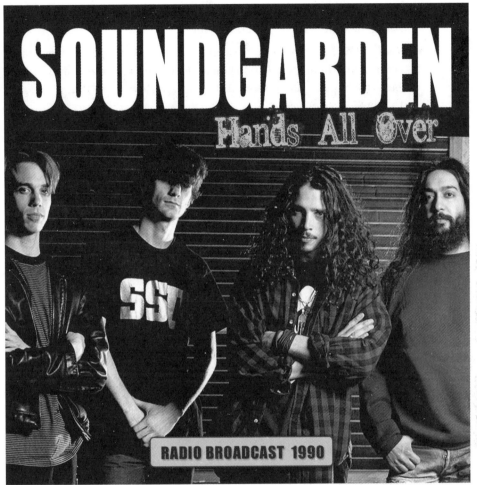

The members of Seattle grunge band Soundgarden seemed so miserable opening for Guns N' Roses during the *Use Your Illusion* Tour in 1992 that GN'R members labeled the band "Frowngarden." *Author's collection*

Angeles Coliseum due to controversy over Body Count's song "Cop Killer."

December 5, 1992: During a concert at River Plate Stadium in Buenos Aires, Argentina, Axl stops the show during "Nightrain" after a fan throws something onto the stage. He calls for an interpreter and proceeds to berate the audience: "We have some really fucking stupid people here tonight . . . who think that throwing things at the stage will relate into a better show." Forced to call upon the interpreter a second time, Axl exclaims to the audience, "If somebody beside you is throwing something, beat the fucking shit out of them."

February 1, 1993: In Melbourne, Australia, Guns N' Roses perform a show in front of approximately 75,000 fans at the Calder Park Raceway in stifling heat. (Sebastian Bach of opening act Skid Row states that it's "hotter than a $5 hooker's cunt.")

February 23, 1993: Guns N' Roses launch their leaner, meaner "Skin and Bones Tour"—which also features an unplugged performance during the middle of the set—at the Frank Erwin Center in Austin, Texas.

March 17, 1993: After just three songs into Guns N' Roses' set at the Boston Garden, a fan throws a glass bottle onstage. The band retreats backstage, causing chants of "Bullshit!" in the crowd. When GN'R return to the stage, they launch into the Misfits' "Attitude," with Duff remarking, "Not that this city needs any!"

April 4, 1993: At the ARCO Arena in Sacramento, California, Duff gets knocked out cold onstage by a Jack Daniel's bottle full of piss that was thrown from someone in the audience. While Duff gets transported to the emergency room, the concert abruptly ends, and Axl informs the audience that the show is over: "So we're sorry, have a good night. And if you find the asshole, kill him." Five minutes later, Slash returns onstage and addresses the bewildered audiences, telling them to "leave peacefully and don't fuckin' fuck with other people or fuck with anything, just cruise on."

June 16, 1993: A totally naked Shannon Hoon of Blind Melon nonchalantly strolls onstage at a Guns N' Roses concert at St. Jakob Stadium in Basel, Switzerland, and delivers a pizza to the band. He then sits down to play the bongos.

June 26, 1993: Footage for the "Estranged" music video is shot at a Guns N' Roses show at Olympiastadion in Munich, Germany.

July 17, 1993: The *Use Your Illusion* Tour ends at River Plate Stadium in Buenos Aires, Argentina. Believe it or not, it would be the last time Axl would perform with Slash until the April 1, 2016, reunion show at the Troubadour. After the gig, Axl, Slash, and Dizzy Reed reportedly retreat to the hotel bar where Axl plays the grand piano and the exhausted band members hang out until 5:30 a.m.

14

Anything Goes Tonight

The Top Ten Most Notorious Guns N' Roses Concerts

We cause some chaos, sure, because we think that's what rock and roll is about. —Slash

In the early days, as they performed at a variety of clubs throughout West Hollywood, Guns N' Roses' gigs were characterized by their sheer unpredictability—leading to a thrilling, raucous, and potentially dangerous experience for everyone in the audience. With the success of *Appetite for Destruction*, things changed overnight, and GN'R started playing huge arenas and outdoor stadiums. Later, as the band started to splinter during the two-and-a-half-year-long *Use Your Illusion* Tour, Guns N' Roses concerts became characterized by frequent delays, unruly fans, security violations, and abrupt cancellations that led to disgruntled crowds that occasionally started riots, most notably at the Riverport Amphitheatre near St. Louis, Missouri, and at Montreal's Olympic Stadium in 1992. During a Q&A session as Guns N' Roses embarked on the 2016 Not in This Lifetime Tour, Axl Rose remarked, "When we were opening for bigger bands, and then when we first started headlining, I don't think anybody knows how violent it was. It was really violent in the crowd . . . You'd have to stop the show. I got a lot of grief for stopping the show 'for no reason,' [but] there was just a lot of really rowdy crowds."

Marquee Club, London (1987)

Appetite for Destruction had not even been released yet when Guns N' Roses traveled to London for a three-night stint at the legendary Marquee Club.

British tabloids like the *Star* sensationalized the band's visit with such amusing headlines as "A Rock Band Even Nastier Than the Beastie Boys Is Heading for Britain." GN'R first took the stage at the Marquee Club (a "famous little sweatbox," according to Slash) on June 19, 1987, where the unruly crowd proceeded to pelt the band with beer and spit (along with hypodermic needles, according to some reports). Undeterred by the rowdy, boisterous fans, (a spirited Axl Rose had taken the stage exclaiming, "It's great to be in fuckin' England, finally!"), Guns N' Roses managed to pull off a reasonably admirable set (despite the circumstances) that featured "Welcome to the Jungle," "Out Ta Get Me" "Rocket Queen," "Nightrain," "My Michelle," "It's So Easy," "Mr. Brownstone," "Don't Cry," "You're Crazy," "Paradise City," "Whole Lotta Rosie," "Move to the City," and "Mama Kin."

Guns N' Roses played two subsequent shows at the Marquee Club, both of which were much better received, and they also performed "Knockin' on Heaven's Door" live for the first time at the venue. During the final Marquee Club show, Axl dedicated "Out Ta Get Me" to "all the fucking critics in the back." Ian Astbury of the Cult was in attendance at one of the Marquee shows and was so impressed with the band that he offered GN'R a slot as opening act on the Cult's upcoming tour. In addition, the band got the opportunity to meet their hero, Lemmy Kilmister of Motörhead, during the London trip. Other bands that performed at the Marquee Club over the years include the Rolling Stones (who performed live for the first time ever at the club's original location on July 12, 1962), the Who, Jimi Hendrix, Pink Floyd, Led Zeppelin, the Clash, David Bowie, Status Quo, the Police, the Damned, and the Sex Pistols, among many others. The Marquee Club closed its doors for good in 1996, and several unsuccessful attempts to resurrect the venue have been made over the years .

Omni Coliseum, Atlanta (1987)

During a November 20, 1987, Guns N' Roses performance opening for Mötley Crüe at the Omni Coliseum in Atlanta, Georgia, Axl jumped offstage during "Mr. Brownstone" and assaulted a security guard (who reportedly was shoving a friend of his in the crowd). He was held backstage while the band decided to forge ahead with a roadie known as "Big Ron" assuming vocal duties on Led Zeppelin's "Communication Breakdown" and the Rolling Stones' "Honky Tonk Women." According to concert promoter Charlie Brusco in a 2016 *Vulture* interview, "I heard this horrible sound . . . I look up, and one of the guys in the road crew was singing." In addition,

Steven Adler pulled off a lengthy drum solo to fill some time. Meanwhile, Axl was hauled off to jail after refusing to apologize to the security guard. He later pleaded guilty to assault and paid a fine in order to avoid a trial.

Monsters of Rock Festival, Castle Donington (1988)

Tragedy struck the Monsters of Rock Festival—a huge outdoor rock show at a racetrack in Castle Donington, England—on a rainy, muddy day before an unruly, surging crowd of more than 100,000 people on August 20, 1988. As Guns N' Roses performed "It's So Easy," two fans—eighteen-year-old Alan Dick and twenty-year-old Landon Siggers—were crushed to death amid the moshing crowd swarming around the front of the stage. Axl repeatedly stopped the set and urged the crowd to calm down, but to no avail. However, the band was not informed of the tragedy until they had already returned to their hotel. Monsters of Rock was cancelled the following year as an official inquest was undertaken by authorities. The festival returned in 1990 with capacity capped at 72,500 fans. In addition to Guns N' Roses, the 1988 Monsters of Rock lineup also included Iron Maiden, Megadeth, KISS, David Lee Roth, and Helloween, a German power metal band that—believe it or not—actually released an album called *Pink Bubbles Go Ape* in 1991. When asked about the Monsters of Rock tragedy in a 1988 *Rolling Stone* article, Axl remarked, "I don't know what to think of it . . . We didn't tell people, 'Drink so much alcohol that you can't fucking stand up.' I don't feel responsible in those ways. I don't want people to get hurt . . . We want the exact opposite."

Los Angeles Coliseum, Los Angeles (1989)

One of rock 'n' roll's most legendary meltdowns occurred during the first concert of a four-night stint at the Los Angeles Coliseum on October 18, 1989, as Guns N' Roses opened for their idols, the Rolling Stones. After a set by Living Colour, GN'R took the stage at 7:30 p.m. However, Axl brought the concert to a screeching halt after the first song and directly addressed the stunned audience of 80,000 fans: "I don't like to do this onstage, but unless certain people in the band start getting their act together, this is going to be the last Guns N' Roses show. I'm sick and tired of too many people in this organization dancing with Mr. Brownstone." During the Rolling Stones set, Mick Jagger dedicated "Mixed Emotions" to Axl.

The following night, Axl threatened not to take the stage unless Slash address the audience about drugs. Slash reluctantly agreed, remarking to

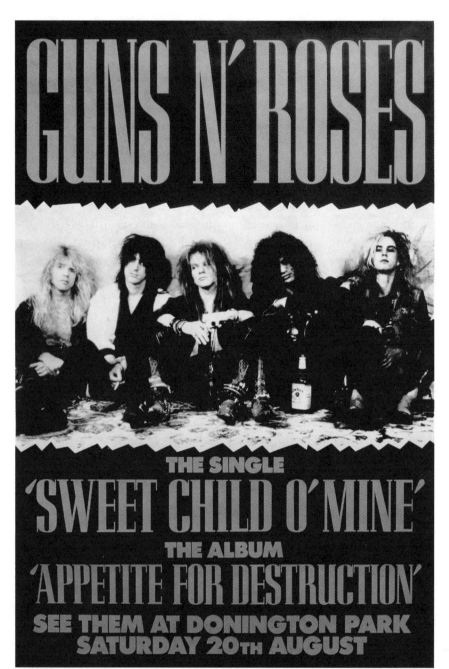

Two fans were tragically crushed to death amid a surging crowd of 100,000 unruly fans during Guns N' Roses' set at the Monsters of Rock Festival in Castle Donington, England, in 1988.   *Author's collection*

the crowd, "There's been a lot written about this band and drugs . . . A lot of it is bullshit, a lot of it is true. Last night, you almost saw the last Guns N' Roses gig . . . Last night I was up here, and I didn't even know it. Smack isn't what it's all about . . . and we're not going to be one of those weak bands that falls apart over it." Axl then made his way onstage and remarked, "I just don't want to see any more of my friends slip away." The band then performed, rather appropriately, "Mr. Brownstone" as the first song of their set. Slash later told VH1, "I knew [Axl's outburst] was directed at me, because I was real strung out at the time. But it was probably one of the things that made me hate Axl more than anything." Duff later lamented in his 2011 autobiography that "Once Axl took his concerns public, the times of being a gang—us against the world—were over. We played the rest of the show, but it was a halfhearted effort at best. Afterward, and really for the remainder of our career, we just went our separate ways. That night officially rang the bell for the end of an era in GN'R."

Forum Copenhagen, Copenhagen (1991)

During an August 19, 1991, concert at the Forum Copenhagen in Copenhagen, Denmark, someone from the audience threw a firecracker on the stage during "Sweet Child O' Mine." Axl abruptly stopped singing and addressed the audience: "You wanna play games like that, we'll go home, it's not a problem." The band resumed the song but security was unresponsive and made no effort to track down the perpetrator, so Axl stopped singing again and remarked, "Stop, stop, stop . . . I didn't come here for anyone in my band to get hurt or for any people in the crowd to get hurt, because somebody wants to be an asshole . . . In fact, we are gonna leave for a bit, until you find the guy." The band exited the stage but returned fifteen minutes later and resumed "Sweet Child O' Mine."

Riverport Amphitheatre, Maryland Heights (1991)

The state-of-the-art outdoor Riverport Amphitheatre (located just outside of St. Louis, Missouri) was the site of one of the all-time most notorious Guns N' Roses concerts (a.k.a. the "Rocket Queen Riot" or "Riverport Riot") in front of 16,000 fans on July 2, 1991. The brand-new Riverport Amphitheatre had just opened a few weeks early with a Stevie Winwood concert. Everything seemed to be going smoothly until the fifteenth song of the set, "Rocket Queen," when Axl noticed a fan near the front of the stage with a video camera and notified security to "get that guy!" Unsatisfied with the tepid response from security, Axl decided to take matters into his own hands by stage diving into the audience and confronting the fan, who was later identified as Billy "Stump" Stephenson. After returning to the stage, Axl exclaimed, "Thanks to the lame-ass security, I'm going home!" He then stormed off the stage, soon followed by the rest of his rather bewildered band members, who had kept playing through the ordeal, briefly hoping Axl would return. The crowd began shouting, "Bullshit! Bullshit!" Chaos quickly erupted throughout the venue.

The ensuing riot left approximately sixty fans injured and caused tremendous damage (estimated at $200,000) to the new facility. Some of the rioters took to the stage and destroyed the band's equipment. An estimated 400 nightstick-wielding police officers descended upon the scene in an attempt to restore order. Fifteen fans were ultimately arrested. According to Axl in the 2004 VH1 *Behind the Music* special on Guns N' Roses, "I jumped offstage and yeah things went haywire after that . . . Maybe I could have handled it better or whatever but no one was really handling anything at that point. So I took it into my own hands with what I could do." Slash remarked that it was "one of the scariest things" he had ever seen as "the whole place just fuckin' collectively destroyed everything." Somehow the band managed to make it out of the situation safely, and they drove their van all the way to Chicago to escape the chaos (along with the wrath of local authorities!). According to Duff, "the threat of violence hung in the air" at every gig after Riverport.

Just over a year later, on July 12, 1992, Axl was arrested at JFK Airport in New York City following the European leg of the *Use Your Illusion* Tour and charged with four counts of misdemeanor assault and one count of property damage stemming from the riot. Although he pleaded innocent to the charges, Axl was eventually given two years' probation and forced to donate $50,000 to charity. As for "Stump" Stephenson, he filed a lawsuit against Axl seeking $2 million in damages. The suit was settled out of court for what Axl called "a very minimal figure" and, for some odd reason, an autograph. In reference to the riot and ongoing controversy, Guns N' Roses added the not-so-subtle message "Fuck You, St. Louis!" to the liner notes of both of the 1991 *Use Your Illusion* albums.

However, Guns N' Roses isn't the only band to have a negative experience at the Riverport Amphitheatre. In 2010, Kings of Leon made an abrupt exit off the stage of the venue (by then known as the Verizon Amphitheatre and now known as the Hollywood Casino Amphitheatre)

While Guns N' Roses served as the opening act for the Rolling Stones at the Los Angeles Coliseum in 1989, Axl Rose stunned the crowd by embarking on his infamous "Mr. Brownstone" rant. The Stones (pictured in an early concert above) were idolized by GN'R."

Riksarkivet (National Archives of Norway)/Wikimedia Commons

after reportedly getting deluged with pigeon shit streaming down from the rafters. Drummer Nathan Followill took to Twitter after the debacle and commented, "[I]t's the fucking venue's fault. You may enjoy being shit on but we don't. Sorry for all who travelled many miles."

Olympic Stadium, Montreal (1992)

Guns N' Roses and Metallica, two of the biggest rock bands of the era, coheadlined a twenty-five-date stadium tour in 1992. What could possibly go wrong? Besides Axl getting struck in the nuts with a cigarette lighter at Giants Stadium on July 29, 1992, during a performance of "Knockin' on Heaven's Door," things went relatively smoothly early on in the tour. Knowing Guns N' Roses' penchant for delays, Metallica even graciously chose to open every show to avoid any hassles.

Everything changed for the worst on August 8, 1992, as the tour stopped at Olympic Stadium in Montreal, Canada. During "Fade to Black," Metallica front man James Hetfield suffered second- and third-degree burns during a pyrotechnic mishap. Metallica drummer Lars Ulrich later told VH1 rather insensitively that Hetfield "looked like the torch that they bring up the stairs to light the Olympic fire." A desperate call was made to Guns N' Roses at their hotel, asking them to head to the stadium and save the day. After a nearly three-hour delay, GN'R finally started their set but Axl stormed off the stage after just nine songs, citing a stage monitor malfunction (along with a sore throat) and announcing, "Thank you. Your money will be refunded. We're out of here." More than 2,000 infuriated fans took their rage out on the venue in a full-scale riot. Police used batons and tear gas to try and quell the unruly crowd. Over a dozen injuries were reported, and damage estimates exceeded well over $300,000. Slash later said he witnessed fans "breaking everything in sight."

ARCO Arena, Sacramento (1993)

In one of the weirdest concert incidents in rock 'n' roll history, Duff was hit in the head and knocked unconscious with what Slash later referred to as a "bottle of piss" about ninety minutes into the Sacramento, California, show at ARCO Arena on April 4, 1993, during the *Use Your Illusion* Tour. Duff was rushed to the emergency room, while Axl announced that the show was over: "I hate to ruin your fun, and I'm fun, but somebody just hit Duff in the head with a bottle, and now he's not able to play. So we're sorry, have a good night. And if you find the asshole, kill him." Bewildered fans in the crowd could not believe the show was over. Five minutes later, Slash took to the stage and reiterated that the concert was indeed over, and urged the crowd to "leave peacefully and don't fuckin' fuck with other people or fuck with anything, just cruise on."

General Motors Place, Vancouver (2002)

Guns N' Roses' first North American tour since 1993 got off to an inauspicious start at General Motors Place (now Rogers Arena) in Vancouver, Canada, on November 7, 2002, when Axl failed to show up (his flight was delayed due to mechanical problems). After concert promoters decided to cancel the show, a riot ensued with fans throwing bottles and rocks, as well as breaking glass doors at the venue. Police responded with batons and attack dogs. Meanwhile, the new Guns N' Roses lineup (sans Axl) remained backstage, totally oblivious to all the mayhem taking place outside.

First Union Center, Philadelphia (2002)

On December 6, 2002, less than one month after the Vancouver melee, a second riot broke out at the First Union Center in Philadelphia, Pennsylvania, after the Guns N' Roses concert was cancelled around midnight (after the crowd had been waiting several hours) due to Axl's "health issues." The crowd threw beers, chanted "Axl sucks," ripped the seats off chairs, and ultimately caused nearly $200,000 in damages. According to Larry Magid, one of the concert promoters, in a 2016 *Vulture* interview, "The managers weren't able to persuade the band to go on . . . Whatever psychological issues Axl was having, he just couldn't get onstage." It has been rumored that Axl was actually still in New York City watching a basketball game on TV. Clear Channel made the wise decision to cancel the remaining dates on the tour. In 2012, during a Guns N' Roses concert at Philadelphia's Electric Factory, Axl addressed the 2002 incident: "I was really sick. It had nothing to do with fur coats or basketball games . . . I love Philly. I came to play here a few times and I really liked it . . . So it's good to be here. I want to apologize for my part of that. You know, so . . . I'm not saying I'm innocent."

15

Can't Wait Here Forever

Ten Bands That Opened for Guns N' Roses

We're not the most relaxed guys. We're not fuckin' Mr. Mister, y'know?
—Duff McKagan

As the *Use Your Illusion* Tour churned on for two and a half years and gradually became more bloated and excessive, a number of up-and-coming bands that served as opening acts for Guns N' Roses got caught in the crossfire, such as Nine Inch Nails, which faced the wrath of 65,000 GN'R fans who didn't like the band's sound, resulting in what Trent Reznor called the worst gigs of his entire performing career. Controversy also followed in Guns N' Roses' wake as they chose Ice-T's heavy metal band, Body Count (which had recorded a song called "Cop Killer"), as an opening act. Other once up-and-coming bands that opened for Guns N' Roses, such as Raging Slab and My Little Funhouse, have unfortunately faded into obscurity.

A diverse range of acts were tapped to open Guns N' Roses' 2016 Not in This Lifetime Tour, such as Alice in Chains, Lenny Kravitz, the Cult (ironically, GN'R had opened for the Cult in the summer of 1987), Chris Stapleton, Wolfmother, Billy Talent, and Skrillex.

Quireboys

Formed in London in 1984, the Quireboys (original name: the Queerboys) opened for Guns N' Roses at the legendary Hammersmith Odeon in London on October 8, 1987 (Los Angeles-based glam metal/punk band Faster Pussycat was also on the bill), and also during the *Use Your Illusion*

Once absurdly touted as Britain's answer to Guns N' Roses, the Quireboys opened for GN'R at the legendary Hammersmith Odeon in London in 1987.   *Frank Schwichtenberg/Wikimedia Commons*

Tour in 1993. Before you know it, the band was actually being touted in some (rather delusional!) circles as Britain's answer to Guns N' Roses. However, they unfortunately also shared with their American counterparts a "dangerous addiction to excessive partying" that served to hinder their development. Original Quireboys band members included Spike (vocals), Guy Bailey (guitar), Nigel Mogg (bass), and Chris Johnstone (bass/piano). The Quireboys' 1990 debut album, *A Bit of What You Fancy*, was well-received and reached No. 2 on the UK charts with four tracks from the album released as singles: "7 O'Clock," "I Don't Love You Anymore," "There She Goes Again," and "Hey You" (which reached No. 14 on the UK charts). The band broke up in 1993 but reunited under various guises over subsequent years before totally fading away.

Raging Slab

Formed in New York City in 1983, this talented Southern-style "boogie" rock group with tinges of both punk and metal had its share of misfortunes over the years accompanied by a series of bad decisions that generally led them to fall into obscurity. For instance, the band, rather unwisely, decided to name their 1987 debut album *Assmaster* (not kidding!). *Guitar World* described Raging Slab's unique sound as "Lynyrd Skynyrd meets Metallica." Arguably the band's greatest success came with the release of their 1989 self-titled third album, which featured the popular singles "Don't Dog Me" and "Bent for Silver." Somewhat improbably, the accompanying music video for "Don't Dog Me" skyrocketed to No. 2 on the MTV Countdown.

In addition to opening for Guns N' Roses at the legendary Ritz in New York City in 1991 (footage of which ended up in the "You Could Be Mine" music video), Raging Slab toured with the Ramones, Red Hot Chili Peppers, Warrant, and Molly Hatchet. Another Raging Slab career highlight was the 1993 release of the double album *Dynamite Monster Boogie Concert*, which actually featured string arrangements by John Paul Jones of Led Zeppelin. The music video to the single "Anywhere But Here" off that album featured a cameo by none other than actor Gary Coleman (*Diff'rent Strokes*) and appeared on season three of MTV's *Beavis and Butt-Head* (with Beavis exclaiming, "They're like Skynyrd, but cool!").

Nine Inch Nails

In various interviews over the years, Trent Reznor has made it clear that opening for Guns N' Roses several times in 1991 during the European leg of the *Use Your Illusion* Tour added up to some of the absolute worst shows that Nine Inch Nails (NIN) *ever* played. Ironically, NIN was fresh off of a successful stint at the first Lollapalooza during the summer of 1991 and gaining momentum as one of the newest, hottest bands out there. Everything changed for the worst when the band took the stage in front of 65,000 Guns N' Roses fans—thousands of whom decided to give NIN the finger at the same time (and one who actually threw a link sausage on stage!)—in Mannheim, Germany

According to Reznor in a 2012 *Q* magazine interview, "It was only a couple of shows and they were some of the worst performances we ever had in front of the most hostile, moronic audiences I've ever experienced . . . They were there to rock; what they didn't want was some homo-looking dudes playing noisy synths and they made that very clear to us." According to Reznor, the band managed to exit the stage "with our lives" and ended up selling a grand total of eight T-shirts that night. In another interview with *The Guardian*, Reznor referred to the GN'R audiences as "a bunch of

Cro-Magnon types." To make matters worse, Skid Row was also on the bill, a band that Reznor cited as "the epitome of what I don't like about spandex rock. Poseur toughness, bullshit. I hate them."

Axl loved NIN and even told Matt Sorum that the band was going to be "huge." Gilby Clarke remembered Axl telling him that he wanted to change the sound of Guns N' Roses and "use more industrial type things" like NIN. Interestingly, guitarist Robin Finck has served as a member of both NIN and GN'R. He joined NIN in 1994 as part of the touring band for their Self-Destruct and *Further Down the Spiral* tours. In 1997, Finck joined Guns N' Roses as lead guitarist on a two-year contract (replacing Slash, who had quit the year before) and started working on *Chinese Democracy*. After his two-year stint ended (and no album had been produced), Finck rejoined NIN in 1999 but returned to GN'R in 2000. He joined the band on several sporadic tour dates in the early 2000s before rejoining NIN in 2008, the same year that *Chinese Democracy* was finally released. Finck played on every track of *Chinese Democracy* and shared credit on the creation of the title track, as well as "Shackler's Revenge," "Better," "Street of Dreams," "Catcher in the Rye," "Riad N' the Bedouins," and "Prostitute." DJ Ashba replaced Finck as lead guitarist for Guns N' Roses in 2009.

Soundgarden

Founded in 1984, immensely popular Seattle grunge band Soundgarden opened for Guns N' Roses during the *Use Your Illusion* Tour in 1992. According to lead singer/rhythm guitarist Chris Cornell in a 1993 interview with *Raw* magazine, "It wasn't a whole lot of fun going out in front of 40,000 people for 35 minutes every day. Most of them hadn't heard our songs and didn't care about them. It was a bizarre thing." In addition, the band felt that they were alienating their hardcore punk rock/indie fans by touring with Guns N' Roses. Cornell also remembered that Axl seemed to be "having a personal crisis" every day on tour.

In fact, the members of Soundgarden seemed so serious, unenthusiastic, bored, and miserable touring with Guns N' Roses that the band was quickly dubbed "Frowngarden." During the last show with Soundgarden, on February 1, 1992, at Compton Terrace in Phoenix, Arizona, GN'R decided to play a prank on the band by interrupting their set with several inflatable sex dolls. Slash, who remembers Soundgarden as being "mortified" by the prank, even took it one step further by getting completely naked onstage. According to Soundgarden bassist Ben Shepherd in *Everybody Loves Our*

Town: An Oral History of Grunge, there was a reason the band got dubbed with the "Frowngarden" mantle: "We weren't party monsters. We weren't motherfucking rock stars . . . We were there to play music. We weren't there for models and the cocaine. We were there to blow your doors off." Reminiscing about the tour for a 2012 *Vulture* interview, Cornell referred to Duff and Slash as "regular, sweet, warm guys," while there was a "Wizard of Oz character behind the curtain" complicating the "ideal situation" of being "the most successful and famous rock band on the planet."

Soundgarden achieved their greatest commercial success with the 1994 release of their fourth album, *Superunknown*, which spawned the hit single "Black Hole Sun." In 1997, the band broke up but reunited in 2010 and released the album *King Animal* in 2012. Incidentally, the band named themselves after a wind-channeling pipe sculpture, *A Sound Garden*, located on the grounds of the National Oceanic and Atmospheric Administration in Seattle.

Smashing Pumpkins

Formed in Chicago in 1988, Smashing Pumpkins featured the original lineup of Billy Corgan (lead vocals/guitar), James Iha (guitar), D'arcy Wretzky (bass), and Jimmy Chamberlin (drums). The band, which opened for Guns N' Roses for two dates on the *Use Your Illusion* Tour in 1992 (Oklahoma City on April 6 and Rosemont, Illinois, on April 9), enjoyed mainstream success with the release of their second album, *Siamese Dream* (1993), which spawned the hit singles "Today," "Cherub Rock," "Rocket," and "Disarm." Smashing Pumpkins' epic follow-up double album, *Mellon Collie and the Infinite Sadness* (1995), which Corgan referred to as "*The Wall* for Generation X," sold over 10 million copies, earned seven Grammy Award nominations, and featured such hits as "Bullet with Butterfly Wings," "Tonight, Tonight," "1979," and "Zero."

In a 2016 *Rolling Stone* interview, Corgan claimed that he saw the Guns N' Roses reunion coming: "I said five years ago it'll definitely happen. It'll just be when and where . . . I just think the band, however you want to quantify it, broke up, or the original lineup didn't endure past a certain point, and the world has changed a lot since then. The band is so great and the music is so great, and the chemistry is such a part of what people love—including me—as a fan. It would seem a crime to not be able to enjoy and appreciate the accomplishment in this era."

My Little Funhouse

What the hell happened to My Little Funhouse? The talented rock band from Kilkenny, Ireland, rose from obscurity to win the Carling Hot Press band competition in 1991 and then signed an absurd mega deal ($2 million, at a time when Nirvana received just $60,000) with Geffen Records, which envisioned them as the next Guns N' Roses, believe it or not! In addition to opening for Guns N' Roses at Slane Castle in Ireland on May 16, 1992, as part of the *Use Your Illusion* Tour (it was only their third-ever gig!), the band even appeared in GN'R's "November Rain" music video.

My Little Funhouse's lineup featured Alan Lawlor (vocals), Brendan Morrissey (guitar), Anthony Morrissey (guitar), Gary Deevy (bass), and Derek Maher (drums), who was replaced by Graham Hopkins in 1993. Their debut album, *Standunder*, was released in 1992. However, things fell apart after the band moved to Los Angeles and began a rapid fade into oblivion. (They split up for good in 1996.) In a 2004 interview with *The Irish Times*, Brendan Morrissey commented, "We made our first record in London, and the second album in L.A. That album cost a fortune, but it was never released. Then we did a third record, also in L.A., and that wasn't released either. I knew two years into the record deal that things were going down-hill . . . Music changed after Nirvana . . . and that meant us and the likes of Guns N' Roses were out the door . . . We were just some Irish kids hanging around L.A., going to clubs every night. I'm still in touch with some of the people from Guns N' Roses, good mates in fact. I've no regrets at all."

Faith No More

Hailing from the Bay Area in California and originally known as "Faith No Man," Faith No More went through several lineup changes during the 1980s (including a very brief stint with Courtney Love as lead singer) before settling on Mike Patton (formerly of rock band Mr. Bungle) as front man in 1989. The band scored hits with "Epic" and "Falling to Pieces," both of which had accompanying music videos that received heavy rotation on MTV. The band joined the massive Guns N' Roses/Metallica stadium tour in 1992 (Axl had initially invited Nirvana, but Kurt Cobain hated GN'R and their music), but they drew a rather tepid response from most fans of the main acts. According to legend, Patton took a shit in Axl Rose's orange juice carton, sealed it up and placed it in Axl's personal refrigerator. Faith No More bassist Billy Gould recounted the insanity of the tour in a *Classic*

Rock interview: "There was a rumor that Axl brought his psychic on tour with him . . . And it would be bad luck in any city that started with the letter 'M.' So he cancelled Manchester, Madrid, Munich, and he did Montreal, and that's when the riot happened." After releasing six studio albums, Faith No More broke up in 1998 but have reunited on several occasions.

Body Count

After Faith No More left the Guns N' Roses/Metallica stadium tour in the fall of 1992, rapper Ice-T's controversial heavy metal band, Body Count, filled the slot for several shows, including Kansas City, Denver, Oakland, and San Diego. However, due to outrage over the band's song "Cop Killer,"—which Vice President Dan Quayle denounced as "obscene"—Motörhead replaced Body Count for a September 27, 1992, concert at the Los Angeles Coliseum, and comedian Andrew "Dice" Clay replaced the band at an October 3, 1992, show at the Rose Bowl. Concert promoters deemed the band "inappropriate" due to negative "perceptions." Axl retaliated in a 1992 *Los Angeles Times* interview, calling the decision "shallow-minded" and regretting the lost opportunity "to play together and show people that we're about artistic expression, not violence or prejudice. It comes down to this—freedom of speech is OK, as long as it doesn't piss off some public official." Addressing the controversy over "Cop Killer," Ice-T once remarked, "If you believe that I'm a cop killer, you believe David Bowie is an astronaut."

Formed in 1990 by Ice-T and lead guitarist Ernie C (both of whom, when growing up, were big fans of Led Zeppelin and Black Sabbath), Body Count made its debut performance at Lollapalooza in the summer of 1991, performed "Body Count" on Ice-T's 1991 album *O.G. Original Gangster*, and released their 1992 self-titled debut album, which, in addition to "Cop Killer," featured "There Goes the Neighborhood," "KKK Bitch," "Out in the Parking Lot," and "Momma's Gotta Die Tonight." Ice-T eventually decided to remove "Cop Killer" from the album, replacing it with a new version of "Freedom of Speech," which had first appeared on the rapper's 1989 album *The Iceberg/Freedom of Speech . . . Just Watch What You Say*. Original Body Count band members also included Mooseman (bass), D-Roc the Executioner (rhythm guitar), and Beastmaster V (drums). In addition to their 1992 self-titled debut album, Body Count has released the following albums: *Born Dead* (1994), *Murder 4 Hire* (2006), and *Manslaughter* (2014). The band's new album, *Bloodlust*, is scheduled for a 2017 release.

Suicidal Tendencies

Founded by lead singer Mike "Cyco Miko" Muir in Venice, California, in 1980, Suicidal Tendencies is known as one of the "Fathers of Crossover Thrash," a blend of thrash metal and hardcore punk rock. In 1983, the band released their self-titled debut album, which spawned the popular single and MTV staple "Institutionalized" ("Drug you up because they're lazy/It's too much work to help a crazy"). In addition to opening for Guns N' Roses during the *Use Your Illusion* Tour in 1993, Suicidal Tendencies toured with Metallica, KISS, Danzig, and Queensryche. Suicidal Tendencies has released twelve studio albums over the years, their latest being *World Gone Mad* in 2016.

Lenny Kravitz

Grammy Award–winning singer-songwriter Lenny Kravitz first took the stage to perform "Always on the Run" with Guns N' Roses in Paris during the *Use Your Illusion* Tour on June 6, 1992. (Kravitz had actually attended high school with Slash in Los Angeles.) Featured on Kravitz's second album, *Mama Said* (1991), "Always on the Run" was cowritten with Slash. The song also appeared on the soundtrack of the 1998 Adam Sandler comedy *The Waterboy* and in the 2008 video game *Guitar Hero: Aerosmith*. The song's catchy riff was once considered for a Guns N' Roses song. Slash also played guitar on "Fields of Joy," the first track of *Mama Said*.

In 2016, Kravitz agreed to open for Guns N' Roses on several dates of the Not in This Lifetime Tour. In a 2016 *Rolling Stone* interview, Kravitz stated, "I don't normally do gigs like this . . . But sometimes you've got to do things for the fun of it, for the experience. I'm looking forward to playing with them and celebrating them coming back together . . . I love the summer, outdoor concert vibe, so we'll rock out and improvise and go deep and get psychedelic and out there." Kravitz was in attendance as a special guest at the Guns N' Roses "warm-up show" at the Troubadour on April 1, 2016, and exclaimed, "It was exciting. I mean, come on. They're a stadium act playing a small room. The energy and anticipation in that room was crazy before they came up. It was high energy."

16

Take a Closer Look

Guns N' Roses and Their Recording Sessions

We did the whole album by getting it on the second or third take. That's where the spontaneity comes from. If you don't get it by then you've lost the feel of it. —Slash, on recording *Appetite for Destruction*

The evolution of Guns N' Roses' sound can be traced through a study of their recording sessions—from the raw immediacy and simplicity of *Appetite for Destruction* to the elaborate additions of strings, horns, and ballads in the *Use Your Illusion* albums to the excessive production of the long-delayed *Chinese Democracy*, which was recorded in fourteen studios with a host of revolving band members at a whopping cost of $14 million.

Appetite for Destruction (1987)

Guns N' Roses' breakthrough album was produced and engineered by Mike Clink and recorded at Rumbo Studios in Canoga Park, California; Take One Studios in Burbank, California; and Can Am Studio in Tarzana, California. The album was mixed at Media Sound in New York City. The band entered Rumbo Studios (which was opened in 1979 by Daryl Dragon of Captain & Tennille fame) in January 1987 to start the *Appetite for Destruction* recording sessions. Clink reportedly picked Rumbo because it was a good distance from the distractions available on Sunset Boulevard in West Hollywood.

Slash's unique guitar sound on the album was produced with a 1959 Gibson Les Paul Standard replica. (He reportedly used the same guitar on every subsequent GN'R recording, as well as those of Velvet Revolver.) The 1959 Gibson Les Paul Standard was built by talented guitar luthier

Kris Derrig, who lived in an old trailer behind Music Works in Redondo Beach. The wood used for Slash's guitar reportedly came from an old barn in Hillsborough, New Hampshire. Sadly, Derrig died of cancer at the age of thirty-two on May 17, 1987, two months before *Appetite for Destruction* hit the record stores. The only other guitar Slash used on *Appetite for Destruction* was a borrowed Gibson SG for "My Michelle." In 2010, Gibson Guitars released their Slash Appetite Les Paul model, proclaiming it "the axe that launched a thousand riffs."

Slash also relied on a Marshall amplifier during the recording of *Appetite for Destruction*. According to Slash, in a 1992 interview with *Guitar* magazine, "I had one when I did *Appetite*, which was great. I stole it from S.I.R. [Studio Instrument Rentals], and when we were rehearsing at S.I.R. after the record came out, my idiot roadie at the time brought that amp down by mistake, and they took it back. When we went back into the studio a couple years later, I had to find the ultimate amp again." In 1996, Marshall introduced the Marshall Slash Signature JCM 2555, an authentic reissue of the Marshall "Silver Jubilee" JCM 2555 first released in 1987. Duff used his advance money for *Appetite for Destruction* to purchase a Fender Jazz Special and Gallien-Krueger 800RB Bass Amp Head.

In a 2009 *Los Angeles Weekly* article about the recording of *Appetite for Destruction*, Slash remarked, "After terrorizing Hollywood all night, we'd still somehow have to get up and be at the studio by twelve noon. And mostly we did it." Slash's daily routine would be to show up at the studio and make a Jack Daniel's and coffee to start things off right. Izzy actually slept in a closet at Rumbo Studios after his girlfriend threw him out of her apartment. According to Clink in *Reckless Road*, "*Appetite for Destruction* did not happen by accident. We really worked hard to make that record. It was a labor of love. I put a lot of love into that record."

G N' R Lies (1988)

Guns N' Roses' follow-up to *Appetite for Destruction* was once again produced and engineered by Mike Clink and was recorded at Rumbo Studios in Canoga Park, California; Take One Studios in Burbank, California; and Image Studio in Hollywood, California. The album was mixed at the Record Plant. Four of the tracks on *G N' R Lies* had already appeared on the 1986 EP *Live?!*@ Like a Suicide*, and the other four songs were recorded using acoustic guitars. Therefore, the songs were recorded in just a few recording sessions.

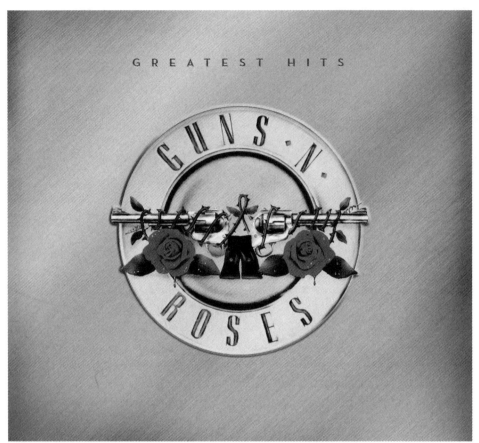

Released by Geffen Records in 2004 without input or authorization from any Guns N' Roses band members, the *Greatest Hits* album was criticized for featuring a plethora of cover versions, including the abysmal remake of the Rolling Stones' "Sympathy for the Devil." *Author's collection*

Use Your Illusion I and Use Your Illusion II (1991)

Both *Use Your Illusion I* and *Use Your Illusion II* were produced by Mike Clink and Guns N' Roses and were recorded at A&M Studios, Studio 56, and Image Studio in Hollywood, California; Conway Studios in Los Angeles, California; and Metalworks Recording Studios in Toronto, Canada. The album was mixed at Skip Saylor Recording in Los Angeles, California. A handful of the *Use Your Illusion* tracks—such as "Back Off Bitch," "Bad Obsession," "Don't Cry," "November Rain," and "The Garden"—had been initially recorded during sessions for *Appetite for Destruction* but were ultimately rejected for that album. Engineer Bob Clearmountain was fired after mixing twenty-one tracks and replaced with engineer Bill Price, who was known for his work with the Sex Pistols. Steven Adler, who was fired by the band in 1990, appears on just one track, "Civil War," from *Use Your Illusion II*, which also served as Izzy's last studio album with Guns N' Roses. (He departed the band in November 1991.)

"The Spaghetti Incident?" (1993)

Guns N' Roses' cover album *"The Spaghetti Incident?"* was produced by Mike Clink and Guns N' Roses and was recorded at A&M Studios, Conway Studios, and Oceanway Recording in Hollywood, California; the Record Plant in Los Angeles, California; Rumbo Studio in Canoga Park, California; CanAm Studios in Tarzana, California; Sound Techniques, Inc., in Boston, Massachusetts; and Triad Studios in Redmond, Washington. The album was mixed at Skip Saylor Recording in Los Angeles, California.

Many of the tracks for *"The Spaghetti Incident?"* had actually been recorded during the *Use Your Illusion* sessions with Izzy Stradlin, whose guitar tracks were re-recorded by his replacement, Gilby Clarke. At least two songs were recorded that did not make it to the album: "A Beer and a Cigarette" (Hanoi Rocks) and an instrumental version of "Down on the Street" by Iggy and the Stooges. (A cover of the Stooges' "Raw Power" does appear on the album.) *"The Spaghetti Incident?"* was the last Guns N' Roses studio album to feature Slash, Duff, Matt Sorum, and Clarke.

Chinese Democracy (2008)

The long-delayed (and much-ridiculed) album *Chinese Democracy*, which cost a staggering $14 million to record, was produced by Axl Rose and Caram Costanzo and was recorded over a period of ten years (1997–2007) at the Village, Rumbo Studio, CanAm Studios, Woodland Ranch, IGA, Cherokee, Capitol, and Sunset Sound in Los Angeles; Battery, Soundtrack, Electric Lady, and Bennett House in New York City; the Palms in Las Vegas; and the Townhouse in London. In a 2000 *Rolling Stone* interview, Axl stated that one of the reasons for the delay was that he was "educating himself about the technology that's come to define rock . . . It's like from scratch, learning how to work with something, and not wanting it just to be something you did on a computer."

Producers who worked briefly on the album at some time during its long gestation include Mike Clink, electronic music pioneer Moby, Youth (founding member of British rock band Killing Joke), Tim Palmer (who mixed Pearl Jam's 1991 debut album *Ten*), and Andy Wallace, who served as engineer on the Aerosmith/Run-D.M.C. collaboration "Walk This Way" with producer Rick Rubin, among others. The final credited producers listed on the album are Axl and Caram Costanzo, who had worked on Pearl Jam's 1994 album *Vitalogy*.

In addition, Brian May of Queen recorded the lead guitar parts for "Catcher in the Rye," but his contributions were removed when the album was finally released. In a 2006 Rhinocast interview, GN'R bassist Tommy Stinson remarked, "We did most of the music as a total collaborative effort a while back, most of the music was recorded [in 2001] . . . [The album's] been pretty much done. It's been through a couple of producers' hands." In a 2015 *Alternative Nation* interview, GN'R guitarist Richard Fortus claimed that Axl recorded all of his vocal parts in less than a week. On a truly bizarre note, eccentric guitarist Buckethead insisted upon the installation of a chicken coop in the recording studio in order to help him get into "his own world" and perform better.

17

Burned-Out Paradise

Tales of Debauchery on the Road

It seems to me that we're a spectacle, a freak show. —Axl Rose

When Guns N' Roses first started playing West Hollywood clubs in 1985, Axl would announce one of their raunchiest songs, "Anything Goes," as the band's "theme song." Whether it involved booze, drugs, sex, or getting into brawls, GN'R was all about excess, which they wrote about in their songs and lived out on the gritty streets of Los Angeles. However, years of self-destructiveness took their toll, and indeed some of the band members are lucky to have survived. (Unfortunately this was not true of some of their friends who tragically died of drug overdoses, including Todd Crew of Jetboy and West Arkeen, who cowrote "It's So Easy" and several other songs for the band.) Duff summed it up concisely in his 2015 memoir, *How to Be a Man: (and other illusions)*, when he stated, "There's nothing elegant about being wasted. There isn't nobility in dying before you get old."

Booze

In the early 1980s, young, hungry bands like Guns N' Roses wandered Sunset Boulevard, getting totally wasted and causing a shitload of trouble. In fact, one of GN'R's best-loved songs, "Nightrain," had its origins in the band members stumbling down the street, swigging from a cheap bottle of Night Train Express, an unusually potent fortified wine that cost just $1 plus tax. In 1984, Razzle from Hanoi Rocks (one of GN'R's favorite bands) died in a car crash during a beer run with a severely inebriated Vince Neil of Mötley Crüe at the wheel. Neil walked away from the accident without a scratch. Hanoi Rocks was never the same after Razzle's tragic death.

In 1987, Steven Adler was eighty-sixed from a bar after he downed approximately twenty kamikaze shots one night and punched the front door

A true rock 'n' roll survivor, Duff McKagan nearly died of acute alcohol-
induced pancreatitis in 1994. After sobering up, he embarked on a strict
exercise regimen centered around mountain biking and martial arts.
Glenn Francis/Wikimedia Commons

of the bar so hard that he broke a finger. Drummer Fred Coury of Cinderella
had to replace Adler on drums for several Guns N' Roses shows. Adler
himself once witnessed El Duce (Eldon Hoke, of the scum-rock band the
Mentors) down an entire bottle of Jack Daniel's, with Adler claiming that
El Duce was "chugging it like it was spring water." (The controversial rocker

was apparently also inebriated when he was struck and killed by a train in 1997.)

At the 1990 American Music Awards, Slash and Duff, both extremely inebriated, caused a major controversy when they spewed profanities, including a couple of F-bombs, during two acceptance speeches that were broadcast live on ABC. In the VH1 *Behind the Music* special on Guns N' Roses, Slash remarked, "Me and Duff were drinking at least a half gallon of vodka or Jack Daniel's a day just trying to sort of keep ourselves on an even keel." During Guns N' Roses concerts, Axl would even introduce Duff as "Duff 'King of Beers' McKagan" because of his prodigious alcohol consumption. Duff soon switched from beer to vodka and then to wine (for health reasons!) and was soon drinking ten bottles of wine a day. Believe it or not, at the height of his alcohol addiction, Duff actually drank his own vomit because it had alcohol in it.

In 1994, Duff suffered a life-threatening bout of acute alcohol-induced pancreatitis at the age of thirty, sobered up, and started a strict workout regimen that involved mountain biking and martial arts/kickboxing. In 2001, at the age of thirty-five, Slash had a defibrillator installed in his heart and was told he had six days to six weeks to live from fifteen years of "overdrinking and drug abuse."

Drugs

Drugs were a major part of the early West Hollywood scene, and Guns N' Roses partied with all the other up-and-coming rock bands, such as Jetboy, Faster Pussycat, and the Wild. The alley located behind the band's rehearsal space on Gardner Street was the site of "the biggest party in L.A." every weekend, according to Axl, and the use (and sale) of heroin was rampant here. In the VH1 *Behind the Music* special on Guns N' Roses, Barbi Von Greif, the inspiration for the song "Rocket Queen," remarked, "Quite often it was a 24-hour-a-day party. Tupperwares full of cocaine . . . Everybody was completely strung out and using Ecstasy." At an early gig at Raji's in 1986, Slash got so smacked out on heroin that he ended up blowing chunks "over the back of [his] amps every five minutes."

In August 1987, Jetboy bassist Todd Crew died of a drug overdose at the age of twenty-two in Slash's room at the Milford Plaza Hotel in New York City. He had been partying with Slash and porn star Lois Ayres. In 1987, Nikki Sixx OD'd in Slash's hotel room at the Franklin Plaza while GN'R was supporting the Mötley Crüe tour. Slash and Steven Adler helped revive Sixx,

Rick Nielsen of Cheap Trick once invited Guns N' Roses over to his house where he challenged Slash to a tequila-drinking contest, got belligerent, and ended up getting into an altercation with Slash, who kicked him in the balls. Nielsen later denied the story.

Kgisborne/Wikimedia Commons

and they called paramedics. He was declared clinically dead for two minutes before being revived by adrenaline. The experience inspired Mötley Crüe's hit song "Kickstart My Heart."

In 1989, after experiencing drug-induced hallucinations, Slash jumped through a glass door and ran naked and bleeding through an Arizona golf resort. Heroin took a big toll on Guns N' Roses, which led to Axl's infamous "Mr. Brownstone" rant in 1989 as the band opened for the Rolling Stones at the L.A. Coliseum: "Unless certain people in this band get their shit together, these will be the last Guns N' Roses shows you'll fucking ever see. Cause I'm tired of too many people dancing with Mr. Goddamn Brownstone."

In fact, Steven Adler was somewhat improbably fired from the band for his severe drug abuse in 1990. (He spent the next two decades in and out of rehab facilities and even appeared on *Celebrity Rehab with Dr. Drew* twice.) During their maiden journey in a 727 leased from MGM Las Vegas for the *Use Your Illusion* Tour in 1991, Slash and Duff "christened" the plane by "smoking crack together" before "the wheels had left the ground." In 1994, Steven Adler returned to rehab, where he was roommates with Layne Staley of grunge/heavy metal hybrid Alice in Chains. Tragically, Staley died of a cocaine and heroin overdose in 2002.

Groupies

During the early days in West Hollywood, GN'R band members hung out with dancers from West Hollywood-area strip clubs, especially the Seventh Veil. Several of the strippers would even dance onstage at early GN'R gigs. Seventh Veil stripper Adriana Smith was immortalized in the song "Rocket Queen" after she agreed to have sex with Axl during a recording session that ended up on the track. The raunchy lyrics of "It's So Easy" serve as an ode to the early groupies that assisted the band in every way possible before they became famous.

Another popular band hangout was a Mexican restaurant called El Compadre, located at Sunset and Gardner, where, according to Slash in his autobiography, "we'd bring chicks . . . and they'd suck us off or fuck us under the table." Steven Adler, in his autobiography, revealed that he, Slash, and Duff held "contests to see who could get the most blowjobs in a single day." Adler claimed that he "won every time." Slash claimed that some of the most embarrassing things he ever did in public, such as passing out "naked in a booth with some chick," took place at the Cathouse, and that he "fucked so many girls on the floor while people were walking over us."

According to Adler in his autobiography, *My Appetite for Destruction*, during the Aerosmith tour, he and Steven Tyler brought about ten groupies back to the tour bus, where Tyler proceeded to assume the role of director, according to Adler, telling the girls, "Now you three, suck his dick. You, sit on his face while he eats your pussy. You two, make out." In his autobiography, Adler boasted: "I fucked them all, fat chicks, skinny chicks, plain chicks, shy chicks—it didn't matter. I was just showing them my appreciation." While touring Europe, Slash admitted spending most of the time between gigs "in and out of a variety of VD clinics."

Fights and Arrests

An unpredictable lead singer combined with raucous, inebriated crowds sometimes turned early Guns N' Roses gigs into total debacles. For instance, during a 1986 gig at Raji's, a total dive in West Hollywood, Axl hit a belligerent female fan over the head with his mic stand and called her a "stupid bitch." After the set, Axl got into a fight with her boyfriend Bob Forrest, lead singer of the band Thelonious Monster. (Forrest would, years later, show up older and wiser as a drug counselor on *Celebrity Rehab with Dr. Drew*.) In 1987, Axl was arrested during a concert opening for Mötley Crüe at the Omni Coliseum in Atlanta, Georgia, after he assaulted a security guard. Less than a month later, Axl started a brawl in a Chicago hotel lobby after being called a Bon Jovi lookalike. The following night, as GN'R opened for Alice Cooper, Axl exclaimed, "Bon Jovi can suck my dick." At the 1989 MTV Video Music Awards, Izzy was sucker punched by Vince Neil backstage for an earlier incident allegedly involving Izzy assaulting Neil's then wife Sharise. Axl stepped into the fray, and the two lead singers exchanged empty threats via the media for several years thereafter.

Axl was arrested in 1990 after one of his West Hollywood condo neighbors, Gabriella Kantor, claimed he hit her over the head with a wine bottle. The charges were ultimately dismissed, but the ordeal inspired the song "Right Next Door to Hell." In a 1990 interview with *Musician* magazine, Axl remarked that "people are always trying to provoke some kind of fight so they can sue me. I'm scared of thrashing an asshole and going to jail for it. For some reason I can walk into a room and someone will pick a fight."

On August 27, 1989, Izzy Stradlin was arrested during a flight from Los Angeles to Indianapolis, Indiana, for urinating in the airplane's galley.

Guns N' Roses' anarchic behavior onstage and off echoed that of the Sex Pistols, who sparked the punk revolution in the mid-1970s.

Riksarkivet (National Archives of Norway)/Wikimedia Commons

According to Stradlin in a 1989 *Rolling Stone* interview, "I was drunk in the middle of a bunch of senior citizen types. I was smoking, and the stewardess came over. I told her to go fuck herself . . . I was drinking so much I had to take a piss. The people in the bathroom . . . man, it seemed like I waited an hour. So I pissed in the trash can instead." During the so-called "Riverport Riot" in 1991, Axl leaped off the stage to stop a fan from filming the concert and then decided the band was going to call it quits for the night. The ensuing riot resulted in approximately sixty fans getting injured and damages exceeding $200,000. Axl was arrested a year later and charged with four counts of misdemeanor assault and one count of property damage stemming from the riot. He was given two years' probation and forced to donate $50,000 to charity.

In 1998, a then reclusive Axl received some unwanted publicity when he was arrested for allegedly threatening an airport security guard, claiming, "I'll punch your lights out right here and now." In one of the most bizarre fights in the annals of Guns N' Roses lore, Axl also got into a scuffle with none other than fashion designer Tommy Hilfiger at a Manhattan nightclub in 2006.

18

History Bears the Scars

Biggest Feuds

A lot of people hold their anger back for a few days. I just explode right away.
—Axl Rose

When Axl and Slash, along with Duff, agreed to embark on the Guns N' Roses Not in This Lifetime Tour during the summer of 2016, they finally buried the hatchet from a contentious feud that has been dramatically played out in the media over the past twenty years. Although Axl vs. Slash easily ranks as the most notorious rift in the band's history (MTV even did a *Celebrity Deathmatch* episode featuring a claymation battle between Axl and Slash; for the record Axl was cut into paper dolls by Slash), many other musicians and celebrities—such as Poison, Bon Jovi, Metallica, Vince Neil of Mötley Crüe, Nirvana, the Offspring, and Eagles of Death Metal—have faced the Gunners' wrath over the years

Let's not forget the rock journalists who were the target of the venomous *Use Your Illusion II* track "Get in the Ring"—Mick Wall of *Kerrang!*, Andy Secher of *Hit Parader*, and Bob Guccione Jr. of *SPIN*—as well as various fans and celebrities alike. One feud that bears mentioning actually spawned not only a GN'R song but also inspired an "Evict Axl" MTV contest. On October 30, 1990, Axl's insane battle with his West Hollywood condo neighbor, Gabriella Kantor, escalated out of control, leading to his arrest (she claimed he hit her with a wine bottle), a lawsuit, and the track "Right Next Door to Hell" off *Use Your Illusion I*.

Indeed, with an anarchic band teetering on the edge of self-destruction every time they took the stage and led by a completely unpredictable lead singer who might fly off the handle at any moment over the slightest

While engaged in a notorious feud with Axl Rose that lasted over twenty years, Slash continued to tour and produce albums such as *World on Fire* (2014), which featured Myles Kennedy and the Conspirators.   *Author's collection*

provocation, conditions were absolutely ripe for a volatile mixture of uncontrolled rage and antagonism. However, according to Slash in the 2004 VH1 *Behind the Music* feature on Guns N' Roses, "As volatile as he is, all the things you might find complicated or difficult about Axl is [sic] what fuels him to be such an amazing performer, such an amazing songwriter." Below are just a few of the most explosive and legendary GN'R feuds (some of which are apparently still ongoing!).

Guns N' Roses vs. Poison

No love was lost between Guns N' Roses and Poison as each band success-fully clawed their way to success in West Hollywood during the mid-1980s. Perhaps best known for their power ballad "Every Rose Has Its Thorn," Poison hailed from the unlikeliest of places, Mechanicsburg, Pennsylvania, and hit the mean streets of Los Angeles in 1983 determined to make their mark on the burgeoning hair metal scene. Both bands were managed by Vicky Hamilton in the early days and battled for many of the same gigs. At a September 20, 1985, show at the Troubadour, Axl sarcastically dedicated the song "Nice Boys Don't Play Rock 'n' Roll" to Poison. In an April 4, 1987, interview with *Sounds* magazine, Axl remarked that "Poison fucked it up for all of us . . . They said that everyone in L.A. was following their trend."

Poison front man Bret Michaels admitted that he penned the band's hit ballad "Every Rose Has Its Thorn" after falling into despair when his strip-per girlfriend cheated on him. The accompanying music video opens with Michaels in bed with a stripper, which is followed by some truly overwrought concert footage interspersed with images of the band partying on the road. "Every Rose Has Its Thorn" reached No. 1 on the US charts and, for a while, was the most popular of the heavy metal ballads released in the late 1980s. Get those lighters out!

Ironically, Slash had actually auditioned for Poison in September 1984 after the band's original guitarist, Matt Smith, quit abruptly and returned to his native Pennsylvania. Slash later recalled that he "played the shit out of those songs," and the band called him back twice. However, he ended up not having a "glam" enough look for Poison and eventually lost out to the much more flamboyant C. C. DeVille, who had no problem slathering on excessive makeup and applying boatloads of hairspray for the cause. According to Marc Canter in *Reckless Road*, Slash "hated [Poison's] image and considered the music lame." In fact, GN'R's general disdain for Poison's image (as well as their music) was shared by many critics, one of whom labeled the band as "cock rock travesties." At one point, someone even gave Slash a "Poison Sucks" T-shirt, and he gave it to Axl to wear onstage at one of the concerts when GN'R opened for Aerosmith.

Michaels later discounted the existence of a feud between the bands in a September 21, 2011, interview with Triple M Sydney radio station, remarking that the feud was more of a media creation than anything else. Furthermore, Michaels claimed, "*Appetite for Destruction* is one of my Top 10 ever favorite records." At least one Guns N' Roses band member, Steven

Adler, in his autobiography, thought Poison was "a cool rock 'n' roll band that was doing exactly what I wanted to do." However, before the band hit the big time, they lived a rather squalid existence as described by Adler in *My Appetite for Destruction*: "The four guys in Poison shared a one-bedroom apartment. It was disgusting . . . The place was crawling with cockroaches. They had four queen-size mattresses set up in the bedroom, so the floor was like one big mattress. They had chicks there all the time."

Axl vs. Jon Bon Jovi

In August 1986, Bon Jovi released *Slippery When Wet*, and the massively successful album spent eight weeks at No. 1 on the US charts, spawning hit singles such as "You Give Love a Bad Name," "Livin' on a Prayer," and "Wanted Dead or Alive." Axl's animosity to lead singer Jon Bon Jovi was intensified when a fan confronted him in a Chicago hotel lobby in 1987 and reportedly told him he looked just like the New Jersey rock star. A brawl ensued, and the next night, when Guns N' Roses opened for Alice Cooper during his *Raise Your Fist and Yell* Tour at the UIC Pavilion, Axl announced to the crowd that "Bon Jovi can suck my dick."

The feud continued for years thereafter. For instance, according to a 2006 *Los Angeles Times* article, "Bon Jovi criticized the amount of media attention Rose still received because he 'hadn't made a record in 13 years,' calling him a 'freak show' and 'recluse.'" However, Axl, Bon Jovi, and Sebastian Bach of Skid Row reportedly resolved their differences in 2012 over fifteen bottles of wine in a London eatery.

Izzy and Axl vs. Vince Neil of Mötley Crüe

At the 1989 MTV Video Music Awards, which took place at the Universal Amphitheatre in Universal City, California, on September 6, 1989, Mötley Crüe front man Vince Neil punched Izzy in the face as the GN'R rhythm guitarist was exiting the stage after performing "Free Fallin'" and "Hearbreak Hotel" along with Axl and Tom Petty and the Heartbreakers. Neil reportedly was reacting to an earlier incident when Izzy allegedly assaulted his then wife Sharise (a former mud wrestler) at the Cathouse while Neil was away on a white-water rafting trip in Idaho with some of his buddies. According to Neil in *The Dirt*, "When Izzy walked offstage, looking like a cross between Eric Stoltz in *Mask* and Neil Young, I was waiting for him . . . 'You fucking hit my wife!' 'So fucking what?' he spat. All my blood

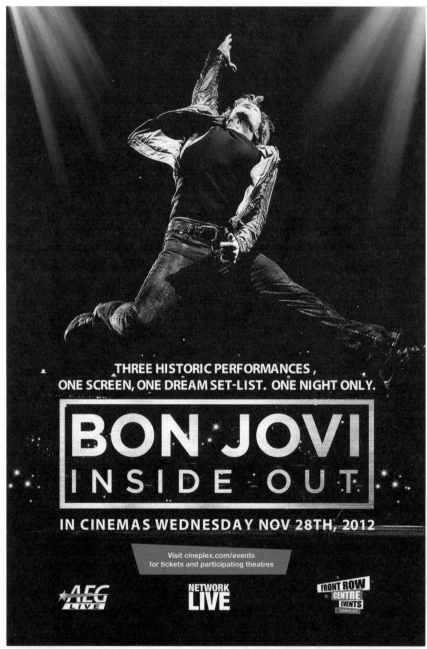

THREE HISTORIC PERFORMANCES ,
ONE SCREEN, ONE DREAM SET-LIST. ONE NIGHT ONLY.

BON JOVI
INSIDE OUT

IN CINEMAS WEDNESDAY NOV 28TH, 2012

Visit cineplex.com/events
for tickets and participating theatres

After getting confronted by a fan who told him he looked like singer Jon Bon Jovi, Axl Rose took the stage at the UIC Pavilion in Chicago in 1987 and shouted, "Bon Jovi can suck my dick."   *Author's collection* rushed into my fist, and I decked him. I decked him good, right in the face. He fell to the ground like a tipped cow."

When Axl (dressed like an "overdressed Doberman," according to the Mötley Crüe lead singer) heard about the incident, he reportedly chased down Neil and his posse as they exited the venue and yelled, "Come on, motherfucker, I'm going to fucking kill you!" Axl quickly went to the media and claimed that Neil had sucker punched Izzy. In the meantime, Izzy had already called Neil to apologize for the Sharise incident. Neil, who boasted of having a red belt in the Korean martial art Tang Soo Do, took to the MTV airwaves and challenged Axl to a public fight. Axl, in turn, responded to Neil in an interview, "Vince, whichever way you want it, man: Guns, knives, or fists, whatever you want to do. I don't care." The fight never took place. The incident with Neil reportedly inspired the GN'R song "Shotgun Blues" from the album *Use Your Illusion II* and its antagonistic lyrics, such as: "An now you're blowin' smoke/I think you're one big joke."

Years later, the animosity between the two rock front men remained strong. After the release of Guns N' Roses' long-delayed album *Chinese Democracy* in 2008, Neil managed to get his digs in, telling *The Sun*, "To fail was pretty crazy after so many years of it being recorded. I heard one track [and] then it just disappeared off the radio. Then the tour got cancelled— a buddy of mine went to play guitar for him. They rehearsed for three months, and Axl never once turned up."

Guns N' Roses vs. Bob Guccione Jr. of *SPIN*

On the outrageously belligerent track "Get in the Ring" off the album *Use Your Illusion II*, Guns N' Roses took the opportunity to lash out at members of the rock 'n' roll media who they felt had somehow wronged the band, such as Mick Wall of *Kerrang!*, Andy Secher of *Hit Parader*, and especially Bob Guccione Jr., publisher of *SPIN* magazine and the son of the *Penthouse* magazine magnate. Interestingly, "Get in the Ring" evolved from a simple song by Duff called "Why Do You Look at Me When You Hate Me?"

"Get in the Ring" features the inflammatory lyrics, "Bob Guccione Jr. at *SPIN*, what, are you pissed off cause your dad gets more pussy than you?" Guccione Jr., who reportedly had nine years of martial arts training, accepted Axl's challenge to "get in the ring," but the fight never took place. In an April 19, 2010, *SPIN* profile, Guccione Jr. wrote that Axl's anger to him and the magazine in general stemmed from an incident after Guns N' Roses "circulated a contract for journalists giving the band ownership and control

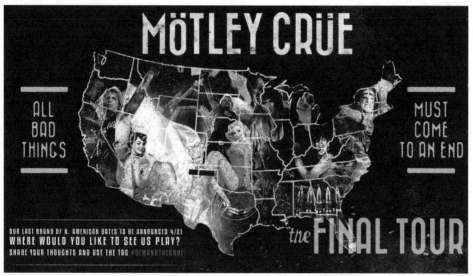

In November 1987, Guns N' Roses supported Mötley Crüe during the *Girls, Girls, Girls* Tour. Axl Rose and Crüe front man Vince Neil would later engage in a lengthy feud that began after Neil punched Izzy Stradlin in the face during the 1989 MTV Video Music Awards.   *Author's collection*

of any interview." Guccione Jr. decided to publish the contract in the magazine and invite readers to submit it to GN'R "if they wanted to get an interview themselves." The band quickly got deluged with thousands of these contracts.

Founded in 1985, *SPIN* ceased publishing its print edition in 2012 and currently operates only as a webzine. On February 19, 2016, *SPIN* published "Every Guns N' Roses Song, Ranked," listing their top ten GN'R songs in descending order as: "You Could Be Mine," "Mr. Brownstone," "The Garden," "Patience," "Better," "Sweet Child O' Mine," "Locomotive," "Nightrain," "November Rain," and "Welcome to the Jungle." Their least favorite Guns N' Roses song? The "sluggish" cover of the Rolling Stones' "Sympathy for the Devil" that appeared on the soundtrack of the 1994 film *Interview with the Vampire*.

Axl Rose vs. Actor Warren Beatty

During a live pay-per-view Guns N' Roses concert at the Paris Hippodrome on June 6, 1992, as part of the *Use Your Illusion* Tour, Axl took the opportunity to dedicate "Double Talkin' Jive" to actor Warren Beatty (*Bonnie and Clyde*) and then launched into a totally bizarre but highly entertaining attack on the aging lothario. It turns out that Beatty had briefly dated Axl's then flame, supermodel Stephanie Seymour, before marrying actress Annette Bening (*American Beauty*). However, Axl was reportedly convinced that Beatty and Seymour were still an item.

During Axl's extensive rant, he repeatedly slammed Beatty, calling him "a man who likes to play games, a parasite, an old man who likes to live his life vicariously through young people and suck up all their life because he has none of his own, a cheap punk." As he roamed the stage in a frenzy, Axl continued bashing Beatty mercilessly, "Well listen home fuck . . . if you think Madonna kicked your ass, I'm betting on Annette, you stupid fuckin' asshole." Needless to say, every fan who shelled out the big bucks for the pay-per-view spectacle certainly got their money's worth. Beatty never publicly responded to Rose's spirited harangue. As for Beatty and Bening's relationship, they have been the very picture of stability since getting married in 1992 and have four children.

Guns N' Roses vs. Kurt Cobain (and Courtney Love) of Nirvana

At the 1992 MTV Video Music Awards on September 9, 1992, Axl got into a heated verbal altercation backstage with Kurt Cobain and Courtney Love, who had wandered out of their trailer and spotted the GN'R lead singer walking with his then girlfriend, Stephanie Seymour. Love reportedly asked Axl sarcastically if he would like to be the godfather of the couple's child, Frances Bean, and the singer yelled to Cobain, "Get your bitch to shut up or I'll take you to the pavement." Cobain turned to Love and nonchalantly remarked, "Shut up, bitch," provoking much laughter from the surrounding crowd. However, in *I Want My MTV*, former GN'R manager Doug Goldstein, a witness to the incident, commented that Love actually remarked, "It's Asshole Rose. It's Asshole Rose." According to Goldstein's account, Love was clearly the instigator in the bizarre incident.

Ironically, Axl had been an early fan of Nirvana (he can even be seen wearing a baseball cap with the band's logo on it in the "Don't Cry" music video) and had previously asked the band to open for Guns N' Roses. He even requested Cobain to perform at his thirtieth birthday celebration. Both offers were promptly declined (if not outright ignored). In a February 1993 interview with *The Advocate*, Cobain remarked, "I can't even waste my time on that band, because they're so obviously pathetic and untalented. They're really talentless people, and they write crap music, and they're the most popular band on the earth right now. I can't believe it."

In early April 1994, a depressed Cobain, who had been struggling with heroin addiction, committed suicide with a shotgun. His suicide note quoted from "My My, Hey Hey," a 1979 song by Neil Young: "It's better to burn out than fade away." Ironically, Duff was one of the last people to see Cobain alive. In his 2011 autobiography, *It's So Easy: and Other Lies*, Duff recalled sitting next to Cobain on a flight from Los Angeles to Seattle on March 31, 1994. Cobain had just skipped out of rehab, and the two "fucked up" rockers talked during the whole flight, "but we didn't delve into certain things: I was in my hell and he was in his, and we both seemed to understand."

As for Love, time apparently heals old wounds, and in 2016 she took to Facebook and commented that Axl has "gotten pretty nice" and went on to say: "We're all in it together! He was under huge pressure and being picked on by millions, myself included . . . He's very sweet these days. I think he was totally misunderstood by us Grungers, although the chicks thing was pretty blatant . . . All of it has been reconciled for years . . . We are all of us in the gutter, some of us [are] just looking at the stars." In April 2016, Axl even borrowed former Nirvana drummer Dave Grohl's "throne" for GN'R's 2016 Las Vegas reunion shows after he broke a bone in his foot onstage during the Troubadour warm-up gig.

The whole Axl vs. Kurt Cobain feud pointed to a shift in the music industry from the hard rock of Guns N' Roses that dominated the late 1980s to the grunge movement out of Seattle that took over in the early 1990s. Nothing better exemplified grunge than Nirvana's "Smells Like Teen Spirit" music video. A blindsiding attack on the senses, the "Teen Spirit" video takes place in a high school gym, an anarchic pep rally that evolves into an intense and disturbing inferno. The impact of the video spread through the music industry like a wildfire, bulldozing the remnants of the glam/hair metal band era, and nothing would be the same again.

Axl vs. James Hetfield of Metallica

The bitter feud between Axl and James Hetfield can be traced to the ill-fated Guns N' Roses/Metallica Stadium Tour, specifically the infamous August 9, 1992, Montreal concert at Olympic Stadium when the Metallica front man suffered second- and third-degree burns from malfunctioning pyrotechnics during a performance of "Fade to Black." After a long delay of approximately three hours, Guns N' Roses finally started their set, but Axl soon stormed off the stage, later claiming that his throat hurt and he was unable to continue singing. A riot ensued among pissed-off fans, and it spilled onto the streets of Montreal and caused extensive damage.

Footage from the concert debacle can be viewed in the 1992 documentary *A Year and a Half in the Life of Metallica, Part 2*, which also contains a scene where Hetfield relentlessly mocks Axl's personal rider requirements: "Horrible truths. The piddly wants and needs of certain folks on the road. Axl 'Pose' dressing room requirements . . . One cup of 'cubed' ham, it's got to be cubed so it can get down his little neck . . . one rib eye steak dinner . . . I didn't know the guy ate meat, looks like a fucking vegetarian . . . pepperoni pizza, fresh—I think that's just for throwing around. One can of assorted Pringles chips, that's the greasy shit so he can grease his hair back . . . it's just fucking crap."

Axl quickly retaliated by calling Hetfield a racist for supposedly firing Body Count—the controversial heavy metal band founded by rapper Ice-T— as opening act off the Guns N' Roses/Metallica Tour. In an April 15, 1993, *Rolling Stone* interview, Hetfield stated, "They're a different type of band— and I use the word *band* loosely. We were out to show people that there was something a little more progressive and hardcore than Guns N' Roses. And to go about it our way. But it was hard going on, dealing with Axl and his attitude. It's not something we'd want to do again."

Guns N' Roses vs. the Offspring

In 2003, the Southern California skate punks threatened to call their seventh album *Chinese Democracy (You Snooze, You Lose)* in an elaborate April Fool's Day joke to make fun of the long-delayed album by Guns N' Roses. Axl immediately filed a cease and desist order against the band, which opted to name its next album *Splinter* instead. Offspring lead singer Dexter Holland later remarked on the band's official website, "It was so damn funny. We felt like we had to do it. The idea of stealing the title of an album someone else has been working on for so long was very funny to us. You snooze, you lose. Axl ripped off my braids, so I ripped off his album title."

Axl vs. Fashion Designer Tommy Hilfiger

Believe it or not, Axl and fashion designer Tommy Hilfiger were involved in a brawl at the Plumm, a newly opened (and now defunct) Manhattan nightclub in 2006. Axl later remarked during an interview with Los Angeles radio station KROQ that he had merely moved Hilfiger's girlfriend's drink so it wouldn't spill. According to Axl, "It was the most surreal thing, I think, that's ever happened to me in my life . . . He just kept smacking me." The girlfriend in question was model Dee Ocleppo, who ended up marrying Hilfiger in 2008. Axl was at the Plumm to give a surprise performance for actress Rosario Dawson on the occasion of her twenty-seventh birthday party. During his set, Axl dedicated "You're Crazy" to "my good friend Tommy Hilfiger." Several years later, Hilfiger sat down with Richard Bradley, editor-in-chief of *Worth Magazine*, and gave his version of events: "Axl pushed me [out of the way], and I said 'That was rude.' [He turned around and] had a huge ring on. He wears all this jewelry. [I'm thinking], if I get hit, it's over. No teeth, no eye. So I hit him before he hit me. It was self-protection. Now we're friends."

Axl vs. Eagles of Death Metal

During the 2006 Guns N' Roses *Chinese Democracy* Tour, Axl dropped opening band Eagles of Death Metal after the first night (a November 24, 2006, show at Quicken Loans Arena in Cleveland, Ohio), calling them out onstage in front of the crowd as the "Pigeons of Shit Metal." Axl's negative reaction caused then GN'R bassist Tommy Stinson, who had recommended the band, to throw his bass guitar to the floor in disgust and exclaim, "Fuck you, that's it." He even threatened to quit the band. On December 2, 2006, Stinson released the following public statement: "Eagles of Death Metal were a suggestion of mine a while ago. Turns out they were the wrong band for our crowd. They were booed and did not play for as long as they were scheduled to . . . In the past I have thrown my bass. I have never thrown it at Axl or anyone else in the band nor has anyone thrown my bass back at me . . . yet. Axl has been a dear friend to me for nine years. We have no problem communicating and wish that people would stay the fuck out of shit they don't know anything about."

Despite their evocative name, Eagles of Death Metal is not a death metal band at all. In a 2003 interview, drummer Josh Homme described the band as a combination of "bluegrass slide guitar mixed with stripper drum beats and Canned Heat vocals." In a September 29, 2015, *BraveWords* interview, Eagles of Death Metal front man Jesse Hughes revealed that he has sent Axl "a very sincere request" every Christmas since being fired from the tour "to come in the studio and record two Christmas songs, and be released as 'the Pigeons of Shit Metal.'" Hughes further explained, "And I always close it with a very judgmental, 'Because I want you to know Axl, I'm willing to forgive you, and I feel like the rest of the world is, too.'"

Tragically, on November 13, 2015, terrorists attacked the audience during a sold-out Eagles of Death Metal performance at Le Bataclan in Paris, killing eighty-nine people. The entire band managed to escape backstage. On November 18, 2015, Eagles of Death Metal issued a statement, thanking "the French police, the FBI, the US and French State Departments, and especially all those at ground zero with us who helped each other as best as they could during the unimaginable ordeal, proving once again that love overshadows evil."

19

Can't Find My Way Back

"The Spaghetti Incident?" (1993)

A great song can be found anywhere. Do yourself a favor and go find the originals.   —*"The Spaghetti Incident?"* liner notes

Guns N' Roses found a great way to pay tribute to some of their diverse musical influences (mostly culled from punk rock but with a few surprises added as well) when the band released *"The Spaghetti Incident?"*—a 1993 album of covers released by Geffen Records (and once again produced by Mike Clink) that served as the final album of the original *Appetite for Destruction* lineup (sans Steven Adler). According to Slash in a March 12, 1994, *Kerrang!* interview: "It was just us doing a bunch of songs that we sort of grew up on. Bands that were out then that you don't hear from anymore. Bands that were icons when I was getting into this stuff, that were hugely significant in the late '70s. It basically started out as simple warm-up jams for *Use Your Illusion*. There was no master plan to it." However, controversy reared its ugly head after it turned out that the album's "hidden track" was "Look at Your Game, Girl," a song written by none other than infamous cult leader/serial killer Charles Manson. In fact, "Look at Your Game, Girl," would be by far the band's most controversial song if it hadn't been overshadowed over the years by the racist and homophobic lyrics in "One in a Million" off of *G N' R Lies* (1988).

The album's strange title came from testimony during the Adler trial (he sued the band after getting fired in 1990 and was eventually awarded $2.5 million in an out-of-court settlement) after a lawyer asked Duff about "the spaghetti incident." (The lawyer was allegedly referring to a food fight between Adler and Axl, but it has also been suggested that it was a hidden reference to Adler's stash of drugs that was kept in the refrigerator near some takeout Italian food while the band resided briefly in Chicago in 1989.) The album cover itself is simply an image of a nasty looking batch of canned spaghetti. However, the strange code near the bottom of the cover is reportedly symbols from the Zodiac Killer that, when deciphered, reveal the message "fuck'em all." The album's inside jacket features images of each band member, except Axl, who is represented by a pair of personalized "Axl" sneakers. By the way, the end of the album's extensive liner notes irreverently exclaims, "And lastly, Guns N' Roses would finally like to thank the world . . . except for the assholes. If you don't know who you are, we do!"

"Since I Don't Have You"

A true anomaly on the album, "Since I Don't Have You" was first recorded in 1959 by the Skyliners, a doo-wop group from Pittsburgh. The song reached No. 12 on the US charts and was featured on the soundtrack of *American Graffiti* (1973). GN'R's extremely bizarre music video for the song boasted a demonic appearance by actor Gary Oldman (*Sid & Nancy*) and served as the last Guns N' Roses video to feature Slash, Duff, Matt Sorum, and Gilby Clarke. Somewhat improbably, "Since I Don't Have You" made an appearance on the 2004 *Greatest Hits* album. (None of the existing or former GN'R members had any input on track selection, which was determined by the record company.) Other artists to cover "Since I Don't Have You" over the years include the Four Seasons, Patti LaBelle, Art Garfunkel, Don McLean, Johnny Mathis, Ronnie Milsap, and others.

Writers: Joseph Rock, James Beaumont and the Skyliners. **Personnel:** Axl (vocals, keyboard), Slash (lead and rhythm guitars), Gilby Clarke (rhythm guitar), Duff (bass), Matt Sorum (drums), Dizzy Reed (piano).

"New Rose"

Guns N' Roses (with Duff on vocal duties) recorded a spirited cover of the punk classic "New Rose," which initially appeared on the 1976 album *Damned Damned Damned* by British punk rockers the Damned. Nick Lowe produced the seminal punk album. Written by guitarist Brian James, "New Rose" was the first single released by a British punk rock group. The single's B-side featured a sped-up version of the Beatles' "Help!" In a February 2013 *MOJO* interview, James commented, "Everyone thinks 'New Rose' is about a girl or a new relationship but it's not. It was about the emerging scene, this lovely buzz that you'd never dreamed could possibly happen. It was like, 'I'd got my own Swinging '60s,' that sorta vibe." The group was the subject of a fascinating 2015 documentary *The Damned: Don't You Wish That We Were Dead.*

Writer: Brian James. **Personnel:** Duff (vocals, bass); Slash (lead and rhythm guitars); Gilby Clarke (rhythm guitar); Matt Sorum (drums).

"Down on the Farm"

British punk band the UK Subs (originally known as the Subversives), originally recorded "Down on the Farm" for their 1982 album, *Endangered Species.* The group, which celebrated its fortieth anniversary in 2016 and still performs 150 to 200 concerts a year, is led by the indefatigable Charlie Harper, the "Godfather of UK Punk." Guns N' Roses performed "Down on the Farm" at Farm Aid IV at the Hoosier Dome in Indianapolis, Indiana, on April 7, 1990, which served as Steven Adler's last live performance with the band before he was fired several months later.

Writers: Charlie Harper, Alvin Gibbs, Nicholas Garrett. **Personnel:** Axl (vocals), Slash (lead and rhythm guitars), Gilby Clarke (rhythm guitar), Duff (bass), Matt Sorum (drums).

"Human Being"

Proto-punk band the New York Dolls were longtime favorites of Guns N' Roses, so the inclusion of "Human Being" served as a tribute to their self-destructive forebears from the early 1970s. Written by David Johansen and Johnny Thunders, the song first appeared on the Dolls' second studio album, *Too Much Too Soon* (1974). In a 1995 interview with *Q* magazine, Dolls' bassist Arthur Kane remarked, "I make more money from Guns N' Roses' version of 'Human Being' than I do from the New York Dolls . . . It's criminal." In addition to vocals, Axl is credited on the kazoo.

Writers: Johnny Thunders, David Johansen. **Personnel:** Axl (vocals, kazoo, Slash (lead and rhythm guitars), Gilby Clarke (rhythm guitar), Duff (bass), Matt Sorum (drums); Dizzy Reed (keyboards).

"Raw Power"

"Raw Power is a boilin' soul/Got a son called rock 'n' roll." Guns N' Roses were big fans of the Stooges, and on this cover Duff shares vocal duties with Axl. The title track of the Stooges' highly influential 1973 album, "Raw Power" featured Iggy Pop on vocals, James Williamson on guitar, Ron Asheton on bass, and Scott Asheton on drums. Interestingly, GN'R nemesis Kurt Cobain of Nirvana wrote in his *Journals* that *Raw Power* was his favorite album of all time. In a May 10, 1973 review of *Raw Power*, Lenny Kaye of *Rolling Stone* exclaimed, "The Ig. Nobody does it better, nobody does it worse, nobody does it, period. Others tiptoe around the edges, make little running starts

Guns N' Roses covered the Stooges' highly influential hit song "Raw Power" on their 1993 covers album, *"The Spaghetti Incident?"* Both Slash and Duff McKagan had performed on Iggy Pop's 1990 solo album, *Brick by Brick*.   *Eddy Berthier/Wikimedia Commons*

and half-hearted passes; but when you're talking about the O mind, the very central eye of the universe that opens up like a huge, gaping, suckling maw, step aside for the Stooges."

Iggy Pop (original name: James Newell Osterberg Jr.) has been acknowledged in some circles as the "Father of Punk Rock." Originally known as the Psychedelic Stooges (and named in honor of the Three Stooges—Moe, Curly, and Larry), the Stooges formed in Ann Arbor, Michigan, in 1967. The band released their self-titled debut album in 1969—which featured the classic track "I Wanna Be Your Dog"—and followed it up with *The Funhouse* in 1970. In the early 1970s, the Stooges' influence extended to such proto-punk and punk bands as the New York Dolls, Suicide, the Sex Pistols, the Damned, the Germs, and Black Flag. In 1990, Slash and Duff made guest appearances on Iggy's tenth studio album, *Brick by Brick*, which features a cool cover by cartoonist Charles Burns. The album has been credited with revitalizing Iggy's solo career.

Writers: Iggy Pop, James Williamson. **Personnel:** Axl (vocals), Duff (vocals), Slash (lead and rhythm guitars), Gilby Clarke (rhythm guitar), Duff (bass), Matt Sorum (drums), Dizzy Reed (keyboards).

"Ain't It Fun"

Guns N' Roses dedicated this Dead Boys cover "In Memory of Stiv Bators." Originally written by Cheetah Chrome (Eugene O'Connor) and Peter Laughner for the proto-punk band Rocket from the Tombs, "Ain't It Fun" first appeared on *We Have Come for Your Children*, a 1978 album by the Dead Boys, an influential punk rock band out of Cleveland, Ohio. Fronted by Stiv Bators (Steven John Bator), the Dead Boys were known for their violent, aggressive, and nihilistic stage shows (the band's motto: "Fuck art, let's rock!"). Original band members included Chrome, Jimmy Zero (William Wilden), Johnny Blitz (John Madansky), and Jeff Magnum (Jeff Halmagy). The Dead Boys played frequently at legendary New York City club CBGB. After Blitz was stabbed multiple times during a street fight, actor John Belushi (*Animal House*) actually filled in on drums during a Dead Boys show at CBGB in 1978. The band called it quits shortly after their second album, *We Have Come for Your Children*, was released. (The band's 1977 debut album, *Young, Loud and Snotty*, featured the punk classic "Sonic Reducer.")

According to *The Rough Guide to Rock*, "The Dead Boys will be remembered and revered for one great album, some demented live performances,

On the GN'R Dead Boys cover "Ain't It Fun"—which appeared on "*The Spaghetti Incident?*"—Hanoi Rocks front man Michael Monroe served as guest vocalist.

Tuomas Vitikainen/Wikimedia Commons

a host of brutal and insensitive imagery, and a unique front man. Modern thrash bands owe them a particular debt of gratitude, and their young, fresh aggression can still be seen as quintessentially punk rock." Bators went on to form the Lords of the New Church with Brian James of the Damned in 1982. He died in 1990 at the age of forty after getting hit by a taxi in Paris. According to legend, Bators' girlfriend snorted some of his ashes and scattered the rest over Jim Morrison's grave at Pere Lachaise Cemetery.

Michael Monroe, lead singer of Finnish rock band Hanoi Rocks, shared vocal duties with Axl on GN'R's Dead Boys cover. In addition, Mike Staggs of the Los Angeles rock band Dumpster played additional guitar on the track. "Ain't It Fun" also appears on Guns N' Roses' 2004 *Greatest Hits* album. In addition, Guns N' Roses liked to cover "Sonic Reducer" during live shows. A cover of "Ain't It Fun" by Henry Rollins appears on the 2001 Rollins Band compilation album, *A Nicer Shade of Red*.

Writers: Cheetah Chrome, Peter Laughner. **Personnel:** Axl (vocals), Michael Monroe (vocals), Slash (lead and rhythm guitars), Duff (bass), Matt Sorum (drums), Mike Staggs (additional guitar).

"Buick Makane (Big Dumb Sex)"

According to his own account, Gilby Clarke, the GN'R rhythm guitarist, used to wear a T. Rex T-shirt every single day until the rest of the band figured they had to include one of the English glam band's songs on the *"The Spaghetti Incident?"* album. "Buick Makane" (which was actually titled "Buick Mackane" in the original version) first appeared on T. Rex's 1972 album *The Slider*, which reached No. 4 on the UK charts and No. 17 on the US charts. Believe it or not, "Buick Mackane" included backup vocals by Slash, who later remarked, "I won't do it again if I can help it . . . I only did it that one time because Axl didn't want to sing it. Beyond that, I'm not the singing type."

The Guns N' Roses version of "Buick Makane" is part of a medley with Soundgarden's "Big Dumb Sex," which appeared on the 1989 album *Louder Than Love*. In a December 9, 1993 review of *"The Spaghetti Incident?"* for *Rolling Stone*, Jonathan Gold wrote, "When Chris Cornell sings, 'I want to fuck, fuck, fuck, fuck you,' in the Soundgarden anthem 'Big Dumb Sex,' Cornell's voice is filled with longing and desire; Axl, reprising that Soundgarden chorus . . . sounds like a guy reading cue cards on the set of a porno movie."

Writer ("Buick Makane"): Marc Bolan. **Writer ("Big Dumb Sex"):** Chris Cornell. **Personnel:** Axl (vocals); Slash (vocals, lead and rhythm guitars); Gilby Clarke (rhythm guitar); Duff (bass); Matt Sorum (drums).

"Hair of the Dog"

Well known for its repeated lyric—"Now you're messing with a son of a bitch"—"Hair of the Dog" appeared as the title track on Scottish rock band Nazareth's 1975 album. Axl grew up listening to Nazareth and remains to this day a huge fan of lead singer Dan McCafferty. In fact, he even tried unsuccessfully to get Nazareth to sing "Love Hurts" at his wedding to Erin Everly in 1990. Nazareth bassist Pete Agnew, in a *Metal Hammer* interview, revealed that "Just before Guns N' Roses broke . . . we played seven gigs in California and they came to every one. Nazareth and Aerosmith were to them what the Beatles and Stones were to us." On the GN'R version of "Hair of the Dog," listen for the refrain of the Beatles' "Day Tripper" as a gag at the end of the song. By the way, according to McCafferty, the song's title is a play on words—"heir of the dog" equals "son of a bitch."

GN'R's cover of "Hair of the Dog" was not the band's only Nazareth connection: Back in 1986, Nazareth lead guitarist Manny Charlton was brought in for an audition to see if he was the right person to produce *Appetite for Destruction*, but it didn't work out because of conflicting schedules. A good friend of Matt Sorum, drummer Mike "The Sack" Fasano, makes a guest appearance on percussion on the "Hair of the Dog" cover.

Writers: Dan McCafferty, Pete Agnew, Manuel Charlton, Darrell Sweet. **Personnel:** Axl (vocals), Slash (lead and rhythm guitars), Gilby Clarke (rhythm guitar), Duff (bass), Matt Sorum (drums, percussion), Dizzy Reed (keyboards), Mike Fasano (percussion).

"Attitude"

Duff assumed vocal duties on the track "Attitude," a song from the Misfits, a hardcore punk band out of New Jersey that was founded in 1977 by singer-songwriter Glenn Danzig, bassist Jerry Only, and drummer Manny Martinez. During a March 17, 1993, Guns N' Roses show at the Boston Garden, a drunken fan threw a glass bottle onto the stage after just three songs. The band retreated backstage for about ten minutes while fans chanted "Bullshit!" the whole time. As soon as GN'R returned to the stage, they immediately launched into "Attitude," with Slash exclaiming, "Not that this city needs any." In addition, "Attitude" made the setlist during Guns N' Roses' appearance at 2016 Coachella. Metallica also covered the Misfits—"Last Caress/Green Hell"—on the band's 1987 release, *The $5.98 E.P.: Garage Days Re-Revisited.*

Writer: Glenn Danzig. **Personnel:** Duff (vocals); Slash (lead and rhythm guitars, background vocals); Gilby Clarke (rhythm gui tar); Duff (bass); Matt Sorum (drums, background vocals).

"Black Leather"

Ex-Sex Pistols guitarist Steve Jones and drummer Paul Cook (along with ex-Lightning Raiders bassist Andy Allen) formed the Professionals in 1979. However, there has been some dispute as to whether "Black Leather" should be considered a Sex Pistols or Professionals song. The album's liner notes attribute the song to "Steve Jones/the Sex Pistols." According to one source, "Black Leather" was actually recorded after the Sex Pistols broke up but before the formation of the Professionals. The Runaways (which featured future stars Joan Jett and Lita Ford) also covered the song in the late 1970s. In 1996, Jones joined Duff, Matt Sorum, and John Taylor of Duran Duran to form the supergroup Neurotic Outsiders.

Writer: Steve Jones. **Personnel:** Axl (vocals); Slash (lead and rhythm guitars); Gilby Clarke (rhythm guitar); Duff (bass); Matt Sorum (drums).

"You Can't Put Your Arms Around a Memory"

Known as ex-New York Doll Johnny Thunders' signature song, "You Can't Put Your Arms Around a Memory" was either a song about heroin or French singer-songwriter, actress, and model Fabienne Shine. The title itself derived from a line that appeared in the "Better Living Through TV" episode of the 1950's sitcom *The Honeymooners*, which starred Jackie Gleason. Duff not only assumed vocal duties on the song but also played nearly all of the instruments, including acoustic guitar, bass, and drums. Richard Duguay of Canadian punk rock band Personality Crisis made a guest appearance on the track playing lead and rhythm guitars. In a March 12, 1994, *Kerrang!* interview, Slash revealed that he didn't even play on this

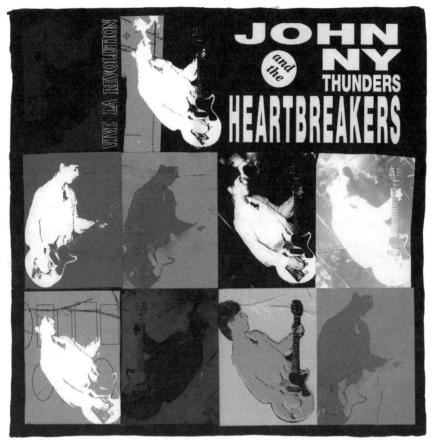

Guns N' Roses opened for punk legend Johnny Thunders, of New York Dolls and Heartbreakers fame, at Fender's Ballroom in Long Beach, California, in 1986. On their 1993 album "*The Spaghetti Incident?*" GN'R paid tribute to Thunders by covering "You Can't Put Your Arms Around a Memory." *Author's collection*

song because "I hated that little fucker!" He went on to explain, "So I really wasn't all that concerned when he died. We worked with him a coupla times, and I didn't like him at all. No disrespect for the deceased, but he's not one of my heroes, let's put it that way! I did like the Dolls . . . but I just wasn't very interested in Thunders."

Writer: Johnny Thunders. **Personnel:** Duff (vocals, acoustic guitar, bass, drums, background vocals); Richard Duguay (lead and rhythm guitars); Dizzy Reed (background vocals); Eddie Huletz (background vocals).

"I Don't Care About You"

Hardcore punk band Fear originally recorded "I Don't Care About You" on their debut album, *The Record*, in 1981. It's a classic punk anthem with a simple message: *"I don't care about you/Fuck you."* Formed in Los Angeles in 1977 by Lee Ving and Derf Scratch, Fear was prominently featured in the 1981 punk documentary *The Decline of Western Civilization*, and they became notorious after a live performance on the 1981 Halloween episode of *Saturday Night Live* upon the instigation of cast member John Belushi, a big fan of the band. In front of a slam-dancing crowd (that included Belushi and caused some major damage to the studio), Fear performed "I Don't Care About You," "Beef Bologna," "New York's Alright If You Like Saxophones," and part of "Let's Have a War," before NBC took an unscheduled, desperate commercial break to get the band off the air.

Fear's "Let's Have a War" was later included on the punk-inspired soundtrack of the 1984 cult film, *Repo Man*, which also featured "TV Party" by Black Flag, "Institutionalized" by Suicidal Tendencies, "Repo Man" by Iggy Pop, "Pablo Picasso" by Burning Sensations, "Bad Man" by Juicy Bananas, "Hombre Secreto (Secret Agent Man)" by the Plugz, and "When the Shit Hits the Fan" by Circle Jerks, among others. In an April 1, 2009, interview with the *Riverfront Times*, Ving remarked, "I have to say, I was really overjoyed when Guns N' Roses recorded a cover of 'I Don't Care About You.' That was . . . lucrative."

Writer: Lee Ving. **Personnel:** Axl (vocals); Slash (lead and rhythm guitars, background vocals); Gilby Clarke (rhythm guitarist); Duff (bass); Matt Sorum (drums); Riki Rachtman (background vocals); S. C. Bailey (background vocals); Blake Stanton (background vocals); Eric Mills (background vocals).

Hidden Track: "Look at Your Game, Girl"

Axl insisted on including this extremely controversial Charles Manson-penned song as the hidden track on the album. It featured Axl on vocals, Dizzy Reed on percussion, and session musician Carlos Booy on acoustic guitar. According to Slash in a March 12, 1994, *Kerrang!* interview, "We buried it on the album . . . We didn't want to draw attention to it . . . The dark humor behind the idea of someone as psychotic as him writing a love song . . . I mean, it's entertaining . . . He complained because we didn't ask his permission. So fuck him!" In a public statement defending the inclusion of "Look at Your Game, Girl" on the album, Axl stated, "The song talks about how the girl is insane and playing a mind game . . . I felt it was ironic that such a song was recorded by someone who should know the inner intricacies of madness." David Geffen addressed the controversy in a 1993 *Los Angeles Times* interview, remarking, "I would hope that if Axl Rose had realized how offensive people would find this, he would not have ever recorded this song in the first place. The fact that Charles Manson would be earning money based on the fame he derived committing one of the most horrific crimes of the twentieth century is unthinkable to me."

In the "Estranged" music video—as well as at a GN'R concert in Milton Keynes, England, in 1993—Axl actually appears to be wearing a Manson "Charlie Don't Surf" T-shirt. Manson's share of the royalties from "Look at Your Game, Girl" was paid to the family of one of his victims. "Look at Your Game, Girl" was originally recorded by Manson in 1967 and appeared on the 1970 album *Lie: The Love and Terror Cult*, which was released to help pay for his defense during the murder trial.

Writer: Charles Manson. **Personnel:** Axl (vocals); Dizzy Reed (percussion); Carlos Booy (acoustic guitar).

20

Nothin' Lasts Forever

Years of Turmoil in the 1990s and Beyond

It's sad, but the history of GN'R is so fraught with barbs and accusatory hand grenades that complete separation seemed to be the one and only answer for a while. —Duff McKagan

The exhausting, two-and-a-half-year *Use Your Illusion* Tour officially ended at River Plate Stadium in Buenos Aires, Argentina, on July 17, 1993. By this time, there were only three members of the original *Appetite for Destruction* lineup left: Axl, Slash, and Duff. Steven Adler had been fired from the band in 1990, and Izzy Stradlin left under his own volition the following year. The band continued to limp along for the next several years with little to no activity taking place. Holed up in his Malibu mansion, Axl became more and more reclusive, while Slash and Duff embarked on several high-profile side projects, including Slash's Snakepit and the Neurotic Outsiders supergroup that Duff organized with Matt Sorum, Steve Jones of the Sex Pistols, and John Taylor of Duran Duran.

After Slash departed in 1996, followed by Duff in 1997, Axl became the only original Guns N' Roses band member left. According to Slash in a 2000 *Kerrang!* interview, "When the 90s rolled around, Axl got really, really into the whole trip and became a more exaggerated version of someone I already knew." Over the next few years, Axl started an extremely slow process of recruiting new musicians, while writing and recording the songs that would eventually find their way into the long-delayed *Chinese Democracy* album (finally released in 2008). The media even started referring to Axl as "Rock's Greatest Recluse" and the "Howard Hughes of Rock" for his J. D. Salinger-like reclusiveness during the mid- to late 1990s. (Ironically, one of the tracks on *Chinese Democracy* would be named after Salinger's most famous novel, *Catcher in the Rye*.) Axl would only resurface periodically and usually unwillingly, such as in February 1998 when he was arrested for disorderly conduct at Phoenix Sky Harbor International Airport after an altercation with security personnel who asked to search his carry-on luggage. According to the police report, Axl exclaimed, "I'll punch your lights out right here and right now. I don't give a fuck who you are. You are all little people on a power trip." He spent a few hours in jail and later paid a $500 fine after pleading no contest to a misdemeanor charge of disturbing the peace.

Where did it all go wrong? How did the band collapse so spectacularly in the 1990s after skyrocketing to fame so quickly upon the release of *Appetite of Destruction* in 1987? In fact, as the band got more and more successful, the factors that got them there dissipated in a sea of drug and alcohol addiction, bad management and personnel decisions, lack of communication, and ever-increasing megalomania.

Steven Adler Gets Fired (1990)

In a band known for excessiveness and self-destructiveness, it came as an ironic surprise that Steven Adler got kicked out of the band for drug abuse in July 1990 (after first being placed on a thirty-day probation period). However, the story goes deeper than that. In 1989, Steven Adler checked into drug rehab, and Don Henley of the Eagles filled in on drums (unbeknownst to Adler) as Guns N' Roses performed "Patience" at the American Music Awards (AMAs). Adler later revealed that he was very bitter that no one in the band had even told him about the AMAs appearance much less that Henley was going to take his spot (on a song that didn't even require any drums or percussion!).

During a recording session for "Civil War" in 1990, Adler (who was once again struggling with drug addiction) had trouble with the complicated drum parts on the track, requiring numerous takes of the song to be meticulously edited together. The stitched-together track ended up on a 1990 charity album to benefit Romanian orphans called *Nobody's Child: Romanian Angel Appeal*, which also featured "Lovechild" by Billy Idol, "Wonderful Remark" by Van Morrison, "Medicine Man" by Elton John, and others. Frustration and impatience soon set in among the other band members since nothing was getting done with the *Use Your Illusion* recordings at Rumbo Studios, and within two weeks Adler was unceremoniously relieved of his duties as GN'R drummer. He was soon replaced by drummer Matt Sorum, formerly of the

Manufactured by Data East, the Guns N' Roses pinball machine made its debut in 1994 and featured images from photographer Robert John's 1993 book, *Guns N' Roses: The Photographic History.*   *Author's collection*

Cult. (The band also considered hiring Martin Chambers of the Pretenders and Adam Maples of the Sea Hags.) Adler's final, awkward performance as a member of Guns N' Roses was an April 7, 1990, appearance at Farm Aid IV (where he took a nosedive on stage as he sprinted up to his drum riser). In a 2013 interview with *The Week*, Slash perhaps summed it up best when he remarked, "With Steven, it was sex, drugs and rock and roll. It was all he lived for. Then it was drugs and rock and roll. Then it was just drugs."

A bitter Adler later sued Guns N' Roses. In and out of rehab for years, Adler managed to get his act together long enough to start his own band, Adler's Appetite, which performed mainly songs from *Appetite for Destruction*. Slash later admitted that the firing of Adler was "kind of ridiculous," "excessively harsh," and "had a big effect on the camaraderie of the band."

Adler's struggle with drug addiction continued for the next two decades and he even made several appearances on *Celebrity Rehab with Dr. Drew*, as well as the show's spin-off, *Sober House*. In the VH1 *Behind the Music* special on Guns N' Roses, Adler confided, "I did everything I possibly could to try and kill myself. I had nothing to live for. Everybody I knew I thought were 'my friends' took everything they could from me and disappeared. I would drink a whole bottle of vodka, just down it, before the sun was coming out, so I could pass out."

Doug Goldstein Replaces Alan Niven as GN'R Manager (1991)

Guns N' Roses fired their original manager, Alan Niven (who had been with the band since the days of recording *Appetite for Destruction*), in May 1991 and replaced him with Doug Goldstein, who quickly was perceived by other band members as Axl's yes-man. According to Slash, Axl's issues with Niven had been "brewing for years." Slash also claimed that Goldstein served as the "catalyst" for the demise of GN'R because of his "divide and conquer techniques."

Izzy Quits Guns N' Roses (1991)

In November 1991, a newly sober Izzy Stradlin decided to call it quits right in the middle of the *Use Your Illusion* Tour. (His final show had been the August 31 Wembley Stadium concert.) In a 1998 *Rolling Stone* interview, Izzy remarked, "Once I quit drugs, I couldn't help looking around and asking myself, 'Is this all there is?' I was just tired of it; I needed to get out." Izzy also later cited becoming increasingly frustrated with the "complications" of daily life in Guns N' Roses, referencing the Riverport Amphitheatre riot on July 2, 1991, and Axl's habitual lateness to concerts as examples. According to Slash in his 2007 autobiography, "Izzy's departure happened so quietly, with no fanfare, and no media awareness. It was such a major change within the band, but to the outside world it was a nonevent."

According to GN'R manager Alan Niven, "Izzy was the heart of the soul of the band," and his departure was a huge loss for Guns N' Roses. The band quickly replaced Izzy with Gilby Clarke, formerly of the band Kill for Thrills. Axl had initially asked Dave Navarro of Jane's Addiction to replace Izzy, but Navarro later explained in a 2011 *Washington Post* article, "Back in those days, I was simply too intoxicated to show up to anything." As for Izzy, he continued to pursue solo projects such as his new band, Izzy Stradlin and the Ju Ju Hounds, which released its self-titled debut album in 1992.

Slash and Duff Sign Away Rights to GN'R Name (1992)

Finding out the circumstances surrounding Slash and Duff's signing over GN'R ownership rights is a regular *Rashomon*—everyone has a different story. According to former Geffen exec Tom Zutaut in a 1999 *SPIN* interview, "Axl told the rest of the band that the only way he would play [on the *Use Your Illusion* Tour] was if they'd give ownership of the name to him. They were looking at canceling the tour and losing millions and millions of dollars, [so] they capitulated."

Guitarist Paul Tobias Makes an Unwelcome Splash (1994)

Paul Tobias (sometimes referred to as "Paul Huge" for some unknown reason), Axl's old buddy from Indiana (the two cowrote "Back Off Bitch" and several other songs), showed up while Guns N' Roses were recording "Sympathy for the Devil" for the soundtrack of the 1994 film *Interview with the Vampire* and just after Axl had dismissed rhythm guitarist Gilby Clarke (without consulting anyone, according to Slash). According to Clarke in a July 1999 *SPIN* interview, "One day my paychecks stopped coming . . . There was no explanation—they just stopped paying me. So I pretty much took that as a hint." Clarke ended up suing the band for back royalties and received an out-of-court settlement. Slash was furious about the personnel change, and in his 2007 autobiography he referred to Tobias as "the least interesting, most bland guy holding a guitar I'd ever met." Early on, Slash claims he did his best to work with Tobias, "but it went nowhere." In 1997, after Slash left the band, drummer Matt Sorum also got into a fight with Axl about Tobias (he had suggested trying to get Slash to return to the band) and was fired. Sorum later referred to Tobias as the Yoko Ono of Guns N' Roses.

Slash Leaves the Band (1996)

Over the years, Slash has referenced the band's "inactivity" and "negative energy" as two of the main reasons for walking away from Guns N' Roses in

1996. He woke up one morning, called manager Doug Goldstein, and told him, "I'm done. I quit." On October 31, 1996, Axl announced Slash's departure via a somewhat deprecating fax sent to MTV: "Slash will not be involved in any new Guns N' Roses endeavors, as he has not been musically involved with Guns N' Roses since April 1994 with the exception of a brief feel period with Zakk Wylde and a 2 week initial period with Guns N' Roses in the late fall of '95. He (Slash) has been officially and legally outside of the Guns N' Roses Partnership since December 31, 1995."

In a 2004 interview with Contactmusic.com, Slash commented, "It was a hard band to quit. But if I hadn't I'd be in the very same rut that Axl's stuck in right now, which is going nowhere. I

Zakk Wylde, a former guitarist for Ozzy Osbourne, auditioned for Guns N' Roses in 1995 and went on to form Los Angeles heavy metal band Black Label Society.

Chascar/Wikimedia Commons

couldn't sit still that way." Slash, who continued working with his band, Slash's Snakepit, also formed the supergroup Velvet Revolver with ex-GN'R band members Duff and Matt Sorum. The Slash vs. Axl feud would continue unabated in the public arena until 2016, when they finally put their differences aside and reconciled for Coachella and the Not in This Lifetime Tour.

Duff Officially Quits Guns N' Roses (1997)

Duff officially quit Guns N' Roses in August 1997, although he later commented in his autobiography that the band had been renting studios for the three years before he quit in 1997 and "still did not have a single song." By this time, Duff had sobered up and was ready to move on to other creative endeavors. He later started a band called Loaded with some of his friends from the Seattle punk scene, and he also formed Velvet Revolver with Slash and Matt Sorum, as well as Scott Weiland of Stone Temple Pilots and Dave Kushner of Wasted Youth.

Axl Hires Slew of New Band Members (1997–98)

As the sole remaining original member, Axl was able to continue working under the Guns N' Roses banner and hire new band members (on contract basis only) since he had legally obtained the band name. In January 1997, Axl filled Slash's vacant slot with Nine Inch Nails touring guitarist Robin Finck. Josh Freese became the new GN'R drummer during the summer of 1997 (replacing Matt Sorum). By the end of 1998, the new version of GN'R included Axl, Finck, bassist Tommy Stinson of the Replacements, rhythm guitarist Paul Tobias, keyboardist Dizzy Reed (who had joined the band in 1990), keyboardist/bassist Chris Pitman, and drummer Josh Freese. However, the only track released by the new lineup by 1999 was "Oh My God," which appeared on the soundtrack of Arnold Schwarzenegger's overblown thriller *End of Days*. Axl later stated that "Oh My God" was an unfinished demo that had been rushed to completion for inclusion in the soundtrack. According to Slash in his 2007 autobiography, "I found it morbidly ironic that, out of all of us, the guy who'd basically browbeat and pressured us into submission into retaining the name had done nothing much with it whatsoever at that point."

Live Era '87–'93 Released (1999)

One bright spot during the latter part of the decade was the November 1999 release of *Live Era '87–'93*, a double-disc collection of concert recordings (from both the *Appetite for Destruction* and *Use Your Illusion* tours). *Live Era '87–'93* served as the first official Guns N' Roses album since "*The Spaghetti Incident?*" in 1993. Axl reportedly communicated with Slash and Duff via managers in order to select the track list. (The album simply states "Recorded Across the Universe Between 1987 and 1993" without naming specific concert dates.) Ten of the twelve songs on *Appetite for Destruction* were represented on the album: "Nightrain," "Mr. Brownstone," "It's So Easy," "Welcome to the Jungle," "My Michelle," "Rocket Queen," "Sweet Child O' Mine," "You're Crazy," "Out Ta Get Me," and "Paradise City." A couple of pleasant surprises were also included such as "Move to the City" from *G N' R Lies* and "Pretty Tied Up" from *Use Your Illusion II*.

In a 2004 *Guitar World* interview, Slash remarked that the album is "not pretty and there are a lot of mistakes, but this is Guns N' Roses, not the fucking Mahavishnu Orchestra. It's as honest as it gets." The album cover is composed of early GN'R flyers from the band's days playing West Hollywood clubs, such as the Troubadour, Whisky A Go Go, the Roxy, Madame Wong's East, Country Club, and others. Interestingly, both Matt Sorum and Gilby Clarke are listed in the album credits simply as "Additional Musicians." The album is "dedicated to the memory of Joni Abbot, West Arkeen, Todd Crew, Shannon Hoon, David Kehrer, and Howard King."

The next Guns N' Roses album didn't appear until *Greatest Hits* in 2004, although Axl was joined by Slash and Duff in an unsuccessful lawsuit to prevent the album's release. (None of the existing or former band members had authorized the album or were involved in the selection of songs that would appear on the album.) Although some of the band's biggest hits were represented on the album—such as "Welcome to the Jungle," "Sweet Child O' Mine," "Paradise City," "Patience," "Civil War," "Don't Cry," and "November Rain"—the release featured a plethora of cover versions, such as "Knockin' on Heaven's Door," "Live and Let Die," "Ain't It Fun," and "Sympathy for the Devil" (arguably one of the band's worst songs). Despite the questionable track selection, the album went on to sell more than 5 million copies.

Axl Makes a Rare Public Appearance at Cat Club in West Hollywood (2000)

Axl shocked just about everyone in June 2000 when he actually made an appearance at the Cat Club (owned by Slim Jim Phantom of the Stray Cats) in West Hollywood and jammed with former bandmate Gilby Clarke and his band, the Starfuckers, on two Rolling Stones tunes, "Wild Horses" and "Dead Flowers," in front of a crowd of about 250 people. Axl had just returned from attending a Roger Waters concert, and the Cat Club appearance was his first live performance since 1993. His brief return to the public eye in a performance role gave Guns N' Roses fans a glimmer of hope that the band would start performing live once again and release some new material. (They would have to wait patiently for another eight years for that to happen!)

21

Never Felt So High

Notable Guns N' Roses Television Appearances

They say you guys are cocky, they say you guys are insolent, they say, honestly speaking, you guys are a bunch of wackos.

—VJ Adam "Smash" to GN'R during their first MTV appearance in 1987

In their prime, Guns N' Roses created full-blown chaos wherever they went—whether they were totally trashing the set of MTV's *Headbangers Ball*, getting shitfaced at the American Music Awards and dropping multiple F-bombs, performing "Used to Love Her" on Fox's *The Late Show*, stumbling around the stage at Farm Aid IV, or battling the likes of Vince Neil and Kurt Cobain at the MTV Video Music Awards. Indeed, the seven-second delay on live TV broadcasts was invented for bands like Guns N' Roses (and in fact may have been implemented as a result of Slash and Duff's booze-addled appearance at the AMAs!), and that kind of in-your-face honesty proved to be truly refreshing. It was obvious from the outset that Guns N' Roses would forge their own path with no shits given at all about their image.

Headbangers Ball (1987)

On October 24, 1987, Guns N' Roses stopped by MTV's *Headbangers Ball* studio to promote their recently released debut album, *Appetite for Destruction*. While the interview with VJ Adam "Smash" was rather sedate, the band perked up after the host invited the band to destroy the set: "You guys, as I understand it, are very well known for your interior decorating capabilities, along with the great rock 'n' roll. I understand you've redecorated many a hotel room, and as I look at this beautiful set we have here . . .

I'm gonna give you thirty seconds to redecorate this room. On your marks, get set, go!" Guns N' Roses proceeded to wreak total havoc on the set in a matter of seconds before hastily departing in one of the most memorable moments of *Headbangers Ball*.

As for the interview itself, Axl did most of the talking (in fact, no one else really said anything of interest, besides Slash rambling off some upcoming tour dates), while other bored band members slouched, fidgeted, and generally ignored the questions. For example, Steven Adler played with a hubcap during the entire interview, while Slash clutched a bottle of Jack Daniel's and at one point even casually flipped off the cameraman. Axl revealed that the Guns N' Roses' negative image among certain critics stemmed from the fact that the band didn't "take garbage off of anybody, that's all, and a lot of people think that's a problem." Adam "Smash" later became a popular DJ at KSHE 95 in St. Louis, and he also went on to front a local cover band called the Smash Band. Interestingly, in his 2007 self-titled autobiography, Slash mistakenly claimed that it was original MTV video jockey J. J. Jackson who had actually interviewed the band that day and invited them to destroy the set.

The Late Show (1988)

"Welcome, Guns N' Roses!" On March 31, 1988, GN'R appeared on Fox's long-forgotten foray into late-night TV, *The Late Show*, to perform raw, energetic versions of "You're Crazy" and the controversial "Used to Love Her" from their upcoming album, *G N' R Lies*. In his 2010 autobiography, *My Appetite for Destruction*, Steven Adler remarked that he remembered the performance so well because the band played the song "the way it was always meant to be played: slower, sleazy, more bluesy, with more feeling," as opposed to the sped-up version on *Appetite for Destruction*. Shortly after GN'R's appearance, Bill Cosby appeared on *The Late Show* to accept his three Golden Raspberry Awards (a.k.a. "Razzies") in the categories of "Worst Picture," "Worst Actor," and "Worst Screenplay" for the truly awful film *Leonard Part 6*.

First aired in 1986 and initially known as *The Late Show Starring Joan Rivers*, the troubled late-night TV show was intended to be Fox's answer to NBC's *The Tonight Show Starring Johnny Carson*. For his part, Carson was reportedly enraged that Rivers took the job without first notifying him, especially since she had been his permanent guest host since 1983. Rivers later revealed that Carson never spoke to her again. After a season of abysmal ratings, Fox fired Rivers in 1987 and hired a succession of equally unsuccessful guest hosts over the next two years, such as Suzanne Somers, Richard Belzer, Robert Townsend, Buck Henry, Arsenio Hall, John Mulrooney, Ross Shafer, and Jeff Joseph (who later joked that he even changed his name to "Jeffsenio Hall" to boost the show's ratings). Fox even considered hiring Howard Stern to take over at one point, as well as David Spade, who, believe it or not, actually turned the network down. After a couple years of dismal ratings, Fox finally pulled the plug and put *The Late Show* out of its misery on October 28, 1988.

MTV Video Music Awards (1989)

Axl and Izzy took the stage with Tom Petty and the Heartbreakers to perform a rather lackluster version of "Free Fallin'" and a much more lively cover of Elvis's "Heartbreak Hotel" at the 1989 MTV Video Music Awards (VMAs), which aired on September 6, 1989. The performance has become totally overshadowed by what happened next: As Izzy exited the stage he was sucker punched by Mötley Crüe's Vince Neil over an earlier altercation involving Izzy and Neil's then wife, Sharise, a former mud wrestler. (See the "Biggest Feuds" chapter for more on this.) Another notorious moment from that year's VMAs took place when comedian Andrew "Dice" Clay launched into his raunchy versions of Mother Goose nursery rhymes while introducing Cher's performance of "If I Could Turn Back Time." Clay was in turn permanently banned from MTV for the clever stunt. (A good friend of the band, Dice had even performed his bawdy act at Duff's bachelor party in 1988 before his brief marriage to Mandy Brixx of the Lame Flames.)

On a positive note, Guns N' Roses captured "Best Heavy Metal Video" honors for "Sweet Child O' Mine" over Aerosmith's "Rag Doll," Def Leppard's "Pour Some Sugar on Me," and Metallica's "One." Ironically, it was Mötley Crüe that presented Guns N' Roses with the award, which was accepted onstage by Duff and Steven Adler. (This happened before the Izzy altercation.) In addition, GN'R was nominated for "Best Stage Performance in a Video" for "Paradise City" but lost out to Living Colour ("Cult of Personality"), the band that had publicly criticized Guns N' Roses for the racist and homophobic lyrics of "One in a Million." Somewhat surprisingly, veteran rocker Neil Young received the "Video of the Year" award for his controversial "This Note's for You." Other memorable performances at the 1989 VMAs included Madonna ("Express Yourself"), the Rolling Stones ("Mixed Emotions"), Tone-Loc ("Wild Thing"), the Cult ("Fire Woman"),

Jon Bon Jovi and Richie Sambora (acoustic versions of "Livin' on a Prayer"/"Wanted Dead or Alive"), Bobby Brown ("On Our Own"), and the Cure ("Just Like Heaven"), among others.

A good friend of Guns N' Roses, comedian Andrew "Dice" Clay was banned from MTV for reciting his raunchy nursery rhymes at the 1989 MTV Video Awards, the same show where Vince Neil punched out Izzy Stradlin.   *Author's collection*

American Music Awards (1990)

The seventeenth annual American Music Awards (AMAs)—which took place on January 22, 1990, and was broadcast live on ABC—would almost be completely forgotten today if not for the notoriously inebriated acceptance speeches by Slash and Duff after Guns N' Roses captured awards for "Favorite Heavy Metal/Hard Rock Artist" and "Favorite Heavy Metal/Hard Rock Album" for *Appetite for Destruction*. The hilarious "performance" involved a great deal of stumbling around, slurring incoherently, and swearing profusely. Upon accepting the first award, which was presented by Stephanie Mills and MC Hammer, a bewildered Duff remarked, "What do we say?" Slash tried to pick up the slack: "OK, so listen, we really didn't even expect this. It's like, just come down to the show and hang out and stuff. We thought we'd come down and hang out for two hours and shit." Before the duo was hustled offstage, Duff exclaimed, "Have a drink on us! Thank you very much!"

During their next and even more notorious trip to the stage to accept the second award, which was presented by Aaron Neville and Lita Ford (who hastily exited the stage), Duff again slurred, "What do we say?" Slash then launched into a rambling diatribe that was fortunately cut off by exit music and a commercial break but not before the damage had been done: "Listen, I want to say a few things I didn't get to say last time, right? I want to thank fuckin' . . . oops! . . . Tom Zutaut for finding us, Alan Niven for fuckin' getting us there, Doug Gold." Thankfully it was over for all involved. However, things got even dumber backstage during a press interview as both rockers rambled on incessantly about their craft, with Duff even declaring, "Record sales is not our main priority whatsoever. Integrity. Sincerity."

As can be imagined, AMAs creator Dick Clark and ABC network executives were not amused. After being flooded with complaints about the "profane" acceptance speeches, ABC issued an apology the following day: "We regret that last night's live telecast of the American Music Awards contained some offensive language. This has not happened before in the seventeen years this awards show has been on the air. We will take precautionary measures to see that it does not happen in future telecasts." As for Slash, he later remarked unrepentantly in a January 24, 1991 *Rolling Stone* interview, "I sort of wanted us to be the fuck-ups there, because everybody else was so polite and stiff and unnatural . . . We were trying to have a good time, and I think out of all the people there, we were the only ones who weren't putting on a façade." By the way, buried among all the assorted "thanks" in the *Use Your Illusion* album liner notes is the name "Dick fuckin' Clark."

Farm Aid IV (1990)

The fourth edition of Farm Aid will not go down as one of Guns N' Roses' brightest moments. The event took place at the Hoosier Dome in Indianapolis, Indiana, on April 7, 1990, and was televised live on The Nashville Network. GN'R turned in a disastrous performance that began immediately when Steven Adler tripped and took a face plant as he sprinted onto the stage toward the drum riser. To add insult to injury, Adler later revealed that no one had even bothered to inform him which songs the band would be playing. Axl (wearing a cowboy hat) took the stage next and addressed the audience with "I'd like to dedicate this to my Uncle Bob . . . who lives in Illinois on a farm." Guns N' Roses opened with "Civil War." It was the band's first live performance of the song, which Adler had struggled mightily with in rehearsals. In addition, Adler didn't even know the next number, a rousing cover of the English punk band UK Subs' quirky "Down on the Farm," which was "the only farm song we know," according to Axl, who added, "Don't take it personal but this song rocks!" Featuring offbeat lyrics such as "I can't fall in love with a barn/when everything smells of horseshit," the song would later show up on GN'R's 1993 album of covers, *"The Spaghetti Incident?"* As the song concluded, Axl threw down his mic and exclaimed, "Thank you and good fuckin' night!" As it turns out, Farm Aid IV would be Adler's last live performance as a member of Guns N' Roses. He was fired just three months later. In his 2010 autobiography, *My Appetite for Destruction*, Adler cried conspiracy: "I believe they wanted me to fuck up on live TV; that would be their evidence. By branding me as an ill-equipped, crappy drummer, they'd be armed with a sound reason for kicking me out."

Farm Aid IV also featured live performances from the likes of John Mellencamp, Elton John, Neil Young, Willie Nelson, Bonnie Raitt, Jackson Browne, Don Henley, Garth Brooks, Gorky Park, John Denver, Arlo Guthrie, Iggy Pop, Carl Perkins, Alan Jackson, Asleep at the Wheel, Bruce Hornsby, Bill Monroe, Taj Mahal, Lou Reed, Poco, K. T. Oslin, and Crosby, Stills, Nash & Young. Highlights of Farm Aid IV included Elton John's moving rendition of "Candle in the Wind," which he dedicated to young AIDS victim Ryan White, who sadly died the following day; Mellencamp's belting out of "Pink Houses" to his appreciative hometown Hoosier crowd; Iggy Pop's spellbinding rendition of "I Wanna Be Your Dog"; and Young's blistering performance of "Rockin' in the Free World."

MTV Video Music Awards (1991)

Guns N' Roses performed a spirited rendition of "Live and Let Die," with Axl rocking it out in a kilt, that was broadcast from a Wembley Stadium concert in London and aired on the 1991 MTV Video Music Awards (VMAs), which took place on September 5, 1991. However, the night belonged to R.E.M., which took home "Video of the Year" honors for "Losing My Religion," along with six other awards. (Interestingly, R.E.M. declined to perform at the show.) Although Guns N' Roses was nominated for "Best Metal/Hard Rock Video" for "You Could Be Mine," the band lost out to Aerosmith for "The Other Side." GN'R also failed to win for "Best Video from a Film" ("You Could Be Mine" from *Terminator 2: Judgment Day*), losing out to Chris Isaak ("Wicked Game" from *Wild at Heart*).

Other memorable performances turned in at the 1991 VMAs included Van Halen ("Poundcake"), Mariah Carey ("Emotions"), Queensryche ("Silent Lucidity"), LL Cool J ("Mama Said Knock You Out"), Metallica ("Enter Sandman"), Don Henley ("The Heart of the Matter"), and Prince and the New Power Generation ("Gett Off"). However, GN'R's longtime nemesis, Poison, turned in by far the most disastrous performance of the night—one that ranks among the worst in the history of the VMAs. The band intended to play "Unskinny Bop," but inebriated guitarist C. C. DeVille had other ideas, as he launched into "Talk Dirty to Me." Everything went completely downhill from there (even though host Arsenio Hall valiantly tried to smooth things over). DeVille and lead singer Bret Michaels even got into a fistfight backstage, and the guitarist was in turn fired from Poison. (He finally rejoined the band six years later.) Last and most certainly least, the 1991 VMAs are also remembered for the return of Paul Reubens (a.k.a. Pee-wee Herman) to the public eye after his notorious arrest at a Sarasota adult theater ("Heard any good jokes lately?").

MTV Video Music Awards (1992)

Best remembered for the escalating feud between Guns N' Roses and Nirvana that spilled over into the performances, the 1992 MTV Video Music Awards (VMAs), which took place on September 9, 1992, had its fair share of bizarre and outrageous moments. Therefore, few rock fans even remember that Van Halen and the Red Hot Chili Peppers both had huge nights—the former winning "Video of the Year" for "Right Now" and the latter

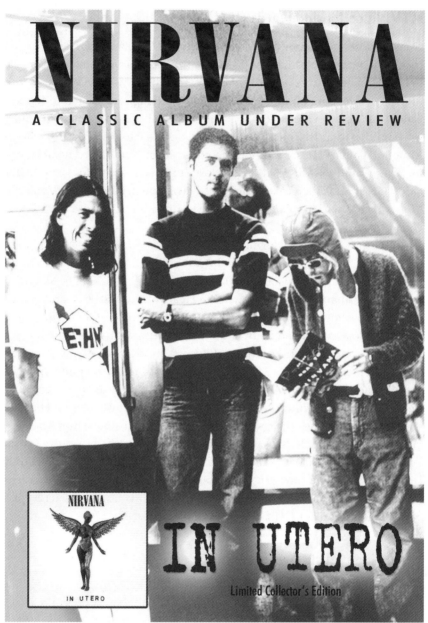

Tensions between Nirvana and Guns N' Roses turned into a full-blown feud after a backstage altercation between Axl Rose and Kurt Cobain/Courtney Love at the 1992 MTV Video Music Awards.   *Author's collection*

capturing "Viewer's Choice" honors. In addition, GN'R won "Best Cinematography in a Video" honors for the epic video "November Rain." When Guns N' Roses also won the "Michael Jackson Video Vanguard Award," Axl ended his acceptance speech by remarking wryly, "Oh yeah, this has nothing to do with Michael Jackson." To top it off, Guns N' Roses joined Elton John, along with a full backing orchestra, for a dramatic rendition of "November Rain." However, 1992 VMA "lowlights" included the Axl/Stephanie Seymour vs. Kurt Cobain/Courtney Love verbal battle backstage (see the "Biggest Feuds" chapter for more on this), Nirvana bassist Krist Novoselic almost getting into a fistfight with Duff (years later the two actually became friends), Cobain allegedly spitting all over the keys of what he thought would be Axl's piano (but which actually turned out to be Elton John's!), Van Halen improbably winning "Video of the Year" for "Right Now" over Nirvana's teen anthem "Smells Like Teen Spirit," Bobby Brown dropping an on-air F-bomb, and Howard Stern's infamous train wreck of an appearance as "Fartman."

In addition, Nirvana turned in a highly entertaining performance of "Lithium" that started with a defiant intro to "Rape Me" and featured Novoselic getting knocked out with his own guitar, Cobain climbing up the amplifiers, and drummer Dave Grohl taking over the mic to taunt Rose ("Hi, Axl!"). Grohl later gave a simple explanation for the animosity his band felt toward GN'R: "Nirvana didn't want to turn into Guns N' Roses." Forgotten in all the total insanity and grotesque posturing was the fact that there were some decent performances that night from the likes of the Black Crowes ("Remedy"), Bobby Brown ("Humpin' Around"), U2 ("Even Better Than the Real Thing," live via satellite from Detroit with VMAs host Dana Carvey playing drums!), Def Leppard ("Let's Get Rocked"), Elton John ("The One"), Pearl Jam ("Jeremy"), the Red Hot Chili Peppers ("Give It Away"), Michael Jackson ("Black or White," from his *Dangerous* Tour in London), En Vogue ("Free Your Mind"), and Eric Clapton ("Tears in Heaven").

MTV Video Music Awards (2002)

A "surprise guest" joined the lineup at the 2002 MTV Video Music Awards held on August 29, 2002—the event's host, Jimmy Fallon, announced the return of a braided Axl Rose and his new lineup of Guns N' Roses, which included guitarists Buckethead and Robin Finck, bassist Tommy Stinson, and drummer Brian "Brain" Mantia, as well as longtime keyboardist Dizzy

Reed. The band proceeded to close the show by performing a three-song medley—"Welcome to the Jungle," "Madagascar," and "Paradise City"—that included two *Appetite for Destruction* classics sandwiching an epic new tune that would appear on *Chinese Democracy*. Reviews of the performance were decidingly mixed with a seemingly out-of-shape Axl huffing and puffing his way across the stage. Believe it or not, this was Axl's first appearance at the VMAs since GN'R's duet with Elton John in 1992. After the set, MTV's Kurt Loder interviewed Axl and asked him about the progress of the long-awaited *Chinese Democracy* album. Axl responded, "You'll see [the album] but I don't know if 'soon' is the word . . . It will come out, and we'll do some more recording and start the American leg of the tour." Soon was most definitely not the word; the album finally appeared *six years* later.

Besides the Guns N' Roses performance, the 2002 MTV VMAs may very well be remembered (sadly) for the tension between Eminem and Moby (as well as Eminem vs. Triumph the Insult Comic Dog!). Eminem ended up having a big night, winning four awards, including "Video of the Year" for "Without Me." The event also featured the spectacle of Michael Jackson accepting a birthday statue that he mistakenly believed to be an "Artist of the Millennium Award." (Britney Spears had referred to Jackson as "the artist of the millennium" when introducing him, and things went downhill from there.)

Late Show with David Letterman (2007)

Fresh off the release of his self-titled autobiography, Slash (introduced as the "guitarist for Velvet Revolver") guested on the *Late Show with David Letterman* on October 30, 2007. (Dave's other guests that night included actress Jennifer Connelly and singer-songwriter Nicole Atkins.) The candid interview covered a lot of ground that included Slash's past drug and alcohol abuse, the source of his nickname, his family being outcasts on a Disney cruise, his longtime feud with Axl, the time Axl jumped out of Slash's car as they sped down Santa Monica Boulevard after an argument, a hilarious story about throwing a bottle of Jack Daniel's through a TV screen, the self-destructive nature of rock stars (which results simply out of "boredom," according to Slash), and the possibility of reconciling with Axl.

Slash informed Letterman that "excessive drinking"—half a gallon of vodka a day at home and "then I would go out," a routine that lasted ten years—led to a cardiomyopathy diagnosis that required an implantable defibrillator at the age of thirty-five. Doctors told Slash that he had six days to six weeks to live, so he stopped drinking and started a moderate exercise routine. He also revealed that his childhood friend Matt's father, actor Seymour Cassel (*The Killing of a Chinese Bookie*), gave him the nickname "Slash" because he was "always in a hurry, always scheming, always hustling, always on the go." In regard to his feud with Axl, Slash remarked, "What I would like to sort of do is clear the air. The media has sort of perpetuated a lot of negative energy about the whole thing and I think I probably helped too because I think when I started doing press when Velvet Revolver first started, I was still bitter about the whole Guns N' Roses breakup."

Jimmy Kimmel Live! (2012)

In a rare public appearance, a slightly uncomfortable Axl appeared on *Jimmy Kimmel Live!* on October 24, 2012, to provide very brief answers to a variety of questions (some of which were provided via fans on Twitter). Subjects included GN'R's upcoming twelve-date Las Vegas residency at the Joint, the band's original lineup, Axl's penchant for tardiness, his infamous cornrows, the US Presidential election (he claimed to be leaning toward Obama), and even "Halloween trees" at Axl's annual Halloween party. (The singer admitted that he once dressed up as "a giant ear of corn.")

In addition, Axl discussed how he hitchhiked from Indiana to Los Angeles at the age of nineteen and worked briefly as night manager at Tower Video on Sunset Boulevard: "I let everybody have beers after work . . . I hired people from the old lineup, I hired all my other friends. We had a great time for a while." Kimmel responded, "You know, I think it's funny because every video store employee thinks they're gonna be a rock star one day. You're the only one that actually did!" At the conclusion of his appearance, Rose surprised the audience with tickets to the Las Vegas Guns N' Roses shows along with gift certificates for Tommy's Burger Truck, which he had conveniently arranged to be parked outside the studio.

22

All My Twisted Dreams

Guns N' Roses Music Videos

It was like Spinal Tap with money . . . I've been asked by students about the metaphorical imagery in those videos, and I'm like "Fuck if I know."
—Andy Morahan, who directed the GN'R music videos
for "Don't Cry," "November Rain," and "Estranged"

TV truly started a revolution when it aired the first music video—
"Video Killed the Radio Star" by the Buggles—on August 1, 1981,
at 12:01 AM, and followed it with videos for "You Better Run"
(Pat Benatar), "She Won't Dance" (Rod Stewart), "You Better You Bet" (the
Who), and "Little Suzi's on the Up" (Ph.D.). However, Guns N' Roses had a
love-hate relationship with MTV best exemplified by Slash, who commented
in *I Want My MTV* that the music video network was "a channel that helped
us out, but that we didn't care for." Initially, MTV stayed clear of the band
because they knew of GN'R's rather sordid reputation and were afraid of
any type of controversy. However, under pressure from David Geffen of
Geffen Records, the network played "Welcome to the Jungle" in the middle
of the night and soon Guns N' Roses held sway over MTV. (Axl Rose was
even instrumental in getting his buddy Riki Rachtman hired as a VJ for
MTV's heavy metal show, *Headbangers Ball*.) After the release of the *Use
Your Illusion* albums in 1991, Guns N' Roses' music videos became more
and more bloated and excessive, with the unofficial trilogy of "Don't Cry,"
"November Rain," and "Estranged" ranking as some of the most expensive
music videos ever made. In fact, "Estranged" itself cost approximately $4
million (say what?).

Over the years, Guns N' Roses was nominated for nine MTV Video
Music Awards (VMAs) and won four times: "Best New Artist in a Video,"
1988 ("Welcome to the Jungle"); "Best Heavy Metal Video," 1989 ("Sweet

Child O' Mine"); "Michael Jackson Video Vanguard Award," 1992; and "Best Cinematography in a Video," 1992 ("November Rain"). During the 1992 VMAs, Axl's hero, Elton John, joined Guns N' Roses for a live performance of "November Rain." First released in 1998, the *Guns N' Roses: Welcome to the Videos* DVD features thirteen GN'R music videos from 1987 to 1993: "Welcome to the Jungle," "Sweet Child O' Mine," "Paradise City," "Patience," "Don't Cry," "Live and Let Die," "November Rain," "Yesterdays," "The Garden," "Dead Horse," "Garden of Eden," "Estranged," and "Since I Don't Have You."

"Welcome to the Jungle"

Guns N' Roses' very first music video (and still arguably their best!) from *Appetite for Destruction* typecasts Axl as a hayseed from the Midwest who arrives in the big city via a Greyhound bus. Footage of the singer sitting in a chair watching disturbing images on TV—police brutality, riots, and various violent insurrections—is interspersed throughout the video, along with scenes of the band performing "Welcome to the Jungle." (Interestingly, Axl sports totally glammed-out hair in the concert scenes.) Izzy appears as a

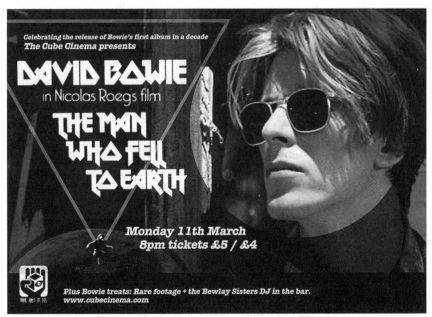

Guns N' Roses' groundbreaking music video for "Welcome to the Jungle" was inspired by such cult movies as *Midnight Cowboy* (1969), *A Clockwork Orange* (1971), and *The Man Who Fell to Earth* (1976). *Author's collection*

drug dealer harassing Axl as he gets off the bus, while Slash shows up very briefly as a homeless drunk slouching in a doorway drinking booze out of a paper bag. Meanwhile, Steven Adler can be seen lying in bed with a sexy blonde (his roommate, Julie Angel) in a cheap hotel. Even Adler's little brother, Jamie, made it into the video. (He's the kid pointing drumsticks at Axl.) Duff is in there somewhere, too (but if you blink you'll miss his cameo). In one particularly disturbing scene, Axl is restrained by a straitjacket while being forced to watch violent images on a stack of TVs. By the end of the video, the hayseed has miraculously transformed into a true L.A. rock star.

According to former GN'R manager Alan Niven, Geffen Records refused to shell out the big bucks for the music video, so they "piggybacked" it on a Great White shoot. Niven came up with the music video's concept, which he claimed was influenced by such "cool movies" as *Midnight Cowboy* (1969), *A Clockwork Orange* (1971), and *The Man Who Fell to Earth* (1976). Predictably, Axl was always late for the shoot, which took place on August 1–2, 1987 (shortly before the band embarked on the Cult tour). In addition, the production crew always worried about what would set the Guns N' Roses lead singer off on his next "tantrum," according to director Nigel Dick, who later committed the blasphemy of actually acknowledging that he "preferred Great White's music" to GN'R's. A portion of the video was shot in Dayle Gloria's Scream Club at the Park Plaza Hotel. (Gloria was known as the "Queen of the Sunset Strip.") Afraid of causing any controversy, MTV only started playing "Welcome to the Jungle" on its after-hours rotation (meaning five a.m. EST on a Sunday when supposedly no one was watching) after a personal request by David Geffen to the network executives. However, before long, "Welcome to the Jungle" became MTV's most requested music video and won GN'R "Best New Artist in A Video" honors at the 1988 VMAs. As an amusing side note, Slash believes he left his VMA in a cab, "which, now that I think about it, is as much as it deserved," he remarked in his 2007 autobiography.

"Sweet Child O' Mine"

Filmed in grainy black-and-white, the brilliantly edited video for "Sweet Child O' Mine" from *Appetite for Destruction* features a clip of the band rehearsing the song at Huntington Ballroom in Huntington Beach, California, while various members of Guns N' Roses' crew, girlfriends, and entourage mill around. (Everyone was given a camera by the director in order to get multiple perspectives for the video.) Since Axl wrote the lyrics to

"Sweet Child O' Mine" about his then girlfriend and future wife Erin Everly, it was only natural that she would appear in the music video. In addition, the video featured all of the other band members' significant others at the time (except Izzy, who brought his dog along), including Slash's girlfriend Sally, Duff's girlfriend and future wife Mandy Brixx of the Lame Flames, and Steven Adler's girlfriend Cheryl. Duff wears a CBGB T-shirt in the video.

Two versions of the music video were shot, the first being a mix of color and black-and-white images, and the second being entirely black-and-white (except for the final color shot of Axl). It was MTV's heavy rotation of the video that popularized the song and allowed "Sweet Child O' Mine" to assume the No. 1 position on the US charts while Guns toured with Aerosmith during the summer of 1988. The "Sweet Child O' Mine" video was directed by Nigel Dick, who remarked in *I Want My MTV*, "After the first couple of takes, I thought, *God, this is awful. It's so dull.* Some execs from Geffen were standing behind me, going, 'This is so fucking cool.' I'm thinking, *'I'm shooting a bunch of guys playing guitar. What's special about this?'* But for whatever reason, people thought it was the hottest thing in the world. There's nothing remarkable about the video at all, except, of course, for the band. Which is exactly how it should be."

"Paradise City"

The "Paradise City" music video expertly captures the meteoric rise of Guns N' Roses from dingy Los Angeles clubs to massive stadium shows. Filmed at Giants Stadium in East Rutherford, New Jersey, with six cameras in front of 77,000 raucous fans, the music video for "Paradise City" from *Appetite for Destruction* cost approximately $250,000 ($45,000 of which served as a payment to the stadium's unions "for carrying a hundred camera cases thirty yards from a parking lot into the stadium," according to director Nigel Dick in *I Want My MTV*). A clever mix of black-and-white and color footage, the video also includes scenes of GN'R band members wandering the streets of New York City, signing autographs, sightseeing, rehearsing, and hanging out in their hotel rooms. Also look for a brief glimpse of a couple in the massive crowd making out, totally oblivious to all of the madness around them. The video was shot when GN'R opened for Aerosmith and Deep Purple on August 16, 1988, as well as when the band performing at the 1988 Monsters of Rock festival at Castle Donington in England (where two fans were tragically trampled to death).

"It's So Easy"

Filmed at the Cathouse in West Hollywood on October 10, 1989, during a rowdy warm-up show before GN'R's four-date gig as opening act for the Rolling Stones at the Los Angeles Coliseum, the black-and-white music video for "It's So Easy" from *Appetite for Destruction* was never officially released (but can be easily found on YouTube). The controversial video features Erin Everly decked out in bondage gear, complete with a ball-gag in her mouth, and tied up backstage. Meanwhile, Axl stage dives recklessly into the crowd several times. The "It's So Easy" music video provides a good glimpse of what an early GN'R show was like during one of the band's many West Hollywood club gigs. Interestingly, David Bowie attended the show during which the video was shot, but Axl accused him of flirting with Everly, punched him, and chased the bewildered "Thin White Duke" down the street. Bowie quickly apologized, and the two rock stars hit the China Club for many rounds of booze.

"Patience"

The music video for "Patience" from *G N' R Lies* was filmed in Los Angeles at the abandoned Ambassador Hotel, where Democratic presidential candidate Robert F. Kennedy was assassinated on June 6, 1968. Performance scenes were shot at the Record Plant, where the song had been recorded. Axl reportedly showed up for the shoot seven hours late, while Izzy arrived with cocaine dripping out of his nose and "sat in a dark corner while we were filming," according to GN'R manager Alan Niven. A conscious decision was made to minimize Izzy's exposure in the video since he "looked wretched."

Filming took place on Valentine's Day, 1989. Each band member was featured in an individual scene (except Izzy, who remained seated in the dark corner), while ghostly patrons of the hotel appear and fade away like those in the Men at Work song "Overkill." In Slash's scene, the guitarist is shown hanging out with his pet snake (a six-foot-long red-tailed boa constrictor named Pandora) on a bed in a hotel room, oblivious to the beautiful models in sexy lingerie that appear and disappear in succession next to him. In another scene, Duff returns a room service tray from his hotel room to the lobby. In Steven Adler's scene, the drummer can be seen briefly in the lobby just hanging out with a couple of gorgeous chicks. Axl is shown in a hotel room picking up a phone, throwing it to the ground, and then stomping it to pieces. At the end of the video, Axl sits alone watching old Guns N' Roses concert footage in a somewhat forlorn state.

According to director Nigel Dick in *I Want My MTV*, "Mostly what I remember about the video is a shitload of chicks and a snake." By the way, *Appetite for Destruction* producer Mike Clink can be viewed at the mixing board during the first part of the video.

"Don't Cry"

Directed by Andy Morahan, the video for "Don't Cry" is the first chapter of the unofficial Guns N' Roses music video trilogy that includes "November Rain" and "Estranged." The videos were based on the short story "Without You," which was written by Axl's friend, Del James, and later appeared in *The Language of Fear* (1995). Blind Melon singer Shannon Hoon (who also hailed from Lafayette, Indiana, along with Axl and Izzy) appeared in the video, as well as Axl's then girlfriend, supermodel Stephanie Seymour. Axl was undergoing regressive therapy at the time and incorporated his experience into the video. In fact, the woman who portrayed Axl's psychotherapist was his actual therapist, Suzzy London, who occasionally accompanied the band on the road.

The "Don't Cry" video begins with Axl traipsing through a blizzard in some sort of medieval garb while clutching a bottle. Then we witness a fight over a gun between Axl and Seymour, followed by a picnic at a cemetery and a catfight in a crowded bar. Next, Slash drives a car over a cliff, and then Axl meets up with his multiple selves, an incident that leads him to therapy. In the final image, Axl stands over his own gravestone, which reads "W. Axl Rose, 1962–1990." What does it all mean? Who the hell knows, but it's entertaining nonetheless. In a 1992 interview with *Metallix* magazine, Axl confessed, "With our video for 'Don't Cry,' and the fight that Stephanie Seymour and I had over the gun, you don't necessarily know what's going on. But in real life that happened with Erin Everly and myself. I was going to shoot myself. We fought over the gun and I finally let her win. I was kind of mentally crippled after that."

Portions of the video—those that include the band playing while helicopters swirl above—were shot atop the Transamerica Center in downtown Los Angeles, while other portions were shot at the Los Angeles County Cemetery. According to Kip Winger of Winger in *I Want My MTV*, Guns N' Roses stole the idea of a car going off a cliff from their video for "Hungry," even though GN'R's version "was way cooler, because they had more money." Look for a sign in the video that reads: "Where's Izzy?" The GN'R rhythm guitarist had recently departed the band for good.

"November Rain"

With a budget of approximately $1.5 million, the bloated and excessive "November Rain" video was one of the most expensive music videos ever made. It also clocked in at more than nine minutes, making it one of the longest videos in music video history. Directed by Andy Morahan, "November Rain" served as the second chapter of GN'R's unofficial music video trilogy, along with "Don't Cry" and "Estranged." The video features Axl popping pills at his bedside, marrying Stephanie Seymour in a very extravagant wedding (Slash serves as best man and of course he misplaces the ring!), and then attending her funeral. All of these sequences are intercut with a live performance from the band, complete with a full backing orchestra. The video abounds with religious imagery, including a bleeding crucifix. In addition, it's rather hilarious to see a poor guy (*Headbangers Ball* host Riki Rachtman) leaping onto the wedding cake during all the commotion created after a violent storm ruins the wedding reception. Look for Axl wearing a leather jacket with Madonna's image on the back (for some inexplicable reason) during the bachelor party scene filmed at the legendary Rainbow Bar & Grill in West Hollywood.

Filming also took place at the Orpheum Theater (with 1,500 extras) in downtown Los Angeles, as well as at a New Mexico church (out of which Slash strolls to play a guitar solo in the desert) used in the 1985 film *Silverado*, a big-budget Western starring Kevin Kline, Scott Glenn, Kevin Costner, Danny Glover, John Cleese, Rosanna Arquette, Brian Dennehey, Linda Hunt, and Jeff Goldblum. About $8,000 of the video's budget reportedly went to Seymour's custom-made coffin. In a 2014 *HuffPost Live* interview, Slash admitted that he had no idea what the music video was about: "The song itself is pretty self-explanatory, but the video is so complex. And I remember when Axl was writing it, it just became . . . It was so epic, it was like a movie." At the 1992 Video Music Awards, "November Rain" won "Best Cinematography," MTV placed the video at No. 1 on their list of the "Top 100 Music Videos of 1992," and it was voted "Best Video Clip" in *Metal Edge's* 1992 Readers' Choice Awards. According to Dave Grohl of Nirvana/Foo Fighters fame in *I Want My MTV*, "When a musician starts to use the phrase 'mini-movie' to describe a video, it's time to quit. Some videos I enjoyed just because they were train wrecks, like 'November Rain.' I looked forward to seeing that on TV because I didn't need those nine minutes of my life anymore."

As for the real-life couple, they broke up in 1993 after Rose accused Seymour of being unfaithful. She later married billionaire Peter Brant. In a 2014 *Vanity Fair* interview, Seymour remarked, "Getting involved with Axl Rose? Clearly a mistake . . . It taught me a lot, though. He was a violent person, and I realized I never wanted to be around that again. The thrill of the whole rock 'n' roll thing wore off. I saw the worst of that world and it soured me."

"Estranged"

If there ever was a "jump the shark" (or in this case "jump the dolphin") moment for Guns N' Roses, this may very well be the leading candidate. The final chapter in GN'R's unofficial trilogy (along with "Don't Cry" and "November Rain"), "Estranged" topped them all as the most expensive music video created by the band (estimated at a whopping $4 million). It was also the strangest of the three videos. "Estranged" deals with a troubled relationship (Axl had split up with Stephanie Seymour by this time). The video also somewhat improbably features Axl actually jumping off an oil tanker and being saved from drowning by a dolphin (not kidding!). Definitions for words like "illusion," "estranged," and "disillusion" keep popping up during the video for some odd reason. Meanwhile, Slash plays a guitar solo in front of the Rainbow Bar & Grill in West Hollywood and then later in the middle of the ocean. There's also a SWAT team breaking into a mansion, and even the US Coast Guard makes an appearance. In addition, throughout the entire video, Axl can be seen wearing a Charles Manson T-shirt with the words "Charlie Don't Surf" on the back. By the way, the abandoned estate that appears in the video was actually Rose's Malibu mansion.

"The Garden"

In the music video for "The Garden," the Gunners descend upon a nightmarish New York City (scenes of urban decay abound), wander around Times Square and through Washington Square Park, and visit a bunch of strip clubs and adult bookstores (which are filmed in color). Duff looks completely strung out (once again!) and lost as he sits on a curb and spits. A somber looking Axl takes the subway. "The Garden" video provides a good glimpse of sleazy Times Square before it was Disneyfied. Otherwise, there's not much here (unless you're in the mood to get thoroughly depressed). By the way, Alice Cooper and Shannon Hoon (of Blind Melon) provided the guest vocals. Jef Rouner of the *Houston Press*, in his 2015 list of the "10 Worst Guns N' Roses Songs," called "The Garden" a "trite pretentious hair metal track" accompanied by an "unforgivably boring" music video.

"You Could Be Mine"

A caption at the beginning of the music video for "You Could Be Mine" reads "Ten years ago they sent a machine from the future to kill Sarah Connor . . . they failed. Now, they have a new target: Guns N' Roses." Since "You Could Be Mine" from *Use Your Illusion II* was featured on the soundtrack for *Terminator 2: Judgment Day* (1991), the accompanying music video for the song boasts an appearance by Arnold Schwarzenegger as the cyborg T-800, who methodically hunts down GN'R band members in between live footage shots of Guns N' Roses performing in concert.

"Dead Horse"

Directed by Louis Marciano, the music video for "Dead Horse" first appeared on a 1993 VHS-only release, *Garden of Eden: Strictly Limited Edition*, along with videos for "Garden of Eden" and "Yesterdays." The "Dead Horse" video was later included in the 2003 DVD *Guns N' Roses: Welcome to the Videos*. The video itself reveals some fascinating footage taken during various concerts during the *Use Your Illusion* Tour. Once again, Axl can be seen wearing the offensive Charles Manson T-shirt at several shows. Slash dons a sombrero at one point, and Duff looks completely out of it. A must-see!

"Since I Don't Have You"

The only music video released from *"The Spaghetti Incident?"*, "Since I Don't Have You" (a cover of the Skyliners' 1958 hit single) was also the last video Guns N' Roses made with Slash and Duff. Arguably GN'R's weirdest music video, "Since I Don't Have You" plays out like some demented acid trip. The video features actor Gary Oldman (*Sid & Nancy*) as a demonic figure who torments Axl, who at several points is shown bound with a gag in his mouth, as the other band members hang out on the beach with several scantily clad beauties. Model Jennifer Driver, who dated Axl briefly, also appears in the video. At the end, Oldman pushes Axl's convertible over an embankment into a body of water. It's all very weird and senseless, but somehow it works. Slash later revealed that Oldman was a partying buddy of his and only appeared in the video because he was hanging around the set. According to Slash, the next time he heard from Oldman, the actor was in rehab.

Other Notable GN'R Videos

In addition to the featured music videos above, several more obscure GN'R videos can be sought out on YouTube, such as the following:

"Yesterdays"

In the black-and-white "Yesterdays" music video, footage of Guns N' Roses rocking out in a huge warehouse is interspersed with images of the band in their early years. It's a minor effort indeed and instantly forgettable.

"Garden of Eden"

For total simplicity, few music videos beat "Garden of Eden"—which features a sped-up, fisheye-lens view of a maniacal Axl singing along with fellow band members rocking it out insanely behind him. It's cool how Axl just collapses to the side at the end. The video first appeared on a 1993 VHS-only release, *Garden of Eden: Strictly Limited Edition*, along with videos for "Dead Horse" and "Yesterdays." The "Garden of Eden" video was later included in the 2003 DVD *Guns N' Roses: Welcome to the Videos*.

"Live and Let Die"

A spirited cover of the Paul and Linda McCartney/Wings song, "Live and Let Die" was turned into a music video in November 1992. The video featured GN'R playing live on stage during various performances along with childhood images of the band. Izzy, who had by this time departed the band, appears on a milk carton (making this his last official appearance in a GN'R music video). Axl, who takes a couple of amazing stage dives, can be seen wearing an N.W.A. baseball cap at one point in the video. It's a pretty cool video but ultimately rather pedestrian and unmemorable.

"Chinese Democracy"

The music video for "Chinese Democracy," from the long-awaited 2008 GN'R album *Chinese Democracy*, features concert footage of the band interspersed with disturbing scenes of violent conflicts around the world. It's one of the few Guns N' Roses videos (okay, it's the only one!) with a political subtext. At the end of the video, a line appears, stating, "dedicated to those fighting oppression."

"Bad Apples"

An unusual choice for a music video is the typically forgotten song "Bad Apples," which appears near the end of *Use Your Illusion I*. In fact, the video came out in 2009, eighteen years after the release of the album. The video features outtakes from the "Don't Cry" video, with the band performing atop the Transamerica Center in Los Angeles. Shannon Hoon, lead singer of Blind Melon, makes an appearance even though he didn't even perform on "Bad Apples." The result is "choppy and oversaturated," according to *Ultimate Classic Rock* magazine.

"Wild Thing"

Last and most certainly least, Slash and Steven Adler were invited to take part in the late, great comedian Sam Kinison's music video for his hilarious cover of the Troggs' "Wild Thing," which appeared on his 1989 album *Have You Seen Me Lately?* and included new lyrics, such as "Everytime I kiss you/I taste what other men had for lunch." The raunchy video, which featured a "cage match" between Kinison and the notorious Jessica Hahn (infamous from the Jim Bakker scandal), also boasted cameos by Rodney Dangerfield, Jon Bon Jovi, Steven Tyler and Joe Perry of Aerosmith, Billy Idol, Richie Sambora and Alec John Such of Bon Jovi, Jonathan Cain and Dee Castronovo of Bad English, Rick Marty of Alice Cooper Band, Tommy Lee of Mötley Crüe, C. C. Deville of Poison, Rudy Sarzo of Quiet Riot, and several members of Ratt. A keg of beer was provided for all of the attendees, and there is a great shot in the video of a drunken Slash falling into an alley trash can.

A former revival-style preacher, Kinison got his first big break on

Both Slash and Steven Adler, along with a slew of other rockers and celebrities, appeared in comedian Sam Kinison's music video for his hilarious cover of the Trogg's "Wild Thing" in 1989.   *Author's collection*

Rodney Dangerfield's *Ninth Young Comedians Special*, which aired on HBO in 1984. Known for his intense style and trademark scream, Kinison unleashed an outrageous and uncensored form of comedy that included angry rants and attacks against conventional norms. In 1986, Kinison had a memorable role as the totally insane "Professor Terguson" in *Back to School*, which starred Dangerfield. Kinison also appeared as Al Bundy's guardian angel in a 1989 episode of *Married with Children*. Tragically, just six days after marrying his girlfriend Malika Souiri in 1992, Kinison was killed in a car accident on US 95 in California at the age of thirty-eight. His epitaph reads: "In Another Time and Place He Would Have Been Called Prophet."

23

Bought Me an Illusion

Guns N' Roses Songs That Have Appeared in Feature Films

That's the sound of a band breaking up right there.
—Slash, on GN'R's cover of "Sympathy for the Devil"

The inclusion of "Welcome to the Jungle" in two high-profile movies—*The Dead Pool* and *Lean on Me*—during the late 1980s helped signal the arrival of Guns N' Roses onto the national scene, and they soon skyrocketed to superstardom. Conversely, GN'R's lethargic cover of the Rolling Stones' classic "Sympathy for the Devil" for the soundtrack of the 1994 film *Interview with the Vampire* signaled the demise of the band's original lineup (as evidenced by the above quote). Through it all, countless films—from low-budget cheapies such as *America Ninja 2: The Confrontation* and *Bad Dreams* to big-time blockbusters like *Days of Thunder* and *Terminator 2: Judgment Day*—have melded the Gunners' slew of electrifying hits into their soundtracks with mixed results.

In addition to the films featured below, GN'R songs have appeared on such widely divergent soundtracks as *Amok: Patrolman 2* (1989, "Knockin' on Heaven's Door"), *The Program* (1993, "Welcome to the Jungle"), *Selena* (1997, "Welcome to the Jungle"), *Grosse Pointe Blank* (1997, "Live and Let Die"), *Can't Hardly Wait* (1998, "Paradise City"), *End of Days* (1999, "Oh My God"), *Big Daddy* (1999, "Sweet Child O' Mine"), *Titans* (2000, "Welcome to the Jungle"), *Gone Baby Gone* (2007, "You're Crazy"), *Terminator Salvation* (2009, "You Could Be Mine"), *Gulliver's Travels* (2010, "Sweet Child O' Mine"), *Megamind* (2010, "Welcome to the Jungle"), *Warm Bodies* (2013, "Patience"), *The Big Short* (2015, "Sweet Child O' Mine"), and *How to Be Single* (2016, "Welcome to the Jungle"), among others.

Several Guns N' Roses songs also feature lyrics woven from classic quotes from well-known movies, including "Civil War" (*Cool Hand Luke*,

1967), "Breakdown" (*Vanishing Point*, 1971), and "Madagascar" (*Cool Hand Luke; Mississippi Burning*, 1988; *Casualties of War*, 1989; *Braveheart*, 1995; and *Se7en*, 1995).

"Move to the City"—*American Ninja 2: The Confrontation* (1987)

"Tell me, what would Japanese assassins be doing in this part of a world? Taking a vacation?" Notable as the first film to feature a Guns N' Roses song in its soundtrack ("Move to the City," which can be found on both *Live?!*@ Like a Suicide* and *G N' R Lies*) and not much else, this overwhelmingly cheesy but highly entertaining martial arts film served as a sequel to *American Ninja* (1985). For the record, in one of the film's early scenes, "Move to the City" can be heard on the radio briefly as a couple of soldiers/mercenaries drive a convertible along a beach in the Caribbean and ogle a bevy of topless bathers.

Released by the Cannon Group (which should give you a good idea of what to expect in terms of quality here!) and directed by Sam Firstenberg (*Breakin' 2: Electric Boogaloo*), *American Ninja 2* features the return of Michael Dudikoff as Sergeant Joe Armstrong, who heads to an unnamed Caribbean island to battle against "an army of mutant Ninja warriors." The relatively unknown cast also consists of Steve James, Gary Conway, Larry Poindexter, Michelle Botes, and Mike Stone (as "Tojo Ken"). As an added bonus, the film contains some priceless dialogue, such as this gem spouted by "Wild Bill" Woodward (Jeff Weston): "I don't like that tiny maggot, I don't like him at all. I mean, what is this? Ninjas? Drug pushers? My men being kidnapped and murdered? This is really beginning to get on my tits."

The *American Ninja 2* soundtrack also features "Wasteland" from undeservedly obscure San Francisco power metal band Ruffians. Believe it or not, *American Ninja 2* spawned three additional sequels: *American Ninja 3: Blood Hunt* (1989), *American Ninja 4: The Annihilation* (1990), and *American Ninja V* (1993). For a humorous, totally outrageous overview of this and other low-budget films churned out over the years by the Cannon Group, check out the 2014 documentary *Electric Boogaloo: The Wild, Untold Story of Cannon Films*.

"Welcome to the Jungle"—*The Dead Pool* (1988)

"Dirty Harry just learned a new game." Clint Eastwood returned for his fifth and final appearance as Inspector "Dirty Harry" Callahan in *The Dead Pool*

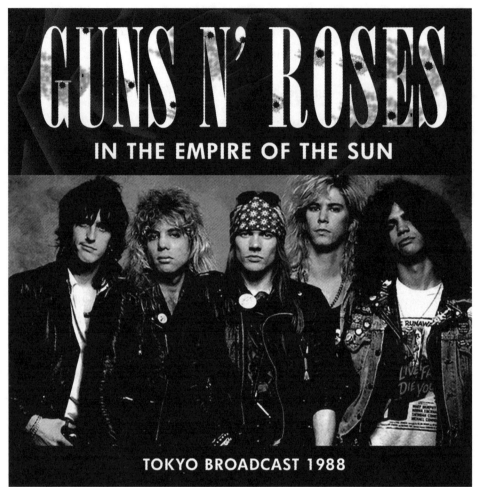

As Appetite for Destruction skyrocketed up the charts in 1988, Guns N' Roses performed in Tokyo, Japan, for the first time and also made a cameo in *The Dead Pool*, which featured Clint Eastwood's fifth and final appearance as Inspector "Dirty Harry" Callahan.   *Author's collection*

(not to be confused with the 2016 superhero film *Deadpool*), which was filmed on location in San Francisco and also starred Patricia Clarkson as reporter Samantha Walker, Liam Neeson as slasher film director Peter Swan, Evan Kim as Dirty Harry's new partner Al Quan, David Hunt as deranged villain Harlan Rook, and a then unknown Jim Carrey (in only his second film after 1985's *Once Bitten*) as drug-addled rock star Johnny Squares. In *The Dead Pool*, which was directed by Buddy Van Horn (*Any Which Way You Can*), Dirty Harry attempts to stop a serial killer who is preying on celebrities and soon finds himself in the psychopath's crosshairs. Along the way, he gets the opportunity to deliver some vintage "Dirty Harry" witticisms, such as "Fuck with me, buddy, I'll kick your ass so hard you'll have to unbutton your collar to shit."

The film's soundtrack features Carrey lip-synching "Welcome to the Jungle" in a truly awful music video that spoofs *The Exorcist*. In addition, all of the Guns N' Roses band members can be viewed in a cameo during the Johnny Squares funeral scene. (If you blink, you'll miss it!) Also, during the filming of the "nightmare scene," Slash accidentally fires a harpoon through a window on the pirate tugboat. Spoiler alert! Dirty Harry himself later wields the harpoon gun against the film's villain in the final scene. As expected, the brief film shoot featured its fair share of GN'R-style debauchery. For instance, Steven Adler in his 2010 autobiography *My Appetite for Destruction* details how he picked up a "stripper chick," who was serving as an extra on the set. After they smoked some weed, Adler noticed that she slipped a brown powder into his cup of tea. According to Adler, "The last thing I remember, she had my head between her legs and was forcing my face against her groin. 'Now I'll show you how to eat pussy,' she purred. She was in control and I was floating, floating away . . . without a care in the world."

As for *The Dead Pool*, the film received rather mixed reviews, with Vincent Canby of the *New York Times* describing it as "a mini-movie in the company of a mythic figure," while the late, great film critic Roger Ebert called it "smart, quick, and made with real wit." The "Dirty Harry" film series also includes *Dirty Harry* (1971), *Magnum Force* (1973), *The Enforcer* (1976), and *Sudden Impact* (1983).

"Sweet Child O' Mine"—*Bad Dreams* (1988)

"When the nightmares come to life, the fight for survival begins." Viewers of this low-budget horror film (with shades of *Nightmare on Elm Street*) will have to patiently sit through the entire eighty-four-minute running time to listen to "Sweet Child O' Mine" playing during the closing credits. (It's not worth it, believe me!) A young girl named Cynthia (Jennifer Rubin, who portrayed Taryn White in *A Nightmare on Elm Street 3: Dream Warriors*) survives the mass suicide of a 1970s hippie cult named Unity Fields (they douse themselves on fire in a particularly gruesome scene), spends the next thirteen years in a coma, and awakens in a psychiatric ward with nightmares of the creepy cult leader (Richard Lynch) beckoning to her from the grave.

Directed by Andrew Fleming (*The Craft*), *Bad Dreams* also stars Bruce Abbott (*Re-Animator*), Harris Yulin (corrupt cop Mel Bernstein from *Scarface*), E. G. Daily (*Valley Girl*), and Dean Cameron (best known for his role as Francis "Chainsaw" Gremp in the 1987 comedy *Summer School*). In his one-star review of *Bad Dreams* that appears on Rogerebert.com, critic Roger Ebert remarked, "It is not surprising to see a violent teen film exploiting the lowest common denominator and preaching a message of nihilism and despair. It is not surprising to see the latest special-effect technology supplying lingering closeups of burnt flesh and other horrors. What is surprising, I suppose, is that nice people would want to wade in this sewer."

"Welcome to the Jungle"—*Lean on Me* (1989)

"A true story about a real hero." Although best known musically for the title theme (a No. 1 single written and recorded by Bill Withers in 1972), the *Lean on Me* soundtrack also features "Welcome to the Jungle" during the opening credits as students of inner-city, graffiti-strewn Eastside High School in Paterson, New Jersey, start another chaotic school day amid various acts of gang violence, vandalism, drug deals, and assorted mayhem. Directed by John G. Avildsen (*Rocky*) and based very loosely on a true story, *Lean on Me* stars Morgan Freeman in a powerful performance as real-life principal Joe Clark, who uses rather unorthodox and controversial methods (including carrying around a bullhorn and baseball bat) to attempt the seemingly impossible task of returning the school to its primary role as an institution of learning. Along the way, Clark spouts such empty platitudes as "Discipline is not the enemy of enthusiasm!"

The *Lean on Me* cast also features Robert Guillaume, Lynne Thigpen, Beverly Todd, Alan North, Robin Bartlett, Michael Beach, and Ethan Phillips. In addition, look for Michael Imperioli (Christopher Moltisanti from *The Sopranos*) as a dumb punk on the stage among the "incorrigible" students expelled from the school by Clark. As for the real-life Clark, he got dismissed as principal soon after the film's release when it was discovered that a troupe of strippers performed a "risqué rap show" at a school assembly. (Clark, who went on to become a popular motivational speaker, referred to the sordid spectacle as an "ethnic dance.") In a March 3, 1989 review of *Lean on Me* for the *Washington Post*, film critic Hal Hinson stated, "The movie's attitude is that the end justifies any means—even taking one young man who is killing himself with crack onto the roof and urging him to jump . . . [The filmmakers] don't seem inclined to acknowledge that

Clark's actions might be questionable or even dangerous, as many believed those of the real Joe Clark were."

"Knockin' on Heaven's Door"—*Days of Thunder* (1990)

"You can't stop the thunder." Directed by Tony Scott (*Top Gun*) from a script by Robert Towne (*Chinatown*), this moderately entertaining stock car racing film stars Tom Cruise as Cole Trickle, an upstart driver on the NASCAR racing circuit. (Cruise's character is reportedly loosely based on driver "Hollywood" Tim Richmond, who died of complications from AIDS at the age of thirty-four in 1989.) The all-star cast includes Nicole Kidman as love interest/neurosurgeon Dr. Claire Lewicki, Robert Duvall as gritty crew chief Harry Hogge, Randy Quaid as arrogant race team owner Tim Daland, Cary Elwes as rookie driver Russ Wheeler, John C. Reilly as Trickle's car chief, Buck Bretherton, and Michael Rooker as Trickle's main rival, Rowdy Burns. *Days of Thunder* also features cameos by legendary NASCAR drivers, such as Richard "The King" Petty, Rusty Wallace, "Handsome Harry" Gant, and Neil Bonnett. (Tragically, Bonnett would lose his life in a crash during a Daytona 500 practice session in 1994.)

The *Days of Thunder* soundtrack features a slightly different version of Guns N' Roses' cover of Bob Dylan's "Knockin' on Heaven's Door" than the track that would appear a year later on *Use Your Illusion II.* It was also reportedly the first song that new drummer Matt Sorum played on with GN'R. (He replaced Steven Adler, whose excessive drug use was adversely affecting his drum skills.) Commenting on recording "Knockin' on Heaven's Door," Slash, in his self-titled 2007 autobiography, stated that he used a '58 Gibson Explorer for the solo and that it was "an amazing take." However, regarding Adler's departure from the band, he felt there was a "definite difference" between the new Guns without Adler and the old Guns: "We had lost a little bit of the mayhem and punk rock, that raw chaotic, seat-of-the-pants feel."

"Knockin' on Heaven's Door" can be heard when Cole is talking to Claire in the garage and then arguing with Harry. The *Days of Thunder* soundtrack also includes "The Last Note of Freedom" (David Coverdale of Whitesnake), "Deal for Life" (John Waite), "You Gotta Love Someone" (Elton John), "Trail of Broken Hearts" (Cher), "Hearts in Trouble" (Chicago), "Break Through the Barrier" (Tina Turner), "Gimme Some Lovin'" (Spencer David Group), "Long Live the Night" (Joan Jett & the Blackhearts), and "Thunderbox" (Apollo Smile).

In a November 10, 2009, *Metro* interview, director Quentin Tarantino claimed that *Days of Thunder* was his favorite big-budget racing movie of all time: "To me *Days of Thunder* is the movie *Grand Prix* (1966) and *Le Mans* (1971) should have been. Sure, it had a big budget, big stars, and a big director in Tony Scott, but it had the fun of those early AIP [American International Pictures] movies. I just don't think it works if you take the whole thing too seriously." Cruise and Kidman, who met for the first time on the set of the film, were married between 1990 and 2001, and together they appeared in two more films that couldn't be more diverse: *Far and Away* (1992), a mediocre romantic adventure directed by Ron Howard, and *Eyes Wide Shut* (1999), an erotic drama that served as acclaimed director Stanley Kubrick's final film.

"Sweet Child O' Mine"—*State of Grace* (1990)

"A family ripped apart by violence. A love corrupted by betrayal. A friendship stained by blood." A gritty crime drama shot on location in New York City, *State of Grace* is notable for featuring a slew of powerful performances from the likes of Sean Penn, Gary Oldman, Ed Harris, Robin Wright, and John C. Reilly. "Sweet Child O' Mine" can be heard during one of several bar brawls in the film, which focuses on the Irish mob (based on the notorious Westies gang) in the Manhattan neighborhood known as Hell's Kitchen and headed by Frankie Flannery (Harris).

In *State of Grace*, Terry Noonan (Penn) returns to the gang after a mysterious ten-year absence and once again starts hanging out with his childhood buddy, Jackie (Oldman), who is Frankie's younger brother, a total loose cannon with stringy hair, a violent streak, and a wild, self-destructive bent. Terry also rekindles his relationship with Jackie and Frankie's sister, Kathleen (Wright, who was married to Penn from 1996-2010). Reilly portrays not-so-bright gang member Stevie McGuire. Also look for Joe Viterelli as Borelli, John Turturro as Nick, and Burgess Meredith as Finn. Not only does this unruly Irish gang have to deal with rival Italian mobsters encroaching on their turf, but also Hell's Kitchen itself is undergoing gentrification (much to everyone's chagrin!). The film's dynamic ending (spoiler!) features a slow-motion shootout at the bar intercut with shots of the St. Patrick's Day Parade.

Directed by Phil Joanou and written by Dennis McIntyre (who tragically died of cancer the year it was released), *State of the Grace* was a box office failure, generating just over $1.9 million during its brief US run. (It didn't help that the film was released around the same time as *Goodfellas*!) The legendary Ennio Morricone provided the score. The stellar soundtrack also features "White City" by the Pogues, "Street Fighting Man" by the Rolling Stones, "I Love You Yesterday" by Lyle Lovett, "Moondance" by Van Morrison, "Drink Before the War" by Sinead O'Connor, and "Trip Through Your Wires" by U2. Joanou also directed U2's critically acclaimed 1988 rockumentary *Rattle and Hum*.

"You Could Be Mine"—*Terminator 2: Judgment Day* (1991)

"The battle for tomorrow has begun." GN'R's "You Could Be Mine" serves as the theme song for the critically acclaimed sequel to *The Terminator* (both of which were directed by James Cameron and starred Arnold Schwarzenegger and Linda Hamilton) before it showed up several months later as a track on *Use Your Illusion II*. The film contains a couple of Guns N' Roses in-jokes: At one point the Terminator is strolling along through a hallway in the mall, and all of a sudden he pulls out a gun from a box of roses. Also, John Connor's friend Tim (Danny Cooksey) can be seen wearing an L.A. Guns T-shirt. The corresponding music video for "You Could Be Mine" featured GN'R concert footage cleverly intermixed with clips from *Terminator 2* as the T-800 mercilessly stalks members of the band.

"You Could Be Mine" was nominated for a Grammy Award for "Best Song from a Movie" along with such distinguished company as "(Everything I Do) I Do It for You" from *Robin Hood: Prince of Thieves* (Bryan Adams, who actually won the award, believe it or not!), "Addams Groove" from *The Addams Family* (MC Hammer), "I Wanna Sex You Up" from *New Jack City* (Color Me Badd), and "Tears from Heaven" from *Rush* (Eric Clapton).

"Patience"—*Cape Fear* (1991)

"There is nothing in the dark that isn't there in the light. Except fear." A remake of the classic 1962 psychological thriller of the same name (featuring Gregory Peck and Robert Mitchum), *Cape Fear* was directed by Martin Scorsese and stars a thoroughly unpleasant Robert De Niro totally chewing scenery as psychopath Max Cady. Cady has just been released from prison and vows revenge on lawyer Sam Bowden (Nick Nolte), who deliberately withheld evidence that could have lessened his sentence for rape. The all-star cast includes Jessica Lange as Bowden's wife, Leigh, and Juliette Lewis as Bowden's troubled daughter, Danielle, as well as Mitchum and Peck in

minor roles. "Patience" can be heard in the background on the radio in the scene when Danielle retreats to her bedroom to avoid her frequently bickering parents as they embark on another major argument. (In fact, *none* of the characters are particularly likeable in this rather unpalatable film.) In addition, look for the Jane's Addiction music video for "Been Caught Stealing" playing on the TV silently during the "Patience" scene.

De Niro was nominated for a "Best Actor" Oscar (but lost to Anthony Hopkins for *The Silence of the Lambs*), while Lewis was nominated for a "Best Supporting Actress" Oscar (but lost to Mercedes Ruehl for *The Fisher King*). Cape Fear served as one of nine collaborations between Scorsese and De Niro, the others being *Mean Streets* (1973), *Taxi Driver* (1976), *New York, New York* (1977), *Raging Bull* (1980), *The King of Comedy* (1983), *Goodfellas* (1990), *Casino* (1995), and *The Irishman* (set to be released in 2018).

"Sympathy for the Devil"—*Interview with the Vampire* (1994)

"So you want me to tell you the story of my life?" According to a review of *Interview with the Vampire* in the April 1995 issue of *Film Threat*, "The film's most egregious misstep is its final coda, in which [Tom] Cruise performs a Freddy-like resurrection from the grave to savage his final victim, all set to the discordant wailing of Axl Rose performing the Stones' classic 'Sympathy for the Devil.'"

Written by Mick Jagger and Keith Richards, "Sympathy for the Devil" (working title: "The Devil Is My Name") was featured on 1968's *Beggars Banquet*, which served as the last album the band released before Brian Jones died under mysterious circumstances on July 3, 1969, at the age of twenty-seven. *Rolling Stone* placed "Sympathy for the Devil" at No. 32 on its list of the "500 Greatest Songs of All Time." In the 2012 Rolling Stones documentary *Crossfire Hurricane*, Jagger cited Russian writer Mikhail Bulgakov's novel *The Master and Margarita* (which remained unpublished until 1967, twenty-six years after the author's death) and decadent French poet Charles Baudelaire as influences for the song. In his 1989 memoir, *Wonderland Avenue: Tales of Glamour and Excess*, rock biographer Danny Sugerman called Baudelaire "the first real rock star" because he smoked dope, stayed up all night, frequented whorehouses, and proceeded to "fuck around so much he finally got syphilis and ultimately died insane and mad, brilliant as he was tragic."

Guns N' Roses' recording of "Sympathy for the Devil" created animosity between Slash and Axl when the latter brought in his old friend, guitarist

Paul "Huge" Tobias, to overdub the former's guitar solo. Slash would end up quitting the band two years later in 1996. In his 2007 self-titled autobiography, Slash remarked, "If there is one Guns track I'd like never to hear again, it is that one . . . From the basic tracks through to the final overdubs, we never saw or heard from Axl . . . [H]is disregard for our time and commitment definitely inspired a *very* uninspired instrumental track." In addition, rhythm guitarist Gilby Clarke was on the road touring for a solo record at the time and wasn't even informed about the recording.

The GN'R "Sympathy for the Devil" cover reached No. 55 on the *Billboard* charts and rather inexplicably ended up on the 2004 *Greatest Hits* album (a Geffen release that Axl and former band members Slash and Duff unsuccessfully tried to block). In a February 19, 2016, ranking of all Guns N' Roses songs from worst to best, *SPIN* magazine listed "Sympathy for the Devil" dead last at No. 79, explaining, "Whereas the Stones are loose and breezy and quick-footed, Guns trudge through their cover—and because the music is so sluggish, Axl overacts to fill up the extra space, his vocal a miserable dramatic interpretation." The film itself, which was directed by Neil Jordan (*The Crying Game*) and based on the bestselling 1976 novel of the same name by Anne Rice, won a Razzie Award for "Worst Screen Couple" for Cruise and Brad Pitt (tied with Sylvester Stallone and Sharon Stone in *The Specialist*). The soundtrack was nominated for the Academy Award and the Golden Globe Award for "Best Original Score" but lost both to *The Lion King*.

"Sweet Child O' Mine"—*The Wrestler* (2008)

"The world don't give a shit about me." Known as Mickey Rourke's comeback film, *The Wrestler* was directed by Darren Aronofsky (*Requiem for a Dream*) and documents the often sordid world of professional wrestling. Rourke portrays washed-up former wrestler Randy "the Ram" Robinson, who is caught between his rapidly fading celebrity and a genuine desire to forge a new life outside the ring. (He has heart trouble, lives in a dilapidated van, works part-time in a supermarket deli, hangs out at a seedy strip club, and scrapes by wrestling the independent circuit in front of sparse crowds on weekends.) The cast includes Marisa Tomei as a jaded stripper named Cassidy, Evan Rachel Wood as the Ram's estranged daughter Stephanie, and Ernest Miller as a fellow wrestler known as the Ayatollah.

"Sweet Child O' Mine" can be heard upon the Ram's final entrance into the ring at the end of the film. (Rourke had reportedly used the song as his intro music when he took up a short-lived and widely disparaged boxing career in the early 1990s.) In addition, the Ram and Cassidy engage in a spirited dialogue on their first "date" at the dive bar as they compare 1980s hard rock to 1990s grunge. As Cassidy remarks, "Fuckin' 80s man, best shit ever," Ram exclaims, "Bet your ass man, Guns N' Roses rules . . . Then that Cobain pussy had to come around and ruin it all . . . I hate the fuckin' '90s."

The film's solid soundtrack also features "The Wrestler" (Bruce Springsteen), "Round and Round" (Ratt), "Metal Health" (Quiet Riot), "Don't Know What You Got" (Cinderella), and "Animal Magnetism" (Scorpions), among others. Rourke received a Golden Globe Award for "Best Actor" for the role but lost out on the Academy Award to Sean Penn (*Milk*), while Tomei also was nominated for a "Best Supporting Actress" Oscar (but lost out to Penelope Cruz in Woody Allen's *Vicky Cristina Barcelona*). During his Golden Globe speech, Rourke, a good friend of Axl Rose, singled out the Guns N' Roses singer, remarking that "We had no money, Axl stepped up to the plate and gave us 'Sweet Child O' Mine.'" The film itself received the Golden Lion Award at the 2008 Venice Film Festival.

24

What Seemed Like a Memory

Cultural and Political References in Guns N' Roses Songs and Music Videos

Everything of worth in a video is stolen from somewhere, so I stole from some cool movies. —Alan Niven, director of the "Welcome to the Jungle" music video

C ertain Guns N' Roses tracks, such as "Civil War" (from *Use Your Illusion II*) and "Madagascar" (from *Chinese Democracy*), contain great samples that reference classic films and historical events relevant to the song lyrics. For instance, "Civil War" not only features a clip from the 1967 Paul Newman film *Cool Hand Luke* but also a quote from a Peruvian Shining Path guerilla officer, as well as allusions to the Vietnam War and to both the John F. Kennedy and Martin Luther King Jr. assassinations. In addition, the "Welcome to the Jungle" music video features several scenes influenced by popular movies, such as *Midnight Cowboy*, *A Clockwork Orange*, and *The Man Who Fell to Earth*.

A Clockwork Orange

It's no coincidence that the scene in Guns N' Roses' 1987 "Welcome to the Jungle" music video where Axl is strapped into a chair and forced to watch insane images on TV mirrors a scene from Stanley Kubrick's disturbing 1971 film *A Clockwork Orange*. In fact, the music video's director, Alan Niven, claimed he stole the idea directly from the film (along with scenes from *Midnight Cowboy* and *The Man Who Fell to Earth*). The dystopian film features Malcolm McDowell as the Beethoven-loving Alex, who leads a gang of thugs (known as "droogs") who go on a spree of rape and "ultra-violence." After he is arrested and sent to prison, Alex undergoes a conditioning process that makes him detest violence, and then he is released to the streets with horrific results. Kubrick adapted *A Clockwork Orange* from Anthony Burgess's 1962 novel of the same name.

Braveheart

Several lines from *Braveheart*—the epic, historically inaccurate 1995 Mel Gibson film about thirteenth-century Scottish warrior William Wallace—are sampled in the powerful song "Madagascar" from the *Chinese Democracy* album. Braveheart captured five Academy Awards, including "Best Picture," "Best Director," "Best Cinematography," "Best Makeup," and "Best Sound Editing."

Captain America

Buried in the lyrics to "Paradise City" is a sly reference to a fictional Marvel Comics superhero: "Captain America's been torn apart/Now he's a court jester with a broken heart." Created by Jack Kirby and Joe Simon, Captain America, a patriotic World War II soldier, first appeared in Captain America Comics #1 in 1941. Other musicians have used Captain America as inspiration, such as Jimmy Buffett's "Captain America" from his rather obscure 1970 album *Down to Earth*, and the Kinks "Catch Me Now I'm Falling" from the 1979 album *Low Budget*.

Casualties of War

"Madagascar" features a sample from the impassioned speech of Private Max Eriksson (played by Michael J. Fox) from the 1989 Brian De Palma Vietnam War film *Casualties of War*: "Everybody's acting like we can do anything and it don't matter what we do. Maybe we gotta be extra careful because maybe it matters more than we even know." *Casualties of War* was based on actual events (known as the "Incident on Hill 192") involving the horrific kidnapping, gang rape, and murder of a young Vietnamese woman by a squad of American soldiers in 1966 during the Vietnam War.

Catcher in the Rye

The title for the seventh track of *Chinese Democracy*, "Catcher in the Rye," was taken from J. D. Salinger's critically acclaimed, controversial, and frequently censored 1951 novel of teenage angst and rebellion that focuses on narrator Holden Caulfield. *Catcher in the Rye* has been associated with several high-profile shootings, such as Mark David Chapman's murder of John Lennon on December 8, 1980, and John Hinckley's assassination attempt on President Ronald Reagan on March 30, 1981. The highly reclusive Salinger published his last original work in 1965 and retreated to a private life in New Hampshire for the last fifty years of his life. He passed away of natural causes in 2010 at the age of ninety-one.

Cool Hand Luke

Both "Civil War" and "Madagascar" contain samples of the famous "failure to communicate" speech by the "Road Crew Captain" (Strother Martin) in the 1967 film *Cool Hand Luke*, which starred Paul Newman in the title role, along with George Kennedy (who won a "Best Supporting Actor" Oscar for his performance as "Dragline"). The stellar cast includes Jo Van Fleet, Luke Askew, Dennis Hopper, and Harry Dean Stanton. *Cool Hand Luke* was based on a 1965 novel of the same name by Donn Pearce, who had spent two years on a chain gang in Raiford Penitentiary in Florida after getting arrested for burglary in 1949 at the age of twenty. According to author Ted Geltner (*Blood, Bone and Marrow*), "Pearce's Hollywood experience was underwhelming. He thought little of Paul Newman, was snubbed by Jack Lemmon during a visit to the set, and [was] ignored by the director [Stuart Rosenberg]." Pearce, whose other novels include *Pier Head Jump* (1972), *Dying in the Sun* (1974) and *Nobody Comes Back* (2005), appeared in a cameo in the film as a convict named Sailor and currently lives in Fort Lauderdale, Florida.

Falun Gong

"Blame it on the Falun Gong/They've seen the end and you can't hold on now." The title track of Guns N' Roses' *Chinese Democracy* album refers to this controversial Chinese spiritual practice that blends qigong exercises with mediation and places an emphasis on morality and cultivation of virtue. In the late 1990s, the Chinese government organized a crackdown on Falun Gong, declaring it a "heretical organization," and Falun Gong practitioners have been subject to a range of human rights abuses.

A sample from the famous "failure to communicate" speech from the 1967 film *Cool Hand Luke* appears in two Guns N' Roses songs: "Civil War" and "Madagascar."   *Author's collection*

Hit Parader Magazine

In "Get in the Ring," which appears on *Use Your Illusion II*, Axl attacked specific rock journalists that he felt printed malicious lies about Guns N' Roses along with "rippin' off the fuckin' kids," such as Andy Secher of *Hit Parader*, who began writing for the magazine in 1979. *Hit Parader* began in 1942 as a popular-song lyric newspaper.

John F. Kennedy

One of the rare Guns N' Roses political songs, "Civil War" references the assassination of President John F. Kennedy in Dallas, Texas, on November 22, 1963, when Kennedy was just forty-six: "And in my first memories/They shot Kennedy/An' I went numb when I learned to see." Kennedy is buried at Arlington National Cemetery in Arlington, Virginia, and his grave is lit with an "Eternal Flame." William Howard Taft (1857–1930) is the only other US president buried at Arlington.

Kerrang! Magazine

Mick Wall of *Kerrang!*, a popular UK-based magazine first published in 1981, was another rock journalist singled out to face Axl's wrath in "Get in the Ring." Wall wrote two biographies related to GN'R: *Guns N' Roses: The Most Dangerous Band in the World* (1991) and *W. Axl Rose: The Unauthorized Biography* (2007). However, Wall believes that Axl became upset after he published an interview in *Kerrang!* concerning the Axl vs. Vince Neil of Mötley Crüe feud.

Martin Luther King Jr.

The following lyrics from "Civil War" refer to the assassination of civil rights leader Martin Luther King Jr. in Memphis, Tennessee, on April 4, 1968: "D'you wear a black armband/When they shot the man/Who said 'peace could last forever.'" During a September 27, 1993, Rockline radio show interview, Duff explained the origins of the song: "Basically it was a riff that we would do at soundchecks. Axl came up with a couple of lines at the beginning. I went in a peace march when I was a little kid with my mom. I was like four years old. For Martin Luther King . . . It's just true-life experiences, really." Samples from several of King's most famous speeches can be heard in "Madagascar," including "I Have a Dream," which was delivered as the keynote speech at the March on Washington for Jobs and Freedom on

August 28, 1963, and "Why Jesus Called a Man a Fool," which was delivered at Mount Pisgah Missionary Baptist Church in Chicago on August 27, 1967.

Kundun

Axl revealed that the title of the *Chinese Democracy* album was inspired by the 1997 Martin Scorsese film *Kundun*, which documents the life of the fourteenth Dalai Lama, the exiled political and spiritual leader of Tibet. The Chinese government voiced their objections to the release of the film and even banned Scorsese from ever setting foot into China. Although the film was a critical success, it totally bombed at the box office.

The Man Who Fell to Earth

Alan Niven, director of the "Welcome to the Jungle" music video, stole the idea of Axl watching a stack of TVs from the 1976 cult film *The Man Who Fell to Earth*, which starred David Bowie as Thomas Jerome Newton, an alien from a doomed, water-starved planet. Directed by Nicolas Roeg (*Performance*), *The Man Who Fell to Earth* is an offbeat, surreal, and ultimately bleak science fiction film. Newton rapidly loses sight of his original mission of building a spaceship and shipping water back to his planet, and he gradually gets enveloped in a purple haze of sex, booze, and endless hours of television. Candy Clark (*American Graffiti*) portrays Mary-Lou, a motel housekeeper who befriends Newton. The cast also includes Buck Henry as patent attorney Oliver Farnsworth and Rip Torn as college professor Nathan Bryce. Ironically, Slash's mother, Ola, a costume designer, worked on the film and even dated Bowie for a short period. *The Man Who Fell to Earth* is based on a 1963 science fiction novel of the same name by Walter Tevis.

Midnight Cowboy

The scene where Axl arrives in Los Angeles in the "Welcome to the Jungle" music video mirrors the arrival of Joe Buck (Jon Voight) to New York City in the 1969 film *Midnight Cowboy*. In an interview with *Rolling Stone*, the music video's director, Alan Niven, remarks, "Axl's character is a corollary to Jon Voight in *Midnight Cowboy*, who comes to a city that's a cauldron of false dreams." Directed by John Schlesinger, *Midnight Cowboy*, which also stars Dustin Hoffman as Ratso Rizzo, was based on the 1965 novel of the same name by James Leo Herlihy. Initially slapped with an X rating, the film went on to win three Academy Awards for "Best Picture," "Best Director," and "Best Adapted Screenplay."

Mississippi Burning

Several lines from the 1988 film *Mississippi Burning*—such as "Where does it come from, all this hatred?"—can be heard in "Madagascar." Directed by Alan Parker, *Mississippi Burning* is very loosely based on the FBI's investigation of three civil rights workers—James Chaney, Michael Schwerner, and Andrew Goodman—in Mississippi in 1964. The film stars Gene Hackman, Willem Dafoe, Frances McDormand, Brad Dourif, Michael Rooker, Stephen Tobolowsky, and R. Lee Ermey. *Mississippi Burning* received seven Academy Award nominations, including "Best Picture," but only won for "Best Cinematography." The film was widely criticized for making FBI agents the "heroes" of the civil rights movement. Social activist Julian Bond referred disparagingly to the film as "Rambo meets the Klan."

Se7en

Two lines from the 1995 neo-noir psychological thriller *Se7en* are sampled in "Madagascar." Directed by David Fincher, *Se7en* stars Brad Pitt, Morgan Freeman, Gwyneth Paltrow, John C. McGinley, R. Lee Ermey, and Kevin Spacey. The plot concerns two detectives, David Mills (Pitt) and William Somerset (Freeman) as they attempt to track down a serial killer obsessed with the seven deadly sins.

Shining Path

"Civil War" features the following particularly chilling quote from a Peruvian Shining Path guerilla officer: "We practice selective annihilation of mayors and government officials, for example, to create a vacuum, then we fill that vacuum. As popular war advances, peace is closer." With the goal of establishing a dictatorship of the proletariat, the Communist Party of Peru (a.k.a. the Shining Path or "Sendero Luminoso") launched a brutal insurgency throughout the country during the 1980s. The specific quote used by Guns N' Roses was taken from a July 9, 1989, *Chicago Tribune* article by George de Lama with the Orwellian title "'More War Will Bring Peace,' Say Peru's Maoists After 15,000 Die." The young guerilla officer, known simply as "Jorge," also remarks, "Only more popular war will bring peace."

Sigmund Freud

"Right Next Door to Hell" details Axl's ongoing battle with a neighbor when he lived in a West Hollywood condo in the early 1990s. The conflict escalated to the point that the neighbor had Axl arrested after accusing him of hitting her over the head with a wine bottle. The song name-drops Sigmund Freud, the Austrian neurologist and founder of psychoanalysis, in the lines, "Hell 'Freud' might say that's what I need/But all I really ever get is greed."

SPIN Magazine

Bob Guccione Jr., publisher of *SPIN* magazine, was one of the three rock journalists singled out in "Get in the Ring" as one of the "punks in the press/That want to start shit by printin' lies instead of the things we said." Guccione Jr., who had nine years of martial arts training, accepted the challenge to "get in the ring" with Axl, but a fight never took place. According to the *Houston Press*, the whole Axl vs. Guccione Jr. feud was a "great moment in douchebaggotry."

Sunset Strip

The rather obscure track "Bad Apples," which can be found on *Use Your Illusion I*, features a direct reference to the fabled Sunset Strip, the portion of Sunset Boulevard that runs through West Hollywood: "I said Hollywood's like a dryer/An we're down on Sunset Strip." The Sunset Strip is home to some of the best-known landmarks associated with Guns N' Roses, such as the Rainbow Bar & Grill, the Roxy, Whisky A Go Go, and Viper Room, as well as the "Riot Hyatt" (now known as the Andaz West Hollywood). The legendary Troubadour, where the "classic" lineup of Guns N' Roses had their first gig on June 6, 1985, actually lies about a half mile south of the Strip at 9081 Santa Monica Boulevard.

Vanishing Point

Lyrics from the song "Breakdown" from *Use Your Illusion II* incorporate Super Soul's "Last American Hero" speech ("The last beautiful free soul on this planet") from the 1971 existential road movie *Vanishing Point*. Directed by Richard C. Sarafian, the film is basically an extended car chase (accompanied by a great soundtrack) with a nihilistic ending. Barry Newman (from the 1970s TV series *Petrocelli*) portrays the mysterious, stoic, pill-popping Kowalski, who makes a bet that he can drive a 1970 Dodge Challenger from Denver, Colorado, to San Francisco, California, in fifteen hours. Meanwhile, an inept array of law enforcement officers fails miserably in their efforts to try and stop him. Along the way, Kowalski encounters several memorable characters, including a crusty snake wrangler/prospector (Dean Jagger), a hippie biker named Angel (Timothy Scott), and a beautiful "Nude Motorcycle Rider" (Gilda Texter). The film also stars Cleavon Little (*Blazing Saddles*) as Super Soul, a blind DJ who uses a police radio scanner in an effort to help Kowalski evade the cops on his trail, and John Amos (*Good Times*) as Super Soul's engineer. The film's energetic soundtrack includes "Super Soul Theme" (the J. B. Pickers), "The Girl Done Got It Together" (Bobby Doyle), "Where Do We Go from Here?" (Jimmy Walker), "Welcome to Nevada" (Jerry Reed), "Dear Jesus God" (Segarini & Bishop), "Runaway Country" (the Doug Dillard Expedition), "You Got to Believe" (Delaney, Bonnie & Friends), "Love Theme" (the Jimmy Bowen Orchestra & Chorus), "So Tired" (Eve), "Freedom of Expression" (the J. B. Pickers), "Mississippi Queen" (Mountain), "Sing Out for Jesus" (Big Mama Thornton), "Over Me" (Segarini & Bishop), and "Nobody Knows" (Kim & Dave, as in Kim Carnes): "Nobody knows, nobody sees, till the light of life stops burnin', till another soul goes free." In a 2011 interview with *Entertainment Weekly*, Steven Spielberg stated that *Vanishing Point* was one of his favorite movies.

Vietnam Veterans Memorial

In addition to referencing the John F. Kennedy and Martin Luther King Jr. assassinations, "Civil War" also alludes to the Vietnam War and the Vietnam Veterans Memorial: "So I never fell for Vietnam/We got the wall of D.C. to remind us all/That you can't trust freedom/When it's not in your hands." The Vietnam Veterans Memorial is located on the National Mall near the Lincoln Memorial in Washington, D.C., and contains the Vietnam Veterans Memorial Wall (designed by American architect Maya Lin and containing more than 58,000 names of US soldiers killed during the Vietnam War), the Three Servicemen Memorial, and the Vietnam Women's Memorial. Listed on the National Register of Historic Places and maintained by the US National Park Service, the Vietnam Veterans Memorial receives approximately 3 million visitors annually.

"When Johnny Comes Marching Home"

Axl whistles "When Johnny Comes Marching Home" at the beginning and end of "Civil War." A popular song of the Civil War, "When Johnny Comes Marching Home" was written by Irish-American bandleader Patrick Gilmore (who for some unknown reason used the pseudonym "Louis Lambert" to publish the lyrics in 1863). Gilmore reportedly wrote the song for his sister Annie, who was betrothed to a Union officer named John O'Rourke. The melody itself originated from a popular drinking song of the day called "Johnny Fill Up the Bowl."

25

Better Off Left Behind

Ten Obscure Guns N' Roses Tracks

I want it to be right—I don't want it to be half-assed . . . We weren't just throwing something together to be rock stars. We wanted to put something together that meant everything to us. —Axl Rose

T o say Guns N' Roses recorded sporadically would be a gross understatement: Over the course of nearly thirty years, the band has produced just six albums—*Appetite for Destruction* (1987), *G N' R Lies* (1988), *Use Your Illusion I* (1991), *Use Your Illusion II* (1991), *"The Spaghetti Incident?"* (1993), and *Chinese Democracy* (2008). Furthermore, four out of the eight tracks on *G N' R Lies* had already been released on the 1986 EP *Live?!*@ Like a Suicide*, and two of those—"Nice Boys" and "Mama Kin"— were covers (of Rose Tattoo and Aerosmith respectively). In addition, *"The Spaghetti Incident?"* is an album of just covers, and the gap between that recording and the next, *Chinese Democracy*, spanned fifteen years. That said, there's quite a bit of GN'R material out there that never made its way onto any of the band's official recordings. Many of these songs have appeared on various Guns N' Roses bootlegs over the years and now can be heard just as easily on YouTube.

By the way, no discussion of obscure Guns N' Roses tracks would be complete without at least a mention of the notorious song "Cornshucker," which dates from 1988 during the recording sessions for *G N' R Lies* and appears on the *Metal Petals* bootleg. "Cornshucker" deals with anal sex, is loaded with raunchy lyrics, and would never have made the *G N' R Lies* album (or *any* album for that matter). Interestingly, scum-rock band the Mentors later claimed they had recorded "Cornshucker" first (although the songs are totally dissimilar except for the titles). Duff later claimed he was

Several unauthorized Guns N' Roses bootlegs and tribute albums have appeared over the years, much to the chagrin of Axl Rose.   *Author's collection*

just "fucking around" and came up with the song. Axl loved it but "the song was too brutal to put out, even for us." Listen at your own risk!

"Ain't Going Down"

Recorded and rejected during the *Use Your Illusion* recording sessions, "Ain't Going Down" ended up on the *Guns N' Roses* pinball machine that was produced by Data East in 1994 and featured the likenesses of Axl, Slash, Duff, Gilby Clarke, Dizzy Reed, and Matt Sorum. One of the highlights of the GN'R pinball machine is a rose-style plunger on the left side and a revolver-style plunger on the right side. In addition, "Welcome to the Jungle" can be heard briefly whenever a quarter is inserted. Clarke, who was fired from GN'R in 1994, sued the band over the use of his likeness on the pinball machine.

Today, Guns N' Roses pinball machines are available on eBay, and prices range from $6,000 to $9,000 each. Other pinball machines released by the now-defunct Data East include *The Simpsons* (1990), *Batman* (1991), *Jurassic Park* (1993), and *The Who's Tommy Pinball Wizard* (1994), among others. As for the song itself, "Ain't Going Down" was first performed live at the Whisky A Go Go on August 23, 1986. (Both "Sweet Child O' Mine" and "Mr. Brownstone" also made their debuts that night.) Besides the pinball machine, the song was never officially released anywhere else.

"Bring It Back Home"

Similar to bluesy rock songs that Aerosmith and Nazareth churned out during the 1970s, "Bring It Back Home" is "greasy, gritty, and full of street-strutting attitude," according to *Rolling Stone*. The song, which features Axl's maniacal laugh at the end, was recording in 1990 during the *Use Your Illusion* sessions but for whatever reason didn't make the cut (but found its way on the *Unwanted Illusions* bootleg).

"Crash Diet"

Cowritten by Axl, along with his old buddies West Arkeen and Del James, and recorded in 1986, "Crash Diet" focuses on the self-destructive nature of the rock 'n' roll lifestyle, specifically drunk driving: "Too stupid to live with nothin' to lose." Arkeen, who reportedly played lead guitar on the track, also cowrote "It's So Easy," "Bad Obsession," "The Garden," "Sentimental Movie," and "Yesterdays" for Guns N' Roses. Tragically, Arkeen died from an accidental drug overdose in 1997. A cover of "Crash Diet" appeared on the 1993 album *Pigs* by San Diego-based rock band Asphalt Ballet. It can also be found on the bootleg *Unwanted Illusions*.

"Going Down"

In the summer of 2013, "Going Down" was leaked via the Internet and features GN'R bassist Tommy Stinson (formerly of the Replacements) assuming vocal duties (with Axl on backing vocals). It was the first Guns N' Roses song to emerge since the release of 2008's *Chinese Democracy*. *SPIN* magazine called the track "a country-tinged, midtempo lighter-raiser," while *Stereogum* characterized it as having "a loose, rock-y feel, much closer to vintage GNR than the hyper-compressed industrial nu-metal of *Chinese Democracy*. It feels like a *Lies* outtake more than anything, really."

"Just Another Sunday"

Another track that ended up on *Unwanted Illusions* and other bootlegs, "Just Another Sunday" concerns the devastating emotional pain of a broken relationship. It was reportedly recorded several times even before the *Use Your Illusion* sessions. According to *Rolling Stone*, the track would have been "one of the poppiest songs on *Use Your Illusion*" and "could have been a classic" if they had spent more time with it.

"Oh My God"

The new lineup of Guns N' Roses released one track in the late 1990s, the industrial rock song "Oh My God," which was written by Axl, Paul Tobias, and Dizzy Reed, and appeared on the soundtrack of the 1999 Arnold Schwarzenegger film *End of Days*. Axl released a statement through Geffen Records stating that the song's lyrics dealt with "the societal repression of deep and often agonizing emotions . . . The fight of good vs. evil, positive vs. negative, man against a seemingly undefeatable, undeterrable, unrevealed destiny, along with the personal and universal struggle to attain, maintain, and responsibly manage free will, can be and often is frustrating to say the least. In America our country's constitutional right to freedom of expression gives us a better chance to fight for that expression than many in other countries enjoy. It can be a big gig, like kickin' the crap outta the devil!"

"Oh My God" won a 1999 *Metal Edge* Readers' Choice Award for "Soundtrack Song of the Year." Upon the song's release, Slash chimed in to *Circus* magazine, stating that the track "convinced me that my departure had been a wise decision and that Axl and I were definitely no longer on the same wavelength musically." Years later, Axl remarked that "Oh My God" was actually rushed into completion for the film's release and should be considered a demo. The *End of Days* soundtrack also featured "Camel Song" by Korn, "So Long" by Everlast, "Crushed" by Limp Bizkit, "Superbeast" by Rob Zombie, "Bad Influence" by Eminem, "Sugar Kane" by Sonic Youth," and "Wrong Way" by Creed, among others.

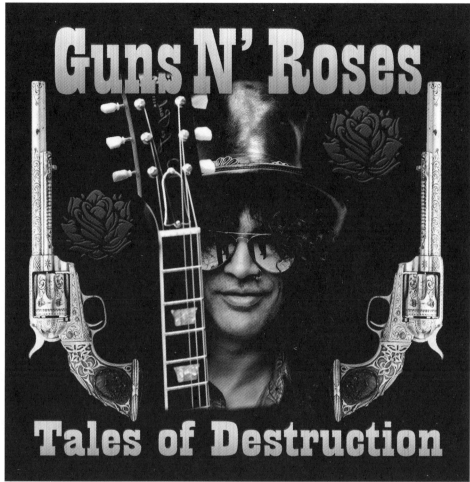

Released in 2016, *Tales of Destruction* features snippets from an interview with Slash about Guns N' Roses that does not lend itself in any way to further insight about the band.   *Author's collection*

"Sentimental Movie"

An early demo from 1986, "Sentimental Movie" was actually recorded by Axl and West Arkeen at "Hell House," a rundown residence located on Fuller Avenue where GN'R band members often crashed. Multiple versions of the song exist. Under their alias, "The Drunk Fux," Guns N' Roses (joined by Arkeen and Del James) performed "Sentimental Movie" at the Coconut Teaszer nightclub on Sunset Boulevard in West Hollywood on January 14, 1988. The setlist also included "I Got a Line on You" (Spirit), "Wishing

Well" (Free), "Communication Breakdown" (Led Zeppelin), "Scarred for Life" (Rose Tattoo), "Yesterdays," "Knockin' on Heaven's Door," "Born to Be Wild" (Steppenwolf), and "Honky Tonk Woman" (Rolling Stones).

"Shadow of Your Love"

An early song from the Hollywood Rose days cowritten by Axl and Izzy, "Shadow of Your Love" was also the first song played in rehearsal by the "classic" lineup of Guns N' Roses in June 1985. According to Steven Adler in *Reckless Road*, "Axl showed up [late] and he grabbed the microphone and was running up and down the walls screaming . . . We knew right then what we had." During a Guns N' Roses performance at Los Angeles Street Scene on September 28, 1985, Axl dedicated "Shadow of Your Love" to "all you rowdy motherfuckers out there." Inevitably, GN'R only released "Shadow of Your Love" as a B-side for both "It's So Easy" and "Live and Let Die" singles. "Shadow of Your Love" (with guitar work by Tracii Guns) also appears on the 2004 compilation album *The Roots of Guns N' Roses*, which was mixed by Gilby Clarke and unauthorized by Guns N' Roses.

"Silkworms"

First performed at a New Year's Eve show at the House of Blues in Las Vegas in 2001, "Silkworms" was cowritten by Dizzy Reed and Chris Pitman. A rather mediocre song rejected off the *Chinese Democracy* recording sessions, "Silkworms" features some unfortunate lyrics such as "pussy for a maggot" and "syphilitic preachers."

"Too Much Too Soon"

Recorded circa 1986, "Too Much Too Soon" pays tribute to one of Duff's earliest influences, Johnny Thunders, who performed with the New York Dolls in the early 1970s. The Dolls' second album, *Too Much Too Soon*, was released in 1974. (Thunders also released a song of the same name on his 1983 acoustic guitar ralbum, *Hurt Me.*) *Rolling Stone* called the Guns N' Roses track "a scratchy boogie-woogie rocker."

26

Seen It All a Million Times

Bands That Have Been Influenced by Guns N' Roses

I want us to make kids feel the way I did watching Guns N' Roses videos as a kid—you need rock star heroes.   —Pete Wentz of Fall Out Boy

As uncompromising iconoclasts, Guns N' Roses have influenced a diverse range of musicians over the years, including Welsh alternative rock band Manic Street Preachers, Mother Love Bone (Seattle precursor to Pearl Jam), Anaheim hard rock band Buckcherry (whose lead singer Josh Todd actually auditioned for Velvet Revolver), and Los Angeles heavy metal band Black Label Society (whose founder auditioned for Guns N' Roses in 1995). In addition, bands that also have acknowledged a debt to GN'R include Welsh heavy metal band Bullet for My Valentine, Huntington Beach heavy metal band Avenged Sevenfold, pop punk band Fall Out Boy, alternative rock band Hinder, thrash metal band Cryptic Warning (which morphed into Revocation), and even Coldplay, which acknowledged the influence of GN'R on the band's hit single "Adventures of a Lifetime."

During a *Hit Parader* magazine interview, when asked about all the bands that have "borrowed" a page from Guns N' Roses in terms of their "musical and stylistic approach," Axl responded, "It doesn't bother me at all except when I feel bands aren't pushing themselves creatively. I don't enjoy being imitated; I'd rather inspire than be imitated."

Manic Street Preachers

Formed in Blackwood, Wales, in 1986, the Manics featured lead singer/lead guitarist James Dean Bradfield, rhythm guitarist/songwriter Richey

Edwards, bass guitarist/songwriter Nicky Wire, and drummer Sean Moore. Bradfield reportedly taught himself guitar while playing along to *Appetite for Destruction*. The alternative rock band's debut album, *Generation Terrorists*, was released in 1992. (Band members boldly predicted it would outsell *Appetite for Destruction*, but it fell far short of that goal!) That same year, the Manics released a cover version of "Suicide is Painless" ("Theme from M.A.S.H."), which reached No. 7 on the UK charts. In 1994, the Manics released *The Holy Bible*, a dark, disturbing, and critically acclaimed album that contained such tracks as "Of Walking Abortion," "She Is Suffering," "Archives of Pain," "Mauseoleum," and "Die in the Summertime."

Tragedy struck the band in 1995 when Edwards, who suffered from alcoholism and depression (and who once carved the words "4 Real" on his arm after an interview questioned the band's authenticity), mysteriously disappeared without a trace and was officially "presumed dead" in 2008. The Manics reached No. 1 on the UK charts for their 1998 album *This Is My Truth Tell Me Yours*, which featured the hit single "If You Tolerate This Your Children Will Be Next." Known for their leftist political bent, the Manics counted Guns N' Roses, the Clash, the Sex Pistols, the New York Dolls, and Wire among their musical influences.

Mother Love Bone

Established in Seattle, Washington, in 1988, Mother Love Bone featured ex-Malfunkshun lead singer Andrew Wood; ex-Green River members Stone Gossard, Jeff Ament, and Bruce Fairweather; and drummer Greg Gilmore, formerly of Ten Minute Warning (Duff's former band) and Skin Yard. Gilmore had actually moved to Los Angeles briefly in 1985 and hung out with Duff and other members of Guns N' Roses before moving back to Seattle. Hearkening to a more classic rock style that definitely evinced a strong Guns N' Roses influence rather than the prevalent late 1980s glam metal scene, Mother Love Bone was only active for two years but proved highly influential. In November 1988, the band signed with Polydor/Stardog and released their debut EP, *Shine*.

Tragically, Wood died of a heroin overdose at the age of twenty-four, shortly before the band released its debut album, *Apple*, in 1990. The album's fourth track, "Chloe Dancer/Crown of Thorns," later ended up on the soundtrack for the 1992 movie *Singles*, which starred Campbell Scott, Kyra Sedgwick, Bridget Fonda, and Matt Dillon. Gossard and Ament would

soon join Eddie Vedder and Mike McCready to form Pearl Jam (original
name: Mookie Blaylock).

Buckcherry

Formed in Anaheim, California, in 1995, Buckcherry released just two
albums—*Buckcherry* (1999) and *Time Bomb* (2001)—before disbanding in
2002. However, lead singer Josh Todd and lead guitarist Keith Nelson
reformed the band in 2005 with a new lineup that included guitarist Stevie
D, bassist Jimmy Ashhurst, and drummer Xavier Muriel. The following
year, the band released the album *15*, which went platinum and contained
the hit singles "Crazy Bitch" and "Sorry." Subsequent Buckcherry albums
include *Black Butterfly* (2008), *Live & Loud* (2009) *All Night Long* (2010), and
Confessions (2013).

Todd was initially considered to become lead vocalist for the band
that would eventually become Velvet Revolver and spent a month in the
studio recording songs with Slash, Duff, and Matt Sorum. However, Todd
was abruptly dropped from the project (he later claimed that Slash "shit-
canned the whole thing") and eventually replaced by Scott Weiland of Stone
Temple Pilots. Slash later remarked that he was displeased with Todd's
vocals. Buckcherry opened for Guns N' Roses for several dates during their
extended *Chinese Democracy* Tour in 2011.

Black Label Society

Zakk Wylde (born Jeffrey Phillip Wielandt), a former guitarist for Ozzy
Osbourne who auditioned for Guns N' Roses in 1995, formed Black Label
Society, a Los Angeles heavy metal band, in 1998. Black Label Society
featured Wylde and drummer Phil Ondich, along with a rotating lineup of
other musicians. The band released its debut album, *Sonic Brew*, in 1998,
and followed it with *Stronger Than Death* in 2000. Subsequent Black Label
Society albums include *1919 Eternal* (2002), *The Blessed Hellride* (2003),
Hangover Music Vol. VI (2004), *Mafia* (2005), *Shot to Hell* (2006), *Order of the
Black* (2010), and *Catacombs of the Black Vatican* (2014).

On an episode of VH1 Classic's *That Metal Show*, Wylde discussed his
GN'R audition in 1995: "We just had some ideas laying around and stuff
like that, but nothing amounted to where Axl sang on stuff and had lyrics
written and everything like that. We just had riffs lying around and stuff
like that, but it was great hanging out." Black Label Society served as

Best known for their controversial 2006 hit single "Crazy Bitch," California-based hard rock band Buckcherry has acknowledged the influence of Guns N' Roses. Buckcherry opened for GN'R during several dates on their 2011 North American tour.   *Jan Brauer/Wikimedia Commons*

opening act for a Guns N' Roses concert in Indianapolis, Indiana, on December 8, 2011, and Wylde joined GN'R onstage for a rendition of AC/DC's "Whole Lotta Rosie."

Bullet for My Valentine

A Welsh heavy metal band formed in 1998 and originally known as "Jeff Killed John," Bullet for My Valentine reveals the musical influence of bands such as Guns N' Roses, Metallica, Iron Maiden, Slayer, Pantera, Machine Head, Sepultura, Alice in Chains, AC/DC, Nirvana, Judas Priest, Korn, and Megadeth. The band, which has been variously described as hard rock, heavy metal, thrash metal, and metalcore, consists of lead singer/rhythm guitarist Matthew Tuck, lead guitarist Michael Paget, bass guitarist Jamie Mathias, and drummer Michael Thomas.

Bullet for My Valentine released its debut album, *The Poison*, in the United States on Valentine's Day 2006. The album spawned four singles: "4 Words (To Choke Upon)," "Suffocating Under Words of Sorrow (What Can I Do)," "All These Things I Hate (Revolve Around Me)," and "Tears Don't Fall." The band then embarked on a US tour in support of Rob Zombie. The band's second album, *Scream Aim Fire* (2008), debuted at No. 4 on the US charts, followed by *Fever* (2010), which debuted at No. 3 on the US charts.

In the summer of 2006, Bullet for My Valentine opened for both Guns N' Roses and Metallica. According to Tuck in a 2008 *Revolver* magazine interview, "When we were on tour with Guns N' Roses, that was a prime example of how not to fucking act on tour. Then with [Iron] Maiden and Metallica, it was the complete opposite. They made us feel so welcome, and anything we wanted, they were more than happy to give us. It was nice to see that though they've established godlike myths about them, when you actually get them one-on-one in a room, they're just Mr. Average. It was inspiring to see that our heroes weren't dicks."

Avenged Sevenfold

Sometimes known simply as A7X, this heavy metal band formed in Huntington Beach, California, in 1999. Avenged Sevenfold's current lineup features lead singer M. Shadows, lead guitarist Synyster Gates, rhythm guitarist Zacky Vengeance, bassist Johnny Christ, and drummer Brooks Wackerman. The band released its debut album, *Sounding the*

Seventh Trumpet, in 2001, followed by *Waking the Fallen* in 2003. With their third album, *City of Evil* (2005), Avenged Sevenfold moved from metalcore to a more traditional heavy metal/hard rock sound. The album spawned the singles "Burn It Down," "Beast and the Harlot," and "Bat Country," which was inspired by Hunter S. Thompson's 1971 novel, *Fear and Loathing in Las Vegas*. The band's 2010 album, *Nightmare*, debuted at No. 1 on the US charts.

Avenged Sevenfold has cited their musical influences as Guns N' Roses, Iron Maiden, Metallica, Megadeth, Motörhead, Black Sabbath, Led Zeppelin, the Rolling Stones, AC/DC, Pantera, Bad Religion, Black Flag, Corrosion of Conformity, Misfits, Slayer, the Vandals, Rage Against the Machine, Korn, AFI, and Suicidal Tendencies, among others. In fact, Machine Head lead singer Robb Flynn sarcastically referred to Avenged Sevenfold's 2013 album, *Hail to the King*, as a "covers album," remarking, "Who knew that re-recording Metallica, Guns N' Roses, and Megadeth songs could be such a worldwide hit!!??" Flynn specifically singled out "Doing Time" as a "Guns N' Roses cover."

Fall Out Boy

Formed in Wilmette, Illinois, in 2001, Fall Out Boy traces their origins from Chicago's hardcore punk scene and features lead singer/guitarist Patrick Stump, guitarist Joe Throman, bassist/songwriter Pete Wentz, and drummer Andy Hurley. The band's pop punk-style debut album, *Take This to Your Grave*, became an underground hit in 2003, and they quickly developed a dedicated fan base. Fall Out Boy's second release, *From Under the Cork Tree*, served as their breakthrough album, going double platinum and spawning two hit singles: "Sugar, We're Going Down" and "Dance, Dance." At the 2006 Grammy Awards, the band received a "Best New Artist" nomination but lost out to John Legend. Fall Out Boy's third album, *Infinity on High*, produced two hit singles: "This Ain't a Scene, It's an Arms Race" and "Thnks fr th Mmrs." Subsequent Fall Out Boy albums have included *Folie a Deux* (2008), *Believers Never Die—Greatest Hits* (2009), *Save Rock and Roll* (2013), and *American Beauty/American Psycho* (2015), which peaked at No. 1 on the US charts and spawned the hit single "Uma Thurman."

The members of Fall Out Boy have acknowledged a diverse range of influences over the years, such as Guns N' Roses, Green Day, the Ramones, Screeching Weasel, Earth Crisis, Metallica, Prince, Michael Jackson, David Bowie, Gorilla Biscuits, Lifetime, and the Get Up Kids. Wentz has referred

Heavily influenced by Guns N' Roses, Fall Out Boy emerged out of the Chicago suburbs in the early 2000s. Ex-GN'R guitarist Gilby Clarke appeared in the music video for Fall Out Boy's hit single "I Don't Care" in 2008, exclaiming, "What the hell happened to rock and roll?"

Lindsey Turner/Wikimedia Commons

to the band's unique style as "softcore"—a blend of hardcore punk with pop sensibilities. (However, don't ever make the mistake of pigeonholing them as an "emo" band!) In a 2013 interview with the *Daily Star*, Wentz remarked, "Why are we the only band willing to take up the challenge of saving rock 'n' roll? . . . I want us to make kids feel the way I did watching Guns N' Roses videos as a kid—you need rock star heroes." Fall Out Boy's 2008 music video for "I Don't Care" features a cameo from former GN'R guitarist Gilby Clarke, chuckling and saying, "What the hell happened to rock 'n' roll? Eyeliner? Energy drinks? And no guitar solos? I've taken shits with bigger rock stars then them!"

As the band's principal songwriter, Wentz has also acknowledged getting inspiration from authors such as Ernest Hemingway (*The Sun Also Rises*), Charles Bukowski (*Factotum*), and JT LeRoy (*Sarah*). According to legend, the band got their name after they were performing in a club and asked the audience what they should be called and someone shouted, "Fall Out Boy" (the name of Radioactive Man's sidekick in *The Simpsons*). Other band names they considered included "Short Story," "Forget Me Not," and "Unhappy Ending." By the way, Fall Out Boy's first gig was opening for a Black Sabbath cover band in the cafeteria at DePaul University.

Hinder

Best known for the hits "Lips of an Angel," "Get Stoned," "How Long," "Use Me," "Without You," and "Better Than Me," Hinder was formed in Oklahoma in 2001 and has been variously described as hard rock, post-grunge, and alternative rock. The band's original lineup featured lead singer Austin Winkler, guitarist Joe "Blower" Garvey, and drummer Cody Hanson. The band released the following studio albums: *Extreme Behavior* (2005), *Take It to the Limit* (2008), *All American Nightmare* (2010), and *Welcome to the Freakshow* (2012). In 2007, Hinder was inducted into the Oklahoma Music Hall of Fame. Winkler departed the band in 2013 and was replaced by Marshal Dutton, who recorded a new album, *When the Smoke Clears*, with the band in 2015. In 2016, Hinder released *Stripped*, a six-song acoustic EP.

In addition to Guns N' Roses, Hinder has been influenced by such bands as Creed, Foo Fighters, Bush, Collective Soul, KISS, Nirvana, Soundgarden, Aerosmith, AC/DC, Ozzy Osbourne, Def Leppard, Mötley Crüe, the Rolling Stones, Led Zeppelin, and others. At one point, Hinder was offered the chance to open for Guns N' Roses during the *Chinese Democracy* Tour but turned it down, as they were aware of GN'R's penchant for cancelling shows and didn't want to upset their own fans. In a 2008 MTV interview, Hinder band members gave *Chinese Democracy* a lukewarm review, with Winkler commenting, "We've heard some of the earlier stuff that's leaked, and the single, and I was just kind of like, 'Eh' . . . Axl's voice sounds great, but that was never a problem. It was him going onstage and working with those other guys that was the problem. I think somewhere Axl's got all these other different guitar players he's tried to work with and he was just whipping them, going, 'More like Slash! More like Slash!' That's what I'm picturing in my mind." Hanson remarked that the album sounded "too artsy" and "overproduced."

Coldplay

It may seem absurd to feature post-Britpop band Coldplay as being influenced by Guns N' Roses, but the group has publicly revealed their debt to GN'R on the track "Adventures of a Lifetime" off their 2015 album, *A Head Full of Dreams.* According to lead singer/pianist Chris Martin during a SiriusXM interview, "I'd been begging Jonny [Buckland] our guitarist for years to make a riff that I like as much as 'Sweet Child O' Mine' by Guns N' Roses, then he showed me that one, and I was like, 'That's it!' so those elements all came together, and we just wanted to kind of embrace or love of joyful music and sort of let it free." A critically acclaimed hit for the band, "Adventures of a Lifetime" reached No. 13 on the *Billboard* charts.

Formed in 1996 by Martin and Buckland at University College London, Coldplay (original name Pectoralz, followed by Starfish) soon added bassist Guy Berryman and drummer Will Champion. The band achieved notice with their hit single "Yellow" in 2000, followed by the release of their debut album, *Parachutes*, the same year. Coldplay's follow-up album, *A Rush of Blood to the Head* (2002), won NME's "Album of the Year." Subsequent albums include *X&Y* (2005) and *Viva la Vida or Death and All His Friends* (2008), which spawned the No. 1 single "Viva la Vida." The album itself won "Best Rock Album" at the 2009 Grammy Awards. Overall, the band has sold more than 80 million records worldwide.

Cryptic Warning

Heavily influenced by both Guns N' Roses and Metallica, thrash metal band Cryptic Warning was formed in Boston, Massachusetts, in 2000 by lead singer/guitarist David Davidson, bassist Anthony Buda, and drummer Phil Dubois-Coyne. The band released its debut album, *Sanity's Aberration*, in 2005. Cryptic Warning changed its name to Revocation in 2006 and has released six studio albums under that name: *Empire of the Obscene* (2008), *Existence Is Futile* (2009), *Chaos of Forms* (2011), *Revocation* (2013), *Deathless* (2014), and *Great Is Our Sin* (2016).

27

Bullshit and Contemplation

Best and Worst Guns N' Roses Covers

I really want to sing with Axl Rose at some point in my life. I've covered enough Guns N' Roses stuff, and it was people like him who taught me how to sing. —Carrie Underwood

What do 1950s teen idol Pat Boone, singer-songwriter Sheryl Crow, legendary blues singer Etta James, country music superstar Carrie Underwood, ska band Voodoo Glow Skulls, lounge singer Richard Cheese, and actor Tom Cruise have in common? Believe it or not, they have all covered versions of Guns N' Roses songs at one time or another (and Crow even won a Grammy Award for her efforts!).

In addition, a hardcore/metal tribute to GN'R, *Bring You to Your Knees: A Tribute to Guns N' Roses*, was released in 2004 to mixed reviews, although the album contains several interesting tracks, such as crossover thrash/metalcore band Zombie Apocalypse's "Welcome to the Jungle," Chicago-based punk/hardcore band Break the Silence's "Nightrain," and New Jersey mathcore band the Dillinger Escape Plan's "My Michelle." Zombie Apocalypse's version of "Welcome to the Jungle" starts with the modified line, "Do you know where you are? You're in the graveyard, you're dead!"

Other *Bring You to Your Knees* tracks include "You're Crazy" (Haste), "14 Years" (Vaux), "It's So Easy" (Unearth), "Anything Goes" (Death By Stereo), "Sweet Child O' Mine" (Most Precious Blood), "November Rain" (Time in Malta), "Paradise City" (Eighteen Visions), "I Used to Love Her" (Every Time I Die), "Out Ta Get Me" (God Forbid), "Rocket Queen" (Bleeding Through), and "Estranged" (the Beautiful Mistake). As an added bonus, listen closely on Unearth's cover of "It's So Easy," as the lead singer shouts out, "Hey Axl, fuck off!"

Pat Boone—"Paradise City," 1997

As insane and meaningless as it seems, squeaky clean 1950's teen idol Charles Eugene "Pat" Boone actually recorded an album of hard rock and heavy metal covers in a jazz/big band style called *In a Metal Mood: No More Mr. Nice Guy* in 1997. The novelty album featured a cover of Guns N' Roses' "Paradise City," as well as "You've Got Another Thing Comin'" (Judas Priest), "Smoke on the Water" (Deep Purple), "It's a Long Way to the Top (If You Wanna Rock 'n' Roll)" (AC/DC), "Panama" (Van Halen), "No More Mr. Nice Guy" (Alice Cooper), "Love Hurts" (Nazareth), "Enter Sandman" (Metallica), "Holy Diver" (Dio), "The Wind Cries Mary" (Jimi Hendrix), "Crazy Train" (Ozzy Osbourne), and "Stairway to Heaven" (Led Zeppelin). Yes, as you can very well imagine, it's as bad as it sounds.

In fact, the whole thing was supposed to be kind of a joke and Boone even appeared at the 1997 American Music Awards (AMAs) wearing leather clothing, a dog collar, a non-piercing earring, and temporary tattoos, accompanied by the "Godfather of Shock Rock" himself, Alice Cooper, as a gimmick to promote the album. Taking stock of Boone's outrageous getup, Cooper remarked, "Well Pat, does this mean heavy metal is dead?" What do you know, the album actually peaked at No. 125 on the US charts, giving Boone his biggest hit record in many decades. (It turns out *In a Metal Mood* was a popular Christmas joke gift among heavy metal fans that year.) However, a lot of Boone's Christian fans were mortified by his brief flirtation with the "devil's music." Defending his actions in an October 4, 1999, interview with *Christianity Today*, Boone remarked, "Christians don't understand the business of what is really happening in pop culture . . . They don't understand that if you don't do something out of the ordinary—something truly eyebrow-raising—to an extent, you're not going to get heard." Boone later appeared on the Trinity Broadcasting Network and apologized if his appearance on the AMAs offended viewers. By the way, Boone was a former neighbor of Ozzy Osbourne, and the two reportedly got along brilliantly.

Sheryl Crow—"Sweet Child O' Mine," 1998

Singer-songwriter Sheryl Crow ("All I Wanna Do") covered "Sweet Child O' Mine" for the soundtrack of the 1999 Adam Sandler comedy *Big Daddy* and also included the song, which was produced by the legendary Rick Rubin, on her third studio album, *The Globe Sessions*. An accompanying music video for the cover featured Crow strumming her guitar in a beat-up car amid a junkyard while a TV in the distance plays scenes from *Big Daddy*. Directed by Stephane Sednaoui (who also did the music video for Red Hot Chili Peppers' "Give It Away"), it was filmed at Sun Valley's now-defunct U-Pick Parts, which also served as the locale for several other music videos, such as Usher's "My Way" and Taio Cruz's "Dynamite." Quite inexplicably, Crow's somewhat mediocre cover won her a Grammy Award for "Best Female Rock Vocal Performance." Crow beat out Tori Amos ("Bliss"), Ani DiFranco ("Jukebox"), Melissa Etheridge ("Angels Would Fall"), and Sarah McLachlan ("Possession") for the award.

As a matter fact, Crow's lightweight take on "Sweet Child' O' Mine" didn't manage to escape criticism. For example, Jeff Gils of *Ultimate Classic Rock* called the cover "a snoozy ballad that not only lacks Slash's signature lead, but also any real reason to exist," and went on to say, "Recorded for one of Sandler's more saccharine comedies, the cover reflects the maudlin nature of the movie's closing moments, recasting a trashy-but-tender ballad as a snoozy lullaby." In addition, Crow's cover placed No. 4 on *Rolling Stone*'s "Top 10 Worst Covers of All Time," joining such classic duds as William Shatner's "Lucy in the Sky with Diamonds," Jessica Simpson's "These Boots Are Made for Walking," Avril Lavigne's "Imagine," Britney Spears's "I Love Rock 'n' Roll" and "Satisfaction," Alien Ant Farm's "Smooth Criminal," Madonna's "American Pie," Limp Bizkit's "Behind Blue Eyes," and Miley Cyrus's "Smells Like Teen Spirit."

Other notorious covers that routinely make these type of "worst ever" lists include "911 is a Joke" by Duran Duran, "Anarchy in the UK" by Mötley Crüe, "Another Brick in the Wall" by Korn, "Bringin' on the Heartbreak" by Mariah Carey, "Dock of the Bay" by Michael Bolton, "Eyes Without a Face" by Paul Anka, "Feel Like Making Love" by Kid Rock, "Fight the Power" by Vanilla Ice, "My Generation" by Hilary Duff, "Ohio" by Devo, "Stairway to Heaven" by Dolly Parton, and "You Shook Me All Night Long" by Celine Dion, to name just a few.

AFI—"My Michelle," 2000

California rock band AFI (A Fire Inside) covered "My Michelle" for the 2000 compilation album *Punk Goes Metal*, which was released by Fearless Records, the first in its ongoing "Punk Goes . . ." series. Other covers on the album include Judas Priest's "Breaking the Law" by Divit, Poison's "Talk Dirty to Me" by Jughead's Revenge, Ozzy Osbourne's "Bark at the Moon" by Strung Out, Skid Row's "I Remember You" by the Ataris, AC/DC's "T.N.T." by Dynamite Boy, and Mötley Crüe's "Looks That Kill" by Diesel Boy, among

California-based punk rock band AFI covered "My Michelle" for the 2000 compilation album *Punk Goes Metal*, which also features contributions from the likes of Jughead's Revenge, Strung Out, the Ataris, Guttermouth, Ten Foot Pole, the Aquabats!, and others.   *Moses Namkung/Wikimedia Commons*

others. Fearless Records' "Punk Goes . . ." compilation series also includes *Punk Goes Pop* (2002), *Punk Goes Acoustic* (2003), *Punk Goes 80s* (2005), *Punk Goes 90s* (2006), *Punk Goes Crunk* (2008), *Punk Goes Classic Rock* (2010), and *Punk Goes Christmas* (2013), among others. AFI had breakout success with *Sing the Sorrow*, the band's 2003 album, which peaked at No. 5 on the US charts and featured the hit songs "Girl's Not Grey" and "Silver and Cold." The band's next album, *Decemberunderground*, debuted at No. 1 on the *Billboard* 200 in 2006. The current AFI lineup features lead singer Davey Havok, guitarist Jade Puget, bassist Hunter Burgan, and drummer/backup vocalist Adam Carson. "My Michelle" was also covered by mathcore band the Dillinger Escape Plan for the 2004 GN'R tribute album *Bring You to Your Knees.*

Voodoo Glow Skulls—"Used to Love Her," 2004

The controversial song "Used to Love Her" from Guns N' Roses' 1988 album *G N' R Lies* received an interesting ska treatment with this upbeat cover from the Voodoo Glow Skulls. The band, which dubs their sound "California Street Music," plays a clever mix of "high octane" ska, rock, punk, and hardcore. The Voodoo Glow Skulls' innovative cover of "Used to Love Her" (which features a mid-song break that veers into "Sweet Child O'Mine") appears on their 2004 release, *Adiccion, Tradicion, Revolucion.* The album also features such classics as "Ghettoblaster" and "Musical Pollution." Formed in 1988 in Riverside, California, the Voodoo Glow Skulls features the three Casillas brothers—Frank, Eddie, and Jorge—along with longtime friend Jerry O'Neill. In 1993, the band released their debut album, *Who Is, This Is?,* for Dr. Strange Records. The Voodoo Glow Skulls' song "Shoot the Moon" appeared on the soundtrack of the dismal 1996 Pauly Shore comedy *Bio-Dome,* while their cover of "Used to Love Her" was featured on the soundtrack for the 2005 romantic comedy/action film *Mr. & Mrs. Smith,* which starred Angelina Jolie and Brad Pitt.

Richard Cheese—"Welcome to the Jungle," 2005

Billed as "America's Loudest Lounge Singer," the frequently hilarious Richard Cheese (real name: Mark Jonathan Davis) belts out "swingin' Vegas versions" of rock and rap songs by "swankifying" Top 40 hits into "retro vocal standards." Since 2000, Cheese, along with his backup band, Lounge Against the Machine, has released twenty albums. The band's present lineup features Cheese (vocals), Bobby Ricotta (piano/keyboards), Billy Bleu (bass), Laighton Millea (drums/percussion), and Becky Running Bear (bongos).

Cheese covered Guns N' Roses with his laid-back version of "Welcome to the Jungle" in the 2005 release *Apertif for Destruction* (which also features a take on the classic *Appetite for Destruction* album cover). *Apetif for Destruction* went full-blown Cheese with other outrageous covers that include "Me So Horny" (2 Live Crew), "People=Shit" (Slipknot), "Brass Monkey" (Beastie Boys), and others, along with "The Girl is Mine" (Michael Jackson/Paul McCartney), which featured an impersonated duet with Stephen Hawking.

Previously, on Cheese's 2002 album, *Tuxicity* (a take on the System of a Down album *Toxicity*), his band recorded GN'R's "Used to Love Her" in true lounge lizard-style, along with the likes of "She Hates Me" (Puddle of Mudd), "Baby Got Back" (Sir Mix-A-Lot), "Insane in the Brain" (Cypress Hill), "Relax" (Frankie Goes to Hollywood), "Hot for Teacher" (Van Halen), "Buddy Holly" (Weezer), and others.

Vitamin String Quartet—Selection of GN'R Hits, 2007

It all started in 1999 with a crazy idea to have a string section perform Led Zeppelin's greatest hits. Since then, Vitamin String Quartet (VSQ) has paid tribute to countless musical artists with their simple formula. According to Tom Tally (VSQ violinist and arranger) at Vitaminstringquartet.com, VSQ "is about applying rock 'n' roll attitude to classical technique." Somehow it all works and VSQ turned their attention to Guns N' Roses with their 2007 release, *String Quartet Tribute to Guns N' Roses*, which features the tracks "Welcome to the Jungle," "Sweet Child O' Mine," "Paradise City," "Don't Cry," "November Rain," "Mr. Brownstone," "Yesterdays," "Patience," "Civil War," "Used to Love Her," "Nice Boys," "Rocket Queen," and "You Could Be Mine." VSQ has also recorded string quartet tributes to such musical artists as Michael Jackson, the Beatles, Black Sabbath, the Red Hot Chili Peppers, Lady Gaga, Adele, Slayer, Iron Maiden, Bruce Springsteen, Queen, the Offspring, Jimi Hendrix, Smashing Pumpkins, System of a Down, the Killers, Radiohead, Muse, Coldplay, Thirty Seconds to Mars, and others. (In fact, their discography features well over 250 albums!)

Gregorian—"Sweet Child O' Mine," 2009

Arguably the strangest cover of Guns N' Roses ever recorded goes to Gregorian, a German band that performs and records "Gregorian chant-inspired" versions of rock and modern pop songs. "Sweet Child O' Mine" appears on the group's tenth album, *Masters of Chant Chapter VII*, which was released in 2009 and also features "One" by U2, "A Face in the Crowd" by Tom Petty, "The Carpet Crawlers" by Genesis, "A Whiter Shade of Pale" by Procol Harum, "Kashmir" by Led Zeppelin, and "Chasing Cars" by Snow Patrol, among others. Another Gregorian album to look out for (or steer clear of, depending on your musical tastes) is *The Dark Side* (2004), which boasts an eclectic mix of tracks such as "Hurt" (Nine Inch Nails),

"My Immortal" (Evanescence), "Close My Eyes Forever" (Lita Ford/Ozzy Osbourne), and "The End" (the Doors). The Gregorian concept was started by Frank Peterson, who reveals the source of his inspiration on Gregorian's online bio at www.gregorian.de: "Years ago, I visited the Escorial Royal Monastery in Spain . . . I was listening to rock music on a Walkman but suddenly some unusual sounds got mixed in: a monastic choir sang Gregorian chants in the hall next door."

Etta James—"Welcome to the Jungle," 2011

Believe it or not, legendary blues singer Etta James (1938–2012) actually recorded a Guns N' Roses song, "Welcome to the Jungle," on her final album, *The Dreamer*, which was released in 2010 and also featured covers of Otis Redding's "Champagne & Wine," Ray Charles's "In the Evening," Johnny "Guitar" Watson's "Too Tired," and Little Milton's "Let Me Down Easy," among others. In a 2012 Associated Press obituary for James, Nekesa Mumbi Moody wrote, "[P]erhaps the most curious tune included on [*The Dreamer*] may be Guns N' Roses staple 'Welcome to the Jungle.' That a 73-year-old icon of R&B would tackle the frenetic rock song—albeit in a pace more fitting her blues roots—might seem odd. But the song may be the best representation of James as both a singer and a person—rambunctious in spirit, with the ability to sing whatever was thrown at her, whether it was jazz, blues, pining R&B, or a song from one of the rowdiest bands in rock." James had another thing in common with Guns N' Roses: The singer struggled with heroin addiction and was in and out of rehab for years before making a musical comeback with the 1989 album *Seven Year Itch*.

Born Jamesetta Hawkins, James gained fame with a slew of hits, such as "I'd Rather Go Blind," "Something's Got to Give," "All I Could Do Was Cry," "My Dearest Darling," "Trust in Me," "Tell Mama," "At Last," and "The Wallflower." Over the years, she garnered six Grammy Awards and seventeen Blues Music Awards. In 1993, James was inducted into the Rock and Roll Hall of Fame along with the Doors, Van Morrison, Sly and the Family Stone, Cream, Creedence Clearwater Revival, Ruth Brown, and Frankie Lymon and the Teenagers. In addition, *Rolling Stone* placed James at No. 22 on its list of the "100 Greatest Singers of All Time." Her mesmerizing autobiography, *Rage to Survive: The Etta James Story*, appeared in 1995. Legendary Atlantic Records producer Jerry Wexler called James "the greatest of all modern blues singers . . . the undisputed Earth Mother."

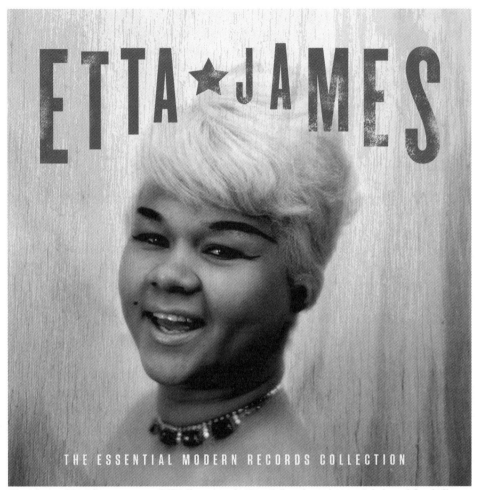

Blues legend Etta James covered "Welcome to the Jungle" on her twenty-eighth and final album, *The Dreamer*, which was released in 2011. The winner of six Grammy Awards, James was also inducted into the Rock and Roll Hall of Fame in 1993.   *Author's collection*

Tom Cruise—"Paradise City," 2012

No discussion of Guns N' Roses covers can avoid mention of Tom Cruise's interesting take on "Paradise City" during the opening and end credits of the 2012 romantic musical comedy, *Rock of Ages*, an adaptation of the hit Broadway musical of the same name. As rock star Stacee Jaxx—"the most unreliable man in the music industry"—Cruise also has a field day performing "Wanted Dead or Alive" by Bon Jovi, "I Want to Know What Love Is" by

Foreigner, "Pour Some Sugar on Me" by Def Leppard, "Every Rose Has Its Thorn" by Poison, and "Rock You Like a Hurricane" by Scorpions. *Rock of Ages* director Adam Shankman called Cruise's performance "a brilliant mashup . . . of Axl Rose, Bret Michaels, Keith Richards, and Jim Morrison." According to an October 11, 2012, review of the movie in the *San Francisco Chronicle*, "No matter how you feel about Guns N' Roses, Tom Cruise as a bandanna-headed Axl Rose type will hit you as the purest bit of genius in the man's entire film career."

Carrie Underwood—"Paradise City," 2013

Critics justifiably praised country music singer-songwriter and *American Idol* season four winner Carrie Underwood after her heartfelt cover of rock anthem "Paradise City" at the 2013 CMA Music Festival. It turns out Underwood has been a lifelong fan of GN'R and told *E!* in a November 21, 2015, interview that she would like to collaborate with Axl Rose one day: "I've covered enough Guns N' Roses stuff, and it was people like him who taught me how to sing. I look at people like him and Freddie Mercury, those people who were doing all these crazy runs. It was so different." Other Guns N' Roses songs Underwood has covered in live concerts over the years include "Sweet Child O' Mine," "Patience," and "November Rain." Underwood, who was inducted into the Grand Ole Opry in 2008, has won seven Grammy Awards, seventeen *Billboard* Music Awards, nine American Music Awards, and twelve Academy of Country Music Awards. She is known for such crossover hits as "Jesus, Take the Wheel" and "Before He Cheats."

Bonus—"Worst Band to Ever Play Letterman"

The *Gothamist* weblog has named a New York City-based Guns N' Roses cover band called Mr. Brownstone the worst band to *ever* perform on the *Late Show with David Letterman* in the show's history, a pretty remarkable feat considering that the *Late Show* catalog consists of more than 4,000 episodes. The hilarious debacle—which featured awful wigs, horrendous singing, and ridiculous posturing—took place on November 19, 2008, as Mr. Brownstone totally butchered a rendition of "Welcome to the Jungle" that has to be seen to be believed. (Although the appallingly bad performance has been scrubbed from YouTube, truly dedicated Guns N' Roses fans can easily find it via a quick Internet search.) Mr. Brownstone band member Dave Godowsky (the "Izzy Stradlin" of the group) told *Gothamist* in a May

New York City Guns N' Roses cover band Mr. Brownstone gained notoriety in 2008 when they butchered "Welcome to the Jungle" and were subsequently dubbed "The Worst Band to Ever Play the *Late Show with David Letterman.*"   *Author's collection*

20, 2015, interview, "I think it's perfectly reasonable to say that the best cover band garners less artistic credibility than the worst original band. In that sense, we were without a doubt the worst band to ever play *Letterman*. Of the five cover bands who have ever graced that stage, we're unequivocally the least impressive. If you're going to be bad at something you might as well go all the way and be the absolute worst." Godowsky admitted that the band didn't even rehearse for the performance and instead "got super drunk."

28

Make It Your Own Way

Solo Efforts, Outside Projects, and Supergroups

We'd started out as a garage band and it became like a huge band, which was fine. But everything was so magnified, drug addictions, personalities, it just became too much.
　　　　　　　　　　　　　　　　　　　　　—Izzy Stradlin

After the massive *Use Your Illusion* Tour finally came to an end in 1993, GN'R band members started pursuing solo projects as they waited for signs from Axl that he was ready to start recording some new material. Well, days stretched into weeks, months, and eventually years as the original core of Guns N' Roses started to fade away and musicians went their separate ways, leading to solo projects like Izzy Stradlin and the Ju Ju Hounds, Slash's Snakepit, and Adler's Appetite, along with the rise of so-called rock supergroups, such as the Neurotic Outsiders and Velvet Revolver.

Izzy Stradlin and the Ju Ju Hounds

Not long after sobering up and leaving Guns N' Roses in 1991, Izzy formed a band called Izzy Stradlin and the Ju Ju Hounds, which also consisted of Rick Richards of Southern rock band Georgia Satellites ("Keep Your Hands to Yourself") on lead guitar, Jimmy "Two Fingers" Ashhurst of Broken Homes/Buckcherry on bass, and Charlie Quintana of Latino punk band the Plugz (and later Social Distortion) on drums. In 1992, the band released their self-titled debut, which *Rolling Stone* called "a ragged, blues-drenched, and thoroughly winning solo debut." Recorded live at Tivoli Theatre in Dublin, Ireland, *Izzy Stradlin and the Ju Ju Hounds Live* was released the following year.

Slash's Snakepit

While still officially a member of Guns N' Roses (although absolutely nothing was going on with the band at this point), Slash started a side project in 1994 known as Slash's Snakepit, which also featured GN'R bandmates Matt Sorum and Gilby Clarke, as well as bassist Mike Inez from Seattle grunge band Alice in Chains and singer/guitarist Eric Dover formerly of Jellyfish, a San Francisco pop band. Slash's Snakepit released their debut album, *It's Five O'Clock Somewhere*, in 1995. Released by Geffen Records, the album was produced by Slash and GN'R producer Mike Clink. It reached No. 70 on the *Billboard* charts. "Beggars & Hangers-On" was the only single released from the album, which *Entertainment Weekly* referred to as "14 lyrically jejune tracks of relaxed headbanging and Southern-tinged blues-rock."

In an April 1995 interview for *Metal Edge* magazine, Slash remarked, "I did what I said I'd never do, which is a solo record, to get it out of my system. [Guns N' Roses had] been doing too many ballads and conceptual records that I started to get a little concerned where it was going. When you listen to everybody's solo albums you can hear the individual input in Guns. Mine sounds like the aspect of Guns that I am."

In 1999, Slash decided to start up Slash's Snakepit once again with a whole new supporting band that included

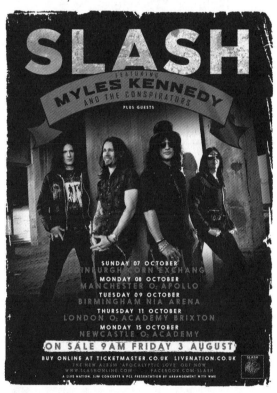

Released in 2010, Slash's debut solo album boasted contributions from three other members of the "classic" Guns N' Roses lineup: Izzy Stradlin, Duff McKagan, and Steven Adler. Other featured performers on the album included Ozzy Osbourne, Ian Astbury of the Cult, Fergie from the Black Eyed Peas, Chris Cornell from Soundgarden, Kid Rock, Lemmy from Motörhead, Dave Grohl from Foo Fighters, and Iggy Pop, among others.
Author's collection

Rod Jackson, Ryan Roxie, Johnny Griparic (a.k.a. "Johnny Blackout"), and Matt Laug. The band's second and final album, *Ain't Life Grand*, was released in 2000. According to *Rolling Stone* in an October 12, 2000, review of *Ain't Life Grand*, the "real problem" with the second album was the fact that "great guitarists need great bands, and the Snakepit dudes are barely functional backup peons who don't even have cool names, except bassist Johnny Blackout."

Neurotic Outsiders

A rock supergroup that had its origins at a Viper Room charity concert in West Hollywood, the Neurotic Outsiders consisted of Duff, Matt Sorum, Steve Jones of the Sex Pistols, and John Taylor of Duran Duran. After suffering near fatal acute pancreatitis in 1994, Duff had conquered his addictions, and his life during this period revolved around "literature, martial arts, healthy food, and mountain biking." Before settling on the name Neurotic Outsiders, the band played early Viper Room gigs as Wayne Neutron, Mr. Moo's Futurama, and Kings of Chaos. They typically performed covers of the Sex Pistols, the Clash, the Stooges, and the Damned. What began as casual jamming led to a million-dollar advance from Maverick Records. The band released its self-titled debut album in 1996 and embarked on a national tour. The Neurotic Outsiders, which also served briefly as house band at the Viper Room, broke up for good in 1998.

Loaded

After his stint in the Neurotic Outsiders ended, Duff formed the band Loaded (initially known as the Gentlemen) in 1999 with some of his Seattle friends, including guitarists Dez Cadena (formerly of Black Flag) and Michael Barragan (formerly of Plexi), and drummer Taz Bentley (formerly of the Reverend Horton Heat). Loaded has featured a variety of different lineups over the years and has released three studio albums to date—*Dark Days* (2001), *Sick* (2009), and *The Taking* (2011)—as well as a live album, *Episode 1999: Live* (1999).

Velvet Revolver

A true rock 'n' roll supergroup that formed in 2002, Velvet Revolver consisted of Slash, Duff, and Matt Sorum from Guns N' Roses; lead singer Scott

In addition to his involvement with Velvet Revolver, Duff McKagan's post-Guns N' Roses activities include stints with the Neurotic Outsiders and Loaded.   *Author's collection*

Weiland from Stone Temple Pilots; and rhythm guitarist Dave Kushner from Los Angeles hardcore punk band Wasted Youth. Weiland was one of several lead singers considered for the Velvet Revolver front man position, along with Sebastian Bach of Skid Row, Josh Todd of Buckcherry, Steve Jones of the Sex Pistols, and Ian Astbury of the Cult. (The search for a lead singer eventually became a VH1 special titled *Inside Out: The Rise of Velvet Revolver.*) However, Weiland was selected since, according to Slash, "he had a John Lennon-ish quality, a little bit of Jim Morrison, and a touch of almost David Bowie." Kushner had known Slash since junior high school and had also worked with him at Tower Video (where Axl was also employed as night manager briefly) on Sunset Boulevard in the mid-1980s. Izzy even jammed with the band for several weeks but he didn't want to officially join up—he preferred to hang out and eventually "just kind of faded from the scene," according to Duff (like Izzy was frequently apt to do). Before settling on the name Velvet Revolver, the band considered several similar names such as Revolver and Black Velvet Revolver.

Velvet Revolver recorded two songs for film soundtracks: "Set Me Free" for *Hulk* and a cover of Pink Floyd's "Money" for *The Italian Job*, both released in 2003. The band's 2004 debut album, *Contraband*, debuted at No. 1 on the US charts and featured such hit songs as "Slither," which reached No. 1 on the *Billboard* Mainstream Rock Tracks Chart, No. 56 on the *Billboard* Hot 100, and won the 2005 Grammy Award for "Best Hard Rock Performance," and the power ballad "Fall to Pieces," which also skyrocketed to No. 1 on the *Billboard* Mainstream Rock Tracks Chart and dealt with Weiland's heroin addiction. "Fall to Pieces" was nominated for a Grammy Award for "Best Rock Song" but lost out to U2's "Vertigo." In addition, *Contraband* received a Grammy Award nomination as "Best Rock Album," which was won by Green Day's *American Idiot*.

After Axl made some unflattering comments about Velvet Revolver in the media, Weiland shot back on the band's official website, exclaiming, "Get in the ring. Go to the gym, motherfucker, or if you prefer, get a new wig, motherfucker. I think I'll resist the urge to 'stoop' to your level. Oh shit, here it comes, you fat, botox-faced, wig-wearin' fuck! O.K., I feel better now. Don't think for a second we don't know where those words came from. Your unoriginal, uncreative little mind—the same mind that had to rely on its bandmates to write melodies and lyrics. Who's the fraud now, bitch? . . . What we're talking about here is a frightened little man who once thought he was king, but unfortunately this king without his court is nothing but a memory of the asshole he once was."

Velvet Revolver's second album, *Libertad*, was released in 2007 and featured "The Last Fight," "She Builds Quick Machines," and a cover of the Jeff Lynne song "Can't Get It Out of My Head." During the summer of 2007, Velvet Revolver teamed up with Alice in Chains for a massive global tour. After both Velvet Revolver and Guns N' Roses appeared together on *Guitar Hero III: Legends of Rock* in 2007, Axl filed a $20 million lawsuit against Activision for "misuse" of GN'R music. (The lawsuit was finally dismissed years later due to the lateness of its filing.) In 2008, Weiland left Velvet

Revolver to reunite with Stone Temple Pilots. Tragically, Weiland's rock career was stymied by drug addiction, and he spent years in a revolving door cycle of rehab facilities. (Sadly, he died of an accidental overdose in 2015.) His ex-wife, Mary Forsberg Weiland, published the memoir *Fall to Pieces: A Memoir of Drugs, Rock 'n' Roll, and Mental Illness* in 2009.

Adler's Appetite

Formed in Los Angeles in 2003, Steven Adler's band featured an original lineup that featured lead singer Jizzy Pearl (Love/Hate and L.A. Guns), guitarist Keri Kelli (Big Bang Babies, Alice Cooper Band, and Slash's Snakepit), and bassist Robbie Crane (Ratt and Vince Neil Band). Their debut (and sole album to date), *Adler's Appetite*, was released in 2005. During live concerts,

Formed in 2003, Steven Adler's band, Adler's Appetite, typically performs songs from *Appetite for Destruction* during live concerts.   *Author's collection*

the band typically performed songs from *Appetite for Destruction*. In *My Appetite for Destruction*, Adler remarked, "I'm giving the fans just what Axl offers: one original member and the music they love . . . Whereas Axl's band sounds disjointed and soulless, our band conveys the hungry, underdog spirit that the original Guns N' Roses possessed." Other Adler's Appetite band members over the years have included Rick Stitch (Ladyjack), Alex Grossi (Angry Salad, Beautiful Creatures, and Quiet Riot), Michael Thomas (Tuff, Beautiful Creatures, and ASHBA), and Chip Z'nuff (Enuff Z'nuff).

29

Just Makin' My Livin'

Later Guns N' Roses Band Members

*If you find your truth you must follow it . . . And if you follow it, stay true
to it, and respect it, you could be in store for the greatest journey you could
ever imagine.*   —Buckethead

B y 1997, all of the original *Appetite for Destruction* band members
(except Axl) had departed—Steven Adler in 1990, Izzy in 1991,
Slash in 1996, and Duff in 1997. In the meantime, keyboardist
Dizzy Reed had joined the band in 1990, Matt Sorum served as GN'R's
drummer between 1990 and 1997 (replacing Adler), and Gilby Clarke
joined the band in 1991 to step in for Izzy on the *Use Your Illusion* Tour.
(Clarke was fired from the band in 1994.)

Therefore, Axl had the arduous task of attempting to find replacements
for his legendary former bandmates. What followed was a revolving door
of musicians over the next decade—from the established, such as Tommy
Stinson of the Replacements, to the truly outrageous, like Buckethead—
joining the band (on a contract basis only) as *Chinese Democracy* took shape
at a snail's pace. Although sometimes dismissed as simply "hired hands," the
talented musicians featured below made some great contributions to GN'R's
legacy through amazing live performances along with recording a few truly
amazing songs that appear on *Chinese Democracy*, such as the title track, as
well as "Better," "Madagascar," "This I Love," "Prostitute," and others.

Dizzy Reed (1990–Present)

Believe it or not, keyboardist Dizzy Reed joined Guns N' Roses in 1990,
making him the longest-standing band member in GN'R next to Axl. Reed
contributed on a majority of the tracks for both *Use Your Illusion* albums, as
well as *"The Spaghetti Incident?"* and *Chinese Democracy*. On the latter album,
Reed cowrote "Street of Dreams" with Axl and Tommy Stinson, and "There

Was a Time" and "I.R.S." with Axl and Paul Tobias. In addition to keyboards, Reed is a sometime percussionist and background vocalist for the band. He has also made several guest appearances on albums for other artists, including playing piano on "Mine all Mine" from Motörhead's 2002 release, *Hammered*.

Darren Arthur "Dizzy" Reed was born in Hinsdale, Illinois, on June 18, 1963, but spent his childhood in Colorado. During the mid-1980s, Reed joined a Los Angeles-based funk/pop band called the Wild, which hung out and partied with members of Guns N' Roses on numerous occasions. Reed notoriously thanked "Hookers and Blow" in the liner notes to *Chinese Democracy*. He was inducted into the Rock and Roll Hall of Fame as a member of Guns N' Roses in 2012 (although he pulled a no-show like Axl and Izzy). That same year, Reed joined the Dead Daisies, an Australian-American supergroup that featured GN'R bandmate Richard Fortus, Marco Mendoza of Thin Lizzy, Jon Stevens of INXS, ex-Whitesnake drummer Brian Tichy, and ex-Mötley Crüe lead singer John Corabi, among others. He also has his own covers band appropriately named (you guessed it!) Hookers & Blow.

Matt Sorum (1990–97)

A former drummer for British rock band the Cult, Matt Sorum was born in Long Beach, California, on November 19, 1960. His favorite musicians when he was growing up included Ringo Starr, Jimi Hendrix, Cream, and the Doors. He joined Guns N' Roses in 1990 after Steven Adler was unceremoniously fired from the band due to his faltering drum skills, which were the result of severe drug abuse. Sorum performed on three GN'R albums: *Use Your Illusion I*, *Use Your Illusion II*, and *"The Spaghetti Incident?"* He also took part in the two-and-a-half-year *Use Your Illusion* Tour. He was fired from the band in 1997 reportedly after he suggested to Axl that he needed to get Slash back in the band to replace Paul Tobias.

In 1995, Sorum joined Slash and Gilby Clarke as part of the former's solo project, Slash's Snakepit. Sorum was also a member of the Neurotic Outsiders with Duff, Steve Jones of the Sex Pistols, and John Taylor of Duran Duran, as well as Velvet Revolver, along with Slash, Duff, Scott Weiland, and Dave Kushner. Sorum's first solo effort, *Hollywood Zen*, was released in 2003 and featured guest appearances from the likes of Slash and Duff. Also, between 2002 and 2014, Sorum was a member of Los Angeles all-star cover band Camp Freddy, which also included Dave Navarro of Jane's

Addiction and others. In 2012, Sorum was inducted into the Rock and Roll Hall of Fame as a member of Guns N' Roses. In comparing the Cult with GN'R in a June 28, 2001, interview with the *Lawrence Journal-World*, Sorum commented, "For whatever reason, Guns took off and the Cult didn't. I believe that American kids tapped into what Axl had to say a little bit. [Ian Astbury's] a bit more mysterious and trippy. I never thought the Cult got their full shake."

Gilby Clarke (1991–94)

Formerly with the Los Angeles rock bands Candy (which released the 1985 album *Whatever Happened to Fun*) and Kill for Thrills, Gilby Clarke replaced Izzy (who he had known from the West Hollywood days during the mid-1980s) as the rhythm guitarist for Guns N' Roses in 1991 as the band embarked on its fabled *Use Your Illusion* Tour. According to Clarke in a November 1992 *Guitar World* interview, "I had to learn 50 songs in one week, and play them in front of thousands of people. My second gig was Madison Square Garden!" Clarke performed on the 1993 GN'R covers album, *"The Spaghetti Incident?"* and also appeared on *Live Era '87–'93* (1999) and *Greatest Hits* (2004). His image also graces the GN'R pinball machine, which was released in 1994. Clarke was unceremoniously fired from the band in 1994 and joined Slash's Snakepit the following year. In the VH1 *Behind the Music* special on GN'R, Clarke remarked, "I knew from day one that it could end tomorrow."

Clarke released his solo debut album, *Pawnshop Guitars*, in 1994. The album boasts contributions from GN'R band members, including Axl singing a cover of the Rolling Stones' "Dead Flowers." Clarke's follow-up effort, *The Hangover*, appeared in 1997 and features covers of the Beatles' "Happiness is a Warm Gun" and David Bowie's "Hang On to Yourself." Clarke has also toured with the likes of Heart and Nancy Sinatra. A motorcycle enthusiast, Clarke once biked 3,000 miles to the Sturgis Motorcycle Rally in South Dakota, where he performed a gig with Heart at the Buffalo Chip Campgrounds. In 2006, Clarke starred on the CBS reality show *Rockstar: Supernova* with Tommy Lee of Mötley Crüe and Jason Newsted of Metallica.

Paul Tobias (1994–2002)

An old friend of Axl Rose (they cowrote "Back Off Bitch" and "Shadow of Your Love" in the early 1980s), Tobias replaced Gilby Clarke as rhythm guitarist on the cover version of "Sympathy for the Devil" for the soundtrack to *Interview with the Vampire* (1994), causing much dissension among the other band members, especially Slash. The song "Oh My God," which appeared on the soundtrack for the 1999 Arnold Schwarzenegger film *End of Days*, was cowritten by Tobias and Dizzy Reed. Tobias performed at several Guns N' Roses' concerts, including Rock in Rio 3. Not one for touring, Tobias quit the band in 2001 and was replaced by Richard Fortus. Tobias contributed to GN'R's sixth studio album, *Chinese Democracy* (2008).

Josh Freese (1997–2000)

A gifted multi-instrumentalist known as the "Bruce Lee of Drums," Josh Freese has performed and recorded with such bands as Guns N' Roses, punk rock band the Vandals, Devo, Nine Inch Nails, A Perfect Circle, Weezer, Suicidal Tendencies, Sublime with Rome, and Paramore. Freese joined Guns N' Roses in 1997, replacing Matt Sorum. During his stint with GN'R, Freese cowrote, with Axl, the title track of the band's 2008 album, *Chinese Democracy*. Born on Christmas Day 1972 in Orlando, Florida, Freese's drumming career began in a Top 40 cover band that performed at the Tomorrowland Terrace Stage at Disneyland in the late 1980s. In 2000, Freese released the album *The Notorious One Man Orgy*. Freese's younger brother, Jason, is a touring member of Green Day.

Robin Finck (1998–99, 2000–08)

A former member of the Nine Inch Nails (NIN) touring band (he first joined the band during the massive Self Destruct Tour between 1994 to 1996 and took part in Woodstock '94), lead guitarist Robin Finck became a member of Guns N' Roses in 1998 (signing a two-year contract as Slash's replacement). After his GN'R contract ended with no new album in sight, Finck took part in NIN's Fragility Tour starting in late 1999. He returned to Guns N' Roses in 2000 and played four shows with the band, which were followed by a brief tour of Europe and Asia in 2002 and the 2002 MTV Video Music Awards.

Throughout 2006 and 2007, Finck again toured with GN'R for concert dates in Europe, North America, Australia, and Japan. In 2008, Finck rejoined NIN's touring band and contributed to the band's next album, *The Slip*. For *Chinese Democracy*, Finck played on every track of the album and also received a cowriting credit for the song "Better." Finck was replaced in Guns N' Roses by DJ Ashba. Early in his musical career, Finck played with several unsigned Atlanta-area bands such as Prowess, Bat Your Lashes, Sik Dik, and Impotent Sea Snakes. Between his NIN and GN'R gigs, Finck served as musical director for Cirque du Soleil. (Axl was simply attending one of the circus shows and found out that Finck used to perform with NIN, one of his favorite bands.) Finck and GN'R bandmate Buckethead contributed to the soundtrack for John Carpenter's 2002 sci-fi horror flick, *Ghosts of Mars*.

Tommy Stinson (1998–2016)

Formerly with the Replacements (considered pioneers of alternative rock), Tommy Stinson replaced Duff as GN'R's bassist in 1998. Between the Replacements (which broke up in 1991) and his stint with Guns N' Roses, Stinson started two bands, Bash & Pop and Perfect. In 2004, Stinson released his solo debut album, *Village Gorilla Head*, which featured contributions from bandmates Dizzy Reed and Richard Fortus. His follow-up album, *One Man Mutiny*, was released in 2011. Stinson's bass playing can be heard on the track "Oh My God," which appeared on the 1999 *End of Days* soundtrack, as well as on Guns N' Roses' long-awaited 2008 album, *Chinese Democracy*. In addition, Stinson found time to perform with Soul Asylum between 2005 and 2012 when not working with GN'R. In 2006, Stinson gained notoriety when he took his bass off and threw it to the stage during a November 24 performance at Quicken Loans Arena in Cleveland, Ohio, after Axl fired the opening act, Eagles of Death Metal (the band that Stinson had recommended), and disparagingly referred to the band as "Pigeons of Shit Metal."

Buckethead (2000–04)

One of the most bizarre, innovative, and prolific guitarists in rock history, guitarist/multi-instrumentalist Buckethead (real name: Brian Carroll) gained notoriety simply by his outrageous getup: a "Michael Myers" mask inspired from the 1988 film *Halloween 4: The Return of Michael Meyers* combined with a KFC chicken bucket embellished with an orange sticker that simply read "funeral," which he wore on his head. In a 1996 interview with *Guitar Player* magazine, Buckethead stated, "I was eating [fried chicken], and I put the mask on and then the bucket on my head. I went to the mirror. I just said, 'Buckethead. That's Buckethead right there.' It was just one of

Guns N' Roses' performance at Rock in Rio 3 in 2001 gave Axl Rose the opportunity to showcase new band members such as guitarist Buckethead.   *Author's collection*

those things. After that, I wanted to be that thing all the time." According to Buckethead's online bio, his strange persona represents a character that was "raised by chickens" and has made it his "mission in life to alert the world to the ongoing chicken holocaust in fast-food joints around the globe." When recording with Guns N' Roses, Buckethead insisted on creating a makeshift "chicken coop" in the studio, complete with a rubber chicken with its head cut off hanging from the ceiling.

Growing up in Southern California, Buckethead's early influences included Angus Young of AC/DC, Swedish "overdrive virtuoso" Yngwie Malmsteen, and the late, great Randy Rhoads, who jammed with the Ozzy Osbourne Band. Buckethead's first band, the Deli Creeps, a San Francisco based metal-funk band, gained a regional following but broke up before recording anything. In 1992, he released his debut album, *Bucketheadland*, followed by several other albums over the years, including 1999's *Monsters and Robots*, which one critic called "post-metal psycho-shred." He also records under the name "Death Cube K" (an anagram for "Buckethead"). Buckethead not only performed with Guns N' Roses at high-profile venues such as Rock and Rio 3 in 2001 and the 2002 MTV Video Music Awards, but he also contributed to the band's sixth studio album, *Chinese Democracy*, which was not released until four years after the guitarist left the band.

In addition to Guns N' Roses, Buckethead has performed and recorded with a host of other musicians, including P-Funk all-stars Bootsy Collins and Bernie Worrell, Iggy Pop, avant-fusion bassist Bill Laswell, Primu, late Miles Davis Quintet drummer Tony Williams, Serj Tankian of System of a Down, and even actor Viggo Mortensen of *The Lord of the Rings* trilogy fame. Buckethead has also contributed to the soundtracks of such movies as *Last Action Hero* (1993), *Mortal Kombat* (1995), *Beverly Hills Ninja* (1997), *Ghost of Mars* (2001), and *Saw II* (2005).

Richard Fortus (2002–Present)

Axl Rose has referred to guitarist Richard Fortus as "an amazing lead player and very technically skilled." Born and raised in St. Louis, Missouri, Fortus studied at the Conservatory of the Arts in St. Louis and Southern Illinois University. Fortus's first band, the Eyes, was formed in 1984 and soon developed a cult following in the Midwest. The band changed its name to Pale Divine in 1990 and embarked on a tour supporting the Psychedelic Furs. (Fortus later became a member of the band.) He then formed a band

The Australian-American musical collective known as the Dead Daisies featured Guns N' Roses band members Richard Fortus, Dizzy Reed, and Frank Ferrer.   *Author's collection*

with Furs' lead singer Richard Butler called Love Spit Love and released a self-titled debut album in 1994. Fortus joined Guns N' Roses in 2001 (replacing Paul Tobias as both a rhythm and occasional lead guitarist), toured with the band, contributed to the 2008 album *Chinese Democracy*, and joined the Not in This Lifetime Tour in 2016. In addition, Fortus has performed and recorded with the likes of Thin Lizzy, Nena, Rihanna, Enrique Iglesias, and others. He has also contributed to the soundtracks for the films *Monster* (2003), *Repo! The Genetic Opera* (2008), and *Role Models* (2008), as well as the long-running *Fast and Furious* action franchise. In 2013, Fortus joined the Dead Daisies, an Australian-American musical collective that also features GN'R bandmates Dizzy Reed and Frank Ferrer.

Bumblefoot (2006–14)

An accomplished guitarist, singer-songwriter, producer, and teacher, Ron "Bumblefoot" Thal released his solo debut album, *The Adventures of Bumblefoot*, in 1995 and quickly developed a cult following. Bumblefoot joined Guns N' Roses in 2006 (replacing Buckethead) and made his live debut with the band at the historic Hammerstein Ballroom in New York City on May 12 of that year (which marked the band's first live show in more than three years). Bumblefoot performed on GN'R's 2008 album, *Chinese Democracy*, and the 2014 DVD *Appetite for Democracy*, and he traveled the globe as part of the *Chinese Democracy* Tour. He left the band in 2014 and explained the reason for his departure in a 2016 *Loudwire* interview: "All I could say is you reach a time when you just know it's time to move on."

Bryan "Brain" Mantia (2000–06)

In addition to his work with Guns N' Roses, drummer Bryan "Brain" Mantia has performed with the likes of Tom Waits, Godflesh, Primus, Praxis, Serj Tankian, and Buckethead. By the way, he got the nickname "Brain" while in the high school concert band because of his "obsession" with Anthony Cirone's classic (and rather complex) book *Portraits in Rhythm: 50 Studies for Snare Drum*. After perfecting his drumming skills at the Percussion Institute of Technology (today known as Musicians Institute), Brain joined Bay Area funk-rock band the Limbomaniacs, who released one album, *Stinky Grooves*, in 1990. He later helped form the supergroup Praxis, which also featured P-Funk veterans Bootsy Collins and Bernie Worrell, as well as Buckethead and producer Bill Laswell. Brain also performed on Buckethead's solo albums *Giant Robot* (1994) and *Monsters and Robots* (1999).

It was Buckethead (who had replaced Slash as GN'R's lead guitarist) who called Axl's attention to Brain's talents, and Brain joined Guns N' Roses in 2000, performing with the band at Rock in Rio 3 in 2001 and the 2002 MTV Video Music Awards. He also helped lay tracks for *Chinese Democracy* (which would not be released until two years after Brain left the band). In the liner notes to *Chinese Democracy*, Brain thanked "Christ, Viagra, and the Right to Choose." After touring with GN'R during the summer of 2006, Brain announced he was taking a hiatus from the band (he was soon replaced by Frank Ferrer). On March 12, 2012, Brain made a guest appearance at the Guns N' Roses show at the House of Blues in West Hollywood and played congas on "You're Crazy" and "Rocket Queen." In a 2012 interview with *MusicRadar*, Brain remarked, "[Axl's] always been good to me. I know he's got his reputation and I've seen it and that's what makes him Axl Rose. He's running the whole ship. He's got a lot of pressure and there's a lot of freaks trying to take shit from him."

Frank Ferrer (2006–Present)

A former member of New York City rock band the Beautiful, as well as Love Spit Love (a Psychedelic Furs offshoot that also included his future GN'R bandmate, Richard Fortus), Frank Ferrer joined Guns N' Roses in 2006 after Bryan "Brain" Mantia took a leave of absence, and Ferrer continues to perform with the band, most notably at Coachella and the Not in This Lifetime Tour in 2016. He contributed to five tracks on *Chinese Democracy* and also appears on the 2014 *Appetite for Democracy* DVD. During downtime between his GN'R commitments, Ferrer has performed with the likes of Wyclef Jean, Tool, Perry Farrell of Jane's Addiction, Gordon Gano of the Violent Femmes, Neil Young, Cheetah Chrome of the Dead Boys, Frank Black of the Pixies, and German pop singer Nena (best known for her 1983 anti-war protest song, "99 Luftballoons"). In addition to playing with two New York City-based bands, the Compulsions and Pisser, when not touring with GN'R, Ferrer also joined Fortus in the Dead Daisies, an all-star rock collective, for the band's 2013 tour.

DJ Ashba (2009–15)

A native of Monticello, Indiana, Daren Jay "DJ" Ashba attended his first concert—Mötley Crüe during the 1987 *Girls, Girls, Girls* Tour—at the age of sixteen. According to Ashba on his online biography, the experience changed his life: "The crowd, the music, the lights! It was the night I realized that no matter what it takes, I was gonna be on that stage one day." At age eighteen, Ashba headed to Los Angeles to make his dreams a reality. Before long, Ashba joined his first band, Barracuda, and spent the next two years touring with the group. His debut instrumental album, *Addiction to the Friction*, was released in 1996.

In 1998, Ashba joined Los Angeles hard rock band Bulletboys (which Steven Adler also joined briefly before returning to his Adler's Appetite project). The following year, Ashba formed the band Beautiful Creatures, which opened for KISS during their reunion tour. Beautiful Creatures released their self-titled debut album in 2001. In 2003, Ashba formed the solo band ASHBA, along with ASHBA Media, Inc., which today is billed as

Guns N' Roses performed at the third annual Sofia Rocks Festival at the Vassil Levski National Stadium in Bulgaria in July 2012 in front of a crowd of 20,000 fans.

MrPanyGoff/Wikimedia Commons

a "scenic fabrication and themed design company based out of Las Vegas, Nevada." In 2005, Ashba joined forces with Nikki Sixx of Mötley Crüe, along with musician and producer James Michael, to form the band Sixx:A.M. (writing music to some of Sixx's old diaries). The band released a 2007 album, *The Heroin Diaries Soundtrack*, which served as musical accompaniment to Sixx's book, *The Heroin Diaries: A Year in the Life of a Shattered Rock Star*, and featured the hit single "Life Is Beautiful." In 2008, Ashba coproduced (with Sixx and Michael) Mötley Crüe's 2008 album, *Saints of Los Angeles*. The following year, believe it or not, Ashba coproduced Neil Diamond's Christmas album, *A Cherry, Cherry, Christmas*.

Ashba was selected as the new lead guitarist of Guns N' Roses in 2009 and joined the band's *Chinese Democracy* Tour. He appears on GN'R's 2014 DVD, *Appetite for Democracy*, which was filmed at the Joint in the Hard Rock Casino in Las Vegas in 2012. In 2015, Ashba announced his departure from Guns N' Roses to focus his attention on Sixx:A.M.

Chris Pitman (1998–2016)

A multi-instrumentalist (as well as a talented painter) who has performed with the likes of Tool, Replicants, Lusk, and (currently) SexTapes, Chris Pitman joined Guns N' Roses in 1998 as the band's second keyboardist and contributed to every track on the 2008 GN'R album *Chinese Democracy* (in addition to cowriting "If the World" and "Madagascar" with Axl). After Pitman left the band in 2016, he was replaced by Melissa Reese. Pitman caused a minor controversy (blown way out of proportion on social media!) when he commented about the upcoming Guns N' Roses reunion during a Facebook chat, claiming, "I quit the Oldies band, they just wanna repeat the 30 year old music over and over . . . boring!" Pitman had previously apologized for a social media post that slammed the reunion: "This is a nostalgia tour, please don't mention those who are there the last 20 fkg years . . . Oh god no! . . . (a money grab) FU." After deleting the post, he sent out an online apology: "I sincerely apologize to GNR, especially the band and crew, for stupid comments about upcoming tour . . . remember kids, don't drink n text!"

Melissa Reese (2016–Present)

A talented and innovative keyboardist, Melissa Reese has performed with Taylor Swift, Vanessa Carlton, Goapele, Chuck D, and Bootsy Collins. She has also worked on several projects with former GN'R drummer Bryan "Brain" Mantia. For their work on the soundtrack for the video game *Infamous 2*, the duo was nominated for "Outstanding Achievement in Original Composition" by the Academy of Interactive Arts and Sciences. Other video games they worked on include *Playstation Home, Modnation Racers, Twisted Metal, Fantasia: Music Evolved*, and *Infamous: Second Son*. In 2016, Reese joined Guns N' Roses as second keyboardist (replacing Chris Pitman) and performed with GN'R at the April 1 "warm-up show" at the Troubadour, as well as at the Las Vegas Reunion Shows, Coachella, and the Not in This Lifetime Tour. She is the first official female member of Guns N' Roses.

30

As the Years Go By

Chinese Democracy (2008)

It's a very complex record, I'm trying to do something different . . . Some people are going to say, "It doesn't sound like Axl Rose, it doesn't sound like Guns N' Roses." But you'll like at least a few songs on there.   —Axl Rose

Fifteen years in the making and the subject of countless jokes about endless delays, Axl Rose's reclusive nature during this period, and the rotating door of musicians involved in its production, Guns N' Roses' sixth studio album, *Chinese Democracy*, was *finally* released in November 2008 and rose to No. 27 on the US charts. When all was said and done, *Chinese Democracy* ended up costing an estimated $14 million to produce, making it the most expensive album in rock history. Things got so bad with the delays that in 2005 Geffen Records pulled funding from the album and released a statement concerning the project's financial complications: "Having exceeded all budgeted and approved recording costs by millions of dollars, it is Mr. Rose's obligation to fund and complete the album, not Geffen's."

Chinese Democracy was released to generally positive reviews. *Los Angeles Times* critic Ann Powers called the album "a cyborgian blend of pop expressiveness, traditional rock bravado, and Brian Wilson-style beautiful weirdness." In a November 27, 2008, review of the album, *Rolling Stone* critic David Fricke commented, "To [Axl], the long march to *Chinese Democracy* was not about paranoia and control. It was about saying 'I won't' when everyone else insisted, 'You must.' You may debate whether any rock record is worth that extreme self-indulgence. Actually, the most rock & roll thing about *Chinese Democracy* is he doesn't care if you do."

In addition to Axl, who wrote or cowrote all of the tracks, Guns N' Roses members who contributed to *Chinese Democracy* during the album's extremely long gestation include Robin Finck (guitar, keyboards), Ron "Bumblefoot" Thal (guitar), Brian "Buckethead" Carroll (guitar), Paul

Tobias (guitar, piano), Richard Fortus (guitar), Tommy Stinson (bass, backing vocals), Bryan "Brain" Mantia (drums), Frank Ferrer (drums), Dizzy Reed (keyboards, piano, backing vocals), Chris Pitman (keyboards, guitar), and Josh Freese (arrangements).

In 2014, Guns N' Roses released *Appetite for Democracy*—a DVD filmed live in 3D in the Joint at the Hard Rock Casino in Las Vegas on November 21, 2012—that features several songs from *Chinese Democracy*, such as the album's title track, "This is Love," "Better," "Catcher in the Rye," and "Street of Dreams." *Appetite for Democracy* also boasts established GN'R classics like "Welcome to the Jungle," "It's So Easy," "Mr. Brownstone," "Estranged," "Rocket Queen," "You Could Be Mine," "Sweet Child O' Mine," "November Rain," "Don't Cry," "Civil War," "Nightrain," "Used to Love Her," "Patience," and "Paradise City," as well as several covers: "Live and Let Die," "Another Brick in the Wall (Part 2)," "The Seeker," and "Knockin' on Heaven's Door."

"Chinese Democracy"

The album's title track was released as a single (with "Shackler's Revenge" as the B-side) on October 22, 2008, and debuted at No. 34 on the US charts. However, the song had been performed live since Guns N' Roses' News Years Eve 2001 concert at the House of Blues in Las Vegas. On that night, Axl introduced the song by remarking, "The [1997 Martin Scorsese] movie *Kundun* was on [TV] about the Dalai Lama . . . And it's not necessarily pro or con about China. It's just that right now China symbolizes one of the strongest, yet most oppressive countries and governments in the world. And we are fortunate to live in a free country. And so in thinking about that it just kind of upset me, and we wrote this little song called 'Chinese Democracy.'" The song served as the show opener during the 2009/2010 *Chinese Democracy* Tour and continued to be part of the band's setlist during the 2016 Not in This Lifetime Tour.

Writers: Axl, Josh Freese, Paul Tobias, Tommy Stinson, Dizzy Reed, Robin Finck, Caram Costanzo, Eric Caudieux.

"Shackler's Revenge"

The industrial rock-style "Shackler's Revenge" appeared on *Rock Band 2* just prior to the release of *Chinese Democracy* in 2008, making it GN'R's first official release since "Oh My God," which appeared on the soundtrack of

Axl Rose took a break from recording *Chinese Democracy* by serving as the voice of "Tommy 'Nightmare' Smith," DJ of classic rock station KDST ("The Dust") in the 2004 video game *Grand Theft Auto: San Andreas.*   *Author's collection*

the 1999 film, *End of Days.* Other songs featured on *Rock Band 2* include "Ace of Spades" by Motörhead, "Let There Be Rock" by AC/DC, "Pinball Wizard" by the Who, "Psycho Killer" by Talking Heads, and "White Wedding" by Billy Idol, among others. During a 2008 chat on a GN'R fan forum, Axl stated that "Shackler's Revenge" was written in reaction to "the insanity of senseless school shootings and also the media trying desperately to make more out of one shooter's preference for the Guns song 'Brownstone' to no avail."

In an interview with Brazil's *Rock Brigade* magazine, GN'R guitarist Ron "Bumblefoot" Thal commented, "I played all the solos [on 'Shackler's Revenge']—the fretless solo followed by the fretted solo, the end tapping stuff and the bends over it—also the rhythms throughout the song with all the riffing in them . . . I like the energy and groove. The vocals really grab ya. I don't think it's what people expect, like tasting somethin' for the first time." Buckethead, who left the band in 2004, is credited as one of the cowriters of "Shackler's Revenge."

Guitarist Ron "Bumblefoot" Thal served as lead guitarist for Guns N' Roses from 2006 to 2014 and appeared on the band's 2008 album, *Chinese Democracy*. He has also launched a line of award-winning gourmet hot sauces.   *Author's collection*

Writers: Axl, Robin Finck, Brian "Buckethead" Carroll, Caram Costanzo, Bryan "Brain" Mantia, Pete Scaturro.

"Better"

Written by Axl and Robin Finck (GN'R guitarist, 1998–2008), "Better" was one of the songs destined for *Chinese Democracy* that was notoriously leaked online through a Guns N' Roses fan site. The song made its live debut during a Guns N' Roses concert at the Hammerstein Ballroom in New York City on May 12, 2006, and was played extensively during the band's *Chinese Democracy* Tour between 2006 and 2007. According to *Rolling Stone*, the song "feels like classic Guns N' Roses—Rose's growling croon in the verses could have floated out of the *Use Your Illusion* sessions." An official music video was made to accompany "Better," but for some unknown reason it has still not been released. The song continued to be performed during the Not in This Lifetime Tour in 2016.

Writers: Axl, Robin Finck.

"Street of Dreams"

Originally titled "The Blues," the ballad "Street of Dreams" was written by Axl and has been performed at Guns N' Roses concerts since 2001. Dizzy Reed plays piano on the track, which reveals once again Axl's debt to Elton John.

Writers: Axl, Robin Finck, Dizzy Reed, Tommy Stinson, Paul Tobias.

"If the World"

In a Wickedinfo.com interview, keyboardist Chris Pitman, who shared writing credits on the song "If the World," claimed that the song is "about environmental decay in its futurist context." The song features the novelty of a flamenco guitar solo by Buckethead. Directed by Ridley Scott and featuring Leonardo DiCaprio and Russell Crowe, the 2008 spy thriller *Body of Lies* features "If the World" played over the closing credits.

Writers: Axl, Chris Pitman.

"There Was a Time"

Featuring a full choir along with strings and a Mellotron, "There Was a Time" made its live debut at the Hammerstein Ballroom in New York City on May 12, 2006, but has been rarely performed by Guns N' Roses since.

Writers: Axl, Paul Tobias, Dizzy Reed, Tommy Stinson.

"Catcher in the Rye"

The song's title refers to J. D. Salinger's 1951 novel of the same name—a classic tale of teenage angst featuring the first-person narration of anti-hero Holden Caulfield. In a 2008 online chat forum, Axl stated that the song was written after he had viewed a documentary on John Lennon's assassin, Mark David Chapman, who became obsessed with the novel. Axl remarked that the song was inspired by "Holden Caulfield Syndrome," which he felt was caused by "how the writing [of the novel] is structured with the thinking of the main character could [sic] somehow re-program, for lack of a better word, some who may be a bit more vulnerable, with a skewed way of thinking." In Axl's view, the novel itself is "utter garbage" and "should be discontinued as required reading in schools." Interestingly, guitarist Brian May of Queen was involved in the initial recording of "Catcher in the Rye" in 1999, but his contributions were eventually excised and replaced by the guitar work of Ron "Bumblefoot" Thal.

Writers: Axl, Tommy Stinson, Dizzy Reed, Robin Finck, Paul Tobias.

"Scraped"

The industrial-style track "Scraped" was first performed live at a Guns N' Roses concert in Osaka, Japan, on December 16, 2009, but has not been played many times since. The song's guitar solo has been attributed to Brian "Buckethead" Carroll.

Writers: Axl, Brian "Buckethead" Carroll, Caram Costanzo.

"Riad N' the Bedouins"

Guns N' Roses was sued by two independent record labels, Independiente and Domino Recording Company, which alleged that the band had sampled

Listed on *Guitar World*'s "25 All-Time Weirdest Guitarists," Buckethead (real name: Brian Carroll) is known for wearing a KFC bucket on his head and a white mask over his face (inspired by *Halloween 4: The Return of Michael Myers*). Buckethead served as lead guitarist for Guns N' Roses from 2000 to 2004.   *Author's collection*

two songs—"Wherever You Are" and "A Strangely Isolated Place"—by German electronic musician Ulrich Schnausson at the beginning of "Riad N' the Bedouins." GN'R manager Irving Azoff rebutted the claims, remarking that "the snippets of 'ambient noise' in question were provided by a member of the album's production team who has assured us that these few seconds of sound were obtained legitimately."

Writers: Axl, Robin Finck, Tommy Stinson, Paul Tobias.

"Sorry"

One of four tracks from *Chinese Democracy* that was performed live during the Not in This Lifetime Tour (the others being "Chinese Democracy," "This I Love," and "Better"), "Sorry" was cowritten by Axl, Bryan "Brain" Mantia, Brian "Buckethead" Carroll, and Pete Scaturro. In addition, Skid Row lead singer Sebastian Bach provided backing vocals. Axl has denied that the song is about either Slash or Guns N' Roses fans.

Writers: Axl, Brian "Buckethead" Carroll, Bryan "Brain" Mantia, Pete Scaturro.

"I.R.S."

In "I.R.S.," Axl sings, "Gonna call the President/Gonna call myself a Private Eye/Gonna need the IRS/Gonna get the FBI." In 2003, the song was bizarrely leaked by New York Mets catcher Mike Piazza on New York classic rock station Q104.3's "Friday Night Rocks . . . With Eddie Trunk." Of the song, Trunk stated, "[It] reminded me of *Use Your Illusion*-era stuff, with some modern flairs to it. The song had a loop track in the beginning, but then, when it kicked in, it was that same dramatic Guns N' Roses hard rock."

Writers: Axl, Paul Tobias, Dizzy Reed.

"Madagascar"

Arguably the most powerful track on *Chinese Democracy*, "Madacasgar," which was cowritten by Axl and keyboardist Chris Pitman, cleverly incorporates several audio samples from two of Martin Luther King Jr.'s most famous speeches ("I Have a Dream" in 1963 and "Why Jesus Called a Man a Fool" in 1967) as well as famous quotes from such movies as *Cool Hand Luke* (1967), *Mississippi Burning* (1988), *Casualties of War* (1989), *Braveheart* (1995), and *Se7en* (1995). The same speech from *Cool Hand Luke* was also used at the opening of "Civil War" from *Use Your Illusion II*: "What we've got here is . . . failure to communicate." First performed by GN'R at Rock in Rio 3 in 2001, "Madagascar" was also part of the band's three-song set (along with "Welcome to the Jungle" and "Paradise City") during their surprise appearance to the 2002 MTV Video Music Awards.

Writers: Axl, Chris Pitman.

"This I Love"

The evolution of the piano ballad "This I Love" dates back to the early 1990s, and Axl has revealed that it's "the heaviest thing I've ever done." In a 2011 interview with *Classic Rock* magazine, DJ Ashba claimed that "This I Love" was probably his favorite song on *Chinese Democracy* "because it's just a great song, lyrically and musically; it goes through a rollercoaster of emotions. It's very heartfelt, you can tell."

Writer: Axl.

"Prostitute"

Written by Axl and Paul Tobias, this power ballad dates from the late 1990s. Actor Nicolas Cage once remarked, "I think Axl is one of the great writers of the last century; his piano playing is amazing and that song 'Prostitute' is incredible!"

Writers: Axl, Robin Finck, Paul Tobias.

31

Real-Time Visionaries

Chinese Democracy Tour

We have to live up to something, have to work a bit harder because
you're living up to the legend or a myth or whatever.   —Axl Rose

Although the actual album *Chinese Democracy* was not released until 2008, the *Chinese Democracy* Tour technically began in 2001. After 2002, the band didn't tour again until 2006. The sporadic tour was rife with cancellations from the outset, spanned ten years, and culminated with a New Year's Eve 2011 concert in Las Vegas. The tour featured Axl Rose, keyboardist Dizzy Reed, bassist Tommy Stinson, and multi-instrumentalist Chris Pitman, as well as rhythm guitarist Paul Tobias (1994–2002), rhythm guitarist Richard Fortus (2002–present), lead guitarist Robin Finck (1998–2008), Buckethead (2000–04), Ron "Bumblefoot" Thal (2006–14), drummer Bryan "Brain" Mantia (2001–06), and drummer Frank Ferrer (2006–present). Below are some of the highlights (and lowlights!) of the *Chinese Democracy* Tour.

January 1, 2001: Guns N' Roses take the stage at the House of Blues in Las Vegas with a lineup that includes Rose, Reed, Buckethead, Finck, Tobias, Stinson, and Mantia for the band's first live performance in seven years. In addition to such classics as "Welcome to the Jungle" and "Paradise City," GN'R perform several new songs such as "Oh My God" and "Silkworms" (unreleased), as well as "Riad N' the Bedouins," "Chinese Democracy," and "Street of Dreams," which would all later appear on the *Chinese Democracy* album. *Rolling Stone* calls the concert a "triumphant return" for the band.

January 14, 2001: On the third night of Rock in Rio 3 in Rio de Janeiro, Brazil, Guns N' Roses take the stage and perform a similar set to the House of Blues concert, along with the addition of "Madagascar." During the set, Axl remarks, "I know that many of you are disappointed that some of

The newly reformed Guns N' Roses performed at the Joint in the Hard Rock Hotel and Casino in Las Vegas on December 29 and 31, 2001. Slash was reportedly banned from attending either of the shows.   *Author's collection*

the people you came to know and love could not be with us here today. Regardless of what you have heard or read, people worked very hard to do everything they could so that I could not be here today. I am as hurt and disappointed as you that unlike Oasis, we could not find a way to all get along." Other musicians to play at Rock in Rio 3 include R.E.M., Oasis, Sting, Foo Fighters, James Taylor, Beck, Iron Maiden,

Dave Matthews Band, Red Hot Chili Peppers, Rob Halford, Neil Young, Sheryl Crow, *NSYNC, and Britney Spears, among others.

December 31, 2001: Slash is denied entrance to the Guns N' Rose concert at the Joint in Las Vegas. According to then GN'R manager Doug Goldstein, "We didn't know what his intentions were. If nothing else, it would have been a distraction. Axl was really nervous about these shows. We decided on our own not to take any risk."

August 23, 2002: Due to technical problems, Guns N' Roses take the stage after 11 p.m. at the Leeds Festival in Bramham Park in England. After the City Council and concert promoters tell GN'R they will have to cut their set short, Axl embarks on a rant: "I think we got a good seven or eight fuckin' songs left at least. And I didn't fuckin' come all the way over to fuckin' England to be told to go back fuckin' home by some fuckin' asshole! All I've got for the last eight years is shit after shit after shit in the fuckin' press and Axl's this, Axl's that. I'm here to play a fuckin' show and we want to play!" The band is allowed to finish their set without incident.

August 26, 2002: Alternative rock band Weezer ("Buddy Holly") open for Guns N' Roses at the London Arena. Several hardcore GN'R fans chant "fuck off" and throw bottles at the stage during the Weezer set.

August 29, 2002: Guns N' Roses perform a medley of "Welcome to the Jungle," "Madagascar," and "Paradise City" to close the 2002 MTV Video Music Awards at Radio City Music Hall in New York City. After the set, MTV's Kurt Loder interviews Axl and asks him if *Chinese Democracy* is going to come out soon. Axl remarks, "I don't know if soon is the word. But it will come out and we will, we'll go back, we'll do some more recording and then we'll start the American leg of the tour. And see how it goes from there." Loder remarks that recording the album "has taken a long time." Axl responds, "Yeah, but it's also how do you rebuild something that got so big and replace virtually every person on the crew, every single thing. And how do you make a whole bunch of guys that are something else into something that already was. I don't know if it's exactly been done like this. And not with the intensity of these players wanting to play the material."

November 7, 2002: Axl fails to show up at a Guns N' Roses show at General Motors Place in Vancouver, Canada, due to his flight being delayed. A riot ensues after promoters decide to cancel the show, with fans throwing bottles and rocks, as well as breaking glass doors at the venue (now known as Rogers Arena). Police try to quell the riot with pepper spray, batons, and attack dogs.

December 5, 2002: Guns N' Roses perform a sold-out show at Madison Square Garden in New York City. According to a review of the concert in *SPIN*, "Guns N' Roses went onstage early and played real fucking rock music for two fucking hours . . . Against seemingly unfathomable odds, the reinvented Guns N' Roses were remarkably awesome."

December 6, 2002: A riot breaks out at the First Union Center in Philadelphia after the Guns N' Roses concert is cancelled around midnight due to Axl's "health issues." The crowd begins throwing beers, chanting "Axl sucks," ripping the seats off chairs, and ultimately causing approximately $200,000 in damages.

March 23, 2004: Geffen Records releases a Guns N' Roses *Greatest Hits* album without the participation or consent of any existing or former GN'R band members. The album reaches No. 3 on the US charts. The track list faces criticism for its overabundance of covers, including "Knockin' on Heaven's Door" (Bob Dylan), "Live and Let Die" (Paul McCartney and Wings), "Ain't It Fun" (Dead Boys), "Since I Don't Have You" (Skyliners), and especially the lackluster "Sympathy for the Devil" (Rolling Stones).

March 30, 2004: Axl issues a press release announcing that Guns N' Roses will not be performing as scheduled at Rock in Rio Lisboa on May 30 by the "untimely departure" of guitarist Buckethead. According to Axl, "During his tenure with the band Buckethead has been inconsistent and erratic in both his behavior and commitment—despite being under contract—creating uncertainty and confusion and making it virtually impossible to move forward with recording, rehearsals, and live plans with confidence."

May 12, 2006: Guns N' Roses take the stage at Hammerstein Ballroom in New York City for the band's first live concert in more than three years. The show serves as guitarist Ron "Bumblefoot" Thal's live debut with the band.

May 18, 2006: Before a surprise Guns N' Roses acoustic show for actress Rosario Dawson's twenty-seventh birthday at the Plumm nightclub in New York City, Axl gets into a fight with fashion designer Tommy Hilfiger. Axl later remarked that he had simply moved Hilfiger's girlfriend's drink so it wouldn't spill, and Hilfiger "just kept smacking me." During the GN'R set, Axl dedicates "You're Crazy" to "my good friend Tommy Hilfiger."

May 27, 2006: Guns N' Roses perform at the Rock in Rio Lisboa 2 festival at the Parque de Bela Vista in Lisbon, Portugal.

June 11, 2006: Izzy Stradlin takes the stage with Guns N' Roses during their set at the Download Festival at Donington Park, England. Stradlin performs with GN'R on "Think About You," "Patience," "Nightrain," "Used to Love Her," and "Paradise City." Skid Row's Sebastian Bach joins the band on "My Michelle."

June 15, 2006: Guns N' Roses perform their first-ever concert in Poland at Stadion Legii in Warsaw.

June 27, 2006: The day after performing at a sold-out Guns N' Roses concert at Globe Arena in Stockholm, Sweden, an inebriated and "very aggressive" Axl is arrested after allegedly damaging property, biting a security guard in the leg, and threatening a police officer at the Berns Hotel. He would later agree to pay a fine of $5,000, along with $1,360 in damages, to the security guard.

July 19, 2006: Guns N' Roses play an abbreviated concert at Metro Radio Arena in Newcastle after Axl gets hit by several objects, including a coin and some bottles, thrown from the audience. Axl later releases a statement regarding the incident, claiming, "Getting hit wasn't a big deal. We stopped the song and gave a warning. We came back and started the song over and completed it. We then said goodnight. The house lights went down and I got hit a second time, in the mouth, by a solid object by someone in the audience. After having warned the crowd that we would leave, and having played more than two hours, we left the stage and called it a night with the full support of everyone in the band, our guests, and management."

July 25, 2006: Halfway through "You Could Be Mine," Axl stops a Guns N' Roses performance at the NEC Arena in Birmingham, England, after he witnesses security roughing up a fan. Axl screams, "What the fuck's wrong with you guys down here? The security guys, you guys are out of control. The guy was having some fun, so you're gonna beat him? You guys gotta go. You're outta here."

July 30, 2006: Guns N' Roses conclude the European leg of the tour with a concert at Wembley Arena in London. After Axl is taken ill and leaves the stage, Sebastian Bach fills in as lead singer for "Nightrain" and "Paradise City."

August 31, 2006: Axl introduces the Killers at the 2006 MTV Video Music Awards by screaming, "Do you know where the fuck you are?" The Killers take the stage and perform "Enterlude" and "When You Were Young."

September 21, 2006: At a Guns N' Roses show at the Warfield in San Francisco, Axl stops the concert during "Sweet Child O' Mine" to reprimand a taunting fan, remarking, "We're trying to have a good time and so is everybody else. I'm not really sure what you want. If you think you're a bigger asshole than me, you've got something to learn!"

October 24, 2006: Guns N' Roses embark on the North American leg of their 2006 tour at the BankAtlantic Center in Sunrise, Florida, with opening acts Sebastian Bach and Papa Roach.

November 10, 2006: Guns N' Roses perform a lively sold-out show at Madison Square Garden in New York City that concludes with Axl remarking, "We wanna get the fuck back here next year!"

November 11, 2006: In New York City, Axl takes the stage and performs "Live and Let Die" at a benefit for the Michael J. Fox Foundation for Parkinson's Resarch titled "A Funny Thing Happened on the Way to Cure Parkinson's." Axl tells *People* magazine, "We actually used a sample of Michael J. Fox from *Casualties of War* in one of our songs ["Madagascar"] that will be on the new album. So I felt, one, I've always been a fan of his. And I also feel for the guy and his situation. I'm for stem-cell research, so I just thought it would be wrong not for me to come when I was asked."

November 13, 2006: The tattooed and pierced rock 'n' roll burlesque group known as the Suicide Girls starts a short stint opening for Guns N' Roses at 1st Mariner Arena in Baltimore, Maryland.

November 24, 2006: During a Guns N' Roses concert in Cleveland, Ohio, Axl fires opening act Eagles of Death Metal onstage, referring to the band as the "Pigeons of Shit Metal." Following the incident, Eagles of Death Metal release a humorous statement directed at Axl's antics: "At first the audience refused to welcome us to the jungle, but by the time we took our final bow, it had become paradise city. Although Axl tried to November rain on our parade, no sweet child o' mine can derail the EODM night train. We say live and let die."

December 14, 2006: Axl releases an open letter to Guns N' Roses fans announcing a tentative release date of March 6, 2007, for the long-delayed *Chinese*

Democracy album: "To say the making of this album has been an unbearably long and incomprehensible journey would be an understatement. Overcoming the endless and seemingly insanity of the obstacles faced by all involved, not withstanding the emotional challenges endured by everyone: the fans, the band, our road crew, and business team has at many times seemed for all like a bad dream where one wakes up only to find they are still in the nightmare and unfortunately this time it has been played out for over a decade in real life."

December 15, 2006: Metallica drummer Lars Ulrich joins Guns N' Roses onstage for a performance of "Out Ta Get Me" at the Oracle Arena in Oakland, California.

December 17, 2006: Izzy Stradlin joins Guns N' Roses onstage for a concert at the Gibson Amphitheatre in Universal City, California, for renditions of "Think About You," "Used to Love Her," "Patience," "Nightrain," and "Paradise City." According to a review of the show in *Variety*, "For a man with so much on the line, [the concert] felt pro forma and desultory . . . Rose took the stage as scheduled, but the combative, charismatic front man was nowhere to be seen."

July 14, 2007: At a sold-out concert at Makuhari Messe in Chiba, Japan, Guns N' Roses perform "Don't Cry" live for the first time in fourteen years.

November 27, 2007: Skid Row's Sebastian Bach releases his solo album, *Angel Down*, which features a guest appearance by Axl on three songs: "Back in the Saddle" (Aerosmith cover), "(Love is) a Bitchslap," and "Stuck Inside."

September 14, 2008: Harmonix releases the *Rock Band 2* music video game, which features the Guns N' Roses track "Shackler's Revenge" from the still-unreleased *Chinese Democracy* (making it the first officially released track from the album). Other featured songs on Rock Band 2 include "Ace of Spades" by Motörhead, "Let There Be Rock" by AC/DC, "Pinball Wizard" by the Who, "White Wedding" by Billy Idol, "Everlong" by Foo Fighters, and others.

October 10, 2008: Directed by Ridley Scott and starring Leonardo DiCaprio, the spy thriller *Body of Lies* is released into movie theaters and features the Guns N' Roses song "If the World" from *Chinese Democracy* playing over the beginning of the closing credits.

November 23, 2008: *Chinese Democracy* is *finally* released in the United States.

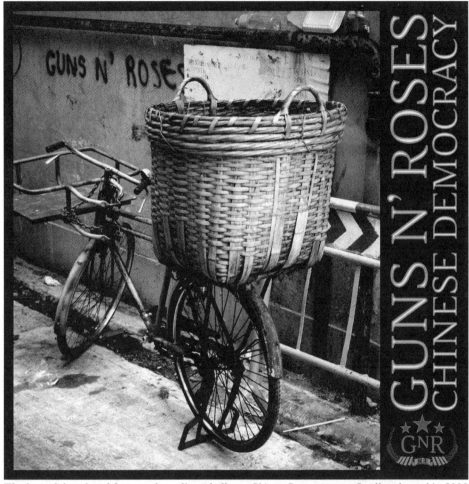

GUNS N' ROSES
CHINESE DEMOCRACY

The long-delayed and frequently maligned album *Chinese Democracy* was finally released in 2008 and debuted at No. 3 on the US charts. The most expensive rock album ever produced, *Chinese Democracy* cost approximately $14 million when all was said and done.   *Author's collection*

December 12, 2008: Axl answers fans' questions during an online message board session, calling *Chinese Democracy* "nothing short of a miracle" considering "the bizarre and ugly conditions" that occurred since the album's conception.

December 11, 2009: Guitarist DJ Ashba makes his live debut with Guns N' Roses at a concert at Taipei City Stadium in Taipei, Taiwan.

Currently the lead guitarist for SixxA.M., DJ Ashba joined Guns N' Roses in 2009 for the *Chinese Democracy* Tour (replacing Robin Finck) and stayed with the band for the next six years. He referred to his GN'R stint as "the most incredible experience of my life."

ThatRockMetalGuy/Wikimedia Commons

December 19, 2009: At the Tokyo Dome, Guns N' Roses perform the longest set in the band's history, lasting three hours and thirty-seven minutes, and comprising thirty-one songs, including seven encores: "Madagascar," "There Was a Time," "My Generation," "Better," "Patience," "Nice Boys," and "Paradise City."

January 28, 2010: During a Guns N' Roses concert at the Air Canada Centre in Toronto, the band dedicates "Catcher in the Rye" to the reclusive author J. D. Salinger, who had died the day before at the age of ninety-one.

February 11, 2010: Guns N' Roses perform a surprise seventeen-song acoustic set at the Varvatos store in New York City at the site of the former CBGB space.

March 25, 2010: The La Explanada Sur Del Estadio Monumental serves as the venue for the first-ever Guns N' Roses concert in Lima, Peru. The band will go on to perform their first-ever show in Ecuador at the Estadio Olimpico Atahualpa in Quito on April 1, their first-ever concert in Panama at the Estadio Figali in Panama City on April 7, and their first-ever show in El Salvador at the Estadio Cuscatlan in San Salvador on April 11.

June 6, 2010: Guns N' Roses take the stage at Ledovy Dvorets arena in Saint Petersburg for the band's first-ever concert in Russia.

August 13, 2010: Due to a technical glitch, Guns N' Roses take the stage at 12:50 a.m. at the seventieth annual Sturgis Bike Rally in Sturgis, South Dakota. Some restless fans start throwing beer bottles and cans at the stage during the long wait.

September 21, 2010: Guns N' Roses play Bucharest, Romania, for the first time ever at Romexpo, followed by a first-ever visit to Belgrade, Serbia, to perform at the Beogradska Arena on September 23.

October 14, 2010: Duff joins Guns N' Roses onstage for the first time in seventeen years for a concert at London's O2 Arena and performs with the band on "You Could Be Mine," "Knockin' on Heaven's Door," "Nice Boys," and "Patience."

December 16, 2010: Guns N' Roses perform at Yas Arena in Abu Dhabi, United Arab Emirates.

October 2, 2011: At Rock in Rio IV in Rio de Janeiro, Brazil, Guns N' Roses take the stage two hours late for their set, much to the chagrin of the event's organizers. According to a Stereogum review of the concert, "the reconstituted Axl-plus-nobodies version of Guns N' Roses earned the wrong kind of attention when they took the stage hours late, looking and sounding like straight dogshit . . . Axl wore a perfectly ridiculous outfit, sounded like a dying baby elephant, and looked like he'd eaten Slash and Duff for dinner that night." The band later released a press release to "set the record straight" on the disastrous Rock in Rio IV performance: "The festival's inadequate production and the downpour of rain delayed the event . . . GNR walked onstage at 2:40 a.m. and played for two and a half hours in the pouring rain. GNR would never seek to intentionally disrespect anyone, especially their fans."

December 7, 2011: Guns N' Roses perform at the Covelli Centre in Youngstown, Ohio, on the day it was announced that the band would be inducted into the Rock and Roll Hall of Fame. Axl refers to the honor once during the three-hour concert, remarking, "I'd like to thank the Rock and Roll Hall of Fame and I'd like to thank our fans. This is your reward."

December 16, 2011: Duff's band, Loaded, opens for Guns N' Roses at the KeyArena in Seattle, Washington. In addition, Duff joins GN'R for a rendition of "You Could Be Mine."

December 30, 2011: Guns N' Roses perform on this date and during a special New Year's Eve show the following night at the Joint at Hard Rock Hotel in Las Vegas.

32

Never Mind the Darkness

The Most Essential Guns N' Roses Biographies

I'm looking forward to people doing a book about us that has a lot of stuff in it that never happened.   —Axl Rose

Three of the five "classic" Guns N' Roses band members have published highly entertaining, informative, and sometimes contradictory autobiographies: *Slash* (2007), *My Appetite for Destruction: Sex & Drugs & Guns N' Roses* (Steven Adler, 2011), and *It's So Easy: and Other Lies* (Duff McKagan, 2012). While we wait patiently for Axl's and Izzy's versions of how events in GN'R's colorful timeline unfolded, there are several other must-read Guns N' Roses biographies, such as Marc Canter's illustrated 2008 classic, *Reckless Road: Guns N' Roses and the Making of Appetite for Destruction*; the 2015 graphic novel *Reckless Life: Guns N' Roses* (2015) by Jim McCarthy and Mark Olivent; and ex-GN'R manager Vicky Hamilton's 2016 *Appetite for Dysfunction*, among others.

Appetite for Destruction: The Days of Guns N' Roses (1991) by Danny Sugerman

"The future of Guns N' Roses, as always, is on the edge. Right where they belong." Anyone familiar with the 1980 bestselling Jim Morrison biography *No One Here Gets Out Alive*, which was written by Jerry Hopkins and Danny Sugerman, may correctly assume that Sugerman's *Appetite for Destruction* will not fit into the mold of conventional rock biography. In fact, hardcore Guns N' Roses fans seeking a conventional history of the band should look elsewhere. However, for those looking for an offbeat, fascinating, and

occasionally pretentious treatise (one of the chapters is titled "The Return of Dionysus") that draws parallels between Axl Rose and the rebellious streak prevalent in such artistic figures and freethinkers as Jim Morrison, Arthur Rimbaud, Charles Baudelaire, William S. Burroughs, Friedrich Nietzsche, Lord Byron, Percy Bysshe Shelley, William Blake, and others while placing their lives in the context of literary, philosophical, and mythological antecedents, this book is for you. In fact, Sugerman's biography is as much about "The Lizard King" as it is about Axl. (Other GN'R band members are definitely given short shrift here.) Indeed, a blurb on the book's back cover comes from none other than Oliver Stone, director of *The Doors* (1991), who exclaims, "[*Appetite for Destruction*] . . . captures the poetry and dark hexagonal of Axl Rose's mind. Sugerman has become an inventor of myth—a Thucydides to an American subculture." In addition, psychedelic guru Timothy Leary calls the book "a wild, exuberant, out-of-control epic poem."

Sugerman, who managed Iggy Pop briefly and also comanaged the Doors' musical and business interests, also authored *The Doors: The Illustrated History* (1983) and the autobiographical *Wonderland Avenue: Tales of Glamour and Excess* (1989). A recovering heroin addict, Sugerman died of lung cancer at the age of fifty in 2005. He is buried in Westwood Village Park Cemetery in Los Angeles and his epitaph reads, "There are things known and things unknown and in between are the doors." Interestingly, Axl discovered *No One Here Gets Out Alive* as a teenager and admitted to reading it about seven times. Axl was so inspired by Morrison's story that he even wrote a poem in his journal about the Doors' lead singer titled "Artistic Death." In "Bad to the Bone," a feature on Guns N' Roses by Sugerman in the November 1990 issue of *SPIN* magazine, Axl discusses a revelation he had while making a pilgrimage to Morrison's grave in Paris's Pere-Lachaise Cemetery: "If you die, the road of excess leads to a dirt plot in a foreign land that people pour booze on and put out cigarettes on."

Guns N' Roses: The Most Dangerous Band in the World (1992) by Mick Wall

"Once in a blue moon a rock 'n' roll band will happen along that so defies the twisted logic of its times that it captures the imaginations of everybody." Before he was placed on Axl Rose's "shit list," British rock journalist Mick Wall had early access to GN'R band members as a writer for *Kerrang!* magazine and conducted a series of insightful interviews, several of which are intertwined with the biographical details throughout this book. Wall's biography was

published just as the band itself was starting to implode, making for a compelling read to say the least. Wall's direct and honest approach to covering GN'R led to conflict with Axl, who felt compelled to attack the journalist (along with several other writers) in the song "Get in the Ring" (which appeared on the 1991 album *Use Your Illusion II*) as one of the "punks in the press/That want to start shit by printin' lies instead of the things we said."

In 1998, Wall became the founding editor of *Classic Rock* magazine. He also has penned numerous other rock biographies, including *W.A.R.: The Unauthorized Biography of William Axl Rose* (2007), *Diary of a Madman: The Official Biography of Ozzy Osbourne* (1986), *Paranoid: Black Days with Sabbath & Other Horror Stories* (1999), *When Giants Walked the Earth: A Biography of Led Zeppelin* (2008), *Love Becomes a Funeral Pyre: The Biography of the Doors* (2014), *Getcha Rock's Off: Sex & Excess. Bust Ups & Binges. Life & Death on the Rock N' Roll Road* (2015), *Lemmy: The Definitive Biography* (2016), and many others.

In an April 18, 2016, blog post on Mickwall.com titled "Getting Out of the Ring," Wall apologized for the tone of his 2007 Axl Rose biography: "It's not that the facts are all wrong or any of that. But the spirit is mean, disgruntled, unworthy. I'm sorry I wrote it. Sorry I wasn't man enough to see the bigger picture. Sorry I squeezed all of the peace, love, and understanding out of the book." Wall stated that he'd just had a heart attack and was "angry at the world" when he wrote the biography.

Guns N' Roses' Use Your Illusion I and II (2006) by Eric Weisbard

"[Use Your Illusion] signaled the end of Guns N' Roses, of heavy metal on the Sunset Strip, and the entire 1980's model of blockbuster pop/rock promotion. [It] marked the end of rock as mass culture." If you are familiar with the popular 33 1/3 series of music criticism books (each focusing on a single album), you know to expect the unexpected, and Eric Weisbard's critical study of the *Use Your Illusion* albums is no exception to the rule. Guns N' Roses fans have generally been outraged by this often pretentious and sometimes incoherent volume that veers off topic on many occasions. (A cursory check of Amazon user ratings reveals it to be one of the lowest-rated books in the entire series!) One amateur critic on Amazon even referred to it as "the narcissistic ramblings of a leftwing bozo, no offense to Bozo." However, for the reader seeking to gain an offbeat perspective on the *Use Your Illusion* albums, the book holds a certain charm (and at just 136 pages, it's a breeze to skim through). Weisbard does provide an interesting glimpse of the early 1990s rock scene as grunge

moved in and quickly crushed "bombastic" stadium rock, exemplified in the author's mind by the *Use Your Illusion* albums and accompanying tour.

Bottom line: This work is such a fascinating anomaly in the world of Guns N' Roses published material that the masochist in you may want to seek it out for fun only *after* you have exhausted all other GN'R resources. If you love Guns N' Roses uncritically, you will most likely hate this book; if you love Guns N' Roses but dislike the "excess" of the *Use Your Illusion* albums, you might like this book; and even if you don't like Guns N' Roses at all, you may find something of interest here if your reading habits tend to be on the eclectic side. Other volumes in the ever-growing 33 1/3 series of books include Love's *Forever Changes*, Neil Young's *Harvest*, the Smiths' *Meat Is Murder*, Pink Floyd's *The Piper at the Gates of Dawn*, Prince's *Sign 'o' the Times*, MC5's *Kick Out the Jams*, the Band's *Music from Big Pink*, Nirvana's *In Utero*, Sonic Youth's *Daydream Nation*, Captain Beefheart's *Trout Mask Replica*, Nick Drake's *Pink Moon*, Tom Waits's *Swordfishtrombones*, Patti Smith's *Horses*, Black Sabbath's *Master of Reality*, Slayer's *Reign in Blood*, Public Enemy's *It Takes a Nation of Millions to Hold Us Back*, Nine Inch Nails' *Pretty Hate Machine*, and many others.

Reckless Road: Guns N' Roses and the Making of *Appetite for Destruction* (2008) by Marc Canter

"When Slash took off in the way I thought he would, I felt there was a potential to capture something special." A true Guns N' Roses insider, amateur photographer, and avid collector of rock memorabilia, Marc Canter attended nearly all of the early Guns N' Roses gigs, as well as those of pre-GN'R bands Hollywood Rose and L.A. Guns. A lifelong friend of Slash's and the current owner of the legendary Canter's Deli (where GN'R members frequently hung out), Canter "became like the sixth guy in the band," according to Duff. "He was always around and had unlimited access to the band, especially in the early days . . . He documented the whole thing, tirelessly." Axl even performed "November Rain" at Canter's wedding.

The results of Canter's Guns N' Roses obsession are vivid throughout *Reckless Road*, a remarkable illustrated biography of the band that traces a line from their early beginnings up to the release of *Appetite for Destruction* in 1987 through fascinating interviews, photos, flyers, concert tickets, magazine covers, news clippings, and more (including plenty of stripper photos for the truly depraved!). In addition, a comprehensive "Cast of Characters" in the front of the book provides a great overview of the whole decadent

West Hollywood music scene during the early to mid-1980s, followed by detailed descriptions of more than fifty early GN'R gigs. The only negative is the prevalence of typos throughout the book, which could have used a good once-over by a quality copy editor. The Independent Publishers Association named *Reckless Road* "2008 Best Pop Culture Book." Bottom line: *Reckless Road* is simply a must-read for any serious Guns N' Roses fan.

Slash (2007) by Slash with Anthony Bozza

"It seems excessive . . . but that doesn't mean it didn't happen." Totally gritty, uncompromising, and raunchy, Slash's autobiography follows his laid-back childhood in a rock 'n' roll family as well as his rise to become one of rock's all-time greatest guitarists, along with the total debauchery of the rock 'n' roll scene and the nightmare of drug and alcohol addiction that followed in the wake of his success. (Slash reveals upfront that fifteen years of continual overdrinking and drug abuse had swollen his heart "to one stop short of exploding" and that doctors had given him six days to six weeks to live.) Through it all, Slash refuses to pull any punches as he discusses his musical influences (basically Aerosmith, Aerosmith, and more Aerosmith), the source of his nickname (actor Seymour Cassel), the peaks and valleys of being a rock star ("we did amazing things every single night that were godlike"), his taste in 1980s porn stars (at one time or another he "dated" actresses Lois Ayres, Traci Lords, and Savannah), his reasons for departing the band in the mid-1990s, how he overcame his many addictions, and the source of his longtime feud with Axl Rose.

In an interview with the *San Diego Union-Tribune*, Slash remarked, "The sole motivation for the book was to straighten out a lot of myths about Guns N' Roses that are still prevalent on the Internet and in unauthorized biographies. I'd love to sound like the book was sort of a deep statement for me. But, in all honesty, it wasn't. It's really everything that's on the surface; I'm way too introverted and shy to bare my soul."

Ironically, Slash takes the time in his autobiography to slam other rock biographies, such as *Hammer of the Gods* (Led Zeppelin) and *No One Here Gets Out Alive* (Jim Morrison), that "were basically written for the authors' own entertainment" and "seemed inaccurate and full of shit." In a 2016 Q&A session to coincide with the Not in This Lifetime Tour, Axl revealed his thoughts on Slash's autobiography, claiming, "Slash and I hadn't talked in nineteen years and when we did talk, I was like, 'You know, you wrote about a lot of stuff that didn't happen, that just . . . is not real.'" Slash's coauthor,

Anthony Bozza, has also penned *Tommyland* (2005) with Tommy Lee, *INXS: Story to Story* (2005) with INXS, *Too Fat to Fish* (2008) with Artie Lange, *I Am the New Black* (2009) with Tracy Morgan, *Purpose: An Immigrant's Story* (2012) with Wyclef Jean, and *Crash and Burn* (2013) with Lange.

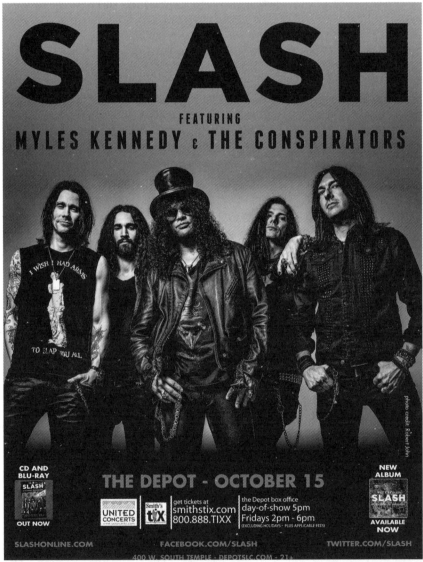

Slash's 2007 autobiography discusses both his time in Guns N' Roses and his many solo projects, such as his frequent collaborations with Myles Kennedy and the Conspirators.
Author's collection

Watch You Bleed: The Saga of Guns N' Roses (2009) by Stephen Davis

"Axl arrived in Los Angeles in the midst of the street battles for supremacy among the top music genres of the eighties: post-punk, thrash, hair metal, and glam." Best known for his controversial, unauthorized 1985 biography of Led Zeppelin, *Hammer of the Gods* (which bassist John Paul Jones called "a very sad little book"), rock biographer Stephen Davis has churned out similar volumes on other musicians over the years, such as *Jim Morrison: Life, Death, Legend* (2004). In *Watch You Bleed*, Davis goes through the motions once again with a standard biographical approach to the Guns N' Roses story punctuated occasionally with the usual salacious details about the band's self-destructive tendencies. It's hard to tell if Davis even enjoys the subjects he writes about, particularly in this case, as a negative vibe encompasses the whole GN'R biography. (In fact, he seems to feel compelled to disparage all of GN'R's work outside of *Appetite for Destruction*, even titling the chapter covering the band's 1987 debut album as "Their Only Good Album.") On a positive note, Davis delves comprehensively into Axl Rose's fucked-up childhood, as well as into the activities of original GN'R band members after the multiple acrimonious breakups in the 1990s and Axl's delays in releasing *Chinese Democracy*. Davis also includes some obscure but interesting details such as Rose's obsession with those *Faces of Death* exploitation videos. (He also apparently had a thing for Stevie Nicks music videos.)

My Appetite for Destruction: Sex & Drugs & Guns N' Roses (2011) by Steven Adler with Lawrence J. Spagnola

"Forty years, twenty-eight ODs, three botched suicides, two heart attacks, a couple of jail stints, a debilitating stroke . . . " An amazingly candid, refreshing, sometimes humorous, and often depressing autobiography from Guns N' Roses' ex-drummer, *My Appetite for Destruction* documents how Steven Adler rose to the height of fame only to be destroyed by his overwhelming addictions, which led to his being fired from the band in 1990. In fact, from the outset of his autobiography, Adler announces that he is "the undisputed all-time booze-chugging, pill-gobbling, drug-shooting, Katrina-caliber fuckup. Throughout my wretched life there isn't a friend, family member, or fantastic opportunity that I haven't shoved into a blender and mutilated." The book's bite-size subchapters feature such great offbeat titles as "Cutting Class, Scoring Ass," "Weed vs. Wine," "Orgies and Orgasms," "Lennon

Hated Blow," "Axhole," "Ayatollah Axl," "One Dumb Fuck," "Nikki Don't Lose That Heartbeat," "Heather Lockjaw," and "The Slurpee Incidents."

It's So Easy: and Other Lies (2011) by Duff McKagan

"These are my stories. These are my perspectives. This is my truth." A more thoughtful, philosophical autobiography than either *Slash* or *My Appetite for Destruction*, *It's So Easy* does plenty of delving into the dark side of fame but also allows the reader to gain insight into some of the bad decisions and regrets along the way through the often poignant musings of ex-Guns N' Roses' bassist Duff McKagan. Believe it or not, the book actually opens with a quote from Upton Sinclair's classic 1906 muckraking novel, *The Jungle*! Most refreshing, *It's So Easy* details Duff's "phoenix-like transformation" as

Duff McKagan's revealing 2011 autobiography, *It's So Easy: and Other Lies* spawned a 2016 documentary of the same name that features archival footage and interviews with the likes of Slash, Matt Sorum, Nikki Sixx, Dave Kushner, and others.   *Wikimedia Commons*

he beat his drug and alcohol addiction (which caused acute pancreatitis that nearly killed him in 1994) through a strict workout regimen that involved a combination of mountain biking and martial arts, along with going back to school and even reading literary classics like the complete works of Ernest Hemingway. (For the record, his favorite Hemingway work is *For Whom the Bell Tolls*.) Duff also provides much insight into the early 1980s Seattle punk scene, which was decimated by the heroin epidemic, as well as his stints in punk bands such as the Fastbacks, the Fartz, and 10 Minute Warning, and the supergroups Neurotic Outsiders and Velvet Revolver. The book also contains its fair share of irreverent details, such as the time Lars Ulrich of Metallica dropped by and took "a big shit" in Duff's bathroom.

It's So Easy: and Other Lies was turned into an insightful 2016 documentary of the same name that features archival footage and candid interviews with the likes of Duff, Slash, Matt Sorum, Nikki Sixx of Mötley Crüe, Mike McCready of Pearl Jam, Dave Kushner of Velvet Revolver, and others (including Duff's martial arts instructor, Benny "the Jet" Urquidez). In the film's trailer, Slash describes his first impression of Duff: "I put an ad in *The Recycler*, and in walked this six-foot-plus guy in a red-and-black, full-length trench coat." In addition, Duff's second memoir (more of a self-help book than a traditional autobiography), *How to Be A Man: (and other illusions)*, was published in 2016.

Reckless Life: Guns N' Roses (2015) by Jim McCarthy and Mark Olivent

"I wonder, if we could see into the future, what would we really do? Would we grab it or would we run from it like hell?" A splendid little graphic biography, *Reckless Life* captures "the rollercoaster tale" of Guns N' Roses through Marc Olivent's amazing artwork blended with a straightforward script from Jim McCarthy. The work, which features more than 200 black-and-white illustrations, takes readers from Axl's troubled childhood in Indiana in the 1960s all the way to the controversy surrounding GN'R's induction into the Rock and Roll Hall of Fame in 2012.

Reckless Life is full of offbeat touches such as "Satan" invading Rose's childhood home, Slash's pet rat "Mickey," Duff's near-death experience, a young Steven Adler playing his drums in the park all day long, President Reagan on the tube promoting "the trickle down theory of economic bullshit," Seventh Veil strippers, cheap breakfasts at Hamburger Hamlet,

GN'R opening for Alice Cooper, Henry Rollins of Black Flag giving the band his blessing, Nikki Sixx OD'ing and then escaping from the hospital, Axl's infamous "Mr. Brownstone" speech and his letter to Erin Everly ("from an asshole!!!"), Slash recording with Michael Jackson, the Charles Manson controversy, Axl vs. Scott Weiland, and Axl on *Jimmy Kimmel Live!* discussing punctuality (of all things!), among others. According to McCarthy, "You can do whatever you want within a graphic novel. You can be very cinematic and put things in that you couldn't in a traditional biography, and maybe not even in a film. You can come at it from different angles, different tenses, different points of view."

Appetite for Dysfunction (2016) by Vicky Hamilton

"Wannabe rockers stand on the curbs, like carnival barkers, passing out flyers for their upcoming gigs, hoping to get the attention of a record label exec, a club booker, or a hot groupie or two." In this highly entertaining autobiography, Vicky Hamilton, a successful music industry executive who served as the original manager for Guns N' Roses (she also worked with Mötley Crüe, Poison, Stryper, Faster Pussycat, and other bands), details some of her adventures and misadventures in the music industry over the years. According to the promo, the book includes fascinating details about Hamilton's "turbulent relationship with Axl Rose and Poison's Bret Michaels, her experience as an A&R rep for Geffen, and above all, *Appetite for Dysfunction* is the story of her rise and fall, and how she regained her life by becoming a Grammy Award winning executive that helped relaunch the career of June Carter Cash in 1999."

Hamilton had a knack for discovering bands and finding them both gigs and eventual record deals. At one point, nearly all of the GN'R band members (except Duff) were living in her tiny West Hollywood apartment. (Yes, they ended up destroying the place!) She even negotiated GN'R's first contract with Geffen Records only to be left behind as their careers skyrocketed. According to Steven Adler, "Vicky was probably the best thing that happened to us in the early days. She dealt with us when nobody else would, and made everything happen for us. I'm grateful for that."

33

Heal the Broken Memories

The Road to Reunion

Rock 'n' roll ended after the '80s. I see bands on TV nowadays, and I could swear it's the same guy I just bought a Whopper from at Burger King. Nobody has a look, nobody really cares.   —Steven Adler

After the endless feuding between Axl and Slash in the media over a twenty year period, as well as Axl's no-show at the 2012 Rock and Roll Hall of Fame ceremony, few Guns N' Roses fans believed the so-called "classic" members of the band would ever reunite again. In fact, Axl squashed a 2009 rumor that Axl and Slash were reuniting, telling *Billboard*, "What's clear is that one of the two of us will die before a reunion and however sad, ugly, or unfortunate anyone views it, it is how it is." In addition, during an impromptu interview with TMZ in 2012, Axl was asked about the possibility of a reunion and he replied, "Not in this lifetime."

So it came as somewhat of a surprise when rumors started cropping up everywhere in 2015 about plans for a Guns N' Roses reunion. For instance, Slash appeared on *CBS This Morning* on May 7, 2015, and seemed to be open for the idea, remarking, "I think the fans would love it. I think it might be fun at some point to try and do that . . . Never say never." On July 27, 2015, DJ Ashba quit Guns N' Roses so he could spend more time with his other band, Sixx:A.M. On August 22, 2015, Slash stated on Swedish TV that he and Axl were friends again. On January 5, 2016, an official Guns N' Roses press release confirmed in grandiose fashion that Slash and Duff would indeed return to the band for the 2016 Coachella festival: "Upholding a three-decade tradition of breaking ground, creating trends, and forever changing the face of rock 'n' roll, Guns N' Roses announce the most significant and anxiously awaited musical even of this century."

Three of the original band members—Axl, Slash, and Duff—took the stage at their old-stomping ground, the Troubadour in West Hollywood, for an April 1, 2016, Guns N' Roses "warm-up show," followed by a Las Vegas Reunion Show, a headlining concert at Coachella, and a summer Not in This Lifetime Tour of North America (that included two shows where Steven Adler joined the band, leaving Izzy Stradlin as the only "classic" band member who refused to participate in any way).

Rock and Roll Hall of Fame Induction (April 14, 2012)

After Guns N' Roses was selected for induction into the Rock and Roll Hall of Fame in 2012, controversy raged about which band members would actually show up to represent the band at the ceremony. Three days before the ceremony, Axl released an open letter addressed to "the Rock and Roll Hall of Fame, Guns N' Roses Fans, and Whom It May Concern" not only declining to attend the ceremony but also requesting exclusion from the Hall of Fame itself (as well as seemingly shutting the door on any possibility of a reunion involving "classic" GN'R band members). Axl mentioned that he had "mixed emotions" when the nominations were first announced but he was "honored" and "excited" and "hoped that somehow this would be a good thing." Of course, he also realized that it would be an "awkward situation" appearing onstage with his former bandmates.

Axl also stated that he did not agree with the Hall of Fame's decision to include certain members and not others for the induction. (For the record, Axl, Slash, Izzy, Duff, Steven Adler, Dizzy Reed, and Matt Sorum were the only ones invited.) The bottom line is that Axl decided to not attend the Rock and Roll Hall of Fame Induction Ceremony and also "respectfully" declined his induction as a member of Guns N' Roses to the Rock and Roll Hall of Fame. He also reiterated that there would be no upcoming reunion of any former Guns N' Roses bandmates from "either the Appetite or Illusion lineups." Such discussion, according to Axl, served as "misguided attempts to distract" from the accomplishments of the current Guns N' Roses lineup (which at that time also featured Dizzy Reed, Tommy Stinson, Frank Ferrer, Richard Fortus, Chris Pitman, Ron "Bumblefoot" Thal, and DJ Ashba). Axl then discussed how Izzy had joined GN'R onstage for a few shows in 2006 and 2011, how Adler had attended an after-show party at the Hard Rock in 2006 after which he spread "reunion lies," and how

Duff joined GN'R for several shows in 2010 and 2011. In order to put the reunion rumors totally to rest, Axl also stated, "Time to move on. People get divorced. Life doesn't owe you your own personal happy ending especially at another's, or in this case several others,' expense." Axl concluded by thanking the Hall of Fame for their nomination and also "the fans for being there over the years, making any success we've had possible and for enjoying and supporting Guns N' Roses music."

Izzy Stradlin and Dizzy Reed also declined to attend the ceremony, with Izzy releasing his own (albeit much briefer) statement: "I have waited up to this point to see what would become of the GN'R induction into [the] Rock and Roll Hall of Fame. I would like to say thank you and gracias to [the] Rock and Roll Hall of Fame for the acknowledgement of our works over the years as a band. Big thanks to all my bandmates who helped get us to where we are today."

Therefore, representing Guns N' Roses at the April 14, 2012, ceremony, which took place at Cleveland's Public Auditorium, were Slash, Duff McKagan, Steven Adler, Matt Sorum, and Gilby Clarke. Green Day front man Billie Joe Armstrong formally inducted GN'R into the Hall of Fame. Referring to *Appetite for Destruction*, Armstrong remarked, "It's the best debut album in the history of rock 'n' roll. Every song hits hard. It takes you on a trip to the seedy world of Los Angeles. The thing that set them apart from everyone else was guts. They never lost their edge for one second." Upon hearing boos in the audiences after referring indirectly to Axl, Armstrong reacted, "Shut up! He was the greatest front man to ever step in front of a microphone . . . But he is . . . crazy. And I can vouch for that." Comedian Chris Rock also took a humorous dig at Axl later in the ceremony, adding "A lot of people are disappointed that Axl Rose isn't here. But let's face it, even if he was going to be here, he still wouldn't be here yet." The former GN'R band members in attendance performed three songs—"Mr. Brownstone," "Sweet Child O' Mine," and "Paradise City"—with Alter Bridge featuring Myles Kennedy on vocals.

Other 2012 Rock and Roll Hall of Fame inductees included the Beastie Boys, the Red Hot Chili Peppers, Small Faces/Faces, Donovan, the Crickets (backing band for Buddy Holly), the Blue Caps (backing band for Gene Vincent), the Famous Flames (backing vocal band for James Brown), the Midnighters (backing vocal group for Hank Ballard), the Miracles (backing vocal group for Smoky Robinson), and Laura Nyro.

Return to the Troubadour (April 1, 2016)

When news of a possible Guns N' Roses reunion first emerged, the ongoing rumor had been that Guns N' Roses would perform at Whisky A Go Go since Steven Adler's band had cancelled a show there scheduled for the same night of April 1, 2016. (However, it turned out that Adler actually cancelled because he was having back surgery.) However, on the night before the show, KLOS-FM broke the story that the concert would take place at the Troubadour in West Hollywood (where the classic GN'R lineup had first performed on June 6, 1985). Starting at 4 a.m. on the morning of the show, fans started camping out for tickets (all of which cost a "retro" price of just $10 each) at the old Tower Records (now a Gibson showroom). The building itself had become transformed into a makeshift Guns N' Roses exhibit.

Guns N' Roses took the stage at the Troubadour just a few minutes past midnight. About 500 fans attended the show, including a balcony full of celebrity friends of the band, such as Lenny Kravitz, Jim Carrey, Andrew "Dice" Clay, and Nicolas Cage. Believe it or not, it had been nearly twenty-three years since Axl and Slash last shared a stage together at River Plate Stadium in Buenos Aires, Argentina, on July 17, 1993. Duff had joined Guns N' Roses sporadically during tours over the last few years. The reunited GN'R lineup at the Troubadour featured Axl, Slash, Duff, Richard Fortus (rhythm guitar), Frank Ferrer (drums), Dizzy Reed (keyboards/percussion), and the first official Guns N' Roses female band member, Melissa Reese (keyboards/effects). Classic GN'R band members Izzy and Adler did not participate in the reunion show, nor would they take part in the Las Vegas Reunion Show, Coachella, or the Not in This Lifetime Tour during the summer of 2016 (although Adler did perform with GN'R for a couple of songs at two of the shows).

The seventeen-song set at the Troubadour featured "It's So Easy," "Mr. Brownstone," "Chinese Democracy," "Welcome to the Jungle," "Double Talkin' Jive" (which had not been performed live since 1993), "Live and Let Die," "Rocket Queen," "You Could Be Mine," *The Godfather* theme song (Slash guitar solo), "Sweet Child O' Mine," "New Rose" (the Damned), "Better," "Knockin' on Heaven's Door," "My Michelle," and "Nightrain," as well as encores "The Seeker" (the Who) and "Paradise City."

Las Vegas Reunion Shows (April 8–9, 2016)

Just before Coachella, Guns N' Roses performed two Las Vegas Reunion Shows at the T-Mobile Arena on April 8-9, 2016, that were only slightly marred by the fact that Axl had broken a bone in his left foot during the Troubadour gig. However, he managed to belt out the set in a "throne" lent to him by Dave Grohl of Nirvana and Foo Fighters fame. The three-hour concert followed closely along the lines of the Troubadour show with the additions of "Estranged," "This I Love," "Coma," "Civil War," "Wish You Were Here" (Pink Floyd cover), "November Rain," and "Patience" (part of the encore that included "Paradise City"). In addition, Skid Row's Sebastian Bach joined Axl for a duet on "My Michelle." As Bach exited the stage, he exclaimed, "I think I can speak for Las Vegas and thank you Guns N' Roses for making us so fucking happy. You're fucking back!" At one point, Axl joked, "How is it I'm working up a sweat sitting on my ass?" Alice in Chains served as opening act for GN'R for both nights.

Coachella (April 2016)

The reunited Guns N' Roses (sans Izzy and Steven Adler) headlined both weekends of the 2016 Coachella Valley Music and Arts Festival held at the Empire Polo Club in Indio, California. Special guest Angus Young of AC/DC took the stage for blistering renditions of "Whole Lotta Rosie" and "Riff Raff." Guns N' Roses dedicated their April 23 concert in memory of Prince.

According to music critic Neil McCormick of the *Telegraph* in an April 15, 2016, review of GN'R's performance, "Rather than serve as a triumphant return to the stage, the GnR performance was more reminiscent of what Christmas is like—if you too had a drunk uncle that always refused to leave the couch while screaming incoherent profanity to the rest of the family from across the room . . . [Because of Axl's injury], the Coachella audience was left with what seemed like a story time session, featuring a largely unrecognizable rock star sweating profusely in his chair, as if enduring a particularly painful deposition, while driving any shred of his badass legacy he had left further into the ground."

Other notable performers at the 2016 Coachella Festival included Ice Cube, LCD Soundsystem, Calvin Harris, Rancid, Underworld, Ellie Goulding, and many others. The inaugural Coachella Festival took place in October 1999, just three months after Woodstock '99. In a column for the *LA Weekly*, Henry Rollins wrote, "The idea of the festival is pretty insane. Drive hours into a very hot part of California and spend three days trying to avoid having your skin destroyed by the sun as you enjoy some of the most popular bands of your lifetime."

Not in This Lifetime Tour (Summer 2016)

Following successful performances at the Troubadour in West Hollywood, T-Mobile Arena in Las Vegas, and Coachella Festival in Indio, California, the newly reunited Guns N' Roses prepared to embark on the massive summer stadium Not in This Lifetime Tour throughout the United States and Canada. The tour's name was taken from an impromptu 2012 interview with TMZ in which Axl was asked about the possibility of a reunion of

Before embarking on the Not in This Lifetime Tour in 2016, Axl Rose filled in as lead vocalist for AC/DC to cover their remaining dates on the *Rock or Bust* Tour due to lead singer Brian Johnson's health issues.   *Author's collection*

"classic" GN'R band members and he remarked, "Not in this lifetime." The official Not in This Lifetime Tour lineup featured Axl, Slash, Duff, Dizzy, Richard Fortus (rhythm guitar), Frank Ferrer (drums), and Melissa Reese (keyboards). The rotating lineup of opening acts for Guns N' Roses during the tour consisted of Alice in Chains, Lenny Kravitz, the Cult, Chris Stapleton, Billy Talent, Skrillex, Wolfmother, Tyler Bryant & Shakedown, and Zakk Wylde.

A typical set during the Not in This Lifetime Tour consisted of a heavy dose of *Appetite for Destruction* songs, including "It's So Easy," "Welcome to the Jungle," "Nightrain," "Mr. Brownstone," "Rocket Queen," "Sweet Child O' Mine," and "Paradise City," along with a representative selection from the *Use Your Illusion* albums and *Chinese Democracy*, such as "Double Talkin' Jive," "Live and Let Die," "November Rain," "Knockin' on Heaven's Door," "Estranged," "You Could Be Mine," "Chinese Democracy," "Better," and "This I Love." In addition, Duff usually sang one of the punk covers from *"The Spaghetti Incident?"* album, such as the Misfits' "Attitude," the Damned's "New Rose," or the Stooges' "Raw Power."

Before embarking on the tour, Axl filled in as lead vocalist for AC/DC to cover their remaining dates on the *Rock or Bust* Tour due to Brian Johnson's health issues. Steven Adler joined the band on drums for two songs, "Out Ta Get Me" and "My Michelle," at both the July 6 concert in Cincinnati, Ohio, and the July 9 concert in Nashville, Tennessee. Prior to this, his last live performance with GN'R (excepting the 2012 Rock and Roll Hall of Fame appearance) had been at the disastrous Farm Aid IV concert on April 7, 1990, which took place shortly before he was fired from the band. On July 15, the band made headlines when they were stopped and detained briefly at the Canadian border for having a gun on board as they were heading for a concert in Toronto the following day. During the concert, Axl joked, "They were understanding. You know, it happens, you can forget you had a fuckin' gun." At a July 23 show at MetLife Stadium in New Jersey, police arrested more than thirty people on a number of charges, ranging from drug possession to lewd conduct.

Times have definitely changed and today's Guns N' Roses experience is quite different from thirty years ago when they performed in smoky West Hollywood dives before raucous crowds. Many of the fans that pack the stadiums these days desire to recapture a bit of their youth, if only for a couple of hours, before they go back to their dreary routine. So they grab a few $10 beers, take a couple of selfies, and record the intro from "Sweet

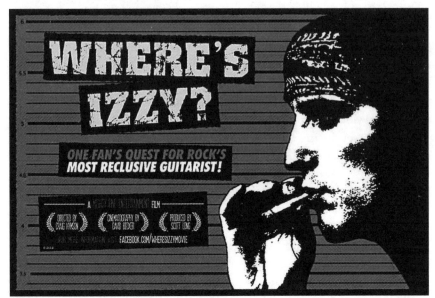

Izzy Stradlin was the only member of the "classic" lineup of Guns N' Roses who had no involvement in the 2016 Not in This Lifetime Tour. The indie documentary *Where's Izzy* highlights one fan's quest to get the reclusive guitarist's autograph tattooed on his arm.
Author's collection

Child O' Mine" on their cell phones to upload for their friends on Facebook. For instance, a *Philadelphia Magazine* review of the Guns N' Roses show at Lincoln Financial Field on July 14, 2016, noted that most of the fans were "completely inebriated" and that "one woman fell down drunk and pooped her pants, and that was within the first hour of the show. Excessive drinking, excessive heat, and excessive crowds are not a good combination."

Selected Bibliography

The following is a list of the most critical sources used in the creation of this rock biography. Many more books and articles exist related to Guns N' Roses. Be sure to seek them out!

Adler, Steven. *My Appetite for Destruction: Sex & Drugs & Guns N' Roses.* New York: It Books, 2010.

Antonia, Nina. *The New York Dolls: Too Much Too Soon.* New York: Omnibus Press, 1998.

Arnold, Gina. *Route 666: On the Road to Nirvana.* New York: St. Martin's Press, 1993.

Bangs, Lester. *Psychotic Reactions and Carburetor Dung.* New York: Anchor Books, 2003.

Berelian, Essi. *The Rough Guide to Heavy Metal.* London: Rough Guides, 2005.

Bronson, Fred. *The Billboard Book of Number 1 Hits.* New York: Billboard Books, 2003.

Burchill, Julie, and Parsons, Tony. *The Boy Looked at Johnny: The Obituary of Rock and Roll.* London: Faber and Faber, 1987.

Canter, Marc. *Reckless Road: Guns N' Roses and the Making of Appetite for Destruction.* Seattle: Shoot Hip Press, 2007.

Christie, Ian. *Sound of the Beast: The Complete Headbanging History of Heavy Metal.* New York: Harper Entertainment, 2004.

Cogan, Brian. *The Encyclopedia of Punk.* New York: Sterling Publishing, 2008.

Davis, Stephen. *Walk This Way: The Autobiography of Aerosmith.* New York: HarperCollins, 1997.

———. *Watch You Bleed: The Saga of Guns N' Roses.* New York: Gotham Books, 2008.

DeCurtis, Anthony, and Henke, James. *The Rolling Stone Album Guide.* New York: Random House, 1992.

Duswalt, Craig. *Welcome to My Jungle.* Dallas: BenBella Books, 2014.

Ebert, Roger. *Roger Ebert's Movie Yearbook 2011.* Kansas City: Andrews McMeel Publishing, 2010.

Ellis, Bret Easton. *Less Than Zero.* New York: Simon & Schuster, Inc., 1985.

Fein, Art. *The L.A. Musical History Tour: A Guide to the Rock and Roll Landmarks of Los Angeles*. Los Angeles: 2.13.61 Publications, 1998.

Fink, Jesse. *The Youngs: The Brothers Who Built AC/DC*. New York: St. Martin's Press, 2013.

Geltner, Ted. *Blood, Bone and Marrow: A Biography of Harry Crews*. Athens: University of Georgia Press, 2016.

Gold, Jeff. *101 Essential Rock Records: The Golden Age of Vinyl from the Beatles to the Sex Pistols*. Berkeley: Gingko Press, 2012.

Hamilton, Vicky. *Appetite for Dysfunction: A Cautionary Tale*. Los Angeles: Vicky Hamilton, 2016.

Heatley, Michael. *The Girl in the Song: The True Stories Behind 50 Rock Classics*. Chicago: Anova Books, 2010.

Hell, Richard. *I Dreamed I Was a Very Clean Tramp: An Autobiography*. New York: HarperCollins Publishers, 2013.

Herman, Gary. *Rock 'n' Roll Babylon*. London: Plexus Publishing Limited, 2002.

Herme, Will, and Michel, Sia. *SPIN: 20 Years of Alternative Music*. New York: Three Rivers Press, 2005.

Heylin, Clinton. *From the Velvets to the Voidoids: The Birth of American Punk Rock*. Chicago: A Cappela Books, 2005.

Hoskyns, Barney. *Waiting for the Sun: Strange Days, Weird Scenes, and the Sound of Los Angeles*. New York: St. Martin's Press, 1996.

James, Del. *The Language of Fear*. New York: Dell Publishing, 1995.

Kendall, Paul, and Lewis, Dave. *Led Zeppelin Talking*. New York: Omnibus Press, 2004.

Kent, Nick. *The Dark Stuff: Selected Writings on Rock Music 1972–1995*. Boston: Da Capo Press, 1995.

Kiedis, Anthony. *Scar Tissue*. New York: Hyperion Books, 2004.

Konow, David. *Bang Your Head: The Rise and Fall of Heavy Metal*. New York: Three Rivers Press, 2002.

Lee, Tommy. *Tommyland*. New York: Atria Books, 2004.

Lovett, Anthony R., and Maranian, Matt. *L.A. Bizarro: The Insider's Guide to the Obscure, the Absurd, and the Perverse in Los Angeles*. New York: St. Martin's Press, 1997.

Marcus, Greil. *Lipstick Traces: A Secret History of the Twentieth Century—Twentieth Anniversary Edition*. Cambridge: The Belknap Press of Harvard University Press, 2009.

Marks, Craig, and Tannenbaum, Rob. *I Want My MTV: The Uncensored Story of the Music Video Revolution*. New York: Dutton, 2011.

McCarthy, Jim, and Olivent, Marc. *Reckless Life: Guns N' Roses—A Graphic Novel.* New York: Omnibus Press, 2015.

McKagan, Duff. *It's So Easy: and Other Lies.* New York: Touchstone, 2011.

Mötley Crüe, with Neil Strauss. *The Dirt.* New York: Regan Books, 2002.

Neil, Vince. *Tattoos & Tequila.* New York: Grand Central Publishing, 2010.

Oseary, Guy. *On the Record.* New York: Penguin Books, 2004.

Pearcy, Stephen. *Sex, Drugs, Ratt & Roll: My Life in Rock.* New York: Gallery Books, 2014.

Perry, Joe. *Rocks: My Life In and Out of Aerosmith.* New York: Simon & Schuster, 2014.

Press, Joy, and Reynolds, Simon. *The Sex Revolts: Gender, Rebellion, and Rock 'n' Roll.* Cambridge: Harvard University Press, 1995.

Quisling, Erik, and Williams, Austin. *Straight Whisky: A Living History of Sex, Drugs, and Rock 'n' Roll on the Sunset Strip.* Chicago: Bonus Books, 2003.

Robb, John. *Punk Rock: An Oral History.* Oakland: PM Press, 2012.

Savage, Jon. *England's Dreaming: Anarchy, Sex Pistols, Punk Rock, and Beyond.* New York: St. Martin's Press, 2002.

Scherman, Tony. *The Rock Musician: 15 Years of Interviews—The Best of Musician Magazine.* New York: St. Martin's Press, 1994.

Sixx, Nikki. *This is Gonna Hurt: Music, Photography, and Life Through the Distorted Lens of Nikki Sixx.* New York: HarperCollins Publishers, 2011.

Slash. *Slash.* New York: It Books, 2007.

Smith, Chris. *101 Albums That Changed Popular Music.* New York: Oxford University Press, 2009.

Spicer, Al. *The Rough Guide to Punk.* London: Penguin Books, 2006.

Stanley, Paul. *Face the Music: A Life Exposed.* New York: HarperOne, 2014.

Stenning, Paul. *Guns N' Roses: The Band That Time Forgot.* New Malden, UK: Chrome Dreams, 2004.

Sugerman, Danny. *Appetite for Destruction: The Days of Guns N' Roses.* New York: St. Martin's Press, 1991.

———. *Wonderland Avenue: Tales of Glamour and Excess.* London: Abacus: 1989.

Turman, Katherine, and Wiederhorn, Jon. *Louder Than Hell: The Definitive Oral History of Metal.* New York: HarperCollins Publishers, 2013.

Tyler, Steven. *Does the Noise in My Head Bother You? A Rock 'n' Roll Memoir.* New York: HarperCollins Publishers, 2011.

Wall, Mick. *Enter Night: A Biography of Metallica.* New York: St. Martin's Press, 2010.

———. *Guns N' Roses: The Most Dangerous Band in the World.* New York: Hyperion, 1991.

———. *W.A.R. The Unauthorized Biography of William Axl Rose.* New York: St. Martin's Press, 2007.

Weiland, Mary Forsberg. *Fall to Pieces: A Memoir of Drugs, Rock 'n' Roll, and Mental Illness.* New York: HarperCollins Publishers, 2009.

Weinstein, Deena. *Heavy Metal: The Music and Its Culture.* Boston: Da Capo Press, 2000.

Yarm, Mark. *Everybody Loves Our Town: An Oral History Grunge.* New York: Crown Archetype, 2011.

Index

THE FAQ SERIES

Johnny Cash FAQ
by C. Eric Banister
Backbeat Books
9781480385405 .... $24.99

KISS FAQ
by Dale Sherman
Backbeat Books
9781617130915 .... $24.99

Led Zeppelin FAQ
by George Case
Backbeat Books
9781617130250 .... $22.99

Lucille Ball FAQ
*by James Sheridan
and Barry Monush*
Applause Books
9781617740824 .... $19.99

M.A.S.H. FAQ
by Dale Sherman
Applause Books
9781480355897 .... $19.99

Michael Jackson FAQ
by Kit O'Toole
Backbeat Books
9781480371064 .... $19.99

Modern Sci-Fi Films FAQ
by Tom DeMichael
Applause Books
9781480350618 .... $24.99

Monty Python FAQ
*by Chris Barsanti, Brian Cogan,
and Jeff Massey*
Applause Books
9781495049439 .... $19.99

Morrissey FAQ
by D. McKinney
Backbeat Books
9781480394483 .... $24.99

Neil Young FAQ
by Glen Boyd
Backbeat Books
9781617130373 .... $19.99

Nirvana FAQ
by John D. Luerssen
Backbeat Books
9781617134500 .... $24.99

Pearl Jam FAQ
*by Bernard M. Corbett and
Thomas Edward Harkins*
Backbeat Books
9781617136122 .... $19.99

Pink Floyd FAQ
by Stuart Shea
Backbeat Books
9780879309503 .... $19.99

Pro Wrestling FAQ
by Brian Solomon
Backbeat Books
9781617135996 .... $29.99

Prog Rock FAQ
by Will Romano
Backbeat Books
9781617135873 .... $24.99

Quentin Tarantino FAQ
by Dale Sherman
Applause Books
9781480355880 .... $24.99

Robin Hood FAQ
by Dave Thompson
Applause Books
9781495048227 .... $19.99

**The Rocky Horror
Picture Show FAQ**
by Dave Thompson
Applause Books
9781495007477 .... $19.99

Rush FAQ
by Max Mobley
Backbeat Books
9781617134517 .... $19.99

Saturday Night Live FAQ
by Stephen Tropiano
Applause Books
9781557839510 .... $24.99

Seinfeld FAQ
by Nicholas Nigro
Applause Books
9781557838575 .... $24.99

Sherlock Holmes FAQ
by Dave Thompson
Applause Books
9781480331495 .... $24.99

The Smiths FAQ
by John D. Luerssen
Backbeat Books
9781480394490 .... $24.99

Soccer FAQ
by Dave Thompson
Backbeat Books
9781617135989 .... $24.99

The Sound of Music FAQ
by Barry Monush
Applause Books
9781480360433 .... $27.99

South Park FAQ
by Dave Thompson
Applause Books
9781480350649 .... $24.99

**Star Trek FAQ
(Unofficial and Unauthorized)**
by Mark Clark
Applause Books
9781557837929 .... $19.99

**Star Trek FAQ 2.0
(Unofficial and Unauthorized)**
by Mark Clark
Applause Books
9781557837936 .... $22.99

Star Wars FAQ
by Mark Clark
Applause Books
9781480360181 .... $24.99

Steely Dan FAQ
by Anthony Robustelli
Backbeat Books
9781495025129 .... $19.99

Stephen King Films FAQ
by Scott Von Doviak
Applause Books
9781480355514 .... $24.99

Three Stooges FAQ
by David J. Hogan
Applause Books
9781557837882 .... $22.99

TV Finales FAQ
*by Stephen Tropiano and
Holly Van Buren*
Applause Books
9781480391444 .... $19.99

The Twilight Zone FAQ
by Dave Thompson
Applause Books
9781480396180 .... $19.99

Twin Peaks FAQ
*by David Bushman and
Arthur Smith*
Applause Books
9781495015861 .... $19.99

UFO FAQ
by David J. Hogan
Backbeat Books
9781480393851 .... $19.99

Video Games FAQ
by Mark J.P. Wolf
Backbeat Books
9781617136306 .... $19.99

The Who FAQ
by Mike Segretto
Backbeat Books
9781480361034 .... $24.99

The Wizard of Oz FAQ
by David J. Hogan
Applause Books
9781480350625 .... $24.99

The X-Files FAQ
by John Kenneth Muir
Applause Books
9781480369740 .... $24.99

HAL•LEONARD®
PERFORMING ARTS
PUBLISHING GROUP

FAQ.halleonardbooks.com